ISBN 978-1-330-40499-7
PIBN 10053986

1 MONTH OF
FREE
READING

at

www.ForgottenBooks.com

English
Français
Deutsche
Italiano
Español
Português

www.forgottenbooks.com

Mythology Photography **Fiction**
Fishing Christianity **Art** Cooking
Essays Buddhism Freemasonry
Medicine **Biology** Music **Ancient**
Egypt Evolution Carpentry Physics
Dance Geology **Mathematics** Fitness
Shakespeare **Folklore** Yoga Marketing
Confidence Immortality Biographies
Poetry **Psychology** Witchcraft
Electronics Chemistry History **Law**
Accounting **Philosophy** Anthropology
Alchemy Drama Quantum Mechanics
Atheism Sexual Health **Ancient History**
Entrepreneurship Languages Sport
Paleontology Needlework Islam
Metaphysics Investment Archaeology
Parenting Statistics Criminology
Motivational

THE

STORY OF MY LIFE.

BY

J. MARION SIMS, M. D., LL. D.,

KNIGHT COMMANDER OF THE LEGION OF HONOR OF FRANCE ; KNIGHT OF THE
ORDER OF ISABELLA THE CATHOLIC OF SPAIN ; KNIGHT OF THE
ORDER OF LEOPOLD I OF BELGIUM ; LATE PRESIDENT
AMERICAN MEDICAL ASSOCIATION, ETC., ETC.

EDITED BY HIS SON,

H. MARION-SIMS, M. D.

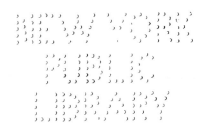

NEW YORK:
D. APPLETON AND COMPANY,
1, 3, AND 5 BOND STREET.
1885.

J. Marion Sims.

EDITOR'S PREFACE.

THIS "Autobiography" was written up to, and including, the year 1863, by my father, just two months prior to his death, while on a visit to the Hon. D. L. Yulee, at Pittsfield, Massachusetts. The "Story" is completed from letters written by him to my mother during his visits to Europe.

To further show the noble character of the man, even as a boy, I have appended a few letters written to his then "sweetheart" while a student at college. I feel under many obligations to my friend Judge Mackey, of Washington, for his able introduction, as well as many valuable suggestions during the preparation of this work.

H. MARION-SIMS, M. D.

267 MADISON AVENUE, NEW YORK, *July 26, 1884.*

CONTENTS.

CHAPTER VII.

CHAPTER VIII.

CHAPTER IX.

CHAPTER X.

CHAPTER XI.

CHAPTER XII.

CHAPTER XIII.

INTRODUCTION.

WHILE the casual reader might deem the following autobiography incomplete, since it terminates nearly twenty years prior to the death of its illustrious author, yet, for all the really useful purposes of a life-record, it is, like the great character whose trials and triumphs it records, fully rounded. It includes the year 1863, at which date he had received general and authoritative recognition, both in Europe and America, as the foremost clinical surgeon of the age. The honors and renown that followed, in later years, were but the natural sequence of the work that he has so graphically recorded. Under the simple title of "The Story of my Life," he has in the most fitting terms narrated the origin and growth of those achievements which, by the general judgment of enlightened men, have stamped him as a benefactor of his race. From that "Story" the reader will perceive that the path he trod to final and deserved success was not strewed with roses.

In the early period of his career in New York, it was almost his fate to furnish a memorable illustration of the historic fact that every pillar in the great temple of Truth rests upon the grave of a martyr. True genius, however, like the moss of Iceland, flourishes best beneath the snow. Dr. J. MARION SIMS never lost "heart of hope," even in the darkest vicissitude of his life. Like the Greek wrestler, Antæus, he arose with renewed strength after every fall. Never did he once lower his lofty crest, but, while his feet were sorely wounded by the thorns that beset his daily path, he kept his sublime head amid the stars. Of all professions the medical is slowest to welcome the reformer. It has always stood to the rearward of reform. The reason is obvious. Its theories are translated into action upon the living human body, and, as it deals with vital problems, it accepts with caution a novelty in theory that might prove mortal in practice.

Hence the great Cullen was severely reproached, for a time, because of his novel views in obstetrics. The immortal John Hunter, after announcing his great lecture on comparative anatomy, through the press, found but a "beggarly account of empty boxes" when the hour for its delivery arrived. His servant-man was his only auditor, and the great anatomist said to him, "William, take that male skeleton down from the wall, and place it in a chair beside you, in order that I may begin my lecture by saying *gentlemen* with grammatical propriety."

Jenner, when he introduced vaccination as a prophylactic against small-pox, was gravely accused of propagating, by such means, the very disease that he was endeavoring to prevent. Harvey's now universally accepted theory of the circulation of the blood encountered trenchant criticism for many years, and even so enlightened a publicist as Sir William Temple not only refused to accord it any credence, but denied that Harvey was its originator. Coming down to our own times, we find that, as late as 1850, Sir James Y. Simpson, of Edinburgh, the great clinical surgeon, not only had to encounter the dissent of the profession when he published his "Notes on the Inhalation of Sulphuric Ether in the Practice of Midwifery," but he was anathematized from the pulpit, as opposing the revealed will of God, declared in the primal curse upon woman, "In sorrow shalt h bring forth children." This extreme conservatism of his profession, in the matter of reform, exhibited itself at its maximum toward Dr. Sims upon his advent in New York, in May, 1853. It was conspicuous and severe, however, only among its recognized leaders. That was doubtless upon the principle that mountains are coldest at the top.

It is due to the medical profession to state the fact, h ch history attests, that no class of men render more exalted and unreserved tribute to the reformer, when the value of his discovery, or improvement, has been shown by actual demonstration. The deliberate and impartial judgment of the majority, once expressed as to the merits of a contemporary physician or surgeon, has never been reversed. Yet its justice is tardy, and, like the sun, it moves slowly in its orbit. Where it does not actively antagonize, it unconsciously, as it were, obstructs the advance of reformatory movement by its *vis inertia*. This is forcibly exemplified by the fact that although Dr. Sims had as early as 1849 cured a large number of cases of vesico-vaginal fistula, and had published his famous paper on that subject, disclosing his method of operating, and applying his silver suture to secure the result, in the "American Journal of Medical Sciences" of January, 1852, yet it was left for him, in person, in 1853, to operate on the first case of vesico-vaginal fistula ever cured in the city of New York.

But a still more impressive illustration is found in the fact that although he discovered, in 1845, the only effective method of curing trismus nascentium, and revealed it to the profession, in the "American Journal of Medical Sciences," in 1846, and subsequently published his "Essay on the Pathology and Treatment of Trismus Nascentium, or Lock-jaw of Infants," in 1864, yet that method has been generally rejected, and has only been fully vindicated since the death of its author. In January, 18... Dr. J. F. Hartigan, a surgeon of deservedly high repute in the city of Washington, D. C., published an admirable monograph in the "American Journal of Medical Sciences," entitled "Trismus Nascentium: its History, Cause, Prevention and Cure." That monograph contains a report of two hundred and twenty-nine cases, and *post-mortem* examinations occurring in the District of Columbia, and presents the result of five years devoted with signal assiduity and success by Dr. Hartigan to the elucidation of this momentous subject.

Referring to the diagnosis of his earliest cases, Dr. Hartigan writes in his monograph: "The extravasation observed in the posterior part of brain and spine, and the relative situation of the bones externally, now attracted attention. It was found that there was usually a depression, or that one side was overlapped by the parietal bone. Here, then, was rational ground for the process of deduction or induction.

"Did these appearances demonstrate cause and effect? viz., mechanical pressure of the occipital or parietal bones on the brain, through the intervening dura mater, finally expending its force on the pons, medulla oblongata, and the nerves issuing therefrom—*a theory which I soon found had been advanced over thirty years before, by Dr. J. Marion Sims, then of Alabama?*

"Time has not changed the views of this distin guished gynæcologist, as I learn from a letter recently received from him, and I believe they will stand preeminent in the history of his great achievements, and their truth it will be my endeavor now to establish wi'h some additional facts."

He has established "their truth," by actual demonstration in a long line of recorded cures, and the commendation which his timely monograph has received from the profession generally gives assured promise that the treatment of this disease, which stands first in the long catalogue of fatal maladies, will not hereafter be (in the language of Dr. Sims) "one of varied empiricism." In his autobiography, Dr. Sims refers to the fact that his doctrines in respect to the pathology and treatment of trismus nascentium had not been adopted or accepted by the profession at large, and adds: "Truth travels slowly, but I am sure that I am right —as sure as I can be of anything. That will be yet fully understood and appreciated by the profession."

Dr. Sims, on learning by a letter from Dr. Hartigan of his success in the treatment of trismus by the "Sims method," wrote him from Nice in April, 1882, in a spirit of just exultation: "You are the very man for whom I have been waiting—lo! these thirty years!"

His was the exultation due to vindicated truth. The wise Athenians embodied in one brief line the history of the true reformer in every age, when they erected a monument to Time, and inscribed upon it, "To him who vindicates."

As the purpose of this memoir is chiefly to supply such salient facts of general interest as transpired with reference to Dr. Sims, after the period embraced in his autobiography, which ends with the year 1863, though incidentally referring to a few later events, it has been deemed proper to present the following brief *résumé* of his career and work after that date. While residing in London, in 1865, he published his "Clinical Notes on Uterine Surgery." That work was issued simultaneously from the English, German, and French presses in London, Berlin, and Paris, and its authority was at once recognized by the profession throughout Europe and America. In his late memoir of Dr. Sims, the distinguished surgeon Dr. Thomas Addis Emmet, of New York, says of it with a nicer sense of justice than has marked some of his criticisms of his early benefactor, "Its publication was the turning-point of modern gynæcology, or, more strictly speaking, American gynæcology, of which he may be justly termed the father."

In 1870, while in Paris, he aided in organizing the Anglo-American Ambulance Corps, for service with the French army in the field during the Franco-Prussian War. He was surgeon-in-chief of the corps, with a staff of seven American and eight English surgeons. He arrived on the field of Sedan just before the battle, and was placed in charge of a military hospital with four hundred beds.

A report of the faithful and efficient service rendered by that corps, under the administration of Dr. Sims, has been published in London, by his first assistant therein, the eminent surgeon, Sir William McCormack. From that report it appears that the Anglo-American Ambulance Corps, with true humanitarian spirit, rendered great and essential service to both of the hostile armies, as, in addition to its vast number of French patients, it treated over a thousand wounded Prussians.

Dr. Sims remained at Sedan a little over a

month, when, the work of his immediate hospital
being completed, he resigned his position, and was
succeeded by his son-in-law, Dr. Thomas T. Pratt,
formerly of Alabama, but now a surgeon in Paris,
as surgeon-in-chief of the Anglo-American Ambulance Corps. Soon after severing that connection,
Dr. Sims returned to the United States, and in
January, 1872, was appointed a member of the Board
of Surgeons of the Woman's Hospital of the State
of New York. On May 1st of that year he entered upon the duties of that position, which he
held until December 1, 1874, when he tendered his
resignation, which was accepted. The point of difference between Dr. Sims and the Board of Managers, that led to his resignation, was one that
vitally involved his self-respect. A large number of
surgeons both from abroad and resident, attended
usually to witness Dr. Sims's operations in that hospital. Such visitors were cordially welcomed by him,
as, the greater the number of medical observers, the
wider became the sphere of the instruction that his
operations imparted.

The board thereupon insisted upon the enforcement of a rule adopted by them which limited the
number of spectators of any one operation to fifteen.

The reason of the rule, as urged by the board,
was, that a due regard for the modesty of patients demanded such restriction. The student of
medical ethics will be sadly puzzled in the effort to

divine by what occult process of reasoning the board arrived at the conclusion that a woman in a state of profound anæsthesia, or otherwise, would have her innate modesty more shocked by the presence of thirty observers than if only fifteen were gazing upon her. Although, for the reason above stated, Dr. Sims earnestly protested against the enforcement of such rule, not only as derogating from the value of the hospital as an agency for diffusing instruction in clinical surgery, but as violative of that immemorial usage that had constituted the attendant physician the "autocrat of the sick-chamber," the board adhered to its resolution, fixing "fifteen" as the limit of endurance, or "high-water mark" of woman's modesty.

Dr. Sims, whose delicate appreciation of all the proprieties of professional life revolted at the arrogance of such an assumed censorship, tendered his resignation, no doubt "more in sorrow than in anger."

He could not but be deeply sensible of the fact that was known of all men, that he was the founder of the Woman's Hospital of the State of New York, and of its parent institution, the Woman's Hospital Association. The ungracious and unwise action of the board was therefore, as to *him*, barbed with ingratitude. It must have led him to recall the story of the wounded eagle, whose pangs were increased when he saw that the arrow that quivered in his breast had been winged in its flight by one of his own plumes.

The American Medical Association, by his election

as its president in 1876, emphasized the approving sanction that the profession generally accorded to Dr. Sims for his action in this matter.

In February, 1877, he revisited for the last time the place of his birth, in Lancaster, South Carolina.

' No more trusty hearts or friendly hands ever greeted him than welcomed him back to the home of his boyhood. They little thought that the head of the young physician, that forty-one years before had been bowed with humiliation at the loss of his first two patients, was destined to leave undying luster in the sky of both hemispheres, when it bowed to its final rest.

Through all the intervening time that true-hearted people had watched his varied career with the deepest interest, and they justly gloried in the fact that General Andrew Jackson, the foremost American soldier, and Dr. J. Marion Sims, the foremost surgeon of his age, were both born and reared in "Old Lancaster."

Nor in the day of their sorest need had he been undmindful of them, while he was winning laurels on fields afar.

In February, 1865, General W. Tecumseh Sherman passed over that section with his army. That commander bore among his baptismal titles, as if in forecast of his military career, the name of a sanguinary Indian savage. The flames of defenseless cities and villages, the smoking ashes of homesteads and schoolhouses, were the monuments of his march through South Carolina. He reared those ghastly columns of his only victories in his own country and among his own people.

Dr. Sims, on learning of the destitution that prevailed in his native county, forwarded five thousand francs from Paris for the relief of the most needy. He subsequently added to that benefaction a sum with which a spacious mansion and sixty acres of land were purchased, as a home for the helpless indigent. The building now shelters some forty needy inmates, and is known as "The J. Marion Sims Asylum for the Poor." Accompanied by his noble wife he spent ten days in Lancaster. With her he there recalled the dear dead summers of the heart, amid the scenes of their early and only love. Ah! well, indeed, did he pay high tribute to her exalted worth and preserve for fifty years, and up to the hour of his death, the rose she gave him there as the pledge of their plighted troth.

He might in very truth have said of her, as Carlyle wrote of the faithful companion of his life-struggles, "She was my angel, and unwearied comforter, and helper in all things, and shone round me, like a bright aureola, when all else was black and chaos."

He went from Lancaster to Columbia, South Carolina, where he spent a few days, and made a filial visit to his *alma mater*, the old South Carolina College.

Thence he went to Montgomery, Alabama. His return to that scene of his earliest professional success, where his genius had been fostered with a generous hand, and where he had made his great discoveries in surgery, was a real triumphal entry. He arrived on March 14, 1877, and was welcomed by the Medical and Surgical Society of Montgomery, and by the citizens generally, with joyful acclamations.

The address of his old and honored friend, Dr. W. O. Baldwin, together with the response of Dr. Sims, on that occasion, form interesting additions to his autobiography, and are therefore included in this volume.

Soon after this brief pilgrimage to the South he returned to New York, and in the following autumn again returned to Paris with his family. He was elected President of the American Gynæcological Society, and served in that capacity in the year 1880.

While in New York, in the winter of 1881, he was attacked with pneumonia, which nearly proved fatal, his recovery being due only to his strong vitalism.

It left deep traces upon his constitution, seriously affecting his left lung, although in a few months he apparently recovered from its effects.

In speaking of it, he was wont to say, "But for that attack of pneumonia, I would probably have lived to the age of ninety."

It did not in any degree abate his untiring energy. His great intellectual forces, which he kept in ceaseless activity, compared with his by no means robust body, suggested the idea of a bright and keen Da-mascus sword-blade, constantly cutting through its incasing scabbard.

It should be stated also that, in 1881, Jefferson University, Pennsylvania, conferred upon him the merited degree of Doctor of Laws. He again left for Europe early in 1882, and remained in Paris until August, 1883, when he returned with his family to New York.

He visited Washington, D. C., October 28th, and spent three days in pleasant communion with his many professional and personal friends at the national capital. He regarded Washington as one of the most healthy cities in the world, and in view of its social and climatic advantages he determined to make it his home. For that purpose he purchased a building-lot in one of the most attractive parts of the city, intending to have erected a suitable mansion upon it, and after two or three years more of active practice to rest from his labors, and to find there that re-pose which every man should seek to obtain, some-where, between the cradle and the grave.

The title-deeds to that property were exe, for it but three days prior to his death. His intent to start for Southern Europe on November he feared the rigor of our Northern w he purchased tickets for himself and fam steamer to sail that day. He was ind earnest appeal of friends to defer his de, although he

17th of that month, in order that he might perform a very delicate and difficult operation on Mrs.
X——, the wife of a prominent citizen of New York.
He performed the operation with marked success, and
was highly gratified at the result. The very favorable
prognosis of that most complex case, together with
his recent purchase of a most eligible site for his
contemplated home in Washington, and the early
prospect of his return to Europe, led him to exclaim
the day before his death, while in the midst of his
happy and most interesting family, "Well, this is one
of the happiest days of my life!" He returned to his
home at No. 267 Madison Avenue about eleven o'clock
on the night of November 12, from a visit to that
patient. He complained of feeling a slight chill, and
his wife handed him a little whisky and water, which
he drank at her suggestion. He had a strong aver-
sion to alcoholic stimulants in every form, and said to
her, "You will never get me to take another dose
of that abominable stuff as long as I live." He retired, but was very restless and unable to sleep. He
aft\l to his wife, "Place your hand over my heart,
appar\el how it beats." He soon after arose and, sit-
In ⸗ in bed, proceeded to make memoranda of
for that 'iat would require his attention on the fol-
lived to tr. After he had been thus engaged for some
It did n, had often to guard him against overwork
His great inible coercion, she put out the light, say-
less activity, will see if you will stop writing."

He continued, however, to jot down memoranda for a little while longer, and then reached over to a glass of water that was near by, and drank a little of it. As he replaced the glass, he sank back, and began to breathe very hard. His watchful wife saw at a glance that he was breathing with great difficulty, and instantly summoned her son, Dr. H. Marion Sims from an adjacent room. He arrived quickly, but came too late.

The great surgeon, the evangelist of healing to woman, had met his God. The worker was at rest. Dr. Sims states in his autobiography, with a mild tinge of superstition, that the 13th of the month was always a "lucky date" with him, and with good reason he esteemed "13" his lucky number.

He instances his birth in 1813; he graduated at college on the 13th; he left Lancaster for Alabama on the 13th; and he arrived in New York on the 13th.

To those coincidences, the mournful addition must be made that he died at about fifteen minutes past three o'clock on the morning of November 13th, 1883.

It proved, indeed, a fortunate day for him, for it was that on which his "mortal put on immortality."

The ancient Romans declared that "Sudden death is given only to the favorites of the gods."

Up to the hour of Dr. Sims's death, his hand had not lost its skill or his eye its brightness. All of his mental faculties were in full vigor, and, although he had nearly rounded his seventy-first year, time had written scarce one wrinkle upon his brow.

He was about five feet eight and a half inches in height, his figure well molded, and though delicate yet not without some degree of robustness. His carriage was erect, with somewhat of a military bearing, and his step quick though well measured. His face was oval, his nose approaching the Grecian type. He had clear, but deep-set eyes, which were, like the original color of his hair, of a deep brown. His eye-brows were heavy, and well curved. His mouth was admirably formed, the lips being of medium fullness, the lower lip somewhat the fuller, indicating decision of character. His smile was one of kindly sweetness. His head was rather below than above the average size, and its unusual height in proportion to its circumference pointed to his Gaelic origin, for, through his mother, the blood of the MacGregors of McAlpin coursed full-proof in the veins of their descendant. His *tout ensemble* suggested, in all respects, Sir John Bell's ideal of the qualities necessary in a truly great surgeon— "The brain of an Apollo, the heart of a lion, the eye of an eagle, and the hand of a woman."

He was brave without being aggressive, though always ready, on proper occasions, to assert the "courage of his convictions." His manliness of nature was joined to the most tender sensibility and trusting simplicity— the strong pinions of the eagle folded around the warm heart of the dove.

He gave largely in private charity, rather considering the needs than the merits of those who sought his aid.   In this respect it may be justly said of him:

"And e'en his failings leaned to Virtue's side."

He always had a long roll of charity patients. He "heard the cry of the poor," and freely gave to them the ministrations of his matchless skill.

Well, indeed, has the Christian derived from the grand profession which Dr. Sims adorned that most endearing title of our Divine Master—"The Great Physician." No class of men give as much unrequited labor to relieve the sufferings of the poor.

He had a lofty scorn of hypocrisy in every guise. It was the inflexible rule of his life to seem what he was and to be what he seemed. He was a hearty hater when smarting under a sense of injury, but ever quickly forgave the regretted wrong that was done him. He was true as well as brave, and never turned his back on friend or foe.

His chivalric spirit came to the front in 1877, when, in behalf of Dr. Crawford W. Long, of Athens, Georgia, he established his claim to the high merit of being the discoverer of anesthæsia, by the inhalation of the vapor of sulphuric ether to produce insensibility to pain in surgical operations, as early as March, 1842.

Dr. Long was then languishing in poverty and neglect, but the appeal of Dr. Sims procured him ample aid in his declining years. He was especially the

2

kindly friend and patron of young men, always ready
to encourage and aid them in the path of honorable
effort. To women he was ever knightly and considerate, and woman in every station trusted in him with
an unreserved faith, whether her heart beat beneath the
royal purple of the queen or under the russet home-
spun of the peasant. His mind was profoundly ana-
lytic. Within the orbit of his investigations he traced
every effect to its ultimate cause.

His inventive powers were of the highest order.
His fertility of resources made him equal to every
emergency, and he either found a path or made one.
He was pre-eminently a grateful man, and during his
long life he left no favor unrequited.

Henri L. Stuart, who befriended him in the day of
his need, "builded better than he knew," when, by his
admirable tact, he enabled Dr. Sims *to introduce himself* to the medical profession in New York. In after
years Dr. Sims lavished his generous bounty on that
uncouth but clever newspaper reporter. But, withal,
he was an earnest Christian, not only by inherited faith,
but from conviction based upon a profound study of
the evidence that supports the sublime verities of Christianity.

His professional fame rests upon his treatment and
cure of vesico-vaginal fistula, before his operation
deemed incurable, he having invented and applied the
silver suture to secure the result of such operation.

Second: His invention of the speculum which bears

his name—the most effective known—to enable the surgeon to make a correct diagnosis in uterine complaints. In the memoir already cited, Dr. Emmet says of the "Sims speculum," "From the beginning of time to the present, I believe that the human race has not been benefited to the same extent, and within a like period, by the introduction of any other surgical instrument. Those who do not fully appreciate the value of the speculum itself have been benefited indirectly to an extent they little realize, for the instrument, in the hands of others, has probably advanced the knowledge of the diseases of women to a point which could not have been reached for a hundred years or more without it."

Third: Upon his exposition of the pathology and true method of cure of trismus nascentium or the lock-jaw of infants.

Fourth : Upon the established fact that he was the founder and organizer of The Woman's Hospital of the State of New York, the first institution ever dedicated exclusively to the cure of the diseases of women.

Fifth: Upon his many valuable contributions to medical literature.

There survive him, his widow and his eldest son, Dr. Harry Marion Sims, of New York, and four daughters, and a brother and two sisters.

His youngest son, William, an amiable young gentleman, survived him but a little more than three months, and reposes by the side of his father in Green-wood Cemetery.

Dr. Sims's teachings abroad were duly appreciated and recognized, by his having conferred upon him the highest decorations of France, Germany, Italy, Belgium, Spain, and Portugal; besides being made an honorary member of numerous scientific societies.

Dr. J. Marion Sims has left a name that the world will not willingly let die. The members of the medical profession throughout the United States may truly exclaim, on contemplating his great achievements, in the words of the inscription above the statue of La Place, in the hall of the French Academy of sciences: " *We* were not needed for *his* glory; he was necessary to ours!"

T. J. M.

CHAPTER I.

Doctors seldom write autobiographies. They never have leisure, and their lives are not so full of adventure or incident as to be interesting to the general reader. It may be presumptuous in me to leave notes of my life; but many of my friends have pressed me to do so. The first man who suggested it to me was the Hon. Henry W. Hilliard—statesman, jurist, divine, diplomatist—whom I knew very well when I lived in Montgomery, Alabama. In 1857 he came to see me in New York, and said the object of his visit was to tell me to begin to make notes of my life-work. He said he had been selected as biographer of the late Hon. William C. Preston, who was so distinguished in South Carolina as jurist, orator, and statesman. He went to Columbia to get material for his work, which to him would have been a labor of love, could he have found enough on which to build the temple of this brilliant, useful life. But he got only some political speeches delivered in Congress, and the record of his brief presidency of the South Carolina College, to which he had been called after his great intellect had been shaken by a paralytic attack. Mr. Hilliard said that he had noticed my rise and progress in my profession while I lived in Montgomery, and had heard of the work I had done in New York, and he thought it worthy of record. I was very much surprised, and blushed like a woman, and told him that all this was a matter of interest only to my wife and children.

In later years I have often been requested by friends to write the story, and I have promised to do so. In 1880, December 19, I was taken suddenly ill, and I sent for Dr. Loomis, who, when asked what was my malady, said, " I am sorry to say you have pleuro-pneumonia."

" Well," I replied, " I shall die on Wednesday or Thursday; certainly by Thursday, the fifth day. I am sixty-eight, and pneumonia kills all old men among us in from three to five days. Very few recover at my time of life. I am ready to die, but my life's labors are not finished. If I had completed my book, and if I had left notes of an autobiography, as I have promised so many of my friends, then my life would have been rounded up, and I would now have nothing more to do but fold my arms and die." But fortunately my life was spared. Skillful management and inherited vitalism carried me through; and, after two years of care and effort, I regained my health.

In May and June, 1883, I had under my professional care a very dear young friend, whom I had known from early girlhood. She had been an invalid for a long time, and was a bed-ridden sufferer. I made her frequent visits daily, as I saw that moral management was of great importance in the treatment of her case. During one of these social visits, when I was in the habit of drawing her away from herself by talking of topics of the day, she asked me a question about myself; when I replied "Oh, that is one of my life stories. You know life is a series of little stories which, when all strung together, make the complete story of the life. I have no time to-day, but to-morrow I will tell you all about it." When the morrow came, and the story was told, she asked other questions of a personal character. And thus she catechised and cross-questioned me, day after day, and at last she even wished me to tell the story of my courtship and marriage. At this I rebelled; but she insisted, and so she had her own way. It all ended in my agreeing to write out the life-notes in their smallest details. I am now surprised to see what an influence this poor little sick girl exerted over me in this regard; for, if I had done this work five years ago, I would only have given an account of my struggles and successes, and left out the inner man, the personal life.

I have now made a long apology for promising to write this life. But I have felt recently more justified in it by Mr. Ruskin's preface to "The Story of Ida." He says: "The lives we need to have written for us are of the people whom the world has not thought of—far less heard of—who are yet doing most of its work, and of whom we may learn how it can best be done."

It is a trite saying, that "every life is a poem, be it long or short." Mine has been a real romance, full of incident, anxiety, hope, and care; some disappointments, and many successes, with much sickness and sorrow; but it has also been full of joy, contentment, and real happiness.

I was born in Lancaster County, South Carolina, the 25th of January, 1813, about ten miles south of the village of Lancaster, and a mile or more west of the old wagon-road from Lancaster to Camden. The ancestors of my father, John Sims, were of the English colonists of Virginia. My mother, Mahala Mackey, was the daughter of Charles and Lydia Mackey, of Scotch-Irish origin. The family came to America about 1740. My paternal great-grandfather, Sherrod Sims, was born in Virginia, 1730. I remember the date well, because he told me he was at Braddock's defeat (1755), and that he was then twenty-five years old. He served through the Revolutionary War, and afterward removed from Virginia with his family to the Beaver Creek neighborhood, in the southern part of Lancaster County, South Carolina. When I was ten or eleven years old, he showed me a document with Washington's name signed to it; but I did not have sense enough to appreciate it, or care to know what it was. He was a tall, raw-boned, splendid old man, six feet high, when I saw him last, in 1824. He died of old age in 1825, at the age of ninety-five, having survived his wife twenty-five years. He had five or six sons and two daughters.

Unfortunately, I never knew much of my father's family. He was an orphan, brought up to "rough it," working on the farm with the negroes, and he was the best worker among them. He never had much love for any of his uncles when he was a boy, for they were rather hard on him. So, when he was grown, and became the father of a family, he saw them but seldom, but always treated them well when any of them came to see him. I never saw but two of his uncles at his house, and that was after he was elected high sheriff, and came to be a power in the county.

My father's family were all long-lived. Sherrod Sims, my great-grandfather, as before stated, lived to be ninety-five. His sons, Sherrod, Stephen, Ashburn, and the others, all lived to very old age.

They were all tillers of the soil. My father was born 27th of December, 1790. He was married to Mahala Mackey, 19th of April, 1812. He never had a day's schooling till I was six months old.

He was therefore over twenty-three when he went to school six months to Dr. Garlick, who lived at Liberty Hill; and he became an accomplished accountant and book-keeper, and wrote a beautiful hand. He was tall, over six feet, well proportioned, and was considered a very handsome man. He was one of the best

of men, and best of husbands. I do not remember ever
to have heard an unpleasant word between my father
and mother. He was always poor, but always lived
well. Being a public man, and well known from one
end of the county to the other, he was obliged to
"treat," as was the habit of the country, to get votes,
but he never drank himself. He kept the village hotel
in Lancaster for several years, and was sheriff for four
years (1830-1834), which gave him occupation and a
living. He was also a surveyor, and his services were
in great demand in all cases of disputed land-titles.

When the war with the mother country broke out,
in 1812, he volunteered, and his company, commanded
by Captain Douglass, was ordered to Charleston, where
it was encamped at Haddrell's Point, in Charleston Har-
bor. He went as subaltern, and became so proficient
a disciplinarian that he rose to the command of his
company. Soon after returning home he organized a
volunteer corps of rifles. It was a splendidly drilled
company. Kennedy Bailey was drummer, and Munson
and Andrews fifers. The uniform of the company was
grey home-spun jeans, made in the hunting-shirt fashion.
It was literally home-spun, for it was made at home.
Every industrious housewife at that time had her own
spinning-wheel and loom. My mother, in early life,
spun and wove the clothing for her husband and children. I never was so proud in all my life as when,
a little boy, I marched with " Captain Jack Sims," as
they called him, at the head of his Hunting-Shirt Rifles.

Colonel Witherspoon was then colonel of the Lancaster regiment of militia, and my father was his adjutant. When Colonel Witherspoon resigned, my father succeeded him as colonel of the regiment; and Governor Miller and Governor Manning, at their annual reviews, in making little speeches to the regiment, always told them that they were the best-drilled regiment, and that they had the best drill-officer, in their colonel, that could be found in the state; and the Lancaster people believed it.

But this was before the days of railroads, telegraphs and newspaper reporters, and I have no doubt that governors always made the same stereotyped, laudatory speech at every review they held throughout the state.

My father was a great marksman. At the age of seventy, with gun and dog, he would bag as many quail as the youngest shot in the country; and with his rifle he could drop his deer, running, at a distance of one hundred yards. In his early life he was a great fox-hunter. He kept a pack of hounds of his own, and about the year 1827 he laid a wager of a hat with one of his fox-hunting friends, Colonel Patterson, of Liberty Hill, on the fox-hunting of one season, which I believe is from October to March. Colonel Patterson caught twenty and my father fifty-two and won the hat. But he came near losing his life; for, at the end of this dreadful winter's exposure in hunting, he got an attack of pneumonia, from which he barely recovered. His physician, Dr. Bartlett Jones, at once advised him to give up his hounds, and he did so, greatly to the happiness of my poor mother. But he never relinquished the quail and deer hunt, to which she had no objection.

He had another sporting habit, which I had almost forgotten, cock-fighting. At that time cock-fighting was not in the hands of the roughs as it is now. Only the rich and cultured bred cocks for fighting, and, like fox-hunting, it was an expensive sport. The great cock-fighters of the country were the Davies, and Greens of Chester, Sims of Lancaster, Dr. Greene and Myers of Columbia, and some other gentlemen in Union County, and the Joneses and Allens of Halifax, North Carolina. These gentlemen were all of purely English descent, and inherited this vicious sport from their English ancestors. Gentlemen now no longer indulge in it. It is in the hands of the uncultured and low and vulgar. I can imagine nothing more inhuman, cruel, and brutal, than the cock-pit and its deadly conflicts.

The only real cause of unhappiness my mother ever had was the time wasted by my father in fox-hunting and billiard-playing. He excelled in billiards, and my mother instilled into me such hatred for my father's three great follies of life, that I have never seen a fox-hunt, nor played a game of billiards, nor bet on a cock-fight. In 1838 my father moved to Mississippi, where he tried farming, but did not succeed very well. In 1853, he moved to New Waverly, Walker County, Texas, where he lived with his eldest daughter, Mrs.

John C. Abercrombie. His last days were spent with Mr. and Mrs. Abercrombie, in the midst of his children and grandchildren, beloved and honored by all who knew him. He was always a young man—never old. The young men of the country were his associates, and he always exercised a great and beneficent influence over young people.

He was a high mason; was master of the lodge in Lancaster, and lived up to the stern principles of the craft. He believed that a good mason was good enough for heaven. In his old days he joined the Methodist Church and became an exemplary Christian. (He was always one before he joined the church.) But he never deserted his masonic faith and works.

There is now a masonic lodge in New Waverly, Texas, named in his honor, the " John Sims Lodge."

No man ever had warmer friends, and he was loved and honored wherever he lived. He had a military bearing, with courtly manners, was generous to a fault, and kind to every one. He did not get rich when he was high sheriff, simply because in the kindness of his heart he assumed so many of the responsibilities belonging to his office which he was obliged to pay in the end.

No man lives as long as he should; the most of us die prematurely, even when we die in old age, because we violate some law of hygiene, or perpetrate some imprudent act that lays the foundation of disease which often terminates in death. The great philanthropist

Peter Cooper died at the age of ninety-three, but died prematurely, because he imprudently exposed himself, took cold, and got pneumonia, which he would not have had if he had taken ordinary care of himself. He ought to have lived to be one hundred or more. So with the distinguished surgeon James R. Wood, and many others whom I could mention. I have come near throwing away my own life several times, by imprudent exposures and unnecessary risks. Even the centenarian Captain Labouche, who died a few years ago in New York at the age of one hundred and eleven, died prematurely, because his life was sacrificed by an imprudent exposure, which at the time was wholly unnecessary, and by which he got cold and had pneumonia. I say that my father died prematurely at seventy-eight, because he did what had been better left undone. In the month of July, 1867, he rode through a hot sun a distance of fifteen miles. After transacting his business he immediately returned home, making thirty miles in the saddle, and all this was done in the heat of the day. He stripped and stabled his horse, and then got his axe and went to cutting wood. There was not the least need of his doing this; but he believed that every man should take so much strong exercise every day to insure good health. He was a great axeman, and delighted to display his skill with it to his grandchildren. After cutting away hard for a whole hour, he suddenly stepped back, dropped his axe, and looked around. His grandson, seeing that something was wrong, ran up to him, saying, "Grandfather, what is the matter? You are sick; come, go into the house with me." This was about twenty or thirty feet distant. When he got there, my sister, Mrs. Abercrombie, says he was paralyzed, and incurably so, aphasia having set in from the very beginning. He lived a year, but very miserably, for he could not write, nor co-ordinate his words so as to make himself understood. The rationale of the attack is this: He was already overheated and fatigued by his thirty mile ride in the hot sun, and the violent chopping overtaxed the heart and lungs, and threw the blood too forcibly to the brain. A blood-vessel gave way in the left side of the brain, front part; he was paralyzed on the right side, the blood was extravasated and formed a clot, which produced, mechanically, all the symptoms of apoplexy and paralysis, with aphasia. And as all this occurred as the result of an imprudent and unnecessary act, I am justified in saying that my father died prematurely at the age of seventy-eight; for I am sure that without this he would have lived to be ninety-five, as his grandfather did before him. He had never lost a tooth, and was in perfect health; straight, erect, active, with every organ and function in normal condition. Even the strongest lose their lives by imprudent acts, while the weak and feeble, compelled to take care of their health, often live to ripe old age.

Charles and Lydia Mackey had nine children. My mother, Mahala, was the youngest. She was born on the 2d of May, 1792, being about eighteen months younger than my father. She was a bright, pretty girl, with black eyes, fair skin, and red hair. I remember her as a handsome, middle-sized woman, with rich, auburn hair. She was the best of wives, the best of mothers, and the most untiring worker I ever knew. She was indeed a helpmeet for her husband. She spun aud wove the cloth, and cut and made the clothes commouly used at home, and did all her own housework in her early life. My father farmed it and kept a little country - store, and after a while got a few slaves, enough to take some of the hardest work off my mother's hands. He then moved from the Hanging-Rock Creek neighborhood, in 1824, to Lancaster village. Here he entered on a new phase of life. He kept the village tavern. It had nice accommodation for travelers, was a bachelors' boarding-house, and headquarters of lawyers during court, which was held twice a year. My mother kept the house well, and my father prospered, notwithstanding his hounds and billiards.

When my mother was about ten years old she was sent to school to Mr. Elijah Croxton. This was in 1802. The schoolhouse was in the pine woods, two miles from her father's house. It was a log cabin about twenty by twenty-five feet—made of pine logs six or eight inches in diameter. There was a window about two feet square at one end of the cabin, and but one door. That was on the side of the house looking east. On the opposite side one log, about three feet from the floor, had been cut out to admit light. This made a longitudinal opening twenty-two or twenty-three feet long and a foot wide. Just under this long opening there was a broad plank, eighteen or twenty inches wide, smoothly dressed, extending the length of the open window, securely fastened to the wall, and sustained by upright posts at each end of the plank and in the center. It made an admirable writing-table. Here the advanced boys and girls, who were studying arithmetic and writing, sat with their backs toward the teacher—whose seat was just at the right of the door as you entered—while the smaller children, learning to spell and read, sat at either end of the cabin with their faces toward the teacher. The chinks or open spaces between the pine logs were covered with boards nailed on outside.

It was summer time. The students of arithmetic were permitted to go out and sit in the shade of the house, or under the trees, till they had worked out the sums allotted to them by the master. When this was done the pupils would come in, and the teacher would look over the slate, and, if the work was satisfactory, he ordered the pupil to transfer the sums from slate to copy-book. Mahala Mackey, on a hot, sweltering day, about 11 o'clock, came in with slate in hand. Mr. Croxton looked it over, and said "all right," and she took her seat about the middle of the long writing-table, with her back to the teacher, and began to copy her sums. The school was unusually quiet. It was the happy season of flies and bees and butterflies and toads and lizards and reptiles of that hot climate. A green lizard, or chameleon, which is green or brown as occasion requires, had been for an hour running around in the open spaces between the logs; the logs had not been peeled, and the lizard's rapid running over the dry pine bark made a great noise. The antics of the cunning little lizard amused the little boys very much, and distracted their attention from their books. They could not refrain from giggling, and the teacher called up two or three of the principal ones and flogged them. Soon after Mahala Mackey had settled down to her copy-book the impudent little lizard came rattling along the open space in front of her seat, and she, not knowing anything of what had happened that morning, grabbed and caught it by the tip of the tail, and, with a shriek, gave it a sling backward. Looking around, frightened at what she had done so automatically and undesignedly, what was her amazement when she saw the lizard hanging to the end of the teacher's nose, while he was knocking away, and crying out with pain at his fruitless efforts to tear it loose from its firm hold. It had caught him by the projecting end of the septum, which separates the two nostrils, and its teeth had gone through and locked. While Mr. Croxton was floundering and knocking away at the lizard, the frightened little red-headed Mahala shot out of the door, by the side of the teacher, and took to her heels, and ran bare-headed to her home, with greyhound speed.

The next day her father went to see her teacher about the unfortunate occurrence of the previous day.

Mr. Croxton's nose was very red and swollen, and he seemed to look upon the affair as a personal indignity; and, strange to say, he refused to allow Mahala to return to the school unless her father would consent to his flogging her. Of course Charles Mackey was indignant, and refused to have his child punished for that which was so purely accidental; and she never went to school to Mr. Croxton again.

Indeed, it was with some trouble that the fiery Charley Mackey was prevented from thrashing the teacher. It is a common saying, " that whatever has happened once can happen again"; but I hardly think it possible that another little school-girl will ever again toss a lizard so as to catch a school-master by the nasal septum.

My mother died at the age of forty, of common bilious remittent fever — a disease that is cured now with the greatest facility, but at that time was attended with great mortality, because they were ignorant of the method of cure.

CHAPTER II.

IN 1781 South Carolina was completely overrun by the British. Lord Cornwallis held quiet possession of Charleston; had defeated Gates and De Kalb at Camden, driven Marion to the swamps of the Pedee, scattered the forces of Sumter, and established his headquarters in the Waxhaws, on the borders of North Carolina, while Tarleton had his on the Hanging-Rock Creek, about thirty miles north of Camden. Davie alone was left with a small force on the west bank of the Catawba, making occasional sorties to harass the outposts of the British.

The Scotch, Irish, and Huguenots of South Carolina were mostly Whigs or rebels. The English colonists were divided; the majority were Whigs, but there were a goodly number of loyal men among them, who conscientiously espoused the cause of the mother country, and were called Tories. Lancaster County was one of the strongholds of the Whigs. The McElwains, Truesdales, Douglasses, Cunninghams, Mc-Mullens, McDonalds, Mackeys, and others of Scotch-

Irish origin, occupied and held the southern portion of Lancaster, and Charles Mackey was their acknowledged leader; while the Crawfords, Dunlaps, Jacksons (Gen. Jackson was then sixteen years old), Whites, Masseys, Dobys, Curetons, and others of the same stock held the Waxhaws, in the northern section of the county. The Whigs had always made Lancaster too hot for the Tories, and had ruthlessly driven them out of the county, to seek companionship and sympathy wherever they might find it.

But the advent of the British turned the tide of war completely, and now the Tories, with Tarleton at their head, had driven the Whigs from Lancaster, some across the Catawba, to join Davie, and some to the Pedee, to join Marion.

Charles Mackey, as the leader of his band, had made himself very obnoxious to the Tories, and they impatiently waited the time for vengeance. He was a man of medium size, very active and energetic, a fine horseman, splendid shot, hot-headed, impulsive, often running unnecessary risks and doing dare-devil deeds. No work was too hazardous for him. Lydia Mackey, his wife, was a woman of good common sense, with clear head, fine judgment, and in her coolness and self-possession far superior to her impulsive husband. They had a young family of two or three children, and Charles Mackey had not seen or heard from them in several weeks. Their home was not more than two and a half miles from Tarleton's camp, on the Hanging-Rock Creek. He knew very well that it would be hazardous for him to return to his home, so near to Tarleton's headquarters; but his anxiety became so great, on account of his wife's peculiar condition, that he could no longer remain in doubt about it; so he cautiously made his way home, where he unwisely loitered for a week, and during this time he had the temerity to enter Tarleton's lines more than once, in search of information which would be valuable to his country's defenders.

Charles Mackey's house was a double log cabin, with cultivated patches of corn and potatoes on either side of a lane leading to the front, while at the rear was a kitchen-garden of half an acre or more, extending back to a large huckleberry swamp, which was almost impenetrable to man or beast. This swamp covered an area of ten or fifteen acres, and was surrounded by a quagmire from ten to thirty feet wide, thus making it practically an island. It was entered by jumping from tussock to tussock of moss-covered clumps of mold, a foot or two in diamater and rising six or eight inches above the black jelly-like mire, which shook in every direction in passing over it. A plank or fence rail served as a temporary draw-bridge, which was pulled into the swamp after passing over.

When the county was infested by Tories, Charles Mackey spent his days in the swamp if not out scouting. At night, he ventured home. He had good watch-dogs, and they gave the alarm whenever any one approached, whether by night or day. If at night, he would immediately lift a loose plank in the floor of his bedroom, drop through on the ground, crawl out into the rear, then run thirty or forty yards across the garden, gun in hand, and disappear in the swamp, pulling his fence-rail draw-bridge after him. There was no approach to the house in the rear, and his retreat was always effected with impunity.

Charles Mackey had been at home now about a week, and was on the eve of leaving with some valuable information for the rebel generals, gained by his night prowlings in and about the headquarters of Colonel Tarleton. But early in a June morning (an hour or two before day), his usually faithful watch-dogs failed to give warning of the approach of strangers, and the first notice of their presence was their shouting "Hallo!" in front of the house. Mrs. Mackey jumped out of bed, threw open the window-shutters, stuck out her head, surveyed the half-dozen armed horseman carefully, and said, "Who is there?"

"Friends—Is Charley Mackey at home?"

She promptly answered "No." Meantime, Charlie had raised the loose plank in the floor, and was ready to make for the swamp in the rear when, stopping for a moment to make sure of the character of his visitors, he heard the spokesman say:

"Well, we are very sorry indeed, for there was a big fight yesterday on Lynch's Creek, between General Marion and the British, and we routed the d—d redcoats completely, and we have been sent to General Davie, at Landsford, with orders to unite with Marion at Flat Rock as soon as possible, and then to attack Tarleton. We do not know the way to Landsford, and came by for Charlie to pilot us." Mrs. Mackey was always cool and collected, and she said that " she was sorry that her husband was not at home."

But her husband was just the reverse, hot-headed and impetuous. This sudden news of victory, after so many reverses, was so in accordance with his wishes that he madly rushed out into the midst of the mounted men, hurrahing for Marion and Davie, and shouting vengeance on the redcoats and Tories; and he began to shake hands enthusiastically with the boys, and to ask particulars about the fight, when the ring-leader of the gang coolly said:

" Well, Charlie, old fellow, we have set a good many traps for you, but never baited 'em right till now. You are our prisoner." And they marched him off just as he was, without hat or coat, and without allowing him a moment to say a parting word to his poor wife. It was now nearly daylight, and they ordered him to pilot them to Andy McElwain's, with the hope of capturing him too; but he was not at home. They then went to James Truesdale's and he was not at home. From there they went to Lancaster village, and then returned to Colonel Tarleton's headquarters, where Charles Mackey was tried by courtmartial, and sentenced to death as a spy.

The next day Mrs. Mackey, not knowing what had happened, gathered some fruits and eggs, and with a basket well filled she made her way to Colonel Tarleton's camp. Hucksters were readily admitted when they had such luxuries to dispose of. On getting within the lines, she inquired the way to Colonel Tarleton's *marquee*, which was shown to her. The colonel was on parade, but a young officer, who was writing, asked her to be seated. After he had finished he said:

"You have something for sale, I presume?"

She replied that she had fruit and eggs. He gladly took what she had and paid for them. She then said that her basket of fruit was only a pretext to get to Colonel Tarleton's headquarters. That she was anxious to see him in person, on business of great importance. She then explained to him the capture of her husband and that she wished to get him released, if he were still alive, though she didn't know but what they had hung him to the first tree they came to.

The officer told her that the colonel was on parade and would not return for two hours, or until he came in for his mid-day meal. Mrs. Mackey was a comely woman, of superior intelligence, and she soon interested the young officer in her sad condition. He expressed for her the deepest sympathy, and told her that her husband was near by, under guard; that he had been tried and sentenced to death as a spy; and that he feared there was no hope of a reprieve, as the evidence against him, by Tories, was of the most

3

positive kind.   He told her that Colonel Tarleton
was as cruel and unfeeling as he was brave, and that
he would promise her anything to get rid of her, but
would fulfill nothing.   "However," said he, "I will prepare the necessary document for your husband's release,
filling in the blanks, so that it will only be necessary
to get Colonel Tarleton's signature.   But I must again
say, frankly, that this is almost hopeless."

It was evident to the most superficial observer
that Mrs. Mackey would soon become a mother, and
this, probably, had something to do with enlisting the
sympathy of the kind young officer.   At 12 o'clock
Colonel Tarleton rode up, dismounted, and entered the
adjoining tent.   As he passed along, the young officer said: "You must wait till he dines.   Another
charger will then be brought, and when he comes up to
mount you can approach him, and not till then."

At the expected time, the tall, boyish-looking, clean-
shaved, handsome young Tarleton came out of his tent;
and as he neared his charger he was confronted by
the heroic Lydia Mackey, who in a few words made
known the object of her visit.   He quickly answered
that he was in a great hurry, and could not at that time
stop to consider her cause.   She said the cause was
urgent; that her husband had been condemned to death
and that he alone had the power to save his life.   He
replied:

"Very well, my good woman; when I return, later
in the day, I will inquire into the matter."

Saying this, he placed his foot in the stirrup and sprang up; but, before he could throw his right leg over the saddle, Mrs. Mackey caught him by the coat and jerked him down. He turned upon her with a scowl, as she implored him to grant her request. He was greatly discomfited and angrily said he would inquire into the case on his return. He then attempted again to mount, when she dragged him down the second time, begging him in eloquent terms to spare the life of her husband.

"Hut, tut, my good woman," said he, boiling with rage, "do you know what you are doing? Begone, I say, I will attend to this matter at my convenience and not sooner!"

So saying, he attempted the third time to mount, and the third time Lydia Mackey jerked him to the ground. Holding by the sword's scabbard, and falling on her knees, she cried:

"Draw your sword and slay me and my unborn babe, or give me the life of my husband, for I will never let you go till you kill me or sign this document," which she drew from her bosom and held up before his face.

Tarleton trembled with rage, and was as pale as a ghost. He turned to the young officer, who stood close by intently watching the scene, and said:

"Captain, where is this woman's husband?"

He answered, "Under guard, in yonder tent."

"Order him to be brought here," and soon Charles Mackey stood before the valiant Tarleton. "Sir," said he, "you have been convicted of bearing arms against his majesty's government. Worse, you have been convicted of being a spy. You have dared to enter my lines in disguise, as a spy, and you can not deny it. But, for the sake of your wife, I will give you a full pardon on condition that you will take an oath never again to bear arms against the king's government."

"Sir," said Charles Mackey, in the firmest tones, "I can not accept pardon on these terms. It must be unconditional, or I must die." And poor Lydia Mackey cried out, "I, too, must die"—and on her knees held on to Colonel Tarleton; and she pleaded with such fervor and eloquence that Tarleton seemed lost for a moment, and hesitated, and then, turning to the young captain, he said, with quivering lips and a voice choking with emotion:

"Captain, for God's sake sign my name to this paper, and let this woman go."

With this, Lydia Mackey sank to the ground exhansted, and Colonel Tarleton mounted his horse and galloped off, doubtless happier for having spared the life of heroic Lydia Mackey's husband.

Lydia Mackey in her old age was a fine talker, and when I was a boy of ten years old I have heard her tell this story with such feeling and earnestness that great tears rolled down her aged cheeks and mingled with those of her little grandchildren, huddled around her knees.

The name of Tarleton was execrated in South Caro-

lina until a very late period. Even fifty years after his
bloody exploits children would tremble at their re-
hearsal. But the Lydia Mackey episode shows that he
was not wholly devoid of sentiment, and that he had a
heart that was not wholly steeled against the nobler
feelings of humanity.

The history of our Revolutionary War can hardly
present a more interesting tableau than that of Lydia
Mackey begging the life of her husband at the hands of
the brave and bloody Tarleton. It is altogether probable that the Lydia Mackey victory was the first ever
gained over the heart of this redoubtable commander;
and it is very certain that Charles Mackey was the only
condemned prisoner ever liberated by him without taking the oath of allegiance to the mother country. This
was about four months before the surrender of Lord
Cornwallis at Yorktown.

CHAPTER III.

My father, feeling the want of an education himself, was determined to educate his children, and so he began with me at a very early age. He then had a little store about a mile north of the Hanging-Rock Creek, on the road leading to Lancaster. This was in 1818. Mr. Blackburn, a Scotchman, had just opened a school in an old field, very near the ford of the creek. Mr. Buck Caston lived a mile north of us, and his children were obliged to pass our door to get to Mr. Blackburn's school. His eldest daughter, Betsey, knowing that my father was anxious to have me go to school, volunteered to call on going by every day and take me to school with them; promising to protect me against all dangers and imposition from other boys in the school. I don't remember much about it, except that the teacher flogged the boys occasionally, very severely, and stood some of them up in the corner with a fool's cap on. I here learned my letters, and to spell in two syllables by the end of the term. The school was only for the summer term.

The next year, 1819, when I was six years old, my father sent me to a boarding-school, some six or eight miles from home. The teacher here was an Irishman, Mr. Quigley, a man about fifty-five years old, and a rigid disciplinarian; altogether very tyrannical, and sometimes cruel. He was badly pock-marked, and had lost an eye by small-pox—otherwise a handsome man. I was very unhappy at his house. He had two grown daughters; one of the daughters was very unkind to me, the other was sympathetic. But my impressions then and my convictions now are that the best place for a child under ten years of age is with his mother. A very curious custom prevailed in this school, which was that the boy who arrived earliest in the morning was at the head of his class during the day, and was considered the first-honor boy. The one who arrived second took the second place, and so on. There was great rivalry among some half-dozen of the most ambitious of the boys. James Graham was about ten years old. He was almost always first in the morning. Although I was so very young, only six, I occasionally made efforts to get there earlier than he did. I suppose the school-house was not more than three quarters of a mile from the teacher's residence, where I boarded; but it seemed to me, at the time, that it was very much farther than that. However, the boy that got ahead of James Graham had to rise very early in the morning. I remember getting up one morning long before daybreak. The dread of my young life was mad dogs and "runaway niggers." I started off for the school-house on a trot, an hour before day, looking anxiously from side to side, and before and behind, fearing all the time those two great bugbears of my young life, viz., mad dogs and runaway niggers, with which the minds of the young were so often demoralized by negro stories. When I arrived at the school-house the wind was blowing very severely. It was in the autumn; the acorns were falling on the clap-boards covering the log-cabin, and I didn't feel very comfortable, and was most anxious for James Graham to come. At last he arrived, greatly to my relief. This was my first and last first-honor day. I was content after this to resign this post to James Graham.

This teacher had one remarkable peculiarity in regard to the admission of small boys to his school. It made no odds whether a boy was good or bad, he invariably got a flogging on the first day. The teacher always sought some pretext to make a flogging necessary, and when he began he seldom stopped until the youngster vomited or wet his breeches. I remember, as if it were yesterday, when a little boy, James Smith, about seven years old, came with his two older brothers to school.

He did not come as a pupil. His mother wished to go to a camp-meeting for a day or two, and sent him with his brothers to school, because she did not wish to leave him at home alone with the negroes. He was a pretty

little blue-eyed, flaxen-haired boy, and wore a red Mo-
rocco-leather Bumbalo cap, and red Morocco shoes, a
checked jacket, and nankeen pants, fitting tight round
the ankles and tied with red ribbons. And his shoulders
were covered with a broad white linen collar, neatly
ruffled. He was as pretty as a picture, the envy of all
the little boys, and admiration of all the little girls in
the school. Old Quigley had that one eye on him all
morning. I wondered if James would be initiated in
the usual way, with all that finery on. If so, I felt
sorry for his vanity and his Sunday clothes. It was
about eleven o'clock. James had been on his good behavior all morning. The teacher would soon go out for
his usual morning leg-stretching; when, unfortunately for
James, he started to run across the school-room. This
was against the rules. In running, he tripped and fell
sprawling in the middle of the floor. Old Quigley lit
on him with a keen, new hickory-switch, and began to
initiate him in his usual way into the mysteries of peda-
gogism. The little fellow yelled and kicked, and
screamed that he would tell his pa. This was of no use.
Old Cockeye whipped the harder. He was not afraid
of any boy's pa. I felt so sorry for the dear little boy.
I had passed along that road. I knew too well what
had to come, and I thought to myself: "Poor little fellow. If you only knew what I do, you would throw
up that breakfast, even to the milk and peaches, or
you would spoil them breeches." At last my mind
was relieved when I saw the nankeens change color.

Thereupon old Quigley immediately stopped whipping.

He made it a rule to whip, when he once began, till the remedy worked either up or down, when he immediately arrested his whipping. This was at a time when it was the custom for the boys to turn out the master a day or two before the term of school ended. Schools were seldom taken up for a longer period than from three to six months. The first quarter of Mr. Quigley's school was about to terminate, and the big boys agreed to turn him out and make him treat before the beginning of the second quarter. It was the teacher's habit, every day, to take a walk of fifteen or twenty minutes, about eleven o'clock in the morning, calling to his desk some of the larger boys to keep order during his absence. No sooner had he descended the foot of the hill leading toward the spring than the three larger boys in the school began barricading the door. There was only one door to the cabin, and by taking up the benches, which were ten or fifteen feet long, and crossing them diagonally, one to the right and another to the left, in the door, the benches projecting as much outside as inside the house, a complete barricade was formed which could easily be defended against assault from without. When the old gentleman saw what had been done he became perfectly furious. He was so violent that he easily intimidated the ringleaders. He swore that he would not give up, and would not treat, and that he was coming into the house whether or no. At last he commenced to climb on the roof of the house, and to throw a part of it off. It was covered with boards held on by poles. The ringleaders, seeing that he was sure to effect an entrance anyway, became intimidated, and agreed to remove the barricade if he would promise not to whip them. After parleying a little while, he promised that he would not flog the ringleaders. He was a man of most violent temper, and, although fifty-five years of age, he was very strong and active. The ringleader of the gang was young Bob Stafford. He was tall, slender, and very strong; but was evidently afraid of the teacher, and showed the white feather decidedly. As Mr. Quigley came in he walked up to young Stafford, who stood trembling in the middle of the room, and said: "Sir," as he drew his big fist back, "I have a great mind to run my fist right through your body!" I had always thought Mr. Quigley would do whatever he said he would do, and I remembered with what horror I looked at Stafford, expecting every minute to see the old gentleman's fist come out through his back.

My father came to see me but once during the six months I was in this school. My mother came to see me about once a month. I was dying to tell her of the bad treatment I received from the teacher and from one of his daughters. The old gentleman was very obstinate, and not only punished me unnecessarily at school, but he would not let me have what I wanted to eat, and would compel me to eat things ab-

solutely distasteful to me. I wished to tell my mother
of all this; of how Miss Nelly used to box my ears
and pull my hair, and how old Quigley used to punish
me, but I was too closely watched. I could never get
her to one side, never see her alone. At last I became
desperate. And right in the presence of the whole
family I told the whole truth of the severe treatment
that I had endured ever since I had been there, and
that she must take me home; if she didn't, I would
run away and leave the place even if I were captured
by runaway niggers and devoured by mad dogs. I
would have run away long before, but for the dread
of mad dogs and " runaway niggers."

As soon as my mother went home, and told my
father what had occurred, he sent and removed me
to my own home again, where I was as happy as the
day was long. I must say, however, that, in spite of
all the disagreeable things of this school, they managed to make the boys learn very cleverly. I used
to lie awake nights, and think about what I could do
to get home. And then it was that the idea of an
elevated road came into my mind strongly. My idea
was that all little boys placed at boarding-schools should
have a trough reaching from the school to their homes,
elevated on posts and girders, ten feet above ground,
so that they could climb up and get into this trough
and run home without the fear of either mad dogs
or runaway niggers.

The next school that I attended was taught by

Mr. John E. Sanderson, an Irishman. I was now seven years old. He taught school alternately in the Wax-haws and Hanging-Rock neighborhoods. The Waxhaws were in the northern part of the county, and the Hang-ing-Rock neighborhood in the southern. He was a fine teacher for arithmetic and writing. But he was very cruel, and whipped the boys often without any provocation at all. He thrashed them even when they were nearly grown, although he was a small man. But he was so violent in his temper and in the govern-ment of his school that the larger boys were afraid of him. There was only one day in the week when the school was happy, and that was Monday. He always got drunk on Saturday night, remained so all day Sunday, and came to school Monday morning as full as he could be, and then was always jolly and good-tempered. He would then pinch the girls' arms, and say witty things to the boys, and he never whipped anybody on Monday, so we were always happy on that day. But when Tuesday arrived he reverted to his old ways of severity. We had one poor fellow named Ike Tillman in the school. He was an orphan, and was for many years under the tuition of Mr. San-derson, and wherever he located a school, whether in one part of the county or the other, Ike Tillman al-ways followed him. He was a bad boy without be-ing very bad. He was very indolent, but not stupid. Mr. Sanderson had begun to whip him when he was seven or eight years old, and the boy had got so used to it that he expected to be flogged every day, even when he was eighteen years old and nearly six feet high. And he was seldom disappointed. At last one or two of the boys, about his own age, said to him, one day, "Ike, you're too big to be flogged; if I were you, I would show fight next time."

"Well," he said, "boys if you'll stand by me I will do it; but if you don't I can't afford it."

They agreed to stand by him. Ike had a slate about twelve by ten inches, and the wooden frame had been broken and lost. The next day Mr. Sanderson called up Ike for a thrashing. Ike came up, with his slate in his hand, leaning it against his bosom, and he said:

"Mr. Sanderson, you have been whipping me, sir, ever since I was a little boy. I am now a man. I will be d—d if I'll stand it any longer! If you come a step nearer to me, I will split your d—d old head open with this slate!"

Mr. Sanderson was surprised, and he changed his tactics immediately, and said:

"Why, Ikey, why, you would not strike me with that slate, would you?"

Ike said: "You come one step toward me and I'll split you open, clean down from your head to your backbone, and," said he, "these boys have promised to see me through the fight!"

"Well, Ikey," said Mr. Sanderson, "we have lived together a long time, but I don't think we can afford to be enemies; and, if you are willing, we'll let by-gones be by-gones, and we'll enter from this day on into a new relationship." The old man saw that the game was up and too strong for him; and, sure enough, so far as Ike Tillman and the larger boys were concerned, the old man was taught a lesson that he never forgot afterward. But he was so cruel to me and my little brother, and other little children, that I swore in my heart that, if I ever got to be a man, I would thrash him, if he were as old as Methuselah. I remember one Saturday meeting him on the road, near my father's house. My little brother and I were riding double on a little pony. He was riding in the opposite direction, meeting us. He was very drunk; and, as soon as he got near enough to us, he commenced striking at us with his stick, and really hurt my brother very much. We got away as fast as we could, and galloped home to tell my father what had happened. But Sanderson was the only teacher in the county, and if a boy didn't go to school to him there was no school for him to go to, and parents had to put up with his cruelties to their children, because they could not help themselves. They were afraid to speak to him about his treatment for fear he would dismiss their children from school.

During the time I went to school to Mr. Sanderson, about two years off and on, Arthur Ingram, a boy about fourteen years old, always came by my father's house, to accompany my brother and myself to the school. I was seven; my brother five. We had then moved to the south side of the Hanging-Rock Creek, and in going to the school we were obliged to cross this creek. We crossed it on a log, and walking through the swamp after a rain our feet became slippery. Ordinarily, the creek was very shallow where we crossed, not more than twelve or eighteen inches deep; but after a rain it would rise to four feet or even five. We were going to school one morning after a severe rain of the night before. Arthur Ingram led the way on the round, smooth log, and went safely over, leading my brother by the hand, and I followed, holding the other hand of my little brother. Just as Arthur had landed on the opposite side of the creek, my brother slipped and fell into the water and I jumped in after him. We were like Siamese twins; whatever one did, the other was bound to do; we were bound up in each other completely. We clasped each other in the water, and, if it had not been for young Ingram, we would both have been drowned. The water was about four feet deep. He stepped in and caught us by the hair of the head, and drew us to the bank, and saved our lives. He was a somnambulist, and often remained over night at my father's house. It was very curious to see him rise from bed fast asleep and wander about in a listless way, not knowing where he was going, or what he wanted to do. My mother would easily coax him back to bed, and he would remember nothing of it the next morning.

My father's partner in business was Mr. Patterson, one of the nicest and best men I ever knew; and he gave me a little lesson once that has lasted me all through life. I was about eight years old. There was a great deal of Jamestown weed growing in the corners of the fences (*Datura stramonium*). He was never very communicative or disposed to talk much to children. He admired them at a distance, and left them quietly alone. However, I was surprised one day when he called me to him, and said: "Do you see this beautiful, bad-smelling weed in the corner of the fence? Some people call it Jimson weed, and some people call it Jamestown weed. Now, will you have the kindness to tell me the proper name for that weed? You have been to school long enough to know."

My bosom swelled with vanity, when the sober, quiet, dignified Mr. Reuben Patterson came to me for information, and I thought I was certain that he did not know, or he would not have asked me the question. I certainly must not appear to be ignorant, so I drew myself up, feeling my importance and thinking I would decide the question very suddenly, and I said, "Mr. Patterson, the proper name of that weed is the Jimson weed, sir."

Mr. Patterson replied: "Young man, the proper name of that weed is the Jamestown weed, and Jimson is only a corruption of Jamestown. I would advise you, hereafter—and lay it up in your memory—as long as you live, never to presume to express an opinion on any subject unless you are thoroughly informed on that subject."

I was never so humiliated in all the days of my life. And I am sure that I have thought of Mr. Patterson and the Jamestown weed a thousand times since then, when I have been called upon to give an opinion and didn't feel competent to do it. I have often profited by the advice he then gave me.

Mr. Sanderson must have educated at least two hundred boys in Lancaster district, and it was said that he had thrashed every young man who had ever gone to school to him except one, George Witherspoon. But George was such a good boy that it was impossible for the teacher to find any pretext to flog him. Mr. Sanderson was certainly an admirable teacher, as far as he pretended to teach, and turned out many young men who were very successful in life afterward.

In 1822, when I was nine years old, I went to school to Mr. William Williams, and he was the first native American teacher that we had had among us. He was a very good teacher, and a very good man, and I used to stand at the head of my class in spelling. Unfortunately, on one occasion some gentleman returning from Camden brought me a jew's-harp. I had never seen one before, but I was perfectly carried away with this senseless little toy. I took it to school with me, and, instead of getting my spelling lessons during the recess, I was off with other little boys displaying the musical powers of my jew's-harp. Time whiled away, books were called, and the boys all hastened to school, and I had forgotten to look over my spelling lesson. About the second round of words that was given out I failed to spell correctly and had to go down. I was very much confused, and failed to spell any word that was given me, and the first thing I knew I was at the bottom of my class instead of standing at the top; and there were about eight little boys in the class. I did not know that Mr. Williams was aware of the fact that I had a jew's-harp, but when the lesson was ended, and I was standing at the wrong end of the class, he said: "Marion, you appear here to-day in a new character; I presume you intend to become a musician."

I was exceedingly mortified when he said that; and he wound up by saying, "Will you have the kindness to spell jew's-harp for us." I felt very much ashamed of my disgrace, and really did not know how to spell it, but I went it on a venture and spelled it "juice-harp." He turned to another boy and asked him if he could spell the word, which he did correctly, to my complete discomfiture. That was my first and last experience with learning music, even with a jew's-harp. I never played it afterward.

When I was a boy I always had a sweetheart. The first one was Miss Caston. It was very natural, when I was only five and she was seventeen, and she was so kind to me, that I ought to be desperately in love with her. But when I was nine years old she no longer went to school, but she had a little sister who went to school to Mr. Williams—Sallie Caston. I somehow had transferred my affections from the big sister to the little one. But the little sister was very unsympathetic, and was altogether a very stupid girl; but it took me some time to find it out. When the school was called at two o'clock it was the habit of the students to run down to the spring-branch and wash their faces and hands. I noticed that Sallie was always among the last, and I concluded that I would be among the last, to get up a little flirtation with her; and being totally ignorant how that could be done, when I was washing near the spring-branch just below her, I said, "Sallie, I am going to throw water on you." She said, "If you do I'll tell master on you." I said, "Oh no, you would not be so mean as to tell the master. If you do that it will be mean." So I took up a little water and sprinkled it on her face, and she commenced crying as though her heart would break. She started for the school-house, screaming as loud as she possibly could, crying, "Oh, Oh dear!" I walked along behind her, saying, "Sallie, you wouldn't tell the teacher, would you?" But she cried all the whole way up the hill, one hundred yards. It was a short one for me. When I got to the school-house, Sallie was 'crying so loudly that Mr. Williams came out to see what was the matter. As she came within ten or fifteen feet of the door Sallie cried out, "Marion Sims, he throwed water all over me down by the spring, boo-hoo!" The master said, "Well, Marion, did you throw water on

Sallie?" I could not say that I didn't, and I had no explanation. My heart was broken for Sallie, and I stammered out, "Yes, sir, I did." As long as I had acknowledged it, there was nothing more to say, and Mr. Williams knocked the love for Sallie out of me in about three minutes, and I never was in love with her again after that. She was a poor little forlorn creature.

Mr. Williams and I were great friends after that. He was my father's deputy-sheriff. He was an admirable teacher, and did the best possible for the advancement of his pupils, and succeeded with all of them who were willing to work. In 1824 my father removed from Hanging-Rock Creek to Lancaster village. I think he went on account of Mr. Williams's school. My brother and myself were left at the old place, in charge of a manager and the negroes. Here we were very much neglected; and white children living among negroes, if they were not looked after carefully by the mother, were sure to become lousy. The servants who had charge of us had neglected us entirely, and I shall never forget the mortification that my mother experienced when my brother and myself went to Lancaster to see her, when she found our heads and clothing infested with these little creatures. They belong always to the black race.

A great hit has been made by Mr. Harris, of Atlanta, Georgia, in regard to the folk-lore of the Africans, in conversations with "Uncle Remus." He gives the story of "Brer Rabbit," "Brer Fox," and other quadruped animals. When I was seven or eight years old a negro by the name of Cudjo used to come every Saturday night to my father's house and tell these African negro stories, about the rabbit and the wolf, etc. He was about four feet high, remarkably well built, and his face was beautiful, but horribly tattooed, just as it appears to us, symmetrically done. He said he was captured and brought to this country when he was a boy. He was a prince in his own country, and would have risen to become a king or ruler of the nation or tribe, if he had remained at home there. It has been questioned by some, whence came these stories of negro folk-lore. From what I remember of this negro, Cudjo, I am satisfied that he brought his stories from Africa, and that a few negroes like himself laid the foundation among the negroes native to this country of the lore that has lately attracted such attention. This man told wonderful stories — ghost - stories — and would eat fire, and knock himself with a stick on the head, when he was telling them. I remember how anxiously I looked for him every Saturday night to tell stories that were really poisoning my mind, and infusing into it and my nature a sense of fear which should not have been cultivated in children. We regularly saved np our little sixpences and gave him all our money for his evening's entertainment; and it was for the money he got out of us little boys in the neighborhood that he went from house to house, giving his Brother Rabbit lectures to little boys.

In 1825 my brother and myself followed our parents to Lancaster, and the days of Johnnie Sanderson as a teacher were about to be numbered. Dr. Jones, Mr. Benjamin Massey, Mr. Sikes Massey, Colonel Witherspoon and my father, all had boys to educate, and they were determined to establish a high-school in Lancaster. They raised a fund for that purpose, organized a board of trustees, built a very nice two-story brick house, thirty-five by twenty feet, and advertised for teachers. Mr. Henry Connelly, of Washington University, in Pennsylvania, was chosen to inaugurate the new educational movement in Franklin Academy, in Lancaster village. He arrived early in December, 1825. There were no railroads, of course, in that day and time, no stage lines from Washington, Pennsylvania, to an obscure country place like Lancaster. The mail was carried across the country on horseback. So Mr. Connelly and the young man who accompanied him as his assistant teacher purchased a horse and buggy in Pennsylvania, drove down through Maryland, Virginia, and North Carolina, to Lancaster, and there sold the horse and buggy, and entered upon the duties of their vocation.

The academy was opened on the fifth day of December, 1825, and the sons of all the "swells" in the village and neighborhood were to study Latin, as well as the several branches of useful English education. I told my father that I thought he was too poor to give me a classical education; that he had eight children; that the other gentlemen whose sons were studying

Latin were all rich men, and that he had better have me prepared for the counting-house and let me help him support his large family. He said, no; that his own education was so entirely wanting, he knew how important it was for every man to get along in the world, and he was determined to give his children a good education, if he did nothing more for them, and that was better than money. So, with the other boys, I went on with my classical studies. The school prospered under Mr. Connelly's administration. He soon established a reputation as a disciplinarian, and as an efficient and successful teacher, and boys were sent from all the counties round. He remained in Lancaster two years, and educated many young men who in after-life rose to distinction. He was a preacher, and belonged to the sect of the Seceders.

The school was for both boys and girls—the lower floor for girls and very little children, and the upper floor for the others. There were about seventy-five in all, boys predominating, some of them over twenty-five years old, down to some not more than ten or twelve. He was certainly a very able teacher, and in two years he left in his school a set of boys who were as advanced as possible for them to advance in that length of time. Like all schools, there were some good and some bad boys. None very bad except one—William Foster. He was a notoriously bad boy from every point of view. He exerted a demoralizing influence on the younger boys of the school.

It was said that Washington never told a lie. I am very sure I am not Washington, for I told one lie in my life, and it was a "whopper"; but I told it very mildly. I always felt sorry that I had to lie, but I can not say I have regretted so much that I did. It happened in this way:

At twelve o'clock was always dismission for play-hours. There was the best of remarkably good boys, Ward Crockett. He always took his seat in the master's chair and sat there studying his lessons while the rest of us were out at play, and he was never known to miss any question put to him. One day Frank Massey came to me and said, "Look here, Marion, I want to break up this Ward Crockett business—sitting in master's chair. Now I tell you what you do. You see this pin?" It was nearly two inches long, as large as a knitting-needle, with a big head and sharp point. Said he, "You take this pin, and I will go and get Ward Crockett and take him to the well. While we are gone you will have half an hour, and you fix that pin in the center of the master's chair. When he comes back and sits down I don't think he will get much of a lesson afterward." I very foolishly agreed to do what he had told me. Presently, Frank Massey and Ward Crockett were seen walking toward the well. I immediately entered the academy; there wasn't a soul in it; everybody was out at play. I very ingeniously arranged the pin in the center of the master's chair-seat, with the point

4

sticking directly upward, and fixed it so that it was
difficult to turn it to either side. Ward Crockett became amused at a game of ball out in the yard with
us, and didn't go into the house that day at all to get
his lessons. At two o'clock the school was called, and
the class of large boys was the first to recite. The
master was walking up and down, in front of the class
with book in hand saying, "Next;" "right;" "next;"
"right," and so on. The answers were all given very
correctly and the recitation was progressing finely. It
was about half through, and after a while the teacher
got tired of walking and went to sit down. He went
down into the chair, but he flew up like a rocket; his
head almost touched the joists above him. He came
down like a stick. Never was a whole school so surprised as at Mr. Connelly's gymnastic feat. Nobody
knew who put that pin in the chair but Frank Massey and myself. But he was certain that one of three
young men in the class had done it. He thought it
might possibly be Frank Witherspoon, but was very sure
that it was either Stark Perry or William Foster, and he
thought he would fasten it on the guilty party. So he
began at the head of the class, and said, "Rush Jones,
did you put that pin in the chair?" He said, "No, sir."

I said, "My God, if he asks everybody the question
separately about that pin, what is to become of me? If
he goes on in that way he will certainly ask me, and
if he finds out that I put that pin in there he will
surely murder me."

"Ward Crockett, did you put that pin in the chair?" He answered, "No, sir."

Suffice it to say that he went on, calling each one by name. Presently he came to Tromp Witherspoon. "Witherspoon, did you put that pin in the chair?" He said, "No, sir." The thing was getting close to me. I said, "Good heavens! Look how pale he is! I think I must tell the truth, and how am I to do it?"

However, before he got to me, he came to William Foster. He thought he had his man. He hesitated, and looked at him, and tried to browbeat him. He said, "William Foster, did you put that pin in my chair?" He said, "No, sir, I didn't; neither do I know who did." The teacher looked despondent after that. Another was asked, and another, and presently he came to the youth beside me, James Adams.

"James Adams," he said, "did you put that pin in my chair?" The teacher well knew that he didn't. I was shivering and felt very cold. He addressed me very mildly: "Marion, did you put that pin in the chair?"

I said, "No, sir," timidly. I thought I would say yes at the last moment, but Mr. Connelly's pale face, compressed lips and clenched hand overawed the truth, and it could not come forth.

Still he went on. Presently he came to Perry. He stopped still, and looked at him fiercely, with a sort of sardonic smile. He thought he had his man at last. He had started out with the expectation of fixing it on

Perry or Foster. Perry was his last hope for revenge. He said, "Stark Perry." "Sir?" "Did you put that pin in my chair?" "No, sir, I did not; and moreover I don't know who did put it there, either."

That pin was always a mystery. No one in the school ever suspected either Frank Massey or me. The little lie I told worried me for some time afterward.

Twenty-eight years after this, when I was living in New York and working to establish the Woman's Hospital, I heard of a preacher by the name of Connelly, who was living in Newburg. I wrote to him, asking him if he was the Henry Connelly who had charge of the Franklin Academy, in Lancaster, South Carolina, in 1825–'27. He answered me very kindly; said he was the same man and that he was coming to see me on a certain day. When he arrived I was not at home, and my wife was out. He had never kept the run of any of his old students, and he did not know what had become of any of them, and he was very glad to hear from me. When he arrived, as I said, I was out and so was my wife, and the children came in to see him, knowing that he was to come, and, as they went up to shake hands with him, he said: "How much this little girl looks like a little girl I had in my school, twenty-five or twenty-six years ago. Her name was Theresa Jones." The little girl said: "Why that was my mamma's name." He replied, "That is very odd, but you look exactly as your mamma did then."

My house was always after this a stopping-place for

him. He always had a room there, and frequently came to see us, and sometimes he staid a day and a night; but he frequently dined with us, or took luncheon with us, when he came to town, and we were ever happy to see him. One evening, while we were sitting at dinner, my two youngest little children got to laughing, and I said, "What are you laughing at?" One of them said, "Oh, nothing; but isn't that the man whose chair you put the pin in when you went to school to him?" I didn't know but what he understood the children, and I said to him, "Mr. Connelly, I have something to say to you which has been on my conscience for more than a quarter of a century." I then told him all about the story of the pin. He took it in very great earnestness and bad humor, and could not enjoy it. He was mortified to death. Of all the seventy-five boys in his school, he said, I was the last one he would have suspected of doing such a thing. Mr. Connelly could not forgive it, and he never came to my house after that day.

I said William Foster was a bad boy, and that reminds me of an incident that occurred just before Mr. Connelly closed his term of school. Foster had given him the nick-name of "Little Teer." There was no sense in the name, but he was very sensitive about it, and didn't like it at all. One day, during intermission, somebody had drawn a face on the blackboard, and written under it, "Little Teer." As usual, the class of big boys were first for recitation. Connelly was walking up and down before the class, as was his custom, between

them and the blackboard. After a while he discovered
the face on the blackboard and the " Little Teer " written under it, and he immediately turned around and
said, " William Foster, did you draw that ? Did you
write those words ! " He said, " Yes, sir, I did ; have
you any objection to it ? I have been wanting a clip at
you for some time." With that they locked. Foster
was a very tall man ; Connelly was short. Connelly was
matured, and strong, and was too much for Foster, and
he threw him out of doors and bruised him considerably.
The next day the trustees of the academy called a meeting and expelled Foster from the school. He ought to
have been expelled long before.

Foster became very dissipated and died two or three
years afterward.

Stark Perry was governor of Florida when our great
civil war broke out. He was very much of a man, and
in many respects a very fine fellow.

Mr. Connelly, before leaving Lancaster, kindly undertook to engage some young graduate to come on from
Washington, Pennsylvania, to take his place, and he was
fortunate in the selection of Mr. John Harris, who entered on his duties at Franklin Academy the first of December, 1827. Of course there were no railroads in
those days, and no stage lines from Washington, Pennsylvania, to Lancaster, South Carolina, so Harris purchased a horse and buggy in Washington, Pennsylvania,
and a young man named Mittag came with him. Then
Mr. Connelly took the same horse and buggy and drove

it back to Pennsylvania. Mr. Harris was a very good teacher, but altogether a different style of a man from Connelly. He admired fine horses, liked a game of whist, and "put on airs" considerably. Still, he was very much liked and was a very efficient teacher. He remained two years, and left in 1829.

CHAPTER IV.

I start to college and get homesick—My first experience with wine not a success.

THE Franklin Academy then passed into the hands of Mr. Niles, of Camden. He was no disciplinarian, and not much of a scholar. Still he prepared boys for college, and in 1830 we all started for Columbia, S. C., about the first of October. There were six of us, all wanting to enter the sophomore rising junior, or junior, except two, who went into the sophomore class. I was admitted to sophomore rising junior. I said previously that in 1825 I did not wish to study the classics; I didn't wish to go to college. In 1830, I still would greatly have preferred to remain at home and take a clerkship in Mr. Stringfellow's store. Not because I objected to college life so much, but I felt that my father was not able to give me a university education. The other young men who were going with me to Columbia were the sons of rich men, planters; and their fathers were able to send them to college. However, college life was a new existence to me. When I went there I was one of the best boys in the world. I do not know that I had

a single bad habit. I didn't swear; I didn't drink; I
didn't gamble; indeed, I had no vices that could be
called such. I was such a good boy that my mother
certainly expected me to be a Presbyterian clergyman,
and my father, I knew, was educating me for the bar.
I knew I should disappoint both of them. When I had
been in college about six months, I became very homesick and wanted to go home. When I thought of all
the money it would cost my poor father to keep me
there, and that he had a family of eight children to support, I decided to relinquish my college course, return
home, and help him to support his family. At last I
became desperate, and, without giving any notice to my
father or the faculty, I left college and went home. I
got a young friend of mine, from Charleston, South
Carolina, Peter Porcher, to answer for me at prayers
and recitations. At prayers it was all right, and he had
only to respond, "Here," when my name was called.
At recitations, if I were called upon, all Mr. Porcher
would have to answer was, "Not prepared, sir"; and
the professor would never look up to see if the right
man gave the answer or not; but would merely put a
mark against my name. When a fellow failed to recite,
it was called a "flash."

My visit home was altogether unexpected to my
family. My father was absent, fortunately for me, and
when I entered the house my mother did not run to
take me to her bosom, as I expected she would, but
looked at me with the utmost surprise and said: "What

in the world, Marion, brings you home?" I told her of my unhappiness at remaining in college, and my great wish to come home and to become a merchant's clerk, and help my father to make a living for us all. My poor mother said: "My dear boy, you are a foolish fellow. Your father knows best what is the proper thing for you, and I am glad that he is not at home to experience the mortification which I feel in seeing you here now. He will not be at home until to-morrow evening, and you must start back to college to-morrow morning before he sees you."

I was exceedingly mortified at having done such a mean thing; and so, with a heavy heart, the next morning I left my dear mother and returned to college. I had been absent about three days, and I was not missed at college during my absence.

Dr. Cooper was president of the college. He was a man considerably over seventy years old, a remarkable looking man. He was never called Dr. Cooper, but " Old Coot." " Coot " is the short for " cooter," a name generally applied south to the terrapin, and the name suited him exactly. He was less than five feet high, and his head was the biggest part of the whole man. He was a perfect taper from the side of his head down to his feet; he looked like a wedge with a head on it. He was a man of great intellect and remarkable learning. Next to President Cooper, Professor Henry was perhaps the ablest man in the faculty. Professor Nott was an able man and a lovely character, but not a man of a great deal of force. The other professors, of mathematics (Wallace), and languages (Parks), were very ordinary men, very old, and without the confidence and respect of the class. Dr. Cooper exerted a very bad influence on the interests of the college. He was a pronounced infidel, and every year lectured on the "Authenticity of the Pentateuch" to the senior class, generally six or eight weeks before their graduation.

There was no necessity for his delivering this lecture. It did not belong to his chair of political economy. Nor was it necessary as president. I have always wondered why the trustees of the college permitted him to go out of the routine of the duties of his office and deliver a lecture of this sort to a set of young men just starting out in the world. I am amazed, at this late day, that a country as full of Presbyterianism and bigotry as that was at that time should have tolerated a man in his position, especially when advocating and lecturing upon such an unnecessary subject. Dr. Cooper lived before his day. If he had flourished now, in the days of Darwin and Tyndall and Huxley, he would have been a greater infidel than any or all three of them put together.

Soon after I arrived at college the new friends I had made there invited me to go to Mr. Isaac Lyons's oyster saloon and join them in an oyster supper. It was always the habit of the young man inviting his compauions to Lyons's to stand the treat of oysters and wine for the crowd. I never had taken a glass of wine in my life before but once. That was the fourth of July, when I was about nine years old. There was a celebration at my father's house, and dinner was served under the great mulberry trees in the yard. A half-dozen boys of us were given places at the lower end of the table. While toasts were being drunk, some gentlemen passed the wine to the boys and they were all allowed to help themselves. I am sure I didn't drink more than two table-spoonfuls of Madeira wine; the other boys drank much more than I did. Everybody was having a good time and enjoying the occasion exceedingly. Unfortunately, I had to be carried to the house, in the course of half an hour, and put to bed, dead drunk. I was exceedingly mortified, and I never drank any liquor after that until I went to college. The first night that I went to supper with the young men at Mr. Lyons's I indulged in a small glass of Madeira. The others drank freely; none of them seemed to feel it. When we started to return to the college I had to go with a man on each side of me. I was so drunk that I would have fallen if left alone. I felt very unhappy about it. I said: "Boys, it is very odd that you can all drink wine and I can not. But I am determined to learn to drink wine."

So this experiment was tried three or four times in two or three months. Each time I had to be taken home to the college, more than half a mile. Then I said to my companions: "See here, boys, I don't understand how this is. There must be something peculiar in my organization. You can all drink and I can not. You like wine and I do not. I hate it; its taste is disagreeable. Its effects are dreadful, because it makes me drunk. Now, I hope you all will understand the position I occupy. I don't think it is right for you to ask me to drink wine when I don't want it, and it produces such a bad effect upon me." They all agreed that they would not ask me to drink wine again.

Since then I have never taken wine or brandy, except in sickness, when it has been prescribed for me and urged upon me by the doctor. Even a drop of brandy put on my tongue is felt instantly in my knees and all over my whole system; and although I have often, over and over again, been compelled to take brandy, I don't think I can recall one single instance in which I have been conscious of any beneficial effects from it. I recall many instances in which it produced decidedly disagreeable and uncomfortable effects.

Mr. Lyons's saloon was patronized by every young man who had ever gone through the South Carolina College, from its foundation up to my day (1832). He was one of the kindest and best of men, to everybody in the world, and particularly to the students. He would trust them to any amount, and for any length of time. He never asked them for money; he lent them money if they wanted it, and he was looked upon as the student's friend always. When I left college I owed him two hundred dollars. I had been there two years, and had not paid him a cent. He was never known to accept interest on a debt any young man had contracted, and he was never known to have charged them for any article that they had not had, or more than it was worth. I said to him: "Mr. Lyons, I am afraid you have lost a great deal of money by us boys." He said: "No, sir; I have never lost a dollar in my life. I have been here twenty years, trusting students, and I have never lost a debt yet. Whenever a student returns home he is almost sure to send me the money very soon or to bring it to me as you have done. If he fails to do it he writes to me and explains why he can not do it. In three or four instances young men have gone away, leaving large debts behind them in my favor. They have been suddenly stricken down by fevers or dysentery, and have died. In every instance the parents have sent me the full sum of all they were owing me, without my even calling on them for it."

Well, I dragged through college in 1831–'32. I was not remarkable for anything very bad or very good. I was known as a self-willed, but amiable fellow. My recitations were about average; not very good or very bad. I was very small when I was eighteen, and weighed but one hundred and eight pounds. Hamilton Boykin, of Camden, South Carolina, was my chum, and he was one of the noblest boys I ever knew. He was a few months younger than I, and was not quite so tall, but looked a little stouter. Still, when we got into the scales, we just balanced each other.

Each of us weighed just one hundred and eight pounds.

I didn't know one card from another until I went to college, and there the students taught me to play whist. The Pedee boys taught me (Cannon, Evans, Williamson, Ellerbe, and four or five others), and we usually had a game of whist two or three times a week. Cannon was a funny fellow. At every game of cards, not with every hand, he would often whistle out and say: "Well, boys—

"There was a man, he had a cow,
  And nothing for to feed her;
  He slapped his hand upon her rump,
  And said, 'Consider, cow, consider.'"

Immediately Ras. Ellerbe would look up and complain of Cannon's senseless couplet. "Look here, Cannon, don't tell that cow to consider any more. Now, you have a private understanding with your partner. When you lay stress on 'consider,' you mean one thing; and when you lay it on *slap*, you mean another; you may as well tell him to lead trumps, or not to lead trumps. I am opposed to your saying 'consider' so often, and insist on your playing the game without bringing up that darned old cow of the farmer who had 'nothing for to feed her.'"

CHAPTER V.

I LIVED in the age of dueling. I was educated to believe that duels insured the proprieties of society and protected the honor of women. I have hardly a doubt but that, while I was a student in the South Carolina College, if anything had happened to have made it necessary for me to fight a duel, I would have gone out with the utmost coolness and allowed myself to be shot down. But my views on that subject were entirely changed, a long, long time ago.

The boys got up a mock duel one day between Frank Massey and Robert Burns. Frank was in the secret but poor Burns was not. But he behaved bravely. They fired cork bullets at each other. I always thought it a hard and foolish game to play off on a good fellow like Robert Burns.

There was a real duel in South Carolina College, just after I graduated. It was between Roach, of Colleton, and Adams, of Richland District. Roach was a young man about six feet high and a physical beauty.

Adams was no less so, though not so tall. Both men were of fine families, and Adams was supposed to be a young man of talent and promise. It occurred in this way: They were very intimate friends; they sat opposite to each other in the Stewards' Hall, at table. When the bell rang and the door was opened, the students rushed in, and it was considered a matter of honor, when a man got hold of a dish of butter or bread, or any other dish, it was his. Unfortunately, Roach and Adams sat opposite each other, and both caught hold of a dish of trout at the same moment. Adams did not let go; Roach held on to the dish. Presently Roach let go of the dish and glared fiercely in Adams's face, and said: "Sir, I will see you after supper." They sat there all through the supper, both looking like mad bulls, I presume. Roach left the supper-room first, and Adams immediately followed him. Roach waited outside the door for Adams. There were no hard words and no fisticuffs—all was dignity and solemnity. "Sir," said Roach, "What can I do to insult you?" Adams replied, "This is enough, sir, and you will hear from me." Adams immediately went to his room and sent a challenge to Roach. It was promptly accepted, and each went up town and selected seconds and advisers. And now comes the strange part of this whole affair: No less a person than General Pierce M. Butler, distinguished in the Mexican war as the colonel of the Palmetto regiment, and who became Governor of South Carolina, agreed to act as second to one of these young men. The other man had as his adviser Mr. D. J. McCord, a distinguished lawyer, a most eminent citizen, a man of great talents, whose name lives in the judicial records of the state as being the author of McCord and Nott's reports. Here were two of the most prominent citizens of South Carolina, each of them about forty years of age, aiding and abetting dueling between two young men, neither of them over twenty years of age.

They fought at Lightwood Knot Springs, ten miles from Columbia. They were both men of the coolest courage. My friend Dr. Josiah C. Nott, then of Columbia, and afterward of Mobile, Alabama, who died some eight years ago in Mobile, was the surgeon to. one of the parties. They were to fight at ten paces distant. They were to fire at the word "one," raising their pistols. There are two methods of dueling: One is to hold the pistol erect, pointing heavenward, dropping it at right angles with the body at the word "Fire!" and then firing at the word one, two, or three; the other is to hold the muzzle down toward the earth, and then at the word to raise it at arm's length and fire. The latter method was adopted at the Roach–Adams duel. When the word "Fire!" was given, each started to raise his pistol; but each had on a frock-coat, and the flap of Roach's coat caught on his arm, and prevented his pistol from rising. When Adams saw that, he lowered his pistol to the ground. The word was then given a second time: "Are you ready?

Fire! One!" They both shot simultaneously; Dr. Nott said it was impossible to tell which was before the other.

Adams was shot through the pelvis, and he lingered a few hours and died in great agony. Roach was shot through the right hip-joint, two or three inches below where his ball entered Adams's body. He lingered for a long time, and came near dying of blood-poisoning; but after weeks and months of suffering, he was able to get up, but was lame for life. I presume he was one of the most unhappy wretches on the face of the earth. He had killed his best friend, became very dissipated, and always, when he was drunk, the murder of Adams was his theme of conversation; doubtless, when he was sober, it troubled his conscience. He studied medicine and went to Philadelphia, to the Jefferson Medical College, and there he gave himself up entirely to dissipation. He had delirium tremens and died in Philadelphia, in an attack of it; I think it was in the month of January, 1836. During the latter part of his illness he was imagining that he was in hell, and begging the author of all torments to pour molten lead down his throat to quench his thirst. This account was given to me by a young man who was an eye-witness of this death-bed scene.

Dueling was the bane of the age in which I lived, in my native state. Many valuable lives were sacrificed to it. I will never forget how the whole country was turned into mourning over the death of Columbus I. Nixon, of Camden, in 1825. He was a young lawyer of very great promise, and unfortunately it was necessary for him to fight a duel. Augusta, just across the Savannah River, was the usual dueling-ground of the South Carolinians. Young Nixon was shot through the heart. I have forgotten who was his unfortunate antagonist; but the sorrow that fell upon the whole community was such that it ought to have put every man's influence against this dreadful method of conflict.

These duels were generally between young and unmarried men; but there were exceptions to this. General James Blair was a noted man in his day and time. He was almost a giant; he was about six feet seven inches high; was symmetrically made. He was a man of great mental as well as physical power. He was very tyrannical and overbearing; he was both loved and feared. Then, politics were altogether of a personal character. There were no great principles at stake; it was simply whether this or that *man* should be elected; and the man that was the most popular, and had the most money, and could buy the most whisky, was generally the man that carried the day. General Blair had fortune and friends, and he was seldom a candidate for any office without getting it. He was a member of Congress, and represented the district of Lancaster, Kershaw, Chesterfield, and Darlington. There was no man in the whole country that could defeat him. He was engaged in several duels. A young man by the name of Evans, married, a lawyer, and the conductor of a weekly paper at Camden, opposed the manner of the canvass made by General Blair, and he had occasion to say something not over-complimentary of the hero of Lynch's Creek, which was very offensive to the General, and the latter thereupon sent him a challenge. Evans didn't want to fight; but public opinion would brand any man as a coward, at that day and time, who refused to fight a duel. So he was obliged to accept the challenge. They went to Augusta, and I have heard Evans recount to my father all the circumstances of the duel: of his sensations; of his firing; of his anxieties as he rode to the field. He said he didn't think that he ever felt so miserable in all his life as he did when the crowd of Georgians, who got wind of the duel and gathered to see the sport, were standing around, and when he and Blair had taken their positions at ten paces distant, with pistols all ready. Just then he heard one Georgian, a rough-looking customer, say to another, "By G–d, Bob, I will bet you five dollars that the big man kills the little one." This was just before he heard the word "Fire!" given; and when he heard the word "Fire!" given, and looked into the muzzle of Blair's pistol, it looked as large to him as a flour-barrel. He pulled away; they fired at the same time; he missed Blair, though Blair was as big as a barn-door and weighed three hundred and fifty pounds. Blair shattered his right arm, and made Evans a cripple for life. It is said that Blair, previously to the challenge, had ridden into Evans's house in a drunken condition, and where Mrs. Evans was sitting beside the cradle where her babe lay, and charged his horse over the cradle. This was the story told at the time all over the country, but I never believed it, though there were plenty of people in South Carolina who did believe it.

As General Blair grew older, he grew more politic, and cared less for fighting a duel than formerly. However, Colonel Hammond, subsequently Governor of South Carolina, who was the conductor of a public press in Columbia, had occasion, in the course of a criticism upon Blair's conduct in Congress, to say some hard things of him; whereupon, Blair, in the heat of the affair, sent Hammond a challenge. Hammond accepted, probably, with thanks. There was nothing else for him to do. They were to fight at the corner-stone of the line dividing North and South Carolina, eight or ten miles from Lancaster. The two parties met in Lancaster. The Blair party stopped at my father's house, and the Hammond party stopped at Gill's Hotel. Colonel Witherspoon, Dr. Jones, the Masseys, and some of the other influential citizens, including my father, were determined that this duel should not take place. For one time, there were men found in South Carolina who dared face public opinion, and save two men, whose lives were useful, from throwing them away so foolishly. The affair was easily settled. It was easy enough for Hammond to say that he didn't mean to offend General Blair by what he had written, and General Blair then could easily retract the challenge. The whole thing was arranged in ten minutes. So the friends of the former agreed to bring Hammond to my father's house, to meet General Blair, which was done. They had never met each other before. I was about eleven years old, and I remember seeing the tall, handsome, and graceful Hammond introduced to the magnificent giant Blair. They shook hands, and both seemed very happy, and everybody else was as happy as they were.

When General Blair was a younger man, he was making a visit to his friend Dr. Bartlett Jones, of Lancaster. While he was sitting in the parlor, talking to the doctor, Mrs. Jones, being in the dining-room adjoining with a very pretty young girl, said to her, "Come here, my dear, and look through the key-hole into the parlor, and you will see the great General Blair." The young girl went softly to the door, looked through the key-hole, and saw the General. She at once drew back, clapped her hands, and, jumping up, exclaimed: "What a splendid-looking man he is! He is just the style of man that I like, and I intend to marry him." And what is strange, this same young lady did eventually become the wife of General Blair. She did not weigh more than one hundred pounds, while the general's weight was over three hundred pounds. The young lady was rich and well educated, and had everything to recommend her. He had social position and power, and was looked upon as a great man in his day and time. But as a representative in Congress he disgraced himself beyond measure. He was continually drunk during the last year he was in Congress, and on one occasion he went into a theatre, and in a state of delirium tremens, while the play was going on, he drew his pistol and fired at the stage. He was removed from the theatre by the police, and to the last day of his life it was a source of the bitterest regret to him.

It is said that cowards sometimes fight duels; that dueling is no evidence of courage or bravery. I am perfectly satisfied of this. A very remarkable duel took place between two Lancaster men about the year 1836. A young man named Herschell Massey (we called him "Hersch"), belonging to one of the first families in the district (a son of Mr. Sikes Massey), often affected the rowdy, and yet there was much of the gentleman about him. He rather wanted to be looked upon as a bully, but he was a man of more heart than the world gave him credit for. He had some personal difficulty with Mr. Mittag on account of an election. Mittag was always antagonistic to the chivalric sentiment that pervaded South Carolina. Massey, thinking Mittag a coward, challenged him. Mittag knew very well that he had always been considered as a coward in that country. He had not been understood. And he said to himself: "I don't think I am a coward; I am going to fight this

thing throngh." So he went to Camden and put himself under the training of the great duelist Chapman
Levy, a man whose advice had always been sought in
every duel that had been fought in the upper part of
South Carolina for many years. Levy put Mittag
through a course of training, and he became a pretty good
shot, and thus worked himself up to the highest pitch
of physical and moral courage. They went to Chesterfield District to fight, and, strange to say, Massey, who
was always regarded as a brave man, was very unwilling
to fight, and it is said that he would gladly have got
out of the affair if it had been possible. Mittag, who
was regarded as a coward, never flinched. He felt that
he had nothing to live for; was without friends and
without sympathy; and he determined to sacrifice his
life, or to prove to the world that he was no longer to
be called a coward.

When they took their stations, Mittag was the picture of coolness and determination. Massey was so despondent in seeing this manifestation of courage that
he was almost disarmed, and fought the duel under dis-
advantageous circumstances; for he was demoralized by
all his surroundings. When the word " Fire!" was
given, both raised their pistols together. Mittag was
shot through the thigh; Massey was not hurt. Mittag
bore his wound with heroism and patience, and he
begged to be tied up to a little sapling and have another shot at Massey; but the seconds interfered and declared that there must be no more bloodshed and risk of

5

life. Massey was my school-fellow. He was two years my junior. With all his bad qualities, he had some noble traits of character. He was kind and generous and sympathetic, and, knowing him as I did when he was a boy, I was surprised that, as a man, he manifested so many characteristics of the bully and rowdy. Mittag was a man of great culture and refinement, and a native of Hagerstown, Maryland. He was educated in Washington College, Pennsylvania, and had gone to South Carolina with John Harris, when he was called to the charge of the Franklin Academy, in 1827. He there studied law with Mr. Howard, and set himself up as a practitioner. However, he failed utterly in all this. He was a ripe scholar, and one of the handsomest men I ever saw. He had a high, classical head, the very picture of Shakespeare to look at, elevated and refined, and more beautiful, if anything, than Shakespeare's; at least, so I thought, of any I have ever seen. He was a philosopher, a scholar, and, in my early days, I loved him dearly. I was fond of him because he had no friends, and because he was kind to me. He took a great fancy to me, and used to write my Greek lessons for me, and gave me advice about my future course of life. From that day to this he has been my devoted friend and occasional correspondent. Many a man has lived before his time; Mittag lived two or three thousand years after his. If he had lived in the days of Socrates or Plato, he would then have been regarded as a great philosopher, for he was learned in the old classics, and had a philosophy of life that was not at all suited to the age in which he lived.

We are what we are by education, and hardly any man is responsible for his opinions, or in his youth for his acts. When I was a boy, in college, I was so imbued with the correctness of dueling that I am sure that if I had been challenged, or thought I had any occasion, I would not have hesitated to put my life in jeopardy in defense of a principle of honor.

CHAPTER VI.

College days continued—A midnight serenade—Almost a murder—The class of 1831—Its *personnel*—Class of 1832—Cole's visit from a ghost—Fire at the college—Cole's heroism.

Two things occurred during my college life which always have been matters of regret and sorrow to me. The first was this: Most of the young men boarded in the Steward's Hall. Many of them got tired of bad bread, bad meat, bad butter, bad manners, and bad everything. It was served at a cheap rate for young men who boarded in the Steward's Hall. Some of us at last got tired, and we went up-town and engaged board in a private house. So about a dozen of us, or possibly fifteen of us, boarded at a house kept by a lady who lived near the old capitol, whose name I have now forgotten. William Boykin sat at the head of the table. At his right sat James Aiken. I sat next to James Aiken; Boykin Witherspoon sat next to me. One day, as we were sitting down to dinner, at one o'clock, James Aiken, who was a very popular, fine young fellow, playfully pulled my chair out from behind me. I happened to see it, and didn't sit down, but mechanically turned around and pulled Witherspoon's chair from under him.

Witherspoon didn't see me, and he fell plump on the floor. He was a man of great dignity, a grand, noble fellow to look at, and a grand, noble fellow from every point of view: morally, socially, and intellectually. He was a man much respected and much beloved. When he arose, I apologized in the humblest manner that I possibly could. I assured him that I did not intend to throw him down, that I regretted it then, and that I was not ashamed to say that I was heartily sorry and should regret it always. I hoped he would receive my apology in the spirit in which it was tendered. He received it very gruffly, saying that he was not at all satisfied. He could not get over the indignity offered to his person. After dinner, he spoke to me of the matter again. Again I repeated the apology; and still he was not satisfied. I then became indignant, and said: " I have done all that a gentleman can do. Now, sir, help yourself." I did not want to appear before my comrades as if I were afraid of anything or anybody. If Witherspoon had been a fool, he would have challenged me. If he had been a coward, he would have knocked me over; for I was a little fellow, and he was a big fellow. He was too much of the man to perpetrate any such outrageous acts. I always felt sorry for it; I never saw him during our intercourse at college without feeling unhappy, though it never was mentioned. He never liked me after that unfortunate day. I never saw him without thinking of it. However, later in our student life, in Charleston, South Carolina, two years after this, my heart was gladdened by a social visit from Boykin Witherspoon. I was glad, and I felt that if he had not forgotten, he had certainly forgiven the unfortunate affair and the foolish freak of a college boy. I had great respect and admiration for him, as for no other young man in all the college. I am now satisfied that if Witherspoon had been foolish enough to have challenged me to a duel, I should have accepted it, even at the risk of losing my own life or of killing him. So much for a faulty education and for a depraved sentiment of public opinion.

Another unfortunate thing, which gave me great regret ever since, occurred during my college life. Rufus Nott was my junior; he was a sophomore when I was a junior. He was the son of the great Judge Nott of South Carolina, one of the younger brothers of the distinguished Josiah C. Nott, already alluded to in this story. One day he said to me, " Marion, do you want to go with me and George Ellis and John Wells, and two or three other boys, out to Barhamville to give the girls a serenade?" This was in the month of May, 1831. Dr. Marks had established a high-school for young ladies at Barhamville, two miles from Columbia, out in the Sand Hills, a mile or more beyond the Lunatic Asylum. Young ladies were sent there from all parts of the State to school, as it was the first and only school of its character at the South. It was of a very high class, and most of the young men of the college had sweethearts, or cousins, or sisters attending this school. "Rufe," as we used to call him, took a loaded gun with him, and also a bottle of whisky; and instead of having a hired fiddler to go out serenading the girls, we had purchased a number of little tin trumpets and school-children's drums. So we went out, thus armed, for our serenade.

The night was beautiful; a full moon shining. It was about eleven o'clock when we arrived. The house was situated on an elevated knoll in the pine woods, surrounded by a beautiful drive and gardens in a state of high cultivation. We marched around this magnificent house, and everything seemed to be as quiet and silent as the grave itself. We were beating the drums, and playing the little tin trumpets, and making a heathenish, hellish noise. After satisfying ourselves with this exploit, we started off. Unfortunately, Dr. Marks had become so incensed that he dressed himself and descended, with a shot-gun in hand, to fire at the boys. We had got nearly down to the gate, some two or three hundred yards from the house, when Dr. Marks came, with his gun in his hand, running in great haste; he fired his gun, loaded with bird-shot. Unluckily, one of the shot struck Rufus Nott in the lower lip, and one or two in the forehead; he bit the shot out of his lower lip. He had a gun in his hand, with a flint-and-steel lock; it was loaded with bird-shot, and he started to run after the doctor, who, after discharging his gun, turned his back and ran for the college. Nott ran after him, and he was not more than ten steps in his rear. He pulled the trigger of his gun, and the fire could be seen rolling to the ground. Two or three times he pulled the trigger back; there was a flash in the pan, and the gun did not go off. If it had, the whole charge would have gone into the back of Dr. Marks. When all this was over, I began to think about it. I saw how foolish an act we had been guilty of; how providentially we had escaped murder and its consequences. "Rufe" Nott is now living in Texas, practicing medicine, and a planter; a man greatly beloved and honored; and doubtless he regrets the foolish act of ours that night out at Barhamville as much as I have for the last fifty years.

The graduating class of the South Carolina College, in 1831, possessed more talent in it, and men of more promise, than any other half-dozen classes that had been turned out of it since the foundation of the institution in 1807 or 1808. Thornwell was first-honor man; Gladney was his great antagonist, and, by common consent among the students, the award of the faculty was the proper one; and students are generally good judges of the qualifications of the members of the different classes. I do not remember all the men of this class who have arrived at distinction; but Gladney, with all his talent, and all his distinction, and all his promise, never got higher than to be the head of a fashionable female academy. McGrath, of Charleston, was a man of great promise, and all thought that he would make his mark in the highest degree. Northrop was a brilliant, meteorie fellow, who graduated in December, 1831, and was returned the next autumn as a member of the House of Representatives from Charleston, and he came back to us a dignified member of the South Carolina Legislature. We were all very proud of him. Such a thing had not happened before, as a graduate of the college going into politics and into the halls of the Legislature within twelve months after he left college. Northrop, though, didn't half fulfill the expectations of his friends; he didn't achieve any great reputation for solidity, but he was an eloquent, good talker, though perhaps too superficial. His death was very sudden; his life was unhappy, and there was something odd about his marriages, his second in particular; but it isn't my business here to record it. During our great civil war, when Sherman was making his march to the sea, and sweeping around through my native State to make his way to Richmond, Northrop had retired from Charleston, and had taken up his abode in a little cabin in Lancaster. He was living in this little cabin, about a mile from the village. When I was there in 1877, the spot was pointed out to me — an oak-tree, on which the Yankees hung Northrop. He was supposed to belong to the upper crust of Charleston, who had taken refuge in that obscure place, and that he must of necessity have money or plate hidden away; and so he was called upon by some of the roughs that went through the country, "hangers-on" upon Sherman's army. He was found at this place and called upon to give up his hidden wealth. He declared that he had nothing in the world to give them. They did not believe him, and said that they had heard that same story before, and too often, and they proposed to bring him to his senses and an acknowledgment of the truth. They tied a rope around his neck and drew him up to one of the limbs of the oak-tree. They let him down again, but he protested that he had nothing, and that if he had, he would give it up if they would spare his life. They did not believe him, and drew him up again; but, unfortunately, they kept him there too long, and life was extinct when he was cut down.

There were in the South Carolina College two societies, literary societies, viz., the Euphradian and the Clariosophic. The number of members was about equally divided; and a county that once had a representation in one society, continued nearly always to send its students to that society afterward. The Lancaster boys were all members of the Euphradian society, and so, of course, I was a Euphradian. Thornwell was the great orator of the society, and there was not a man who could measure arms with him. Vincent would have been considered a good argumentative member if there had been no man superior to him; but Thornwell was the great orator of the society, and he was such a giant in intellect that, when it came to the discussion of a subject, he overrode everything with the strong will of his mighty genius, and everybody else seemed to be a mere pygmy in his grasp. Thornwell was perhaps one of' the greatest intellects that the South Carolina College has ever produced, and second only to John C. Calhoun. Calhoun knew him well, and looked upon him as the coming man for the South. He thought that he would eventually fill his own place in the councils of the nation. Thornwell was the son of a poor man living near Darlington District, South Carolina. He was a poor, dirty-looking, malarial-looking boy, weighing about ninety or one hundred pounds when he joined the junior class of the South Carolina College. He was very small, very thin, very pale, and looked as if he had never had enough to eat. He was very frail, and looked like he could not have run a mile without fatigue. He was a hard student, and had a wonderful memory, a great command of language, great logical powers, and altogether he was one of the most brilliant men I have ever known. When he graduated he went home, and we all expected that he would study law, and predicted for him a brilliant career; for in that day and time everybody looked upon the law as the stepping-stone to preferment, and to power, and to position.

I shall never forget the disappointment I felt when Thornwell, so I had heard, had joined the Presbyterian Church, and that he would not devote himself to the law and to politics, but that he would go into the ministry. He was no more religious than I was when he was in college; still he was a power, and a good man. After he went home he studied law, or began to, and he happened to meet his old friend Dick Baker, who was a class-mate of mine. Baker invited

him to come down to Sumpter District for a visit, and
he went down during the summer. Dick had a sister,
a beautiful and accomplished young woman. Thornwell fell in love with her, and wanted to marry her.
She was a rigid member of the Presbyterian Church,
and they talked a good deal about religion, and he
professed to be inquiring the way of salvation. They
had many conversations on the subject, and some persons had given him one book on the subject, and some
another, for him to read. He read and studied them
all, and at last he was as far from the convincing evidence as ever. Then this beautiful woman told him
if he would take the ordinary Confession of Faith, and
study that, she thought that there he would see the
truth. He did so, and he rose from its perusal a
converted man; and from that time he determined
to give himself to the Church. But, what is strange,
Miss Baker did not marry him. I do not know that
I could blame her; for physically he was nothing,
though intellectually he was a giant. Thornwell subsequently became President of the South Carolina College; he became a power in the State politics, though
he never held any political office; he was the head
of the Theological Seminary; he was a power in the
Presbyterian Church, and a great power outside of it.
His brilliant talents were given to preaching Jesus
Christ and him crucified; to educate the youth of the
State, to writing polemic theological disquisitions, and
to beating the air with abstractions in religion, and

teaching doctrines all of which must eventually pass away. He was a great man, and I shall have more to say of him and his theology by and by.

If the class of 1831, which graduated that year, was so conspicuous for its talent, my own class, which graduated in 1832 (December), represented the other extreme, and was equally conspicuous for its want of talent, excepting possibly Lessesne and Mitchell. Previous to the class of 1832, the class honors had usually been distributed to about a dozen; though of course below the fifth honor there was little or no importance attached to it. However, in Thornwell's class, they had given thirteen honors, while in my own they had given only one, divided between Lessesne and Mitchell. It was the verdict of my class that Mitchell should have the first honor. Still, Lessesne was a very good student, but was not equal to Mitchell in his qualifications and his claims. Still, as Lessesne was about to marry the daughter of President Cooper, it was very likely that this fact had something to do with getting the first honor divided with Mitchell. There were none given after that, and very justly; for none of them were worthy of anything.

We can not always judge of a man by his looks. Some small, puny men, like Thornwell, are men of very great force. There was an illustration of this in a young man named James P. Cole, who was a junior when I was senior. He came from Abbeyville District. He was a small man. I always had sympathy for small men, for I was a little fellow myself, and had an unbounded admiration for large men, and always admired and envied them. Cole was a quiet, unobtrusive fellow, had some friends, but had few warm ones among the students. He was a good student, had few or no bad habits, and was never seen at Mr. Lyons's at an oyster supper, and never drank wine. He always made good recitations, and was altogether a model young man. Soon after he joined college, he was sitting one night about ten o'clock in his room, studying very hard, and there was a rap at his door. He said, "Come in." The door was opened and a ghost appeared, in the shape of a tall man, with a sheet wrapped around him, and a dough face. Cole was no more frightened at that ghost than he was at himself. He just quietly looked around and said, "My young friend, I advise you not to repeat that experiment." The fellow was very much disappointed in seeing Cole's coolness, and never spoke a word; and went away, closing the door after him.

Cole thought it very likely that this ghost would repeat the visit at some future time, and so he prepared himself. He had a pistol, which he laid out at the end of his table, loaded and cocked; determined, if the ghost appeared again, he would give him a "pop." About a week or ten days after this time, at the same hour at night, it tapped again at the door, which was heard by Cole, and who thought that perhaps it was his ghost that had come again to make him another call. So he laid his hand on his pistol and said, "Come in," in response to the knock. Sure enough, it was the very ghost again. Cole did not say one word. He simply raised his pistol and fired at the ghost's head. The ghost fortunately jerked its head away just in time to prevent the bullet perforating its brain. It struck the facing of the door, just on a level with the ghost's head. Nobody ever knew who that ghost was; it was a profound secret to the ghost and the college boys. But one man was always suspected, and that was a tall, slender fellow, named Cosnahan, from the Peedee District. He was always suspected of being that ghost.

Cosnahan was the only fellow in the college who didn't seem to have a warm bosom friend. He was always treated politely, but nobody loved him. Nobody cared for him. He was a great novel-reader and a great smoker; a dirty-looking fellow, without any of the characteristics that engender enthusiasm.

During my last year in college, one day in the spring of the year, it must have been as early as March, for it was the time when fires were very rare but when it was necessary to have one occasionally in our rooms, an alarm of fire was given in the south college, and at the west end of the south building, which was three stories high, the smoke was pouring out from the top of the roof. The fire-bells were rung, messengers were sent up-town, and we were waiting the appearance of the fire-department with great anxiety. Our hearts were breaking to see our college on the eve of being destroyed. We were standing on the campus, with our eyes and mouths wide open, wondering if the fire-companies could not get there sooner, when all at once a small man was seen to emerge from the cupola on the same building, and to walk along on the cone of the roof, with a bucket poised in each hand, deliberately walking to the place where the roof was on fire, and from which the smoke emanated. He was followed by some colored men, and two or three of the students afterward. When we looked up and saw that this young man, Cole, was the organizer of this voluntary little fire-department or brigade, shouts of "hurrah!" rang out in the wildest enthusiasm from the boys who stood on the campus below. Cole, by his heroism and daring example of courage, had saved the college building, while the rest of us were standing idly on the campus below waiting to see it burn down. From that day Cole was a hero, and everybody admired and loved him. He still lives near Galveston, Texas, has risen to honor and eminence in his profession, that of the law, become the father of a family, and is greatly honored and respected in the town where he has lived so long.

CHAPTER VII.

I GRADUATED from Columbia College in December, 1832. I never was remarkable for anything while I was in college, except good behavior. Nobody ever expected anything of me, and I never expected anything of myself. I felt real sorry that the time was drawing near that I would have to assume the stern duties and responsibilities of real life and of manhood. I left college with a heavy heart at sundering pleasant relations that had existed between us for at least two years, and returned to my home in Lancaster. When I left, two years before, it was a happy home; when I returned it was a very unhappy one. My mother had died two months before this, in October, 1832. As before related, my father was left with a large family of children. I was the eldest, and there were five boys and two girls—little children without a mother. I was unhappy on another account. I was dreadfully in love, was too poor to talk about marriage, and too young to propose marriage, for I was only twenty years of age. My sweetheart was having beaus from all parts of the State, and I feared that she would forget the attachment which had existed between us ever since we were little children at school. Another great source of unhappiness to me was the fact that my father would be disappointed .in me. I knew very well that he had educated me with the view of my studying law. My mother hoped that I would study divinity and go into the Presbyterian ministry. My mother never knew the disappointment that awaited her, for she died two months before I left college. Knowing how great my father's disappointment would be, I did not dare to speak to him on the subject of studying a profession, and I waited for him to speak to me. He was very kind in allowing me a whole month's vacation, with nothing to do. I grew very tired, and kept wishing every day that father would say something to me about going to work.

At last he said to me one day, "Come, my boy, is it not time that you were buckling down to professional studies?" I replied, "Yes; I have been thinking of it for some time." I have been asked many times why I studied medicine. There was no premonition of the traits of a doctor in my career as a youngster; but it was simply in this way:

At that day and time, the only avenues open to a young man of university education were those of the learned professions. A graduate of a college had either to become a lawyer, go into the church, or to be a doctor. I would not be a lawyer; I could not be a minister; and there was nothing left for me to do but to be a doctor—to study medicine or to disgrace my family; for it was generally thought that a man who had gone through college, and came back and settled down as a merchant's clerk, couldn't have had much in him if he didn't take to a profession. So there was nothing else left for me but to study medicine. One day my father said, " I guess you had better go down and see Mr. Howard about your beginning your studies with him."

I said: "Father, I know that I have been a great disappointment to you. I knew from the outset that you wanted me to become a lawyer. It is impossible for me to be a lawyer; I have neither the talent nor the gifts necessary for the profession. I can not enter Mr. Howard's office." He said: "What in the world are you going to do, then?"

I said: "If I hadn't gone to college I know what I should have done. I would have accepted Mr. Stringfellow's offer of three hundred dollars a year, and gone into his store two years ago, and by this time I should be getting five hundred dollars a year. But as it is, I suppose I must study a profession, so long as I have had a university education, and there is nothing else left for me but the study of medicine, if I *must* take a profession."

He said to me: "My son, I confess that I am disappointed in you, and if I had known this I certainly should not have sent you to college."

I replied: "I did not want to go; I knew that you were not able to send me there, and I knew that you would be disappointed, and that I should make you unhappy. I am sure that you are no more unhappy about it than I am now. But if I must study a profession, there is nothing left for me to do but to study medicine."

He replied: "Well, I suppose that I can not control you; but it is a profession for which I have the utmost contempt. There is no science in it. There is no honor to be achieved in it; no reputation to be made, and to think that *my* son should be going around from house to house through this country, with a box of pills in one hand and a squirt in the other, to ameliorate human suffering, is a thought I never supposed I should have to contemplate."

However, he told me to go and see Dr. Churchill Jones, and make arrangements to study medicine. The next morning I felt happily relieved at having been enabled to pass through that terrible ordeal with my poor disappointed father. I began immediately to read medicine with Dr. Jones. Dr. Churchill Jones was a man of very great ability. The people in the country around had very great respect for and confidence in him as a physician. But, unfortunately, he drank. That, for a time, seemed to unfit him for the duties of his profession. Besides, he had no facilities for medical instruction, for he had few or no books; and I read anatomy, read the practice, and all the medical books I could get hold of, without any teacher, or reading to any profit whatever. I was very glad when I was able to leave his office, and go to attend medical lectures. But he was a very great surgeon, and from him I imbibed a desire to distinguish myself in surgery, if I ever should become a doctor.

In November, I left home for Charleston, where I was to attend medical lectures, and to take a course in the medical school there. I arrived there on the 12th of November, 1833. I began the study of medicine on the — day of February, 1833, with Dr. Jones. I remember the date very well, because, I stopped at Miott's hotel, and I remember the day of the month when I arrived there so accurately, because, when I arose the next morning, everybody was talking about the falling stars, which exhibition had occurred just before day on the 13th of November. I was always provoked that I was such a profound sleeper that I was not up to see this wonderful display of Nature's fire-works. The Charleston Medical School was opened a very few days after my arrival. Dr. Samuel Henry Dickson was the Professor of Theory and Practice of Medicine. I well remember the introductory lecture; it was a brilliant effort, and I never heard such eloquence from a teacher's desk. He was a small man, very handsome, with a sweet, musical voice; a man of great literary acquirements, a fluent speaker, logical in his reasoning, convincing in his argument, and most captivating in his manner. But as a practical teacher I do not think that I ever learned much from him. The purity of his diction, and the eloquence of his discourse, and the beauty of his teaching captivated the ear, so that I was carried away entirely from the substance of what he attempted to instill into my mind. Wagner was Professor of Surgery. Holbrook was Professor of Anatomy, and he was a great teacher. He had but one equal, I think, as a teacher of anatomy, and that was Ballou, of Jefferson Medical College. I was diligent in my studies, and I felt that, as I had failed in my duty as a student in my college course at Columbia, the responsibility of life was now doubly on me, and weighed heavily upon my shoulders. I felt that I had to prepare for a period that I looked forward to not with pleasurable anticipations but with dread. Most of the young men that I had associated with all my life, from ten years old upward had looked forward to manhood with joy and satisfaction; but with me, it was exactly the reverse. I was afraid to be a man; I was afraid to assume its responsibilities, and thought that I did not have sense enough to go out into the rough world, making a living as other men had to do. I was small in stature, and I did not feel that I had intellect enough to grapple with or to pit myself against such opposition as I should encounter in my life.

I said before, that when I went to Charleston I

went to work in real earnest. I worked diligently; I attended lectures, earnestly taking notes of what I saw and heard. I worked in the dead-house with interest. It was fascinating, and besides I derived a practical knowledge from it which I could appreciate, and could understand, and carry away, and know that I was doing something toward laying deeper the foundation for knowledge to come. I had the good fortune to meet my old friend Dick Baker there as a fellow-student. He had been in college with me, and had graduated the year before me. He was my senior in college by a year. He was a jolly, companionable fellow, and one of the best of men; always in good humor, always had something funny to say, and was full of wit. We worked hard all the week, and usually went on a frolic somewhere or somehow on Saturday night, or went to the theatre. One Sunday he asked me to go sailing with him over to Sullivan's Island. He said he had hired a boat and a man to sail it. He said that we would sail over there, and walk about the beautiful island, and look at the great sea, and pick up shells on the shore, and spend a quiet day, and come back in the afternoon. I was afraid of the sea when I was a young man, but I had never seen it before. I was afraid of little boats. However, he said there was no danger. We got into the little boat, the man raised his sail, and in the course of an hour or so we were at Sullivan's Island, a distance of five miles. We loitered around for an hour or two, and in fact several hours, and talked over old times, our prospects in life, and the preparation for its great duties. By and by it was time to return home, and so we got into our boat and started again for the city. When within about a mile and a half from the city, we looked off to the south and to the left, and I saw a little ripple on the sea, and I said, "Oh, see that beautiful sea; how pretty it is, and the water is agitated over here to our left!" He said, "Yes, that is very pretty." The words had hardly left my mouth before a squall struck us, and the boat was soon bottom side up in the water. I could not swim a stroke, and never could, and of course I shall not learn now. I was very much alarmed, for there we were, with the little vessel on its beam-ends, and we climbing on the side of it. Of course, I thought all was lost, and I expected the water would rush into the hold, and all would be lost, and that the vessel would sink, and where should I be? The vessel seemed to be held down by the jib-boom, and still it was under water. The sailor took out his knife and cut the cords that held this jib-sail, and let it drop into the water, and the little vessel righted itself, and we got safely to land. This was an adventure that frightened me so much that I have never recovered from it to this day. Nothing would induce me to cross the Hudson River in a little boat, either a sail or row boat. I do not mind crossing the ocean in a big magnificent steamer, and I never felt afraid; but when you come to a little sail-boat or row-boat, I certainly would not risk my life in one of them on any account.

I have always said that my friend Dick Baker was full of frolic and fun, and so he got me into a dilemma, only two or three days before we left Charleston for our homes. He came to me one day and said, "See here, Marion, there's to be a masquerade ball at Fayall's ball-room next Saturday night, and I tell you I want you to go with me. I will go as a country wagoner just come to town, and you will go with me as my daughter."

I said, "Dick, that won't do, for I am afraid it will be discovered. I don't want to put on girl's clothes and do that."

"Oh, well," he said, "but it is a masquerade, and you have a right to do as you please, so long as it's a masquerade, and while they all have on masks. I will play my whip and flourish it around, and play that I'm a country wagoner."

"But what shall I do about the clothes?" I asked.

"Oh, that is easy enough," he replied; "you never mind about that, for I have cousins here in the city, and I can get the clothes from them. You will go as a country lassie, and you will make a capital one, too."

After some further conversation, I agreed to go, and the time for the start was also fixed upon. So he went to see his cousins, and got some dresses, and a set of ear-rings, which were tied on to my ears with strings, and I was dressed up in the most outlandish

6

and fantastic way that you can imagine. I wore a turban to hide my short hair, and the ear-rings dangled nearly down to my shoulders. I was dressed in a fashion altogether peculiar and unlike anything of the kind I had ever seen before. When the hour for the ball came, we marched down to Fayall's. There had been a very hard and severe rain that afternoon, and Mr. Fayall, thinking that the rain was to continue until into the night, had put up a notice on the door saying that the masquerade ball was postponed indefinitely on account of the rain. Dick was despondent; but I said I was glad of it, and that I was out of the scrape; and besides, I had had enough of this sort of sport. We accordingly started for my boarding-house. As we walked along Queen Street, Dick brightened up, and he said: "By George! I have an idea. Let's go to the theatre. That is the thing. We will certainly have this frolic out, for there is no telling if we will ever have another chance. Nobody will know but that you are a country girl, and I am big enough and ugly enough to pass for a country farmer."

In an unlucky moment I said, "Well, we will go." Dick bought the tickets, and we started up into the gallery. I said:

"Dick, I must insist that we sit on the back seat, for I am dressed in such an outlandish and awkward way that we might be discovered, and it would sound rather bad to be carried before the police in the morning, and have it known that two young medical students were arrested, and one of them in woman's clothes at that."

He said, " You shall sit just where you please." So we went up-stairs. To my horror, the house was brilliantly illuminated. At least, I thought that I had never seen anything like it. When we were about to enter the compartment that we had been directed to by the usher, I wanted to sit on the back seat. But the Southern people are exceedingly courteous, especially to the ladies, and so they insisted on our taking a front seat whether we wanted to or not. They differ from us here at the North in that respect. Two young gentlemen on the front seat arose and said to Dick: " Here, sir, is a seat for yourself and your lady." There was nothing for us to do but to comply, and so to the front seat we went, they having made room for us two. Both took me by the arm, and one said, " Miss, will you have a front seat?" and the other said, " Miss, have this front seat?" I blushed and said, " I thank you, I can't sit on the front seat;" I insisted on sitting on the back seat, and everybody insisted that I should sit on the front seat, and that with so much of earnestness that it was impossible to do anything else but comply. So I took my seat in the gallery, and in an instant every opera-glass in that theatre was leveled at me, and not on the play, until I was nearly crazed. My condition was not pleasant, and I was very unhappy, and I said, " Dick, for God's sake, take me out of here." He thought it was the greatest joke that he had ever seen or heard of in this world. I shall never forget that play—it was "The Lady of Lyons"; nor shall I ever forget how the beautiful women of Charleston stared at the strange bird sitting in the balcony with the countryman, Dick Baker.

After we had been there about half an hour, Abram McWillie, who was a class-mate of ours in Columbia College, and whom we hadn't seen since we left there, entered, and took a seat by me. He looked over and saw Dick Baker, and they had a hearty shaking of hands. Baker asked him many questions, and talked about old times, and I sat there looking dignified, though he was one of my warmest and best of friends. Now, in another character he did not know me, and so he did not speak to me, nor I to him. Dick enjoyed the joke as long as he could possibly do it, and then he said:

"Abe, old fellow, I want to introduce you to your old friend, Marion Sims."

Abe raised both hands, and he said, "My God!" and then he became very confidential, and I said:

"Abe, it isn't proper, when you are introduced to a young lady, to become so intimate on short acquaintance and all at once. You are entirely too confidential. Just look at all these opera-glasses leveled on us. Now, if you felt as unhappy as I do, you would be making tracks out of this place very soon."

Suffice it to say that these two old friends of mine

kept me there in durance vile till the theatre was dismissed and the curtain fell. I was not happy until I got safely home to my quarters, for every minute I expected that I should be taken up by the police, and carried before the court the next day for appearing in public in women's clothes. I have never seen Dick Baker from that day to this. He studied medicine, graduated with honor, returned to his native place in Sumter, South Carolina, got married, was very successful as a physician, and filled an important station in life. He lived to a ripe old age, and spent a useful and profitable life.

CHAPTER VIII.

THE day after I arrived in Charleston I started out in search of a boarding-house. I was directed to Mrs. Murden's, in Society Street, where I had a comfortable room and excellent board at a reasonable price, and a happy home during my winter's sojourn in Charleston. Mrs. Murden was a poetess, and an enthusiast about everything that she undertook. She had four beautiful daughters — Malvena, Octavia, Valeria, and Rosaline—all of them highly educated and very accomplished young ladies. They had a school, and were patronized by the aristocrats of the city. The school is in existence even to this day, and one of the young ladies is still devoting her life to the work of teaching her young countrywomen. She alone is left of all the family. Mrs. Murden was a very peculiar woman. If she had lived in this day and time, how she would have enjoyed life. I remember well with what eagerness she always looked for the morning papers.

The first thing she looked for was the column of deaths, which she gloated over and discussed thoroughly. Then she looked for the horrors, like shipwrecks and murders, and accidents of all kinds by sea and land, and all the other terrible things of which life is made up and in danger of. The list seemed to give her food for contemplation, and she really enjoyed the horrors that occurred around her every day. In this day and time, when we have all the horrors and horrible things occurring in every section of the great globe brought to the very doors of everybody, and all centered in one small column, it would have been food for Mrs. Murden for a whole week. I was very happy in the Murden family. I worked hard, and if I ever had a spare hour it was given to a game of chess with one of the young ladies.

During this term of lectures at Charleston Medical College, I made the acquaintance of Ben Robinson, of Fayetteville, North Carolina, and we became very intimate. We agreed then that we would go to Philadelphia for our next course of lectures, and we were to meet the next October at Jefferson Medical College, and there work for graduation. About the last of February the lecture term at Charleston was concluded, and I returned again to my home in Lancaster, where I resumed my studies with my old friend and preceptor Dr. Churchill Jones. I got through the summer as well as I could, but it was impossible for me to learn anything, except when he took me out to see some $\mathcal{E}\mathcal{J}$ poor, cal operation, and then I felt that I had carried away with me something that would be of profit to me in after-life.

One night I was dissecting alone in the dissecting-room, where there were ten or twelve dead bodies on as many tables. I had found an anomalous distribution of the tracheal artery, and was anxious to trace it out. I had but a single candle. There was no other light in the room. I told Robert, the supervisor of the dissecting-room, not to wait for me. I happened to knock the candle over, and I was in the dark and had no matches. So I was obliged to desist from my work. I am not afraid of anything, but I must confess that I did not feel very comfortable as I threaded my way out in search of the door of exit.

And this reminds me of a similar experience of my friend Williams Sims Reynolds, of Charleston, when he was a medical student there in 1832. He was alone, at ten o'clock at night, dissecting the parts concerned in an inguinal hernia.

A dissecting-table is about six feet long, and twenty inches wide, and thirty inches high.

To dissect the muscles of the abdomen, we place a billet of wood eighteen or twenty inches long and ten inches in diameter under the loins. This renders the muscles of the abdomen tense and prominent. This is increased by drawing the subject down toward the lower end of the table, so as to let the legs and thighs gravitate eagard the floor, while the body is held firmly in place by a chain a yard long with a hook at each end. One hook is hitched into the scalp of the subject, and the other is hooked over the upper end of the table. If the hook should break loose the body would, by the weight of the legs, shoot over the lower end of the table. Reynolds's only candle was necessarily resting on the epigastric region of the subject. He had been at work all the evening on the right inguinal ring. He started to pass round the lower end of the table for some purpose, when he ran against the subject's projecting legs. This jostled the body so as to knock loose the chain at the upper end of the table, whereupon the body, having the roller billet of wood under the back, was, by the weight of the lower limbs, suddenly jerked to the floor in the upright posture, and its arms were forcibly thrown over Reynolds's shoulders. The light was of course put out. I think I should have left that body to the force of gravity. But Reynolds took it under the arms and replaced it on the table.

The last of September (1834) I started for Philadelphia. It took a whole week to go from Lancaster to Philadelphia. We had to stage it the whole of the way, over the mountains of Virginia. Arriving in Philadelphia, I soon met a number of young gentlemen from the South, students there, and they were all very clannish. They readily got acquainted, and stuck to each other. The first boarding-house I got into was just opposite the Jefferson Medical College. I paid $4 a week, which was very cheap; but, really, the living was excessively poor,

and I came very near starving. After a while, I got
acquainted with a young fellow named Krenshaw, from
Wake Forest, North Carolina. He was a very eccentric
fellow, as green as cheese, and as good as gold. He was a
great Baptist, and made many friends among that denom-
ination and in that church, among them a young medical
student, named Roberts, who lived near Sixth Street ;
and whose mother, who had married a second time, was
the wife of Dr. Lewis Roberts, got acquainted with Krenshaw through the Baptist church. Then Roberts told
him of a Miss Edmunds's school for young girls, in Sansom Street, just opposite the church. He said that she
had some vacancies, and would take a few medical students as boarders. Krenshaw went to Miss Edmunds's,
was delighted with the place, and, when he found out
that I was starving in a little house just opposite the
college, he kindly offered to introduce me to Miss Edmunds, which he did, and I engaged board there with
her. I was very glad, indeed, to make the change, and
Miss Edmunds was enabled to give me a very good
room, and one for my friend, Mr. Rush Jones, of Lancaster, who was soon to be there. As far as our boarding-house was concerned, I was perfectly happy. There
was plenty to eat, we had a good room to sleep in, and
everything bright and cheerful. At breakfast and din-
ner-time there were three or four pretty girls to talk to,
and I do not think that a set of young men ever attended lectures at Jefferson Medical College, that winter at least, who were more fortunately situated than

we were. Miss Edmunds was an old lady, a good deal the other side of fifty, and had taught school all the days of her life. She was a charming woman, and a good mother to all of us. She was devoted to her pastor, the Rev. Dr. Gillette, father of the present distinguished Dr. Gillette of New York. Dr. Gillette was the pastor of the Circular Church, which is now a livery stable, in Sansom Street. Miss Edmunds used to marshal us all to church there every Sunday morning.

During my stay in Philadelphia a most unfortunate thing occurred, resulting in the death of some of the students. A subject who had been brought into the dissecting-room had died of small-pox, and I do not know how many of the students contracted small-pox from it. Two or three of them died; among them a handsome young fellow from Alabama by the name of Lucas. I got acquainted with Lucas soon after lectures began. We became good friends, and he knew many persons that I knew in his section, and he had family connections in South Carolina. When Lucas was taken sick we missed him at lectures, and I immediately went to his boarding-house to inquire what was the matter with him. I found him very ill, and I went there to nurse him at night. I sat up with him, night after night, not having the remotest idea of what was the matter with him. He was very ill, and one night I sent for Professor Patterson, who was attending him, to come and see him. When Professor Patterson came, he examined the patient carefully, and prescribed for him, and I said : " Dr. Patterson, what is the matter with my young friend Lucas ? "

Dr. Patterson replied : " Why, he has the small-pox, and he is going to die to-night. I thought you were acquainted with what was the matter with him."

" My God, small-pox ! " I said. " I have never been vaccinated ; I do not remember to have ever been vaccinated in all my life ! " So I hurried around to Dr. George McClellan to be vaccinated. I was very much alarmed at having been in a room with a small-pox patient. I found him at home, and told him what had happened. He asked me if I had never been vaccinated, and I said I had not been.

" Well, then," he said, " pull off your coat and roll up your sleeves." He was about to scratch my arm with his lancet, when he said, " You have as fine a mark on your arm as there is on any fellow's arm in the whole college."

I said, " I *have* been vaccinated, surely," and there, sure enough, was the mark. " Come to think of it, now I remember all about it. I remember a little epidemic of small-pox in Columbia, South Carolina, in 1831, three years ago. At that time I met Mr. Gladney, one of the honor-men of his class (1831) on the college campus, and he said to me, ' Do you know there is small-pox in town ? ' I said I did not. He asked me if I had been vaccinated, and I said that I had not. So I went into his room and he had a fresh pustule, and he said, ' It is just right for the work, and I know just how to do it.'

He scratched my arm, and put in some virus. It went through the several stages to maturation; but it made so little impression on me that I had forgotten all about it, from the time it was done until now, and I did not remember that it had ever been done. But for that, of course, I should have been in very great danger from having attended my friend Lucas so long." My friend Lucas died that night, his death creating a great commotion among the students; but none of them left. Every man stuck to his post, and attended to his duties.

I had always passed for more than I was worth. My young friends commonly thought I had more talent than I possessed, and gave me credit for more than I deserved. At Charleston, when the class was about to break up and separate, the students held a meeting, at which I was not present, and knew nothing of. They appointed a committee to select a class valedictorian. I do not think that I ever was so surprised in my life as I was when that committee called on me and said they wanted to have me deliver that valedictory address. I declined, of course. So when young Lucas died, and there were two or three other young men who also died of small-pox from the college, in January, 1835, the students held a meeting and appointed a committee to select a eulogist in commemoration of the young men who had died. Again, to my surprise, the surprise of my life, of the three or four hundred young gentlemen students there, the committee waited on me and requested me to perform that office. In both these instances, feeling my incompetency for such a thing, I had the good sense and courage to decline the proffered honor.

Miss Edmunds was always fond of telling anecdotes, and I liked to hear her tell them. I always managed to have her tell them when I had invited any of my young friends to come there to take tea with me. One I especially liked to hear her tell, and it was this: She said that when her mother was about seventy years of age they lived in North Sixth Street. Her mother and her aunt were often in the habit, Sunday evenings, of going around and visiting her brother, who lived in Second Street, four blocks away, and not far north of Walnut Street. One evening, about ten o'clock, these two old ladies, Mrs. Edmunds and her sister, expected a nephew to come and walk home with them. The young man did not come, and the servants having retired, there was no one to accompany them home. At last they said, "We should know that we can go by ourselves, for our age will protect us." So the two old ladies started out by themselves. They were two very delicate, dried-up specimens of women, and in the darkness they looked like girls more than they did like grown women. The houses in that part of the city were quite far apart, and it was not to be wondered at that they were somewhat afraid to go out at night all alone. Besides, the neighborhood was infested by sailors and roughs. They hadn't gone twenty steps from their brother's house before they were accosted by two sailors. It was before the days of gas, and the streets were lighted by miserable lamps, which never threw a particle of light across the street. When they were accosted by these two sailors, the fellows began to make violent love to them. They both cried out, for they were sorely frightened, "We are not young women; we are both old women." But the sailors replied, by way of jest : " Yes, we understand that : we have heard the same kind of talk before. We know old women from young women at any time." So each one grasped a woman, and one of them took his under his arm and running with his trophy across the street, held her face up to the dim lamp-light. Seeing his mistake, he shouted out to his companion, " Patrick, you may drop yours, surely, because the one I have is as old and as ugly as the very divil !" Thus they escaped from their captors and, frightened almost to death, hurried on their way home.

In Jefferson Medical College, and a great gun, was the famous McClellan. He was a great surgeon, and he was a *man* as well. He was very eccentric and erratic as a teacher. His delivery was very spasmodic, but he talked sense all the time. Not that he had much system, but whatever he said was to the point ; it was practical—it was *teaching*—it was a thing that one could carry home and remember always. At the time I was a student in Jefferson College, the distinguished General George B. McClellan was a little boy, four or five years old. I have often reminded him of the time, which he could not remember. I used to pat him on the head, and give him six-pences to buy ginger-bread and taffy with.

Professor McClellan frequently honored me by an invitation to assist him in surgical operations, and I remember one very remarkable case on which he operated. It created a great sensation at the time. It was a case in which he exsected a portion of a necrosed rib, without injury to the pleural cavity He talked to the patient all the time of his operation, for it was before the days of anæsthetics, and when it required great nerve to be a good surgeon. He would gouge and chisel and work away, and say to the man, "Courage, my brave fellow, courage; we wound but to heal. It will soon be over." Then he would work away again, and again he would cheer up the patient, by saying, " Courage, my good fellow; be brave, for we wound but to heal; it will soon be over. Courage, my dear fellow; it will soon be over."

He was a great teacher, a great surgeon, and a great man; and he was the founder of Jefferson Medical College. He died comparatively young, and left a reputation that is imperishable.

In 1847 McClellan left home one bright May morning to make his daily rounds. He walked erect along Chestnut Street, seemingly full of health and vigor, going from house to house to see his patients, while his coachman drove leisurely along, waiting wherever his master entered. Soon he was seen slowly descending the steps of a marble mansion bent over with agonizing pain. He entered his carriage and was driven rapidly home. His medical advisers were summoned. In a few hours he was in collapse, and in sixteen he was dead.

He died of perforation of the bowel just below the sigmoid flexure. The cause of death was septicæmia and shock. And thus passed away one of the great surgeons of the age.

Professor Patterson was the best lecturer on anatomy then living. The next best to him was Hurlburt, of the Charleston College. It made no odds what the subject was, the student was always chained to it as long as he chose to speak. We never tired of his enthusiasm or his eloquence. He had one very bad habit, a dreadful peculiarity and a disagreeable one, especially for those who occupied the front seats. When he became very enthusiastic, and went to the highest pitch of his eloquence, he would forget himself and all around him, and would splutter and slobber and spit, the saliva flying in every direction, so that those who sat within a yard of him would be spattered all over. Of course the young gentlemen were too polite to say anything, and they would wipe off the drops from their faces when he was so earnestly teaching them and so eloquently discoursing to them. Every man in whose face he would happen to splutter his saliva would watch, before he passed the amphitheatre, before raising his handkerchief to wipe it off.

Patterson was very kind to the students, and always managed to help them out of their scrapes. He lent them money, and patronized them in every way that he could. He was a father to the students, and sympathized with them in all their efforts.

I graduated from the Jefferson Medical College, in Philadelphia, on the first day of March, 1835. I studied very hard all winter, and even found time for the dissection of a few subjects. Few students found time for dissection during the graduating course, but I did and heard the graduating course of lectures besides. When I graduated, I felt absolutely incompetent to assume the duties of a practitioner. Professor Patterson had advertised a private course of lectures for a month, and I, with thirty or forty others, young men like myself, who felt that they didn't know much, concluded to take the private course. He delivered a course on "Regional Anatomy and Surgical Anatomy." When I graduated I presume I could have gone into the dissecting-room and cut down upon any artery, and put a ligature around it, but I knew nothing at all about the practice of medicine.

CHAPTER IX.

I RETURNED to my home in South Carolina about the middle of May, 1835. I went home with everything prepared to begin the practice of medicine. I had had no clinical advantages, no hospital experience, and had seen nothing at all of sickness. I had been able to buy a full set of instruments for surgical operations, and I laid in a full stock of medicines in Philadelphia. My father rented me an office on Main Street. I had a sign painted on tin, that would reach one third of the way across the end of my office. It was certainly two feet long, and, like all young doctors just starting, I wanted to let people know where I could be found. I attended my office, and was ready for consultation and for patients. One morning, at the end of two or three weeks, as I was sitting in my office quietly, surrounded by my library, which consisted of seven books, octavo volumes, safely locked up in one of the little drawers in my bureau, Mr. Mayer, an important personage in the town, came whistling along. Mayer had been its mayor; he had been my tailor from the time I was a little boy. He had made coats for me before I was permitted to wear tails to them.

He said, " Good morning, Marion " (for nobody called me doctor). I had lived there all my life, knew everybody in the town, and everybody called me Marion. " Have you had any patients yet ? "

I said, " No, Andy, I haven't had a patient yet."

" Well," he said, " I wish you would go up to my house and see my baby. It is very sick, and has been sick for some time. I wish you would go up pretty soon."

I said, " Very well, I will go up immediately." He passed on to his shop, and I walked up to his house. I thought to myself that this was a good beginning, really. Here is the most important personage in the town who is my first patient, and if Andy Mayer patronizes me my successs will certainly be assured. When I arrived I found a child about eighteen months old, very much emaciated, who had what we would call the summer complaint, or chronic diarrhœa. I examined the child minutely from head to foot. I looked at its gums, and, as I always carried a lancet with me and had surgical propensities, as soon as I saw some swelling of the gums I at once took out my lancet and cut the gums down to the teeth. This was good so far as it went. But, when it came to making up a prescription, I had no more idea of what ailed the child, or what to do for it, than if I had never studied medicine. I was at a

perfect loss what to do, but I did not betray my ignorance to the mother. I blandly said :

"Mrs. Mayer, if you will have the kindness to send
Jennie down to my office in the course of an hour from
this time, I will have medicine ready for the baby, and
write out the directions how to give it."

I hurried back to my office, and took out one of my
seven volumes of Eberle, which comprised my library,
and found his treatise on the " Diseases of Children." I
hastily took it down, turned quickly to the subject of
" Cholera Infantum," and read it through, over and over
again, to the end most carefully. I knew no more what
to prescribe for the sick babe than if I hadn't read it all.
But it was my only resource. I had nobody else to consult but Eberle. By the by, he had a peculiar way of
filling his books with prescriptions, which was a very
good thing for a young doctor. He was a good writer,
and a very practical man, and would be considered good
authority even at this time. The most natural thing in
the world for me to do was to begin. At the beginning
of his article of twenty or thirty pages there was a prescription, but I do not remember whether it was a pow-
der or a mixture. There was chalk in it. So I com-
pounded it as quickly as I knew how, and had everything in readiness for the arrival of Jennie. She took it
back to the house, and the mother began to give it
according to the directions, which were written out. I
was very impatient for the time to come when I should
make my visit, and see the effects of the medicine and

the Eberle prescription. I was there punctually on time. I was very much surprised to find the baby very much as in the morning; no better and no worse. I saw that as the medicine had done no good it was necessary to change it. And so I requested Mrs. Mayer to send Jennie down to my office again at a given time for a new prescription for the baby. I turned to Eberle again, and to a new leaf. I gave the baby a prescription from the next chapter. Suffice it to say, that I changed leaves and prescriptions as often as once or twice a day. The baby continued to grow weaker and weaker. "Is it possible," I thought, "that this child can die? Did any young doctor ever lose the first patient he ever had, and just as he was starting out? Providence could not be so cruel as to allow me to lose my first patient, in a little town like this, with everybody talking about it, and especially the child of so important a personage as Mr. Mayer." I felt very unhappy about it.

Meantime, an old nurse was asked to come and take care of the child. It is well understood that there is a curious antagonism between old nurses and young doctors. They have an idea that young doctors don't know a great deal, and the old nurses are not very far from right. This old nurse seemed to scrutinize me, and very particularly watched everything I said and did. Nothing escaped her, and I felt very uncomfortable in her presence. I wished that she had never come there. However, one night I was sitting by the baby, in an anxious mood of mind, and wondering what was to turn up next. I was feeling its pulse, and watching it carefully. The old nurse sat on the opposite side of the bed, when she said, " Doctor, don't you think that this baby is going to die?" I said, "No, madam, I do not think so, not at all." Externally, I was very calm and self-possessed ; but internally I was not, for I really did not know what that child would do. Presently the child stopped breathing, and I thought it a case of syncope. I never dreamed that it could die. So I jerked the baby from the bed, and held its head down, and shook it, and blew into its mouth, and tried to bring it to. I shook it again, when the old nurse laid her hand on my shoulder gently, and said : " No use shakin' that baby any more, doctor, for that baby's dead!" Well, I laid the baby back in the bed, and my feelings can well be imagined at the idea that I had lost my first patient. I attended the funeral ; I was the chief mourner of all. Certainly its father and mother did not feel so badly over the loss of their child as I did at the loss of my first patient. I was very melancholy and sad, for I thought that everybody in town would know that I had lost my first case, and Mayer's baby at that, and everybody was sorry for him and for me.

About two weeks had rolled around, and the depression which I had felt had somewhat subsided, when Mr. Elias Kennedy came to my office one morning. Mr. Kennedy was foreman for Mr. Mayer, and I had known him all my life. He came in in somewhat of a hurry, and said :

"Marion, my baby is real sick, and I wish you would

go up to my house and see it. I hope you will have better luck with it than you did with Andy's baby."

I said, "Elias, if I don't, I'll quit the town." I went up to see Mr. Kennedy's baby, and, as bad luck would have it, it was about the same age and same size as Mayer's baby, the same prostrating condition of things, and the same disease. I was nonplused. I had no authority to consult but Eberle; so I took up Eberle again, and this time I read him backward. I thought I would reverse the treatment I had instituted with Mayer's baby. So, instead of beginning at the first of the chapter, I began at the last of the chapter, and turned backward, and turned the leaves the same way, and reversed the prescription. The baby got no better from the very first. I did not have any consultation in the first case, for there was no doctor in town to counsel with; for my old preceptor, Dr. Jones, had gone to Tennessee on a visit to his sister, and he was the only doctor in the town besides myself. He returned while I was in attendance upon Mr. Kennedy's baby. As soon as he came home I went to see him. I said: "Dr. Church," (everybody called him Dr. Church) "I lost Andy Mayer's baby since you have been away. If you had been here he would have lived. But he is dead; and now Elias Kennedy's is sick and I want you to go and see it and save it."

"I will go," he said, "with pleasure, Marion."

"But I want you to go at once," I said; "there is no time to wait."

So the dear, good old doctor went up with me to Elias's very cheerfully, and went into the room. He was clear-headed and looked at the patient carefully, and, at the first glimpse, he knew all about it. No questions were necessary, and immediately afterward he was satisfied. He proposed that we would have a consultation, and so we went out for that purpose. It was pretty hot in the house, and so we went out on the shady side, in the corner of the chimney. The first thing he said to me, when we got there, was: "Well, Marion, that baby is going to die."

I said, "The devil, you say; you don't say that this baby is going to die?"

He said that it could not recover.

"Then," I said, "if this baby dies, doctor, I shall never be your successor in this town, for I shall leave."

He replied, "Marion, that baby is going to die; it will die to-night." And it did die, and it died that night. Again I had to be chief mourner at the funeral of another little lost citizen of Lancaster. I went home sadder than ever. I just took the long tin sign-board from my office door. There was an old well back of the house, covered over with boards. I went to the well, took that sign with me, dropped it in there, and covered the old well over again. I was no longer a doctor in the town of Lancaster.

I was then so demoralized, and so disgusted with my beginning in the profession, that if I had had money enough, or any money at all, even the small sum of

7

five thousand dollars, I would not have given another dose of medicine. But there was no other alternative for me. Being obliged to continue in the profession that I had started in, I was determined to make up my deficiency by hard work; and this was not to come from reading books, but from observation and from diligent attention to the sick.

I then made up my mind to leave my country for my country's good, and establish a home in the far West. I had had the misfortune to lose my first two patients, and the thought of it was too terrible to be borne. I had never heard of such terrible luck, and never thought that such misfortune could ever happen to any young man in the world. However, I had one other patient in Lancaster, and he was the rich man of the town, old Captain McKenna, who owned half of the village and one hundred slaves. He would get on sprees occasionally, lasting two or three weeks, and they always wound up with delirium tremens. He was on one of his regular old "blow-outs," and, to my great surprise, he sent for me. I attended him very carefully for two days and nights, and got him over his frolic. He was delighted, and gave me a ten-dollar bill. That was the first money I ever made in the practice of medicine, and the only money I ever got in Lancaster. The patients that ought to have lived died, and the one that ought to have died got well.

On the 13th of October (1835) my father and I started for Alabama. The "thirteenth," by the way, has always been a lucky day with me, and so has Friday. I was born on Friday. Some years ago, when I was one of the surgeons in the Woman's Hospital, we met, four of us, to select operating days, each having a separate day, and I said at once: "Gentlemen, I will relieve your minds, so far as I am concerned, and in regard to the day, by selecting Friday as my own, and you can divide the other days among yourselves to suit your ideas." My father had furnished me with a fine horse and a little Yankee carry-all, and in this my medicines, instruments, and the same old library of seven volumes, were safely stowed away in the back of the wagon. My destination was Marengo County, Alabama. I had heard glowing accounts of the country and its richness, and of the opportunities afforded to young men who located there; especially if they had energy and enterprise. It took us about three weeks to go from Lancaster to Mount Meigs, Montgomery County, Alabama. When we arrived at Mount Meigs we made a halt of a few days, for we had many friends living there who had removed from South Carolina at a previous date. All of them began to persuade me to remain there at Mount Meigs, where there were people that knew me when I was a boy. I was not disposed to do so; but my father said, "Why should you go farther? You had better stop where people here know you, and have an interest in you, than to go to Marengo, where no one will have any personal interest in you." Rather against my will, however, for I didn't like to give up the idea that I had started out with, I consented to stop at Mount Meigs.

There were two doctors there. Dr. Charles Lucas was a man about fifty years of age, a splendid man, who had a great reputation as a doctor. He was a great politician, a great talker, a great planter, was very rich; owned two or three hundred slaves, made large quantities of cotton, and was a man who exerted a vast influence in the country. He was an old bachelor and kept "open house" and good cheer for everybody that called. The other was Dr. Childers. He was a very much older man, and he was a character. He had an enormous reputation as a doctor. He bled and purged, and gave medicine from the time he was called to the patient until the patient was called away. If the patient survived Dr. Childers and the disease together, he had a lease of life that would carry him up to old age. Dr. Childers never lived more than two years in any one place. He had practiced in every little town and village all through Georgia, from Augusta to Columbia; was quoted as authority in medicine all over the States of Georgia and Alabama, though I do not know that he had ever written anything. Still he was a very wonderful man, and he always left an impression with everybody that he knew a good deal more that he really did. I must say that in medicine he was learned. He was a very peculiar looking man. He was small, rather stoop-shouldered, always walked with his hands as if he was tired, holding one hand on each lapel of his coat, his head stooped over to one side—he seemed to be pulled over in that direction by an enormous nose. He had a pleasant voice, and seldom raised it above a whisper, and he always spoke, in the main, in a sort of confidential way to everybody and on any subject. He was never in a hurry, was always prompt in his attention to the duties of his profession, and was one of the kindest of men. He believed in the lancet, and it was rarely that he didn't bleed his patient; it made no difference what the disease was.

I well remember his inviting me to go out into the country once, a distance of three or four miles, to see a patient, a Miss Ashurst. She was a very beautiful woman in the last stages of consumption. She had the usual afternoon hectic flushes of this ruthless disease. She was nothing but a skeleton, and certainly had but a few days to live. But Dr. Childers's theory was that the lancet was necessary wherever the patient had the least appearance of fever. In our afternoon visit to this beautiful, dying, angelic women, he found her in the usual exacerbation of hectic. The skin was hot and dry, and the pulse about one hundred and twenty a minute. What was my surprise when Dr. Childers said, "Miss Ashurst, I believe, as you have a good deal of fever, I will have to draw a little blood from you." This was said in the sweetest, mildest, most gentlemanly tones possible. So he took from his pocket a cord, and drew it over the little skeleton arm above the elbow. Presently the blood came trickling down from the elbow, and, when a tablespoonful had run, the poor little woman fainted and fell over. "Ah," said he, "that is just what I wanted. Now she will be better"; and she was better, but it was the "better" that comes with death. The practice at that time was heroic; it was murderous. I knew nothing about medicine, but I had sense enough to see that doctors were killing their patients; that medicine was not an exact science; that it was wholly empirical, and that it would be better to trust entirely to Nature than to the hazardous skill of the doctors.

Dr. Childers had then been about eighteen months in Mount Meigs, and it was about time that he was preparing to leave there. He was very glad of the opportunity to welcome me to Mount Meigs, provided that I would buy him out. I had no money with which to do this; and yet it was something to have his influence; indeed, it was a good deal. However, he agreed to take my note for two hundred dollars, give me his books and medicines, and recommend me to his patients generally in the country. Two hundred dollars at that time was about equal to one thousand dollars now. Of course the bargain was a very good one for me and not a very bad one for him; for he was going away anyhow. So I was soon regularly installed at Mount Meigs as a practicing physician. This was about the middle of November, 1835. The first patient that I had there came in this way:

Dr. Lucas, I said, was a great politician. He was a

bank director, and, as a bank director he wielded a great power in the country. He had become a bank director of the State of Alabama, and it was necessary for him to go to the Legislature, which then met at Tuscaloosa, in the western part of the State, and two or three weeks were required for the electioneering necessary for this directorship. . . . I think he was gone more than a month, and I am quite sure that he was away five or six weeks before he could be certain of his election. Mr. Evans arrived one morning, about eleven o'clock, from the neighborhood of Union Springs, Macon County. He said that he had come for Dr. Lucas, but, as he was away, he would be glad if I would go with him to see Mrs. FitzGreene, who was very ill with puerperal fever. She was the daughter of Mr. Benjamin Baldwin. They were people of fortune and favor, and, of course, a call to such a family was a very important one. But I said, "No, I can not go with you; you want an older man than I am, and a man with experience. I haven't the knowledge that will satisfy the case, and I think that you had better go to Montgomery and get some of the swell doctors there to attend to the case."

He said "No;" that everybody spoke well of me in Mount Meigs, and recommended me highly, and he would not be satisfied unless I would return with him. I had then been in Mount Meigs about a month, or rather about two weeks. However, he persuaded me to go with him, and we started in an hour afterward. We rode all that evening, and did not arrive at Mr. Baldwin's until nine o'clock that night. We passed through a wilderness country occupied by the Indians, whose camp-fires we could see in every direction, a country without roads, and the only way of reaching the place was by going along little Indian trails, and in one instance through the swamp of Cubahatchee. It was very cold; the country was wild, and the wolves were howling in every direction. With Indian camps, and the howlings of the wolves, the scene was a novel one for me, indeed.

Mr. Baldwin lived in a double log-cabin, surrounded by twenty or thirty negro-houses, distant a few hundred yards from his cabin. The country was being partly cleared up for the cultivation of cotton. Everything was so rough and uncouth on the outside that I did not expect to find anything on the inside to contradict the impression made by the external appearance of things. When I went in, Mr. Baldwin was sitting with his feet to a blazing big fire, and the room was altogether very cheerful and comfortable. He was glad to see me, and welcomed me as if I had been a real doctor. I had forgotten to say that, though I was twenty-two years old, I had no beard and looked like a boy. About as soon as I entered the room, I discovered a piano. I said to myself, "I didn't expect to find a piano in this wilderness; who would have dreamed of it?" In about twenty minutes I heard a door open and a rustling, and, looking behind, there was one of the most beautiful young women I have ever seen in all my life. She was tall, graceful, highly-educated, handsome, and accomplished. If I had not been then engaged to be married, I am sure I should have yielded to the beauty, and to the charms and fascinations of the surroundings of this lovely young woman. But we soon became very good friends, and I made a confidante of her, and that put us on very good and warm social relations. Her sister was the patient, and, after they gave us something to eat, I was invited into the sick-room. I found Dr. Bronson in attendance. He was a man over fifty years of age, had had the advantages of a good medical education, but, unfortunately, he drank—had even been drunk during the management of this case, which was very critical. I went with him to the sick patient. The child had been born about six days before. The mother was extremely ill, and I had sense enough to see that she was dangerously so, and I also had good sense enough, in our consultation, to see that a little tact was necessary. I said, "My dear doctor, I find that you have managed this case strictly in accordance with the principles laid down by our very best medical authorities." That was politic, for, as I said, I really did not know. I told him that I approved entirely of the course pursued, and that I had nothing to do; no alteration or suggestion to make in his treatment. This, too, was politic; for I didn't know what to suggest. They were very much pleased with my gentlemanly deportment and kindly manner, and would not let me think of returning home the next day.

I found myself most comfortably situated, with this

beautiful girl as a companion, and she had a first cousin, a Miss ——, who was certainly as beautiful and as accomplished. These girls had just returned from a high school in Georgia, where they had had the advantages of the best education that could be obtained for young ladies at that day and time. I remained there two or three days, going through the formalities, two or three times a day, of consulting with the doctor, and leaving him to manage the case as he pleased, while the girls and myself galloped through the country on fleet horses, visiting places of interest in the wilderness.

Just before I came away, Mr. Evans said to me, "Doctor, Mrs. McElroy's overseer is very sick, and has had two or three doctors to see him within the last fortnight, and we think that he is going to die." People living in a wilderness had to send thirty or forty miles for a doctor, and put off post-haste if anybody was seriously ill. The doctors would come once, prescribe for the patient, and would never come back again. That poor fellow had had two or three doctors, one from Troy, in Pike County, and another from somewhere else. Still he was very ill, and so Mr. Evans asked me if I would go over and see him. I said I had rather not, and he had better send for somebody else, some of the big doctors. I said, "He won't care to see me; I haven't the knowledge and reputation sufficient to take the charge of such a case as that. It has baffled the skill of all the doctors, and I have no desire to undertake anything that I know so little about." However, he insisted on my going. So the two girls and I mounted our horses, and we galloped over to Mrs. McElroy's, distant about three miles.

A very unfortunate thing happened to me on the excursion. On the road, we came to an Indian old field, about three hundred yards across. The girls bantered me for a race across that old field; and so we all put spurs to our horses, and went it like madcaps. Just as we got to the end of the race (of course the girls beat me) I drew up my horse suddenly, straightened myself in the stirrups, when I heard something go " r-r-r-rip," and then I heard, to my horror, something tear loose about my breeches. I had purchased a new pair of pantaloons just before starting on this visit to Mr. Evans, and, to my dismay, they were split down behind, right in the very middle. I laid my handkerchief down on the pommel of my saddle, and said, " God bless the man who invented frock coats." When I got to the place, I was in a quandary. I didn't know what was to be done, for the breeches were torn open about six inches in the crotch. But I made a joke of it, and told the girls that I was a ruined man. So when we got into the house they kindly offered to repair the damage; and so I was sent into another room, and, taking the garment off, passed it through the door to them, to be sewed up. While they were so engaged they had a good frolic over the affair. I put the pantaloons on, and we had a hearty laugh over the accident. They were sensible girls and appreciated the affair as well as a boy would.

By and by Mr. Evans arrived, and he said, "Now, doctor, we will go into the cabin and see Mr. Adams, the 'overseer.'" He had apprised Mr. Adams of my arrival, and when I entered the room the poor, suffering man turned himself to one side, and, rolling his keen eyes up to me, said to Mr. Evans, "My God, Evans, do you call that thing a doctor? Take him away; take him away. I have got no use for such a looking man as that. I am too a sick a man to be fooled with. Take him away." Really, I did not blame the poor fellow, for, had I been as sick a man as he was, I should have been of his opinion. I did not get into a bad humor, as many a foolish doctor does, or would have done, on such an occasion, but simply said, "Mr. Adams, I haven't come here to see you as a doctor, but simply to gratify Mr. Evans; I haven't the least desire to prescribe for you. I have great sympathy for you, and for everybody else who is sick, and I want to see them get well. I haven't the knowledge or experience necessary to treat any man who is as sick as you are, or as you seem to be."

He was quieted down by my kind words and suave manner, and said, "You will forgive me, won't you?" I said, "I have nothing to forgive you for. I did not come here either to prescribe for you, or even to investigate your case." He said, "I will give you my history, since you are so good as to come and see me, and you have been so kind." And then he gave me a minute account of his attack and sickness. I made no prescription, and left him soon after, and rode back to Mr. Evans's; the next day I rode back to Mount Meigs, after this very curious experience in the wild woods of Macon County, in the Creek Nation. The lady who had puerperal fever died the day after I left.

Just exactly four weeks from that day, which brought it up to the 17th of December, Mr. Evans came to Mount Meigs again, for Dr. Lucas to go and see Mr. Adams, who was still very ill. Dr. Lucas was in Tuscaloosa, and so he came after me. I said: "I will not go; I met the man once, and I am not the man he wants to attend his case. I do not know anything about his case, and I can not go."

Mr. Evans said, "Since you were there we have had eight or nine doctors to see him from different parts of the State, and one from Georgia, and nobody does anything for him, and you *must* go with me."

Most unwillingly, so far as the patient was concerned, but most willingly, so far as the recollection of those two charming young ladies was concerned, I mounted my horse, and went with Mr. Evans to see Mr. Adams. I found Mr. Adams emaciated to a skeleton, and so changed that I should hardly have known him. He was very willing for me to investigate his case, for he was used to having doctors investigate it, and all to no profit. Nobody seemed to understand what was the matter with him. But my having seen him previously, and having gotten from him a minute history of the case in the early stages of it, this experience was now of some service to me in arriving at a diagnosis of the case. When I came to turn him partly over on his back, and pat him on the liver, the right side, and the abdomen, I found that the right side of the abdomen was higher than the other; and, when I discovered that there was fluctuation, I immediately said: "There is matter here, and it must come out, or this man will die. It will have to be opened and come out." Mr. Adams said, "But how can that be so, when so many doctors have seen and examined me, and none of them have found it out?"

I said: "Of this I am sure. I am not much of a doctor, but when it comes to seeing and feeling and handling things, I know something, and I know that there is matter in this belly, and it either comes out or you will die. There is a young doctor living in your neighborhood, that you have never heard of."

"Who is he?" asked Mr. Adams.

"He is Dr. Baker; a graduate of my own college in Philadelphia, a year ago; a young Yankee, who has come down to seek his fortune in the South, and he lives not far from here."

"Yes," said Mr. Evans, "I have heard of him."

I said: "I wish you would send for him to come over here. As soon as he comes, he will know what is the matter with you, and he will have good sense enough to see it as I do. He will indorse what I have to say, because he has had the same training in the same great medical school from which I was graduated."

That required a day, and I didn't mind, as I had the two pretty girls to talk to. Dr. Baker was sent for, and he came over the next day (the 18th), in the morning. We examined the patient very minutely, and then we went out and sat on the fence, under a white-oak tree, for a consultation. I said:

"Well, Baker, there is some matter there."

He said, "No, I don't think so."

I said, "Well, what is it then?"

He replied, "Fungus hæmatodes."

I said: "If he has fungus hæmatodes, he will die; and if he has matter in there he will die, if you do not put a knife into it. If he has fungus hæmatodes, we ought to give him a chance for his life, by sticking a knife into it."

He said: "I am opposed to any surgical operations."

That blocked the game completely. But I was not willing to see the man die without any effort made to save him. So I proposed a council. Mr. Billy Dick, who was the great authority in that neighborhood, to whom everybody appealed and looked for advice, and three or four of his neighbors, were called in. Mr. Dick was a clear-headed man, of sound judgment, capable of weighing evidence, and much respected in the community.

"Gentlemen," I said, "our consultation results in a difference of opinion between us. There is no doctor in the neighborhood to decide, and I will make a statement of the case, and leave you gentlemen to decide what should be done. It is my opinion, gentlemen, that Mr. Adams has pus in his abdomen, probably in the liver. It is the opinion of Dr. Baker that it is not pus, but that it is a malignant disease. Be it one or the other, he will die if left as he is. If it is pus, it should be evacuated, and he will get well almost immediately. If it is what Dr. Baker thinks, sticking a knife into him might shorten his life a little, but not much. Death is certain if we do nothing. I think we ought to open it and see what it is. We leave it to you, gentlemen, whose advice to follow—mine or Dr. Baker's."

Mr. Dick spoke up at once, saying: "We will follow your advice."

I said, "Very well." So we went into the room—it was before the days of anæsthetics—and, pulling out a bistoury, I plunged it into his belly. I think it was one of the happiest moments of my life when I saw the matter flow and come welling up opposite that bistoury. It discharged two quarts of matter at once, and continued discharging for two or three days. A few days after that Mr. Adams was able to walk out, and a week after he rode over to Mr. Dick's, seven miles, and dined. He subsequently married Mrs. McElroy. It was my first surgical operation in Alabama. He became a rich man, went to Texas, and he has descendants in that State now.

Of course, this operation and its success gave me a great reputation in the neighborhood, and it was reflected back to Mount Meigs. I had engaged board at Miss Judkins's, and it made me a comfortable and pleasant home. My prospects were brightening. I was making friends every day, and before six weeks had rolled around I felt so secure in my new position and location, and especially in my prospects, that I thought that I could safely return to my native town to get married to the girl whom I had loved from the time of my schoolboy days. It was about the 1st of February, 1836, that I arrived in Lancaster, having been a week on the road in the stage. When I said that I had come to claim the hand of my affianced, and take her to my home with me in the West, her mother begged and implored me to wait until the following December. I was greatly disappointed, but I was obliged to bow to the wishes of my sweetheart's mother.

CHAPTER X.

The Seminole war—A journey to Philadelphia and New York—An experience in Charleston—An expedition against the Creek Indians—A sickly season—An attack of fever.

At that time the Seminole war had just broken out, and my brother and all the other young men of Lancaster were forming a volunteer company to go to the war. After three days' notice they started, and I was so fired with the war spirit by my visit to South Carolina that I was ready for anything, and was exceedingly anxious to follow my comrades and the friends of my youth to Florida. I was determined to do it; but my father begged me not sacrifice my foothold in Alabama, and said that if I went I should lose everything that I had gained there. He had been for a long time wishing to send my sisters, one of whom was twelve and the other ten, to Philadelphia to school. And, more out of a pretext for keeping me from going to the Florida war than to take them to Philadelphia, he begged me to go with them to Philadelphia, as he was not able to go. He did not intend to send them for perhaps a year, but used this as a pretext to keep me from going to Florida.

We left for Philadelphia about the 10th of February,

1836. It was a cold winter, and the severity of the season killed the orange and China trees at the South in great numbers. We had a very bad time getting North, traveling by stage all the way. There were snow and ice from the time we struck Charlotte, North Carolina, and we were obliged at different places to stop on account of the blockade. At Fredericksburg we had to remain four days, and when we arrived at Washington we were obliged to remain three or four days there. In Baltimore we had to remain two or three days before we could go on to Philadelphia. The snow was deep and the ice obstructed travel in every direction. At last we landed in Philadelphia, about the 1st of March. We were more than two weeks going. During the three days that I was in Washington I went to the capitol, and had an opportunity to see the great men of the nation. Among them were Henry Clay, Daniel Webster, Benton, Calhoun, Van Buren (who was President then), John Quincy Adams, and others of note.

Arriving in Philadelphia, I placed my sisters in Miss Edmunds's school, where I had been boarding a year before. I remained there a week or ten days, renewing acquaintance with my old friends, and then took my departure for the South, by way of New York. It took twenty-four hours to go from New York to Philadelphia, a distance now covered in ninety minutes. I remained in New York about a week, and I recollect one Sunday—I was boarding in Beekman Street, at a Quaker boarding-house, not far from where the "Times" office is now located—walking out into the country with a young medical student. We walked and walked till I was tired, and we went into the fields where they were building some new houses, which were very beautiful. I wondered why they should be building houses away out there in the fields. I said, the town can certainly never grow enough to come away up here. The fields I visited then, and the new houses I saw building, and thought were so far in the country, were in what is now Washington Square and Lafayette Place.

I took the steamer for Charleston, and arrived there the first of April, without a dollar in my pocket. I hoped that, being in my own native state, it would be easy enough for me to raise money, and I was sure that I should see friends and get from them money enough to return to Alabama. I stopped at the best hotel, the "Carolina Coffee-House," and I immediately looked over the list of arrivals to see if there was anybody there that I knew from the up-country! There was no name that I was familiar with. Then I went to the Planters', to Miott's, and looked all over town, to see the registers, and to see if there was any one there, and, to my utter amazement and dismay, there was not a name that I had ever seen or heard of before. The next day I made the same rounds of the hotels, and all in vain; and then the next day, but I could find not a name that I knew or ever had heard of before. Then I was in utter despair; what to do I did not know. I could not stay there much longer; I was obliged to go home, and yet hadn't a penny in my pocket. I was too proud to go and ask any of the professors in the Medical College to lend me money. Indeed, during the winter that I was there, I was so reticent that I did not make many acquaintances among the professors, and knew none of them very well, except the demonstrator of anatomy, Dr. John Bellinger. At last I remembered having heard my. father speak of a commission-merchant in Charleston, by the name of John Robinson; that a good many years ago he used to trade with him, and bought a great many groceries of him, and other supplies, such as were usual in the stock of an ordinary country store. The idea occurred to me that I would go to Mr. Robinson, and tell him frankly who I was and my condition, and ask him to help me. So I inquired the way to his office, and was directed, and then I walked down to the pier and looked in. I could not have the heart to ask a stranger to lend me fifty dollars. I soliloquized: "What if he thinks that I am an impostor? What if he thinks that I am really the son of Colonel Sims, and yet might be a swell swindler?" So I went back to the hotel to pass another night, wondering what I should do. I took the round of the hotels, thinking that perhaps some one from the up-country would be in the city, but all to no avail. The next morning, in a state of despair, I went again to Mr. Robinson's. The first time I inquired for him I was told that he was not in his office. I stood there with an aching heart and bewildered mind. The second time I timidly inquired if he was in, and was told that he was not, but that he would be back soon, in the course of half an hour. I was glad that he was not in, I was so heavy-hearted and sad and unhappy, and I scarcely knew what to do. But, by and by, after standing lounging around at his office for a little time, the half-hour passed, and he returned. I went into the store, and was shown into his private office and counting-room. He was a splendid, fine-looking old fellow, a Scotchman I thought from his accent. I said :

"Mr. Robinson, I am Dr. J. Marion Sims, of Alabama, and I am the son of Colonel Sims, of Lancaster. I left home not long ago to go to Philadelphia with my sisters, leaving them at school. I have journeyed thus far on my return home. I have been a little improvident, not extravagant, and not dissipated. Unfortunately, I am out of money, entirely so, and now I leave it to you to judge whether I am an impostor. I know I am an honest man, and I ask you to lend me fifty dollars to carry me to my home in Mount Meigs."

"I will gladly do it," he said, in a minute. "I know your father very well, and I know that you are just what you represent yourself to be, and what I take you to be."

I never was so relieved in all my life as I was by his generosity and kindness. He said, "When will you leave?"

I replied, "Just as soon as I can settle my bill at the hotel. I have been here now four days, looking at the hotel registers, thinking I might find somebody from Columbia, or some other up-country town, from my home. I could find no one, and in my state of despair I have thrown myself on your generosity. I will return the money as soon as I get to my home in Alabama."

He said, "If you will wait until the day after to-morrow, my son William is going to Marengo. He is a good traveling companion, and I think you will like him very much."

I waited, and on the day named I started, with young Mr. Robinson as a traveling companion, and arrived safely at my destination. But that visit made a deep impression on me, and the kind reception I received sank deep into my heart. I know that I have paid the money I borrowed of Mr. Robinson, over and over again, to many a man in want. I hadn't the conscience to decline when called upon, as I reflected on my feelings that I experienced that morning in Charleston. I have helped many a man unworthily, simply because I thought it was better to let money go in that way than to turn a man away who was deserving of assistance.

Soon after we passed into the Creek Nation the war broke out. Indeed, the stage that we went on was about the last that was allowed to pass, or that went from Georgia to Montgomery, Alabama, and a day or two after that the stages were attacked by the Creek Indians, and the passengers and drivers murdered. The whole country was in a turmoil, and volunteers were

called from every quarter to keep the Indians within
bounds, and to prevent their raids upon the settlers,
until the forces of the regular army could be conceen-
trated. As there were no railroads then, it took a long
time for General Gaines to get sufficient troops into
the Creek Nation to quell the turmoil. Volunteers
were called for, and Mount Meigs sent its quota. Captain Merrill Ashurst issued the call for volunteers, and
in three days he was at the head of one hundred and
twenty of the finest-mounted young men in the country!
They were armed with shot-guns and rifles, and each
with his private arms. I was in the ranks. A regiment had been called out from Montgomery, and I was
offered the position of assistant surgeon in the regiment.
But I preferred to go under Captain Ashurst's command, with my friends, as a private. We were in the
Creek Nation five weeks—a little over a month—where,
as I have often said to my friends, I "have fought, bled,
and died for my country." Captain Ashurst had a difficult position to fill, for every man was the equal of every
other man, and every man felt that no other man was his
superior; and so he had the most unruly set of fellows
entirely to manage. Dr. Hugh Henry, of Montgomery,
was the major in command of the battalion. Ashurst's
men were very unruly and impatient, and they didn't
want to be confined to the military drill and discipline;
and they wanted to be on the move and scouting all the
time. Major Henry hardly knew what to do with
them. At last, Captain Ashurst went to him one day,

and he said: "Major, I don't know how I am to manage these young men, unless you just give me the privilege of doing as I please. They are all of the very best blood in the country, and I can't drive them. I couldn't drive them to heaven, and yet I know that I could lead them to hell. Just give me the privilege of going into Tusceega to-morrow."

The major said: "I will send you off as advance-guard." And so we marched off to Tusceega. When we arrived at Tusceega at night, we pitched our tents, and the spies of Opothleo-ho-holo, the chief of the Creek Nation, so we found out afterward, reported to him that one hundred and twenty volunteers had arrived at Tusceega, and were easy to cut off. He was a wise old man, and he said: "I do not believe it. White people are not fools. They would not send a hostile force of only one hundred men to Tusceega. That is his advance-guard, and on either side of the town is a regiment behind them. I shall not molest them;" and it was to his distrust of his spies that we all owe our lives; for he could easily have annihilated the entire hundred without trouble.

It was a war without bloodshed. General Gaines arrived in time to send us all to our happy homes in five weeks, and that was enough to satisfy our love of adventure, and the exposure was sufficient to satisfy us with the honors of war. We reached Mount Meigs again on the 5th of June, a hot, dusty day, glad enough to return to that peaceful abode. This five weeks for me was a great thing. I went into that command perfectly

8

unknown, and a boy in appearance, but a man in spirit; and I came out of it with one hundred and twenty friends. All of the command were devoted friends of mine and to me. It laid the foundation of my popularity so deeply that I was soon sent for as the doctor for all the fellows that had been with me in that little excursion into the Creek Nation.

I was not at home a week before I found myself with plenty to do; and during June and July I was sent for in every direction to see sick people, and there was sickness enough in all conscience. The whole country was down with malarial fever. There were not enough well people to wait on the sick ones, and so it was that in private families people suffered for the want of medical attendance and the want of nursing, and Death seemed to me to walk in the wake of the doctors. I have never known such a mortality as there was at that time. I had never had a day's sickness in my life, and never thought that I could be sick. On the 4th day of September I went to the plantation of Mr. John Ashurst. The Ashurst family had taken me up as a doctor—John, Robert, and Merrill, and Ward Crocket, who had married a sister, Miss Ashurst, and the same boy that I had stuck the pin in the chair for when we were schoolboys together at Lancaster— and through their influence I had plenty to do.

On the 4th of September I went to John Ashurst's, who had a white house two miles from the village of Mount Meigs, where there were twenty or thirty sick negroes. I went from cabin to cabin, prescribing for them, and I felt very tired from the day's work. About twelve o'clock in the day, when I had made my rounds, I felt a little shiver run down my back. I made my way to the overseer's house, and soon I had a heavier chill, and half an hour later a raging fever with delirium. The fever passed off, moderately, toward night, and I was then barely able to mount my horse, and ride slowly back to Mount Meigs, where I went to bed. The next day Dr. Lucas came to see me; he was exceedingly kind to me and prompt in coming, although he was worked to death, going day and night, with more to do than he could possibly do well. When he came in, he examined me very minutely. Looking around, he saw a little mulatto girl, Anarcha, in the room, and he said, "Bring me a string, and a little cotton, and a bowl; I am going to draw a little blood from the doctor."

I said, "My dear, good doctor, you are not going to bleed me, are you?"

He said, "Yes, sir, old fellow, I'm going to bleed you."

I said, "Doctor, do you think I will die to-night, or before to-morrow, if you don't bleed me?"

He replied, "No, by God! you won't die before to-morrow if I do not bleed you."

"Then, doctor," I said, "you will excuse me if I am not bled to-night."

"Well," he said, "that is just as you please; but

you ought to be bled. I had an idea that you were **a**
d——d contrary fellow, and now I know it."

If I had been bled I should never have got well
nor been here to tell you this story. I was very ill;
the fever raged, and I didn't know how to arrest its
progress by the treatment with quinine. This was before the days of quininism, and fevers were allowed to
take their course. Patients were bled, purged, administered tartar emetic, and given fever-mixtures every
two hours during the twenty-four; the patients were
salivated, and the patients died, some of them sooner
than others. Those who were bled and purged the
strongest died the quickest. I got worse day by day.
At last the fourteenth day came, and the fever still
continued. By that time there were no doctors to be
had. Often I was three days without seeing a doctor.
I had no nurse; poor Mrs. Judkins was down sick; one
son was expected to die in the same house, and all the
servants were sick. A little negro girl would sleep in
the room with me, and hand me a drink of water occasionally. But I had no treatment, and nothing to arrest
the progress of the disease or of the fever. On the fourteenth day of my illness a young Englishman, living in
Montgomery, a druggist, named Thomas B. Coster, having been out on a collecting excursion, happened to
arrive in Mount Meigs about sundown. He stopped at
the village hotel kept by Colonel Freeney. While at
supper he said to Mrs. Freeney, " You have a young
doctor living here, a nice young fellow, whom I know

very well. Last June I was in the Creek Nation with him. He was in Captain Ashurst's company. He is from South Carolina. Can you tell me about him?"

"Yes," said she, "I can tell you all about him. He *is* a nice young fellow, and we all think a great deal of him, and we are all fond of him; and he has made friends with everybody. But he isn't going to be with us long; he is going to die to-night, they tell me."

"What? Is that possible?" he said. "Where does he live? Where is he? I must go to see him."

"Right up the street, about one hundred yards," Mrs. Freeney said.

So he came up to see me at once. I was an emaciated skeleton, in the last agonies, and with little or no pulse, and a cold, clammy sweat. My pulse had not been felt below the elbow for some time; but my mind was perfectly clear. He said, "Doctor, what are you taking? Who is attending you?" I said, "I haven't seen a doctor for three or four days."

"But," he said, "are you taking nothing? Don't they give you any brandy? Don't they give you any quinine? Have you no nurse?"

"No," I said, "I have no nurse, for there are not well people enough to wait on the sick. Poor Mrs. Judkins is sick in the next room; her son is going to die, and there is nobody to wait on the well people or the sick ones. I feel that I am dying; I think that I shall die to-night."

"Who is to sit up with you?" he asked. When I

told him that I expected nobody, he continued, " Then I will sit up with you, and see you through the night."

I turned over and wept like a child to see such kindness, which was perfectly disinterested. All that I remember was that, during the night, a soft hand like a woman's would be placed back of my head, and his tender voice, saying, " Drink, doctor; take this drink; drink just this; it is only a little brandy;" and very soon again the brandy would be poured down me, and then again the same voice would say, " Here, doctor, I have some quinine that I travel with, and I am going to give you some on my own responsibility." I swallowed some of the most nauseous doses that night, but I felt that the hand of a ministering angel had been tending me.

The next morning he left me. He bade me not despair; that many a man had recovered from a prostration as severe as mine, and he hoped that I would get well. That was the turning-point in my disease. The reaction was brought about by the administering of the proper remedies in the hand of my friend Mr. Coster. The pulse returned, and although he could feel it when he went away that morning, and said he hoped that I would get well, still he has told me many a time that he never expected to see me alive, or lay his eyes on me again. My recovery was very, very slow indeed.

Alabama never saw so sickly a season as that. Scarcely a single family escaped, and the whole country was left in mourning. One poor fellow, living across the way from us, who had moved there only six months before from Georgia, lost his wife and two children and the only negro that he had. When he went to bury his wife there was no one to help him, or that was well enough to follow her coffin, but himself and two or three negroes that officiated at the grave. That year's sickness was a great lesson to me. I learned much from observation and from experience, and especially how much mortality followed the practice of the doctors. I became exceedingly conservative; I never bled, and gave as little medicine as possible. But it was not long before the practice of the country was completely revolutionized. The writings of Fearne and Erskine, in Alabama, were the first to throw light upon the proper method of treating malaria and malarial fevers. Until their day, the doctors were in the habit of bleeding and physicking people until the fever disappeared, and then giving them quinine, a grain or two, three times a day. But Fearne and Erskine and others preached the doctrine of giving it without any regard to preliminary treatment, giving it always in the beginning, if possible, and giving it in sufficient doses to affect the system at once. But to return to myself: I was confined to the house, in all, about two months; for my convalescence was very slow, and, indeed, I sometimes despaired of getting well at all. It left me with an enlarged spleen, and I had occasional attacks of intermittent fever. But about the 20th of November I felt strong enough to undertake the journey to South

Carolina. I improved every day from that moment, and by the time I arrived at home, which was about the first of December, I felt strong enough to walk two or three miles. I improved very rapidly. Of course, I lost my hair, but that soon grew out again.

CHAPTER XI.

My courtship — Obstacles and difficulties — My secret engagement — My marriage.

WHEN I was about eleven years of age, and living in Lancaster village, I was standing by my mother one Saturday afternoon, about five o'clock, looking out of the window, when I saw a young girl coming along the street, leading her little brother by the hand. I said, "Oh, see, ma; what a pretty little girl! Isn't she a beauty? Who is she?"

My mother replied, "That is the daughter of Dr. Jones, and she is coming here to see me. I have dressed you up in your best clothes expressly to receive her." Presently the girl came in, leading her little brother. I was so shy and confused that I could not approach to be introduced; but from that time I was dead in love with her. Soon after this the Franklin Academy was started and opened for pupils. During all the time I was there I was loyal to Theresa. She was my ideal and my idol. I was devoted to her from the time I was eleven and she eight. After I went to college at Columbia she was sent to Barhamville, to Dr. Marks's school, near Columbia, and I used occasionally to go out to the school to make her visits, and also to see some other young ladies who came from the same region of country that I did, and whom I knew. By and by she graduated at the school, and returned home a year before I did. She was now sixteen or seventeen, and had grown to be a fine woman, tall, handsome, and very soon was a great belle, while I was a comparative pigmy.

After I left college and returned home, I began to study medicine with Theresa's uncle, Dr. Churchill Jones. I found her then a blooming young lady, a leader and a belle in society, greatly admired, with beaus coming from every direction. She was a dashing girl, a fine rider, with fine accomplishments and great beauty. She had some little fortune, which I regretted very much, for I had none. As I was now twenty years old, I was very much afraid that she might forget the tender attachment between us as children. She had many and rich beaus, talented, excellent, splendid fellows, of good families and of fortune, so that I was exceedingly anxious to let her know that I had the same affection for her that I always had. I was afraid that she might become engaged to some of the young men that were flying around her, and so I determined to let her know that childhood love had only increased with manhood growth. I tried my best to tell her about it, but I could not. My love was so profound that I could not find the tongue to express it. I arranged to take walks with her, but I never could speak. I talked about everything but the thing I would like to have talked about. At last, seeing that it was impossible for me to speak to her, I sat down and wrote her a note. It was dated the fifth day of March, 1833—fifty years ago. I told her that I had always loved her, that I was too young to propose marriage, and too poor to marry; that I wanted her to know of my affection, and I wished very much to know whether she returned it or not. I felt that, having written to her once, I could talk to her when opportunity presented itself. My brother took the letter.

I shall never forget with what anxiety I watched for him to return and tell me all that happened. She read the letter, so he said when he returned, and did not seem angered, nor did she throw it back to him. I went to see her, but I could hardly bring myself to talk. I said: "You have received a letter from me." She said that she had. That ended it. The thing went that way for a whole month. I was very anxious to know what she meant. At last, one evening, we took a walk, partly to go out to Mr. James Witherspoon's, her brother-in-law, who lived in Cooterborough, one of the suburbs of the town of Lancaster. We walked out there with a party of young people. It was more than half a mile, but I could not talk on the subjects that I wanted to talk about. I was pretty sure that she loved me, and yet I feared that perhaps she did not. I thought that I would have the thing over before we got to Mr. Witherspoon's to tea. We returned by a longer route, as an excuse for a longer walk. It was a beautiful moonlight night, and we had walked about half a mile without my coming to the point. I said to myself, "What a fool I am, that I can not talk to this girl frankly and openly." My heart was in my throat, and my mouth so dry that I could hardly speak. Looking ahead I saw Mr. Locke's blacksmith shop, and I vowed not to pass that shop without knowing. There was a large locust-tree there, and we stepped under it. I said:

"Theresa, I wrote you a note a month ago. You are seventeen years old this very day, and you are old enough to think of what that note contained. I did not ask you to marry me, but I do ask you now—will you marry me?"

She said, in a low, tremulous voice, "No, Marion, I can never marry you."

We never spoke after that during the rest of the walk. It was the longest quarter of a mile I ever walked in my life. I led her up the steps of her house and timidly said "Good night," and went away. I think I was the most miserable wretch that was ever in love. I did not know what in the world to do. I did not sleep a wink that night. If I had been fond of liquor I should have gone off and got drunk. But I never drank, and would not get drunk. I had passed through college (two years) and had never smoked a cigar. But I went up town and bought some common American cigars, and sat down and smoked one, and I felt very badly. I said, "I have a great mind to get drunk." And then I said, "No, I will not; I wish I were dead. I don't know what I was born for, anyhow. I am of no account, and I will never make love again. She is right; she ought never to marry me. The world looks dark to me. I wish I were dead."

I was very unhappy, taking it altogether. I lived a half a mile from the village. And from Dr. Jones's, where I studied medicine, I could see my sweetheart's house, and could occasionally see her walking in the garden! My whole life was changed; I was embittered, and I did not know how to judge her. I said, "She is like all women; she will sell herself for money. She is venal." How unkind and cruel was it in me to speak of her in that way; I could not understand it. Perhaps it was because her brother, and her mother, and the family opposed me. If she had only said that she loved me and would be constant to me! I said, "I know what it is; there is some young fellow from North Carolina, who has a fortune, and is a matured man, and everything for a girl to love. She liked me as a schoolboy, but not now that she has grown to be a magnificent woman." So I soliloquized. First, I upbraided her, and then abused myself. Then I wished that I were dead, or that I had never been born, and at last, in despair, I went to my father, and I said:

"Father, I know you are very poor, but don't you think you could manage some way to allow me to leave this place? If I had a few hundred dollars I could go to Alabama, or go somewhere?"

He said, "My son, are you crazy?"

I said, "No father, I am not crazy, but I will tell you what is the matter. You know that Theresa and I have been sweethearts all our lives. The rich North Carolina fellows are flourishing around her, and I made up my mind some little time ago that I would tell her all about my love for her. But she rejected me, and so I would like to go away from here; I can not stand it. I can not study, and I do not know what to do." He said, "My dear boy, I am very sorry for you, but I can not help you. I couldn't give you one hundred dollars to save my life. I advise you to accept the inevitable. I have known Theresa from her infancy, and have seen how devoted and attentive you have been to her. I have seen her grow up to be beautiful and accomplished, and she is certainly one of the finest women I have ever seen, and nothing would have made me so happy as to have called her my daughter. But you must accept your fate; you must work on; not give up, but make a man of yourself, and do not get despondent, or neglect your studies. Go to work, that is my advice."

I never went to the village in the daytime, but remained out in the edge of the forest, occasionally going to the village at night to see some of the boys of the town, and then I would sneak home by a back way. I never went along the main street, for it was almost impossible to go into the village of Lancaster without going by Dr. Jones's door. I never passed it; on the contrary, I avoided it.

One day I happened to meet Betsey Witherspoon.

She was a cousin of Theresa Jones, and her bosom and intimate friend. Soon after we met she said, "Cousin Marion" (we always called each other cousins although we were no kin), have you seen Theresa lately?"

I said, "No, only at a distance."

"Well how are you and Theresa getting on these days? Tell me all about it."

I said, "Cousin Betsey, you surprise me by the question, and it also hurts me very much."

She said, "What?"

I said, "I am wounded by your putting that question to me. You know what has occurred."

She said, "What do you mean? I do not understand you. I know nothing that has happened, and I ask you for an explanation."

I said. "Are you in earnest in what you say?"

She said, "Perfectly so."

"Then," I said, "I will tell you. Three months ago I asked Theresa to marry me when I got a profession. She said 'No,' and that is all that has passed between us. Since then I haven't passed her house, nor been in town in daytime. I am a changed man; I am nobody."

She said, "Cousin Marion, now I understand things; I have noticed something very peculiar about Theresa lately. She has been very reticent, and rather sad, but has never mentioned your name to me, and I thought it was very odd. Now I know that she loves you just as well as you love her. I know that the family do not want her to marry you, and I presume she has been trying to obey her mother, and has sacrificed her heart for the peace of the family. She has been as dumb to me as you have been all this time."

I said, "Ah, if I thought this were so I would go back to her again, because she has complete possession of my heart."

She said, "I think if I were in your place I would at least see her, and know exactly what her feelings are on the subject."

I replied, "I have not been to town in daylight in three months, but have been prowling around like a night-owl. I haven't passed by Mrs. Jones's house since the 4th of last April."

The next morning, which was July 23, 1833, I left my house and went to the village, not knowing exactly where I was going, or what I was going for. But as I was walking along the street by the garden of Mrs. Jones (it was one of those old-fashioned, scolloped-paling fences), to my great surprise and delight, on the opposite side of the palings was Theresa, walking alone, with a rose-bud in her hand. So I stopped suddenly, bowed, and said, "Good morning, Cousin Theresa."

She said, "Good morning."

"You have a pretty rose-bud in your hand; will you give it to me?" She gave me the bud through the garden fence; and now, my dear readers, whenever you may call to see me, I will show you that rose-bud. This was just fifty years ago.

We had a long talk that morning, and she told me frankly that she had been as miserable as I had been; but she tried to please her mother by saying No to me. That as soon as she had sent me away she relented, and would have gladly welcomed me if I had come back. She said that she had never spoken to her cousin Betsey, nor to anybody, and had carried her own heavy heart, as I had carried mine. We came to a mutual understanding, which was this:

I said, "Now, I will love you forever. I will seem not to care anything for or about you. I will never come to see you or come to your house, unless I am invited. I will not even dare to walk with you to or from church. I will never persecute you, or presume to follow you. Nobody in this world must know that there is anything between us, and you must know that I have the utmost confidence in you, for you may carry on all the innocent flirtations that you please, and I beg of you to have the same confidence in me."

With that understanding we parted, and I saw nothing more of her, excepting at a distance; but my heart was tranquil, and I was happy. I knew that she returned my affection, and that was all I wanted to know. I was happy enough to see her in the distance, and my heart was throbbing for her, as I knew that hers was for me. I was poor, and she waited for me a long time. I went to Charleston and attended lectures, and came home. I never had a fear that she would not prove true and faithful to me. I wrote to her, and directed

the letters to my brother. When he saw the initials
" J. M. S." on the seal of the letter, he knew it was for
her. This thing we carried on until I graduated in
Philadelphia and came home.

Two years had passed, with this secret hidden from
everybody but two—Betsey Witherspoon and my brother. When I came home and put up my shingle in
Lancaster as a doctor, I could not claim her hand, as
I had no money, and no home to take her to. If she
were willing to wait until I could make her a home, I
was happy. When I returned from Philadelphia, in
May, 1835, I found my friend Thornwell settled in
Lancaster as pastor of the Presbyterian church. Theresa
was a member of his church, and her family were also
members of it, and her uncle, Dr. Dunlap, was one of the
deacons, and one of the lights of the church. Theresa
had made a confidant of Mr. Thornwell, knowing that
he was my bosom friend in college. She told him all
our love story and trials, and he heartily sympathized
with her. When I returned home from Philadelphia,
he immediately came to see me, and told me that he
knew all about the affair; so I threw off the mask entirely. I went to Theresa's house every day or two,
went to church with her, walked with her, rode with
her, and was a good deal in her society. Her mother
became quite uneasy, and was very anxious and unhappy, and talked with her brother, Dr. Dunlap, and
her son, Dr. Rush Jones, about the matter. She said,
" He is a very nice fellow; I have known him ever since

he was a little boy; but Theresa must not marry him, and the affair must be ended."

At last, my friend Thornwell came down to see me at my office, and he said, "Well, Marion, old boy, there is about to be an explosion. The secret must come out now. Annie" (Annie was Theresa's maid-servant, a mulatto girl, a little older than she was, but who was in the secrets of her mistress), "Annie came over to tell me to go and see Miss Theresa. She told me that the family had been having a consultation, and that she had listened and heard Mrs. Jones say, 'I am going to tax Theresa with this business, and ask her if she is going to marry Marion Sims. I thought all this matter was dead and buried long ago, but now it seems to be resuscitated.' This young colored girl heard every word of the consultation from an adjoining room, and went at once and told her mistress, Miss Theresa, all about it. Then she sent the girl to me, and said that I must come at once to see her."

I said, "Thornwell, I am going to write a note to Mrs. Jones and make a clean breast of the whole affair."

"That's right," said Thornwell; "there is nothing else to do. I will read a newspaper while you write the letter."

In about five minutes I had written a nice little note to Mrs. Jones, in which I said that Theresa and myself had been sweethearts all our lives, and that we had been engaged for the past two years; that I did not propose marriage now, at all; that I had no means with which to support a wife, but that I hoped when I had made a position for myself and a home for Theresa to obtain her consent to our union. My friend Thornwell read the note, and said I had done exactly right, and then added, " Now, old fellow, we will see what can be done."

So he took the letter up to Mrs. Jones's. Mrs. Jones received it, read its contents carefully, cried bitterly, and after a while she said she could not give her consent to the marriage, either now or prospectively.

My friend Thornwell said, " Pray, what is your objection to him ? " She had no particular objection to me, only that I did not belong to the church. To this Thornwell replied : " Two years ago, I was not a member of the church myself. I was in college with Marion Sims, and I know that there he was a fellow of good morals. He swears a little bit occasionally, but he can be cured of that. He has no really bad habits, and now that he has a profession he will be able to make his way in the world. Now, as I view it," said Thornwell, continning, " when two young people's hearts have clung to each other as long as theirs have, from childhood up, the interference of parents and friends is a very serious matter, unless there is the best reason for it ; and here there is absolutely none."

Thornwell told her that she was all wrong in this matter, and that her opposition was not well founded. He said, " I know Marion Sims well. He is an honorable young man, and will never elope with or do anything to disgrace your daughter. He will, I am sure, be a good husband to her, and a dutiful son-in-law. It is impossible for you to separate these two young people, and I advise you, as your pastor, to dismiss the whole of this nonsense, and let them come together now, and be married whenever he has a home to which he may take her, and not till then, be the time near or remote."

There were ten days of crying and grief, all of which time Theresa was kept a prisoner in her little room upstairs, except when she came down to her meals. I, too, was quarantined by Mr. Thornwell at my office. These were days of anxious solicitude truly, and I was hoping every day for the termination of the unhappy affair. At last, Mrs. Jones accepted the inevitable, after the plain advice given her by her pastor and friend Thornwell. She sent for her daughter and kindly told her that she consented to the union. Mr. Thornwell came running down to me with the joyful news, and told me I could call at Mrs. Jones's. Of course, I was promptly there on time. Mrs. Jones met me with a smile and a welcome, making no allusion whatever to any of the disagreeable things that had occurred. Everything was happily understood, without our talking about it.

This was in the month of June, 1835. I spent the summer in Lancaster, as I have before said. My unhappy medical experience there has already been related.

On the 13th of October, I left for Alabama. I have already told the story of my experience there, and of my return to South Carolina on the first of December, 1836, to be married. We were married on the 21st of that month, by the Rev. Mr. Thornwell. We were the first couple he ever married.

I propose now to go on with this narrative, which will show how, in the end, much of my success in life has been due to my wife's co-operation, and to her wise and good advice.

About the middle of January we went to Alabama. I had already engaged rooms at Mrs. Judkins's, where we were very comfortably and cozily located. Soon after our arrival Mr. Henry Lucas kindly offered me the use of a vacant house he had in the village. This we furnished very simply, and began housekeeping. I had succeeded in making many friends, as I before stated, and very soon I was pretty well occupied. We spent the year 1836 at Mount Meigs. I was content with my position and business, expected to remain there, and had no intention of changing my residence. But, in 1837, Dr. Blakey, who practiced medicine, and planted on a large scale, desired to give up a part of his practice, and offered me a partnership. He resided about ten miles east of Mount Meigs, at a place in Macon County, near Cubahatchee Creek. His offer was so favorable that I, of course, accepted it. He at once introduced me into a very large practice, in the Abercrombie neighborhood. The Abercrombies were all rich and influential, and, with Dr. Blakey's indorsement and their patronage, I soon had as much as I could possibly do. I was exceedingly happy in my new position. I had a little piece of ground, upon which there was a log-cabin with one room, and I had an addition built to it, making two, and there our first two children were born.

CHAPTER XII.

I think of abandoning the profession—A severe attack of fever—My wife
and children ill with fever—I resolve to seek a new home— Journey
to Lowndes County—Final determination to settle in Montgomery.

I am an example of a man who has never achieved
the ambition of his early life. My successes have been
in a direction that I never dreamed of when I started.
I had no particular interest in my profession at the beginning. I studied away at it, and at the end of five
years had become quite a respectable physician, and, I can
say, a tolerably successful one. Still, I was really ready,
at any time and at any moment, to take up anything that
offered, or that held out an inducement of fortune, because I knew that I could never make a fortune out of
the practice of medicine. I, of course, never dreamed of
making any other than a local reputation.

While I was comfortably situated with Dr. Blakey,
and getting on so well, I received a letter from George
Brown, of Philadelphia, who was a cousin of Miss Edmunds, and whom I had known very well when I was
a medical student there. He wrote that some capitalists
there had offered him a credit of one hundred thousand
dollars in Philadelphia, if he would take a stock of cloth-

ing, go to Vicksburg, Mississippi, and set up a large clothing-house. He offered to make me, without any money consideration, a half-partner, if I would quit the practice of medicine and join him in this commercial enterprise. I immediately said, "What is the use of my struggling here always, for two thousand or three thousand dollars a year, with no prospect of any advancement in life, when such an offer comes to me unsought and unsolicited?"

So I immediately informed Dr. Blakey of the offer, and of my determination to give up the profession and become a clothing-merchant in Vicksburg. I sold out my little home, got four hundred dollars for it, and was preparing to go to Vicksburg in the month of October (1838). Just as I got ready and was about to leave, I received news from Mr. Brown that the whole thing had exploded, and that he could not go to Vicksburg. Financial embarrassments among the men that wanted to set him up in business had caused the trouble. I had acted hastily and unwisely. I was greatly disappointed, but had nothing else to do but to return to my practice again. Dr. Blakey was only too glad to have me remain, but, having sold my house, I moved across the Cubahatchee Swamp, into what was called Cubahatchee, only about a mile and a quarter from Dr. Blakey's. I there went to work again and in real earnest, giving up all ideas of getting rich fast. In 1839 I had all the practice I could possibly attend to. I had the confidence of the community in which I lived, and

9

even the affection of everybody. I was perfectly happy. I had a beautiful wife, whom I loved to distraction, and two lovely children, and was making three thousand dollars a year. I had a double-barreled shot-gun, a pointer dog, and I took life lightly. There never was a fellow so happy as I, and I expected to remain there forever. I never dreamed that any misfortune could ever drive me away from the place in which I was seemingly so firmly anchored. Everything was going on smoothly and carelessly, as it were. When I was sent for to go to a plantation to see sick negroes, I mounted my pony, with my gun on my shoulder, and my medical saddle-bags behind me, and with my dog trotting by my side; so, if in galloping along through a piece of piney woods, or in the swamps, any small game made its appearance, like a covey of partridges or a squirrel, I would blaze away, bring down my game, dismount, secure my prize, and then I would jump on my horse and gallop off. I never made a visit in daytime that I did not succeed in bagging a partridge or squirrel, and sometimes a wild duck.

The year 1839 came and went in this free and easy way, and 1840 also came and was passing. But it was a sickly year, and malarial fevers were everywhere, often assuming a congestive form, in which men would die sometimes in eight hours; often less. It was an awful thing to see a man walking about to-day strong and well, and in the enjoyment of perfect health, suddenly stricken down with a little chill, going into a collapse, and dying in a few hours. There were many such deaths as that during the summer; more than I had seen any season before.

Early in July (1840), about the 5th or 6th, as I was returning from Mr. Abercrombie's plantation, I felt a slight chill pass over me, and the sensation ran down my spine. I soon reached home and went to bed. There was a slight reaction afterward, and I did not consider myself a sick man. The next day I visited patients, had no paroxysm of fever, and did not fear any return of it. The next day, however, at eight o'clock in the morning, my wife and myself were walking in the garden, looking at the peas and beans, and other little things, growing so finely, when, all at once, a little shiver ran down my back. I went into the house and was put to bed. This chill increased in severity, and it was nothing like I had had two days before. At twelve o'clock, four hours from the first sensations of chilliness, I was in a complete collapse, with no pulse above the wrist, and a cold, clammy sweat on me, with great internal heat, jactitation, and labored breathing, and the utmost prostration—yet with my intellect clear and undisturbed.

There was no doctor anywhere near. My wife and two sisters, and Mr. George Brown, who a year before wished to make a merchant of me, were there. They gave me stimulants and had me wrapped up in mustard-plasters. I felt that I was dying. There was no reaction; I was rubbed and plastered, and there was

nothing else to be done, or that could be done. I felt
that I could possibly live but a few hours; that I must
certainly die. But how hard is death for the young,
when life is full of promise; and how hard it was
for me to leave my wife and children, knowing that
they would have to struggle with the cold world and
its hardships, without much money to aid them; for
when we were married I had nothing, and Theresa
had only a little. I did feel at one time that I would
speak to her; I hated to think of her ever loving
and marrying another man. All these thoughts came
to me when I thought I was dying. Then I said to
myself, " I will not be so mean as to speak to her
and annoy her on this subject; I will die as I am, and
Providence will take care of her." No man ever died
with more of the consciousness of death than I experienced then. I am sure that I was in a moribund state.

I felt that I was sinking and disappearing from the
world. As I lay on my back, things became smaller,
and my wife and sisters seemed to be sinking more and
more, and gradually to be receding from me and from
the room. I seemed to be sinking down into a narrower and narrower and lower channel; and then I
would shut my eyes and immediately open them again.
Calling reason to my aid again, I would try to discover
the manner and secret of death; and, although but a
second would elapse from their opening, still it seemed
to be an eternity. I looked upward, and I thought my
friends were twenty or thirty feet away from me. I

could hear their voices quite distinctly and understand all that was said ; but I gradually sank lower, and lower, and lower, till I looked up through the narrow channel in which I lay, and I could see them fifty or one hundred feet above me.   When I called again my own reason, I knew that I was on the same level with them. But I had the sensation that I was sinking lower and lower, getting weaker and weaker, that soon my eyes would be closed, and I should see them no more forever.

Almost at the last, when I seemed to be a great distance below my wife and sisters, I whispered, " Can you not make a mustard-plaster as broad as my back and as long? I feel that I am dead in everything except my intellect, and that is so obscured that I seem to be a great distance below you ; and yet my senses tell me that I am on the same level with you." As quick as it could be done, the plaster was spread, just as I had ordered.   I was rolled over, and the plaster was placed on the spine, from the nape of the neck, the whole length, and as broad as the back itself. I turned over upon this, and in the course of I know not how long—it might have been fifteen minutes, and it may have been an hour, for I had no way of measuring time—I felt a slight sensation of warmth in the region covered by the plaster.   That warmth was agreeable ; it was not at all uncomfortable as it increased ; and, strange to say, just in proportion as the burning increased on the back, in just that proportion

I seemed to experience relief. I began to improve with the burning; for when it was placed there I was sinking down, down, down; but, as the plaster began to burn, it resisted this sinking oppression, and I felt myself gradually rising, gently, gently, gently, getting nearer to my wife and my sisters, until I was within a few feet, seemingly, of the top of a great pit, into which I had been sunken. After a while the burning increased in my back, and I looked around on the same level with the rest of my family. I could breathe freely, and I felt that life was coming back to me again. Strange to say, at the time I seemed to rise to the surface the cold, clammy sweat was beginning to disappear; warmth began to return to my body generally, and in the course of four hours it was seen that there was a possible chance for me to recover. I was in a collapse, from twelve o'clock until eight.

By eight o'clock at night I had got a pulse; my skin was warm and dry, my head was clear, and I was saved. These were the sensations of death that I know I should have had if I had died. If it had not been for the providential application of the mustard-plaster, and the proper remedies, at the proper time, I should surely have died.

Every day, at the same hour, my case was attended with dangerous symptoms; but they were those which we find in new countries, West and South, as the result of malarial poisoning, coming from a decomposition of vegetable matter in alluvial soils, which endanger health. The conditions are favorable to engendering chills under such circumstances. When they assume a congestive character they are pernicious, and are always dangerous. It is uncommon for one to escape the third chill. I knew this, and I realized the danger in which I was placed. The chills that anticipate are more dangerous than those that procrastinate. My first chill was a little trifling thing, at eight o'clock in the day; the second was an enormous congestive chill at twelve o'clock in the morning; thus anticipating four hours. I feared that the next would come at four o'clock in the morning, or forty-four instead of forty-eight hours later. If it came then I knew that I must die.

I sent a messenger at once for Dr. Holt, at Montgomery, and one of the most eminent practitioners of that city. He was engaged in an enormous practice. I had no claims upon him; I knew him but little; but, when he heard that a young brother was thus dangerously ill, he left his practice and came twenty miles to see me. There were no railroads at that time, and he had to drive in his sulky to Mount Meigs. As soon as he got a history of my case, he said:

"Well you must not have another chill at four o'clock to-morrow morning. If you do you will die. But we will prevent it. Thirty grains of quinine, taken between now and midnight, will save it. You must take it until you feel a little ringing sensation in your ears; keep your bed, keep warm, and keep up good courage. Above all, take the quinine; for bed, and warmth, and good courage alone can not save you. They are only assistants to the specific remedies that will certainly prevent a paroxysm."

How anxiously I looked for that four o'clock the next morning. At midnight I was snug and comfortable and warm, with quite a pulse and soft skin; but I could not feel safe until four o'clock came. At four o'clock I was asleep; but yet I could feel that the secret enemy was at work. To my joy, and as I expected, of course, I did not have a chill. At four o'clock, precisely, my nose began bleeding, and that the ancients would have termed a critical discharge. The chill did not come.

In a few days I was up, and in a month my wife was down with intermittent fever, my children were sick with it, my servants were attacked, I had a recurrence of it, and altogether we were a sorely-afflicted family.

I had been very happy there, and I thought that nothing in the world would ever induce me to leave Cubahatchee. I had everything in the world that a man wanted or needed to make him comfortable and happy, and to make him satisfied in life. But I said to myself: "What is life without health? Three thousand dollars a year is nothing, though it is a great deal for a young man to earn in this day and age of the world. I would rather live in the piney woods, or in any place in the world, and be sure of health, and just have enough to get along with." So I counseled with my wife, and I

said: "We can not stay here. We have good friends
that love us dearly, and who would be sorely afflicted
to give us up, but what is the use of our staying here
when we see that we must always be sick?"

She agreed with me, and seemed to be perfectly willing to go, though she regretted leaving friends whom
we had made there. My first idea was to go to Lowndes
County, where my brother-in-law, Dr. Rush Jones, resided. He practiced medicine and planted cotton extensively. He had a fine plantation; was doing admirably
well from every point of view. I thought I would be
very happy in his neighborhood, as we had been boys
together and always were bosom friends. I started off,
very feebly, in the month of November (1840). I went
to Montgomery, twenty miles distant, which was nearly
half way to my brother-in-law's. There I stopped at
" Montgomery Hall."

I happened to be very well acquainted with Dr.
Goff, a young man of fine family, well educated, and
a very promising young doctor. But, while he had
money, he also had bad habits. He was not strictly a
drunkard, but he got drunk. He played cards, and neglected his business altogether, so that he never could have
been expected to rise to any great eminence in his profession, with his habits of life. He happened to stroll
into " Montgomery Hall " just after I had arrived there.
In the course of the conversation I told him how very
ill I had been, how ill I was then; that I was broken
down with intermittent fever, and told him all about

my family, and that I was so used up I had made up my mind to leave Cubahatchee.

"That is very unfortunate," he said, "for I have never heard of a young fellow doing so well as you are doing there. Everybody loves you, and everybody speaks well of you, and what are the people up there going to do without you? What are you intending to do, or where are you going?"

"I am on my way to Lowndes County," I replied, "to see my brother-in-law, Dr. Rush Jones, in search of a location there with or near him."

"Not to find health, are you? You will not find it there, my dear fellow. It is a worse place than where you are. In place of going there to Lowndes County, why do you not locate here in Montgomery?"

"Come to Montgomery!" I said. "That is impossible. I am nothing but a little country doctor, from the pine woods, with no money and no reputation to start on, and a family of children dependent upon me, and I must go to some place where it would be easier to get practice, and where people would be obliged to employ me, whether they wished to or not. And besides, you have too many great doctors here in the profession, and I would starve to death with you."

"O, no, Dr. Sims, you would not," he quickly replied; "you would not starve to death. You are a man of industry, and such application, such courage, and such devotion to your profession as you have shown, rest assured, old fellow, would soon be appreciated in

Montgomery. You would make hosts of friends and a place among us here; and, what is more, you would hold it too. You had better think of what I am telling you, and if you must leave where you are, where you seem to be so pleasantly located, and where you are loved, and respected, and honored, think seriously of coming to Montgomery, and not of spending your time in such a place as Lowndes County, with your brother-in-law."

It had never occurred to me to think of going to Montgomery. I was too diffident of myself, and too modest in my aspirations, to dream of looking so high, and that in a city which was full of older men, high up in their profession. So I left the very next morning for Lowndes County. But I could not get rid of the idea that Joe Goff had put into my mind. It haunted me all the way that I went, and all the next day. When I neared my brother-in-law's house, every cabin that we passed had sick people in it. Everybody looked as if he was malarially poisoned. I went by no house where there was not one or more beds stretched out before the door, with servants fanning some members of the family that were down sick with the malarial or intermittent fever.

I arrived at my brother-in-law's house, and found that he was in a nest of intermittent fever. His negroes were sick, and he was not well himself. His overseer was sick, and there was sickness everywhere. around. That satisfied me that I must not think of locating there; that I might just as well remain where I was at Cubahatchee as to come down to Lowndes County. Joseph Goff's idea about coming to Montgomery had lifted me so up out of myself that I could not very well get rid of it. I went home and had a consultation with my wife. She saw the situation at once, and immediately said, "Montgomery is the place, and to Montgomery we will go."

I was greatly elated about it, and still I was very unhappy at the idea of leaving Cubahatchee. I was really afraid to tell the Abercrombies—Charles, Milo, and John, three brothers—that I was going to leave. I dreaded to leave them. I managed to let them find out my plans through the neighbors, for I knew that we would have a scene. Two days after, Milo Abercrombie came to my house. I saw him in the distance and I knew what he was coming for. He hitched his horse to the fence, and walked into the house where my wife and children were, looking like a mad bear. He said, gruffly, "Good morning."

I said, pleasantly, "Good morning, Mr. Abercrombie."

He said, "I have just come down to see if you have lost your senses. I am told that you are going away from here."

I replied that there was too much sickness there for me. He retorted by asking me where I expected to get away from sickness, and, if I did find such a place, how I expected to live. "Look here, old fellow," he continued, "are you a fool? I have come here to give you a piece of my mind. You have friends here that love you and who do not want to give you up. Of course we are a little bit selfish in this, but we have an interest in you, and want to see you do well in this world, for you are worthy of it. If you go to Montgomery, and settle down there with your family, expecting to support yourself by practicing, and with nothing else to support yourself—if you expect that, you will be very much mistaken. I advise you to let well enough alone, and stay where you are, among us, where you will be well taken care of and live like a lord, honored, and respected, and beloved, with plenty to do and everything flourishing around you. What more can a man want in this world? You must not leave us."

I said, "Milo, I am very sorry to leave you and go to Montgomery. But I have had a consultation with my good adviser, in whose judgment I put the utmost confidence—my wife. We have thought seriously about this matter. It is not a sudden or impulsive thing, my wife and I having reasoned it out together. We have made up our minds to go to Montgomery. We leave with a great many regrets, and with many thanks for all the kindnesses you have shown us since we have been here. You will always find us to be grateful to you, for you have been friends to us when we needed friends."

Still, Mr. Abercrombie was not satisfied. Suffice it to say, that we got ready and removed to Montgomery. Mr. Cromelin, a very eminent lawyer, whom I had known favorably before I went to Montgomery, when

I was the family physician of Mr. Lucas and his wife at Mount Meigs, Mr. Cromelin's wife being a niece of Mr. Lucas, was prepared to welcome us to Montgomery at once, and promised us his practice. He gave me a handsome house to live in at a rent of three hundred dollars a year, feeling very sure that he would have to pay me that much money, so that the rent of the house would be paid for in practice.

We went into this house on my favorite 13th day of the month of December (1840). We had no money, and always lived from hand to mouth. Everything was on the credit system in that day and time. Nobody had any money but once a year, when the cotton crop was sold and went to market, the first of January. This was a settling time with everybody. So when I went to Montgomery everybody was willing to give me credit for dry-goods, groceries, etc., and whatever I might need. Everybody else was in the same fix. At the end of the year we had to settle. Well, unfortunately, the day after we entered the house, my poor wife had a chill, and I don't think she saw a well day for six months. In the course of twelve months from the date of my first attack of congestive chills, I had seventeen different attacks. They recurred at periods varying from two to three and four weeks. We were all completely malarialized and demoralized. The negroes were also sick. Strangely enough to say, my two sisters escaped, neither of them having intermittent fever.

I lived a whole year in Montgomery, most of the time

in bed. By-and-by, my health began to improve. At
the end of two years, I was getting into practice among
the rich people of the city. I had the Cromelins, the
Pollards, the Balls, and others. These belonged to the
upper-crust; and the fact of my being physician of these
aristocratic families naturally interested others. But
really, I had to begin at the very bottom. The first
people who took me up were " free niggers."

Finally, I became physician to the Jewish population of the town, of which there were several families.
They were people who always had money in plenty, and
were liberal with it. They were very clannish, and as one
or two of the leaders would go, so all the rest followed.
I had all this Jewish practice, which was a large and
agreeable one.

I was the first man at the South that had ever
successfully treated club-foot. I was also the first man
that had ever performed an operation for strabismus,
or cross-eyes. At the end of five years, I had established a reputation as a judicious practitioner and as a
skillful surgeon, and was getting as much as I could do.
Montgomery had always had an able set of medical men.
They were talented, and I never saw a town where there
was so little bickering and jealousy between doctors. A
few valuable and able men at the head of the profession
kept the others in the proper line, and in the right way,
so that their influence was salutary. When head men
fall out, the small men follow. There were not many
small men among the profession in Montgomery. They

were nearly all men of the highest character as gentlemen, and they were skillful physicians besides of
learning and ability. The leading men of the day were
Drs. Holt, McCloud, Ames, McWhorter and Henry, and
all of them were busy, with as much as they could do.
Each had a successful practice, and there were never
too many doctors for the work to be done. The men
of my own age were Drs. Boling, Baldwin, Birney and
Jones.

CHAPTER XIII.

THE year 1845 was a memorable era in my life. It seemed to be a turning-point in my career. Up to the time that I went to Mount Meigs, I was willing to turn aside to do anything excepting to practice medicine. But when I went to Montgomery, I gave away my dog and sold my gun. I have never loaded and shot a gun since. I devoted myself to my profession, determined to do my best in it. I had an ambition for surgery—general surgery—and performed all sorts of beautiful and brilliant operations. This was before the days of anæsthetics. I had made, in five or six years, such a reputation for surgery that people came to me from forty miles off. Sick people were brought to me sometimes from the country, by those who would bring in a bale of cotton or two on a cart, and a sick patient would be brought along also. That was a reputation worth having. I was proud of it—I was very happy over it.

I had surgical cases of all sorts coming to me from

the country around. I was very successful as a surgeon. In the latter part of 1844, there came to my office one day a young woman from Lowndes County, who was about thirty years old. She had on a double thick veil, blue, folded double. She could not show herself in the street, so hideous was she. She walked into my office with her face veiled, and said:

"I have heard of your achievements in surgery, Dr. Sims, and I have come to see if you could do anything for me. I was born with a hare-lip, and I am so ugly that I have had to wear a veil to prevent my face from being seen by any one, even by my own family."

I said, "Raise your veil, and show me your face." When she did raise it, the sight was horrible. I had never seen such a bad case of hare-lip before. It was sickening. Out from the end of her nose was a little bone—a snout—and from the tip end of her nose there was a small piece of skin, about three fourths of an inch long, looking like a shriveled-up gobbler's snout. She had no teeth, and I could look clear down her throat. Altogether, her malformation was frightful.

I said, "I can cure you in a month."

"You can?" she eagerly replied, as a ray of hope came across her.

I said, "Certainly; I will give you a new set of teeth, so that you can eat like other folks, and whistle, if you want to, and you will know the value of the society and association of your friends."

To make a long story short, in the course of a month

she was entirely cured. She had a very presentable mouth, and Dr. Belangee, who was the leading dentist of the town, took a cast of the roof of her mouth, and made her a set of four handsome teeth. When he had finished his part of the work, she was a very presentable person indeed, and really a pretty woman. Her life, of course, was enlivened and revolutionized.

The curing of this woman from Lowndes County was of itself a very small affair, but it was the beginning of one of my little life stories, and plays a by no means unimportant part in it. The plaster cast made by Dr. Belangee for the roof of the woman's mouth was given to me, and for some time it lay on my mantel-piece. Everybody who came in looked at it, and I said, "That is the plaster cast of Miss So-and-so's mouth, of Lowndes County." Dr. Harris, of Baltimore, the founder of the Baltimore College of Dental Surgery, the first of the kind in this country or the world, and his friend Dr. Lipscomb, came to visit Montgomery in the year 1846. Through the Lipscomb interest in the county and among the wealthy classes, Dr. Harris was called to so many of the aristocratic families that for two or three months he entirely displaced my friend Dr. Belangee. He was a magnificent man, of fine physical beauty, a gentleman of great intellect, great kindness of heart, and a very accomplished dentist. He was perhaps the very best of that day in the world.

One day he strolled into my office. I had been to call on him, and he returned it. Having an eye quick to discern anything pertaining to his profession, he walked up to the mantel, and picked up the plaster cast lying there.

"Doctor, what is this?" he asked, after he had looked it over carefully, and examined the wonderful cast. I gave him a history of the case, as above related. "I will tell you what, Dr. Sims, I would like you to do. I would like you to write an account of it for the September number of my 'Journal of Dental Surgery.'"

I said, "Doctor, I can't write anything. I never wrote anything in my life."

"But," he said, "write it as you would talk it, or as you have told it to me. That is all; I will risk you."

"I should be ashamed," I said, "to see anything of mine in print. I am counted as a great worker, to be sure, and I always keep notes of my cases; but I can not write. I never wrote anything in my life. It is not my forte."

He insisted, however, and I sat down and wrote a history of the case in the simplest manner possible, and gave it to him. I was ashamed of it, however, when I gave it to him. In the course of two or three months after I had written the article, Dr. Harris sent me a number of the "Journal of Dental Surgery," containing my article, and a little wood-cut illustrating the plaster cast. I read the article, and was ashamed of it, and determined that I would not show it to any of my medical brethren. I arrived at this conclusion because there were a number of *literati* among them; and, though I was not ashamed or afraid to perform any operation before them, or even in the presence of the best of them, still I did not feel that I was competent to write; especially when compared to Ames, or Bowling, or Baldwin.

Bowling was a most voluminous writer. He had written some really valuable and meritorious articles for the medical literature of the country, which marked the era in which he lived, and which have been incorporated into the literature of the profession, especially his articles on the "Endemic Diseases of the South." He had also written on fevers, pneumonia, and had discussed a variety of surgical questions. But the man that I feared was Ames. Of course, I was on the most friendly terms with all the doctors in Montgomery. Ames was a man that everybody respected, but whom nobody loved very much. On the contrary, they were all rather afraid of him. He had the best practice of the country. He was a quiet, dignified, reticent, skillful man, who filled a very useful and prominent place in his profession. His opinion was sought on all questions, and on all occasions of great importance; and no man in high life ever died, in any other physician's hands, unless Dr. Ames was called in consultation.

I liked and admired him, and I also feared him. He was hypercritical, especially in literary matters. I was not afraid to perform any operation before him, because I was a surgeon, and he was not. He took a kindly interest in me and patronized me. He at one time offered me a partnership, but I was too smart to take it. I saw that he had an immense practice, but as I had as much as I could do, and the work was growing, I had only to eliminate the least desirable part of my practice as it increased among the higher walks of life. Dr. Ames was enjoying the full fruition of all that he could have achieved. I knew that, if I accepted a partnership, I would be compelled to do all his country work, which would break me down. As I was doing well enough, I wisely concluded to let well enough alone, and suggested as a suitable partner in my stead another young man in town who had nothing to do, and whom he afterward accepted.

Well, when the "Journal" arrived I read the article, and I determined that Ames should not see it, nor Baldwin, nor Bowling, nor anybody else. I knew that there was not another copy of the work taken in the city. I walked into my library, which, by the way, had increased beyond the seven volumes of Eberle, and stepped up to my book-case, and on a shelf, level with my eye, pulled out a large volume, and put the "Dental Journal," behind it, standing it up on its edge, behind the books on the shelf, with the flat surface to the wall. I then replaced the book in its proper position. Some months after this, Dr. Ames happened to walk into my office; he had called to make me a social visit, as we frequently exchanged neighborly visits. After we had talked over endemic diseases and the other topics of the day, he walked up to the book-case, with the inquiry, "Have you got in any new books lately?" I said "No." I stood there, and he looked at all the books on the shelf, and pulled out, with his left hand, the very identical one behind which I had hidden the "Dental Journal" six months before. As he pulled it out, his quick eye saw something in a new cover hidden away. While he held the book with his left hand, he reached up with his right and pulled out the offending "Journal," of which I had been so choice, and which I had resolved that no one should see. If anybody had told him, he could not have gone more deliberately to the place and found it. To-day, it is the most unexplainable thing that ever happened to me. He did not look into the large book, but he held in his hand the fresh "Dental Journal," and commenced turning over the leaves, one after the other. He had never seen the "Dental Journal" before, and it excited his curiosity, so that he became very much interested in it, and all the more interested because it was new.

I said to myself, "My God! if he goes on in this way, he will come to the article on the 'Lowndes County Girl's Hare-Lip,' and he will give me fits." I was trembling like a leaf, as I stood there like a schoolboy. Still he stood there, turning over leaf after leaf, and, when he got to where the case was described, he did not look up at all, or say a word, but stood there, reading it down on the first page, and then on the other page, deliberately reading it through. It just occupied two pages. My heart was in my throat. As he finished the article he stood perfectly still, and I also stood perfectly still, trembling. As he turned around I thought, "I shall get it now."

In a moment he said, "What would I give if I had the faculty of expressing myself in writing like that?"

I said: "My dear doctor, you have lifted a great load from my heart. Here I have been bewildered all this time, and you have frightened me almost to death, and I don't know what you mean."

"I have never read a thing so natural in my life as your description of the case," he replied; "I could not write that way to save my life. What I do write is labored; but what you write comes natural, it seems. Now let me give you a piece of advice. I have seen you perform many beautiful operations, and many difficult ones, and, as long as you have this power, I advise you to report them for the press. Seeing that you are so timid, and lack confidence in yourself, if you will send your productions to me, I shall be very glad to make such suggestions as are necessary, and to return them to you for your consideration." I accepted his generous proposition; and, but for the encouragement that Dr. Ames gave me, I would not have written anything at all; for I was not aware that I possessed any capacity in that direction.

When I was a boy at school, I never could write compositions, and I had a good many scoldings, and one or two thrashings very nearly, because of that neglect. Somehow or other I always begged off, and got away from composition writing. I always felt quite ashamed of myself; for the other boys in the school could write compositions on any given subject, while I could not write a word. It was impossible for me to put my ideas on paper on any subject assigned to me. I supposed they were always mere abstractions, about which I knew little or nothing. I had an instinctive propensity to write too long, without being able to represent any lengthy disquisitions on the subjects. When I went to college every man was expected in the senior year to write five compositions. Nothing was required of the juniors in this line. These five compositions had to be presented before the close of the summer term, or the summer vacation, which was generally about the first of July. I passed through my senior year without having to write a single one. When I returned in October, to begin the studies preparatory to graduation in December, Professor Henry, who had supervision of the composition department, sent for me. He had a colored man by the name of Jim, whom the boys in the college called "Sheriff Jim." He was the man of the faculty, and carried all their messages and notes. One day "Sheriff Jim" came to my room about the middle of October. He said, "Professor Henry wants to see you, and he is waiting in his study now, in the library."

I said: "What does Professor Henry want of me, Jim? What in the world does he want?"

"I don't know, sah," he replied; "he sent me over to tell you that he wanted to see you at his room, and you got to go." So there was nothing left but for me to obey the command, and I put on my hat and

10

went along with "Sheriff Jim." It happened that there were a good many boys standing out on the campus, and in the door-ways, and looking out of the windows, and when they saw me following after "Sheriff Jim" they wondered what under the heavens I could have been doing to make it necessary to call me before the faculty. When I appeared before his august highness, Professor Henry, he bluntly remarked:

"Mr. Sims, according to the rules of the college, and according to its requirements, you are expected to write five compositions for your senior year, between the first of January and the last of June. In looking over the list, I find that you have not written one. How is it that you have not complied with the rules of the college?"

I said: "Sir, I have never felt able to write a composition which would be creditable, and I did not think it was worth while to send one to you that was not of some value."

He said, "Your record has been excellent except in this particular. There are due from you to the college five compositions, and, as you are on the eve of graduation, you must give a good deal of your time to the preparation for it. I will be very lenient toward you, Mr. Sims, and, if you will send me two compositions this week, I will consider that you have complied with the rules of the college. You can go, sir," he said; "unless you comply with this requirement, you can not go forward in your graduation."

I bowed myself out, and went, without the "Sheriff's" accompanying me there, to my own room, and I had resolved in my own mind that I would write no compositions. As I walked through the campus, back to my own room, a little humiliated by being "trained" before the faculty, as it were, the boys were all on the lookout for me, and they said: "What in the world have you done to be taken before the faculty to be trained for? and what have you had to be taken off by the 'Sheriff' for?"

"I haven't complied with the rules of the college in composition writing," I replied.

John Rice was from Union district, and my junior by nearly two years. We were very good friends. He was very much devoted to me, and he said, "Well, Marion, you know that you have got to write the compositions."

I said, "John, I am not going to write a composition. I can not and will not, and I will see the college and Professor Henry in purgatory before I write one."

He said, "But, Marion, you are unreasonable. Professor Henry is obliged to insist on your compliance, and he has asked you to do so on certain conditions. He has let you off very mildly indeed."

I replied, "John, you are very kind, but I can not write one, and I do not intend to try to do it."

"Well," he said, "if you do not, you will not graduate. He is obliged to be as good as his word, and he will not allow you to come forward to receive your degree. It would be disgraceful for you to go home without your diploma. What would your father and the world say about it?"

I replied, "John, I don't care a cent what anybody says. I do not intend to write a composition. If I can not pass on my merits as a scholar, I don't think that I could do it by having written a few compositions. I have said that I will not do it, and I will not."

John Rice felt very unhappy about the matter, as he was exceedingly interested in me. The next morning he came down and happening to see "Sheriff Jim" going along the campus he beckoned to him to follow him. On reaching my room he said: "See here, Marion, don't be a d—d fool any longer. As I do not want to see you miss your graduation, I have just written two compositions for you on 'Memory,' and I have signed your name to both of them. Of course Professor Henry will never read them, and I am going to send them to him, so that you have complied with the *spirit* of the law. You haven't written five, but you have got two." The "Sheriff" was called in, and John Rice said: "Here, Jim, will you have the kindness to take these papers over to Professor Henry, with the compliments of Marion Sims, and say to him that they are his compositions which he promised to write last night." Jim took the papers, and that was the last that I ever heard about the five compositions. Of course Professor Henry never read them, or criticised them, and he didn't care a cent whether I ever wrote them or not, but was obliged to enforce the rules of the college in that respect.

So it was that I always felt timid about writing, and never dreamed that I could write until the circumstance related, in connection with my friend Dr. Ames. Even to this day the finding of that "Dental Journal" is inexplicable to me. I do not believe there are any accidents in this world. I do not look upon that as an accident, but as a Providential affair. However, I acted on the suggestion of my friend Dr. Ames, and immediately began to write out the histories of my surgical cases, which he suggested to me that I should do. I sent them to him for criticism, and in a day or two he would return them to me. I was very much surprised that he found so little to criticise, and what few suggestions and criticisms and alterations he had to make. He made no alterations that were of any great importance. I continued to write articles and send them to him, and he was very kind always in looking over them, and making corrections when they were necessary. He always wrote me a little note, very kindly worded, for me to preserve, and saying that it was hardly necessary for me to send my papers to him for him to read. This was, as I have already said, in the year 1845, and it was also an eventful year to me in my professional career.

CHAPTER XIV.

In April (1845) Mr. Henry Stickney, having a plantation near Montgomery and a residence in the suburbs of the town, called at my house about tea-time, as he frequently did, to make a social visit, and took occasion to say that his negro woman, Sally, had recently been confined with twins, and that one of them was very ill. He said that it had spasms, and could not suck, and he said that he would like to have me go out and see the babe. After asking him a few questions, as we talked the matter over, I made up my mind what was the matter, and I said: "Mr. Stickney, the baby has what we call trismus nascentium, or lock-jaw, and it is always fatal, no case as yet ever having been cured. I can do the child no good; but, as a study, I will come out to see it and investigate the case. But I can do nothing for it at all."

So I went to the house, as I agreed, and found the child lying in a cradle, on its back. It had been in spasms for two days and nights, and looked as if it were dying. Its respiration was very rapid, and the pulse could hardly be counted. Touching it would throw it into convulsions; laying it on its face it would cause spasms; any noise would produce them. It could not swallow, could take no nourishment, and it was impossible for it to suck. It was covered with a cold, clammy perspiration; its hands were tightly clinched, so that the finger-nails were almost cutting into the flesh on the palms of its hands. The legs and arms were as stiff as a poker, and the whole body was rigid, because of tonic contraction, and every few minutes there would be spasms independent of the tonic contraction. Its face was drawn around so that it wore a sort of sardonic grin. Altogether, the picture was a disagreeable one to look upon. After examining the child for a while, I ran my hand under its head to raise it up from the deep cradle in which it lay. I raised the child, and found it as stiff as could be, and, instead of bending, it came up like raising a pair of tongs, in its rigid condition. While in the act of raising it, my hand detected a remarkable irregularity in the relations of the bones of the head. I sat the child against my knee, because it was so stiff that it could not sit on it, and began to examine its head. At the back of the head I found that the occipital bone was pushed under deeply on the brain, and the edges of it, along the lambdoidal suture, were completely overlapped by the projecting edges of the parietal bones. This was certainly the most unnatural thing that I had seen, and

I immediately suspected that the spasms, both tonic and clonic, were the result of mechanical pressure on the base of the brain, effected by the dislocation of this bone by the child lying on its back. It took some minutes for me to make this examination. After I became thoroughly familiar with the physical condition observed, I turned my attention again to the child, and was surprised to find that by the erect posture removing the pressure from the base of the brain the pulse could be counted, and that the respiration had fallen from one hundred and twenty to about seventy.

As a matter of course, the child died. The next day we held a post-mortem examination. The case was one of so much importance that I invited Drs. Ames, Baldwin, Bowling, and half a dozen other medical men to be present at the post-mortem. I was convinced that the mechanical pressure on the base of the brain had produced all the symptoms I had seen; but what I wanted to find was this: what was the *rationale* of that pressure? In making a post-mortem examination, we found that the spinal marrow was surrounded by a coagulum of blood—extravasation of blood between the spinal marrow and its membranes. I thought that this was the cause of all the symptoms, and I published an article on the subject, in which I elaborated a very ingenious theory going to show that the compression at the base of the brain had strangulated the spinal veins in such a way that the blood could not be returned from the spinal column, and had therefore burst through its thin vessels. Subsequent experience, however, compelled me to modify this view of the case, and I wrote a second article on the subject, showing that this extravasation was not the cause of the disease, but was the result, and that the child might not have died of trismus nascentium had it been laid on its side, where the pressure could be removed from the base of the brain. As a matter of course, the treatment of a case of trismus nascentium is not by medicine, but when it is produced by mechanical causes of this sort it is simply by a lateral position that takes the pressure from the base of the brain. Such cases should be placed first upon one side and then upon the other, and should never be put in a cradle or crib at all. A new-born child especially should be placed upon a pillow, lengthwise of the pillow. If this were done always, there would be no cases of trismus nascentium. I have seen a great many desperate cases cured in a few minutes' time, simply by placing the patient on the side. But, as I have written this subject up, in part, in another treatise, it is not worth while to dilate upon it further here. My doctrines in respect to the pathology and treatment of trismus nascentium have not been adopted or accepted by the profession at large; but I am satisfied that they are true. They have been adopted by a few doctors, here and there, and many cases of trismus nascentium have been cured, which were reported in the medical journals of the country. Dr. ———, of Anderson, South Carolina, reported in the " American Journal of Medical Science " for April, 1875, a dozen cases that he had cured ; whereas, before my discovery, medical literature had not reported a single case of trismus nascentium having been cured on any recognized principle applicable to any other case. Truth travels slowly, but I am sure that I am right—as sure as I can be of anything. This will yet be fully understood and appreciated by the profession.

I consider this my first great discovery in medicine. The next occurred only two months later. I had been a doctor now about ten years. I had established a good, solid reputation as a surgeon, and surgical cases were coming to me every day from all parts of the country. I was also considered a successful family practitioner. I was perfectly satisfied with my position and prospects. I had nothing whatever to do with midwifery, excepting when called in consultation with Dr. McWhorter or Dr. Henry, or some of the older doctors, who wished me to perform some delicate surgical operation. I never pretended to treat any of the diseases of women, and if any woman came to consult me on account of any functional derangement of the uterine system, I immediately replied, " This is out of my line; I do not know anything about it practically, and I advise you to go to Dr. Henry or Dr. McWhorter."

Early in the month of June (1845) Dr. Henry asked me to go out to Mr. Wescott's, only a mile from the town, to a case of labor which had lasted three days and the child not yet born. He said, " I am thinking that you had better take your instruments along with you, for you may want to use them." We found a young colored woman, about seventeen years of age, well developed, who had been in labor then seventy-two hours. The child's head was so impacted in the pelvis that the labor-pains had almost entirely ceased. It was evident that matters could not long remain in this condition without the system becoming exhausted, and without the pressure producing a sloughing of the soft parts of the mother. So I agreed with Dr. Henry that the sooner she was de-livered the better, and without any great effort the child was brought away with forceps. She rallied from the confinement and seemed to be getting on pretty well, until about five days after her delivery, when Dr. Henry came to see me, and said that there was an extensive sloughing of the soft parts, the mother having lost con-trol of both the bladder and the rectum. Of course, aside from death, this was about the worst accident that could have happened to the poor young girl. I went to see her, and found an enormous slough, spreading from the posterior wall of the vagina, and another thrown off from the anterior wall. The case was hopelessly incur-able.

I went home and investigated the literature of the subject thoroughly and fully. Then, seeing the master of the servant the next day, I said: "Mr. Wescott, Anarcha has an affection that unfits her for the duties required of a servant. She will not die, but will never get well, and all you have to do is to take good care of her so long as she lives." Mr. Wescott was a kind-hearted man, a good master, and, accepting the situation, made up his mind that Anarcha should have an easy time in this world as long as she lived.

I had practiced medicine ten years, and had never before seen a case of vesico-vaginal fistula. I looked upon it as a surgical curiosity, although a very unfortunate one. Strange to say, in one month from that time Dr. Harris, from Lowndes County, came to see me, and he said: "Well, doctor, one of my servant girls, Betsey, a young woman seventeen or eighteen years old, married last year, had a baby about a month ago. Since then she has not been able to hold a single drop of water."

I replied, "I am very sorry, doctor, but nothing can be done for her. There is a similar case here in town."

He said, "I thought myself it was incurable. But I am going to tell my overseer to send her up to you to-morrow and let you examine her case." So the next day Betsey came, and I examined her. The base of the bladder was destroyed, and her case was certainly a very miserable one. I kept her a day or two in Montgomery and then sent her home, writing a note to the doctor, giving him my opinion of the case and its incurability. I supposed that I should never see another case of vesico-vaginal fistula.

About another month after this, however, Mr. Tom Zimmerman, of Macon County, called on me. I was his family physician when I lived in Cubahatchee, but I had not seen him since I left there, four or five years before. He began immediately by saying that his negro girl, Lucy, about eighteen years old, had given birth to a child two months ago, and that since that time she had been unable to hold any water.

I said, "Tom, I know all about this case, and there is no doctor in this town or country who can afford any relief. I have just been reading up the subject; I have consulted all the authorities I can find in every doctor's library in this city. She has fistula in the bladder—a hole in it. It may be no larger than a pipe-stem, or it may be as large as two or three inches in diameter; but, whether big or little, the urine runs all the time; it makes no odds what position she is in, whether asleep or awake, walking or standing, sitting or lying down. The case is absolutely incurable. I don't want to see her or the case. You need not send her to town. I have just seen two cases, one in this town, and another that was sent to me from Lowndes County, and I have sent the last one back because there is no hope for it."

"Is there no chance for your being mistaken about the case, without having seen it?"

I said, "No, there is no chance for me to be mistaken. It is absolutely incurable."

"Are you not disposed to investigate it," he said, "and see if there is not some chance?"

I said, "No, I don't want to see it."

"But you would have done so before you moved from the piney woods and came to the city. Moving to a city sets a man up wonderfully. You are putting on airs. When you were my family doctor, and used to see my family or my niggers, you never objected to an investigation of their cases, and you didn't say what you would do and what not. I am going to send Lucy in. What day do you want her to come down?"

I said, "I don't want to see her. I can do her no good."

"Well," said he, "I am going to send her down to you at your office, by Monday's train, whether you want to see her or not." And so, sure enough, Monday came, and Lucy was at my office. I had a little hospital of eight beds, built in the corner of my yard, for taking care of my negro patients and for negro surgical cases; and so when Lucy came I gave her a bed. As soon as I could get to her I examined the case very minutely. I told her that I was unable to do anything for her, and I said, "To-morrow afternoon I shall have to send you home." She was very much disappointed, for her condition was loathsome, and she was in hopes that she could be cured. I told her that she must go home on the next afternoon.

It was my usual habit to start off at nine o'clock to visit my patients, and I seldom had less than from eighteen to twenty visits to make in a morning. Just as I was starting off, and was about to get into my buggy, a little nigger came running to the office and said, "Massa doctor, Mrs. Merrill done been throwed from her pony, and is mighty badly hurt, and you must go down there right off to see her, just as soon as you can get there." So, as this was a surgical case, and not knowing whether it was a fractured limb or a broken skull, I looked upon it as a case of urgency, and instead of making my usual morning round, I started upon "the hill," three fourths of a mile, to see old Mrs. Merrill. She was not an old woman, but she was the wife of a dissipated old man, who was supposed to be of not much account, as he was gambling and leading an otherwise disreputable life. Mrs. Merrill, however, was a respectable woman who obtained a living by washing and taking in sewing, and was much appreciated and respected among her neighbors. She was about forty-six years of age, stout and fat, and weighed nearly two hundred pounds. She had been riding along on a pony, and when within about fifty yards of her own house a hog lying by the roadside, in the corner of the fence, jumped out and made a noise that frightened the pony, and it sprang from under the rider. She fell with all her weight on the pelvis. She had no broken bones. She was in bed, complaining of great pain in her back, and a sense of tenesmus in both the bladder and rectum, the bearing down making her condition miserable.

If there was anything I hated, it was investigating the organs of the female pelvis. But this poor woman was in such a condition that I was obliged to find out what was the matter with her. It was by a digital examination, and I had sense enough to discover that there was retroversion of the uterus. It was half turned upside down, and I took it for granted that this sudden dislocation, or disturbance of the pelvic organs, was the result of the fall on the pelvis. The question was, what I should do to relieve her. I remembered, when a medical student in Charleston Medical College, that old Dr. Prioleau used to say: " Gentlemen, if any of you are ever called to a case of sudden version of the uterus backward, you must place the patient on the knees and elbows—in a genu-pectoral position— and then introduce one finger into the rectum and another into the vagina, and push up, and pull down; and, if you don't get the uterus in position by this means, you will hardly effect it by any other." This piece of information at the time it was given went into one ear and out at the other. I never expected to have any use for it. Strangely enough, all that Professor Prioleau said came back to me at once when the case was presented. So I placed the patient as directed, with a large sheet thrown over her. I could not make up my mind to introduce my finger into the rectum, because only a few days before that I had had occasion to ex- amine the rectum of a nervous gentleman who had a fissure, and he made so much complaint of the examina- tion that I thought that this poor woman was suffering enough without my doing so disagreeable a thing. So, as she raised herself and rested on her knees, just on the edge of the bed, and by putting one finger into the va- gina I could easily touch the uterus by my pushing, but I could not place it in position, for my finger was too short; if it had been half an inch longer, I could have put the womb into place. So I introduced the middle and index fingers, and immediately touched the uterus. I commenced making strong efforts to push it back, and thus I turned my hand with the palm upward, and then downward, and pushing with all my might, when all at once, I could not feel the womb, or the walls of the vagina. I could touch nothing at all, and wondered what it all meant. It was as if I had put my two fingers into a hat, and worked them around, without touching the substance of it. While I was wondering what it all meant Mrs. Merrill said, "Why, doctor, I am relieved." My mission was ended, but what had brought the relief I could not understand. I removed my hand, and said to her, "You may lie down now." She was in a profuse perspiration from pain and the unnatural position, and in part from the effort. She rather fell on her side. Suddenly there was an explosion, just as though there had been an escape of air from the bowel. She was exceedingly mortified and began to apologize, and said, "I am so ashamed." I said: "That is not from the bowel, but from the vagina, and it has explained now what I did not understand before. I understand now what has relieved you, but I would not have understood it but for that escapement of air from the vagina. When I placed my fingers there, the mouth of the vagina was so dilated that the air rushed in and extended the vagina to its fullest capacity, by the natural pressure of fifty-five pounds to the square inch, and this, conjoined with the position, was the means of restoring the retroverted organ to its normal place."

Then, said I to myself, if I can place the patient in that position, and distend the vagina by the pressure of air, so as to produce such a wonderful result as this, why can I not take the incurable case of vesico-vaginal fistula, which seems now to be so incomprehensible, and put the girl in this position and see exactly what are the relations of the surrounding tissues? Fired with this idea, I forgot that I had twenty patients waiting to see me all over the hills of this beautiful city. I jumped into my buggy and drove hurriedly home. Passing by the store of Hall, Mores & Roberts, I stopped and bought a pewter spoon. I went to my office where I had two medical students, and said, "Come, boys, go to the hospital with me."

"You have got through your work early this morning," they said.

"I have done none of it," I replied; "come to the hospital with me." Arriving there, I said, "Betsey, I told you that I would send you home this afternoon, but before you go I want to make one more examination of your case." She willingly consented. I got a table about three feet long, and put a coverlet upon it, and mounted her on the table, on her knees, with her head resting on the palms of her hands. I placed the two students one on each side of the pelvis, and they laid hold of the nates, and pulled them open. Before I could get the bent spoon-handle into the vagina, the air rushed in with a puffing noise, dilating the vagina to its fullest extent. Introducing the bent handle of the spoon I saw everything, as no man had ever seen before. The fistula was as plain as the nose on a man's face. The edges were clear and well-defined, and distinct, and the opening could be measured as accurately as if it had been cut out of a piece of plain paper. The walls of the vagina could be seen closing in every direction; the neck of the uterus was distinct and well-defined, and even the secretions from the neck could be seen as a tear glistening in the eye, clear even and distinct, and as plain as could be. I said at once, "Why can not these things be cured? It seems to me that there is nothing to do but to pare the edges of the fistula and bring it together nicely, introduce a catheter in the neck of the bladder and drain the urine off continually, and the case will be cured." Fired with enthusiasm by this wonderful discovery, it raised me into a plane of thought that unfitted me almost for the duties of the day. Still, with gladdened heart, and buoyant spirits, and rejoicing in my soul, I went off to make my daily rounds. I felt sure that I was on the eve of one of the greatest discoveries of the day. The more I thought of it, the more I was convinced of it.

I immediately went to work to invent instruments necessary for performing the operation on the principles that were self-evident on the first inspection of the first case. The speculum, or retractor, was perfectly clear from the very beginning. I did not send Lucy home, and I wrote to her master that I would retain her there, and he must come and see me again. I saw Mr. Wescott, and I told him that I was on the eve of a great discovery, and that I would like to have him send Anarcha back to my hospital. I also wrote to Dr. Harris, saying that I had changed my mind in regard to Betsey, and for him to send her back again. I ransacked the country for cases, told the doctors what had happened and what I had done, and it ended in my finding six or seven cases of vesico-vaginal fistula that had been hidden away for years in the country because they had been pronounced incurable. I went to work to put another story on my hospital, and this gave me sixteen beds; four beds for servants, and twelve for the patients. Then I made this proposition to the owners of the negroes: If you will give me Anarcha and Betsey for experiment, I agree to perform no experiment or operation on either of them to endanger their lives, and will not charge a cent for keeping them, but you must pay their taxes and clothe them. I will keep them at my own expense. Remember, I was very enthusiastic, and expected to cure them, every one, in six months. I never dreamed of failure, and could see how accurately and how nicely the operation could be performed.

It took me about three months to have my instruments made, to gather the patients in, and to have everything ready to commence the season of philosophical experiment. The first patient I operated on was Lucy. She was the last one I had, and the case was a very bad one. The whole base of the bladder was gone and destroyed, and a piece had fallen out, leaving an opening between the vagina and the bladder, at least two

inches in diameter or more. That was before the days of
anæsthetics, and the poor girl, on her knees, bore the
operation with great heroism and bravery. I had about
a dozen doctors there to witness the series of experiments that I expected to perform. All the doctors had
seen my notes often and examined them, and agreed that
I was on the eve of a great discovery, and every one
of them was interested in seeing me operate. The operations were tedious and difficult. The instruments were
on the right principle, though they were not as perfect as they were subsequently, and improvements had
to be made slowly. I succeeded in closing the fistula
in about an hour's time, which was considered to be very
good work. I placed my patient in bed, and it does
seem to me now, since things were so simple and clear,
that I was exceedingly stupid at the beginning.

But I must have something to turn the urine from
the bladder, and I thought that if I could make a catheter stay in the bladder I could succeed. But I knew
that the books said that the doctors had tried to do it for
ages past and had never succeeded. The great Würtzer,
of Germany, attempted to cure fistula, many years ago,
and, failing to retain the catheter in the bladder, he
adopted the plan of fastening the patient face downward,
for a week at a time, to prevent the urine from dripping
through into the vagina. I said, "I will put a little piece
of sponge into the neck of the bladder, running a silk
string through it. This will act as a capillary tube; the
urine will be turned, and the fistula cured." It was a

very stupid thing for me to do, as the sequel will show. At the end of five days my patient was very ill. She had fever, frequent pulse, and real blood-poisoning, but we did not know what to call it at that day and time. However, I saw that everything must be removed; so I cut loose my sutures, which had been held by a peculiar mechanical contrivance which it is not necessary here to detail. Then I attempted to remove the little piece of sponge from the neck of the bladder. It was about two inches long. One inch occupied the urethra, half an inch projected into the bladder, and half an inch into the meatus. As soon as it was applied, the urine came dripping through, just as fast as it was secreted in the bladder, and so it continued during all the time it was worn. It performed its duties most wonderfully; but when I came to remove it I found what I ought to have known, that the sponge could not rest there simply as a sponge, but was perfectly infiltrated with sabulous matter, and was really stone. The whole urethra and the neck of the bladder were in a high state of inflammation, which came from the foreign substance. It had to come away, and there was nothing to do but to pull it away by main force. Lucy's agony was extreme. She was much prostrated, and I thought that she was going to die; but by irrigating the parts of the bladder she recovered with great rapidity, and in the course of a week or ten days was as well as ever.

After she had recovered entirely from the effects of this unfortunate experiment, I put her on a table, to examine and see what was the result of the operation. The appearance of the parts was changed entirely. The enormous fistula had disappeared, and two little openings in the line of union, across the vagina, were all that remained. One was the size of a knitting-needle, and the other was the size of a goose-quill. That encouraged me very much in the operation, for I said, " If one operation can produce results such as this, under such unfavorable circumstances, why may it not be perfectly successful when I have something to draw the urine that will not produce inflammation of the soft parts ? "

This operation was performed on the —— day of December, 1845. It inaugurated a series of experiments that were continued for a long time. It took Lucy two or three months to recover entirely from the effects of the operation. As soon as I had arranged a substitute for the sponge, I operated on Betsey. The fistula was favorable, and would be considered a favorable one at the present day. Of course, I considered it very unfavorable. The fistula occupied the base of the bladder, and was very large, being quite two inches in diameter. I repeated the operation, in the same way and manner as performed on Lucy, with the exception of placing in the bladder a self-retaining catheter, instead of the sponge. I started out very hopefully, and, of course, I waited anxiously for the result of the operation. Seven days rolled around; she had none of the chills or fever, either violent or sudden, or the disturbance attending the previous operation. At the end of seven days the sutures were removed. To my great astonishment and disappointment, the operation was a failure. Still, the opening had been changed entirely in character, and, instead of being two inches in diameter, it was united across entirely, with the exception of three little openings, one in the middle, and one at each end of the line of union. The line of union was transverse.

I thought I could make some improvements in the operation, and Anarcha was the next case. Anarcha was the first case that I had ever seen, having assisted Dr. Henry in her delivery. She had not only an enormous fistula in the base of the bladder, but there was an extensive destruction of the posterior wall of the vagina, opening into the rectum. This woman had the very worst form of vesico-vaginal fistula. The urine was running day and night, saturating the bedding and clothing, and producing an inflammation of the external parts wherever it came in contact with the person, almost similar to confluent small-pox, with constant pain and burning. The odor from this saturation permeated everything, and every corner of the room; and, of course, her life was one of suffering and disgust. Death would have been preferable. But patients of this kind never die; they must live and suffer. Anarcha had added to the fistula an opening which extended into the rectum, by which gas—intestinal gas—escaped involuntarily, and was passing off continually, so that her person was not only loathsome and disgusting to herself, but to every one who came near her.

I made some modifications in the suture apparatus, such as I thought important, and in the catheter, and then operated on the fistula of the bladder. But, like the others, she was only partially cured. The large fistula was contracted, leaving only two or three smaller ones in the line of union, as in the other two instances. The size of the fistula makes no difference in the involuntary loss of urine. It will escape as readily and as rapidly through an opening the size of a goose-quill as it will when the whole base of the bladder is destroyed. The patient is not cured so long as there is the involuntary loss of a single drop of urine. It would be tiresome for me to repeat in detail all the stages of improvement in the operation that were necessary before it was made perfect. These I have detailed in a surgical history of the facts, and to professional readers are still well known. Besides these three cases, I got three or four more to experiment on, and there was never a time that I could not, at any day, have had a subject for operation. But my operations all failed, so far as a positive cure was concerned. This went on, not for one year, but for two and three, and even four years. I kept all these negroes at my own expense all the time. As a matter of course this was an enormous tax for a young doctor in country practice. When I began the experiments, the other doctors in the city were all willing to help me, and all seemed anxious to witness the operations. But, at last, two or three years of constant failure and fruitless effort rather made my friends tired, and it was with difficulty

11

that I could get any doctor to help me. But, notwithstanding the repeated failures, I had succeeded in inspiring my patients with confidence that they would be cured eventually. They would not have felt that confidence if I had not felt confident too; and at last I performed operations only with the assistance of the patients themselves.

So I went on working without any progress, or at least permanent result, till my brother-in-law, Dr. Rush Jones, came to me one day, and he said:

"I have come to have a serious talk with you. When you began these experiments, we all thought that you were going to succeed at once, and that you were on the eve of a brilliant discovery that would be of great importance to suffering humanity. We have watched you, and sympathized with you; but your friends here have seen that of late you are doing too much work, and that you are breaking down. And, besides, I must tell you frankly that with your young and growing family it is unjust to them to continue in this way, and carry on this series of experiments. You have no idea what it costs you to support a half-dozen niggers, now more than three years, and my advice to you is to resign the whole subject and give it up. It is better for you, and better for your family."

I was very much surprised at what he said. But I said: "My dear brother, if I live I am bound to succeed; and I am as sure that I shall carry this thing through to success as I am that I now live, or as sure as

I can be of anything. I have done too much already, and I am too near the accomplishment of the work to give it up now. My patients are all perfectly satisfied with what I am doing for them. I can not depend on the doctors, and so I have trained them to assist me in the operations. I am going on with this series of experiments to the end. It matters not what it costs, if it costs me my life. For, if I should fail, I believe somebody would be raised up to take the work where I lay it down and carry it on to successful issue."

The experiments were continued at least a year after this conversation with Dr. Jones. I went on improving the methods of operating, eliminating first one thing and then another, till I had got it down to a very simple practice. Then I said: "I am not going to perform another operation until I discover some method of tying the suture higher up in the body where I can not reach." This puzzled me sorely. I had been three weeks without performing a single operation on either of the half-dozen patients that I had there. They were clamorous, and at last the idea occurred to me about three o'clock one morning. I had been lying awake for an hour, wondering how to tie the suture, when all at once an idea occurred to me to run a shot, a perforated shot, on the suture, and, when it was drawn tight, to compress it with a pair of forceps, which would make the knot perfectly secure. I was so elated with the idea, and so enthusiastic as I lay in bed, that I could not help waking up my kind and sympathetic wife and telling her of the simple and beautiful method I had discovered of tying the suture. I lay there till morning, tying the suture and performing all sorts of beautiful operations, in imagination, on the poor people in my little hospital; and I determined, as soon as I had made my round of morning calls, to operate with this perfected suture. Just as I had got ready to perform my operation I was summoned to go twenty miles into the country, and I did not get back until late in the night. I looked upon it as a very unfortunate thing, and one of the keenest disappointments of my life, because it kept me from seeing all the beautiful results of my method. However, the next day, in due time, the operation was performed on Lucy. When it was done, I said, "Could anything be more beautiful? Now I know that she will be cured very soon, and then all the rest must be cured." It was with great impatience that I waited a whole week to see what the result of the operation would be. When I came to examine it, it was a complete failure.

I then said to myself, "There must be a cause for this. I have improved the operations till the mechanism seems to be as perfect as possible, and yet they fail. I wonder if it is in the kind of suture that is used? Can I get some substitute for the silk thread? Mettaer, of Virginia, had used lead, and I had used a leaden suture and failed. What can I do?" Just in this time of tribulation about the subject, I was walking from my house to the office, and picked up a little bit of brass wire in the yard. It was very fine, and such as was formerly used as springs in suspenders before the days of India-rubber. I took it around to Mr. Swan, who was then my jeweler, and asked him if he could make me a little silver wire about the size of the piece of brass wire. He said Yes, and he made it. He made it of all pure silver. Anarcha was the subject of this experiment. The operation was performed on the fistula in the base of the bladder, that would admit of the end of my little finger; she had been cured of one fistula in the base of the bladder. The edges of the wound were nicely denuded, and neatly brought together with four of these fine silver wires. They were passed through little strips of lead, one on one side of the fistula, and the other on the other. The suture was tightened, and then secured or fastened by the perforated shot run on the wire, and pressed with forceps. This was the thirtieth operation performed on Anarcha. She was put to bed, a catheter was introduced, and the next day the urine came from the bladder as clear and as limpid as spring water, and so it continued during all the time she wore the catheter. In all the preceding operations, where the silk was used for a suture at the base of the bladder, cystitis always resulted. The urethra was swollen continually, and the urine loaded with a thick, ropy mucus. With the use of the silver suture there was a complete change in these conditions.

I was always anxious to see the result of all experiments; but this was attended with such marked symptoms of improvement, in every way, that I was more anxious now than ever. When the week rolled around —it seemed to me that the time would never come for the removal of the sutures—Anarcha was removed from the bed and carried to the operation-table. With a palpitating heart and an anxious mind I turned her on her side, introduced the speculum, and there lay the suture apparatus just exactly as I had placed it. There was no inflammation, there was no tumefaction, nothing unnatural, and a very perfect union of the little fistula.

This was in the month of May, I think, though possibly it was June (1849). In the course of two weeks more, Lucy and Betsey were both cured by the same means, without any sort of disturbance or discomfort. Then I realized the fact that, at last, my efforts had been blessed with success, and that I had made, perhaps, one of the most important discoveries of the age for the relief of suffering humanity.

CHAPTER XV.

DURING the time these experiments were being performed, from 1845 to 1849, everything was flourishing with me. I had all the practice that I could attend to, and more than I ought to have attempted. Many a time I said to my wife: "We are too happy; I have never seen a man in my life that was satisfied with his surroundings, but I am perfectly satisfied, and have nothing more in this world to desire. I am happy in my home, in my wife and children, in my friends, in my position, in my prospects for the future. I am perfectly content, and nothing could induce me to leave Montgomery. I have no ungratified ambition or desire." I had been solicited to go to New Orleans, by my friends Professor Stone and Erasmus D. Fenner, as that would offer me a wider field, and they even spoke of making me a professor in the medical college. I had no desire or capacity for a professorship. I said to my wife, "Can these things be; and can such things last always? Can these good things always be, and will not a blow come some time or another? Where will it strike? It is so unusual to see a man in the frame of mind that I am, that I fear something dreadful will happen to us."

The blow came in the prolonged sickness of my little three-years-old son, a beautiful boy, our second son. His death was the first time that death invaded our household. It was a dreadful blow to me, and that was the beginning of our sorrows. He was born on Christmas-day, 1845, and had passed through all the dangers of early childhood, but in 1848 he contracted diarrhœa, and died in October.

Six weeks after my successes with the silver suture, and just as I was beginning to revive from my long series of exhausting experiments, I completely collapsed. I was broken down, and had contracted diarrhœa, and so I took my family and went to Butler Springs. I carried three or four of my uncured patients with me, who were suffering from fistula, to operate on; but I was too ill to do anything. I was utterly prostrated. My disease grew apace; it could not be controlled, and I saw that I was on the verge of going into that chronic state in which, in that day, there was such an attendant mortality. Being very anxious about myself, I concluded to go to the North for a time, and for a necessary change of climate. I was so weak and emaciated that I could hardly make the journey to New York. My wife accompanied me. I was there during July, August, and Sep-

tember (1849). I got no better; I was a little better at
times, but there was no permanent improvement. I returned to Montgomery in October, not much better than
when I left, if any. But soon after my return I gradually grew worse. My friends saw that I was fading
away. I was extremely emaciated; I could take no food
that seemed to nourish me, and I was reduced to eating
milk and bread, and that ran away from me almost like
pouring water through a funnel.

My friends came to see me and to sympathize with
me; but they looked so distressed and unhappy, and my
senses became so acute, that I dreaded the thought of
seeing any one, and at last I said to my wife, "I wish
that I could escape from my friends; their visits are painful to me. They try to comfort me with words; but I
read in their faces, 'This poor fellow, what a pity to see
him going off so fast and so soon, but his fate is inevitable.'" My wife, seeing how unhappy I was, suggested
that I should go to Columbus, on a visit to our relatives
there. She had an uncle, Robert Kyle, and his family,
there.

I was glad to escape the visits of my friends, and
said, "Get my things ready, and I will go to-morrow."
I walked around to Montgomery Hall, about one hundred yards from where I lived, that being the stage
office. Colonel Jim Powell, who was then the great
mail-carrier and stage-coach man of the country, ran a
line of coaches, or rather omnibuses, every morning to
and from the train, and took passengers going north and

east. I said to Mr. Powell, " I want to go to Columbus to-morrow morning; will you have the kindness to direct your man to call for me at my house, and take me to the railroad station ? "

He said, "Certainly, doctor, with the greatest pleasure."

The next morning I sat on the portico, as emaciated as a skeleton, with my wife and children waiting to see me get into the stage. At last eight o'clock came, the hour I was to start. Eight o'clock came and no stage. So I walked around to the stage-office, and being sick and cross, I said some very irritable and disagreeable things to Mr. Powell. He apologized for disappointing me, and said that he would surely send the stage for me on the following morning, there being no other on that day. I was very unhappy all that day long. It made me disappointed and despondent not to have gotten off. But the next morning the stage came in time. I took my seat in the cars—there was but one passenger-coach; it was a short train, and there was not a great amount of travel. Having purchased a morning paper as I went along, I took my seat in the rear end of the coach. I held my paper up before my face, to keep the people from seeing me or talking to me.

Just after I sat down I saw Colonel McLaquelly, of Mississippi, who had been Governor of that State, and whom I had known when I was a little boy, and after I was a grown-up man. He was a great friend of my father's, having known him during the war of 1812, as they were both young soldiers together in Charleston. He was coming North with his wife and two children. He was leading a little boy by the hand, about seven years old, and sat down about the middle of the car, in front of me. I said to myself, " I will not speak to him. I have not seen him for some ten or twelve years, and I will not introduce myself to him, because I will have to recount to him the history of my painful illness, and speak to him of my dark future." There I sat, and the cars rolled off. About two hours had passed, and I sat there looking out of the window, with no one to talk to. At last the colonel's little boy said, " Father, I want a drink of water." His father got up, took him by the hand, walked to the baggage-car, in front, and gave him the drink of water, and came back. Just as he was going to sit down, his eyes rested on me, and as I looked up I involuntarily said, " Colonel McLaquelly." He came up to me, slightly reaching out his hand, and I said, as he evidently did not know me, as I rose, " I am Dr. Marion Sims, of Montgomery. I used to know you when I was a little boy."

"I am glad to see you," he said; " but, doctor, what is the matter with you, you are so changed ? "

I said: " Colonel McLaquelly, I recognized you as soon as you entered the car, and would like to have spoken to you, but I knew that you would ask me this question, and the subject is a painful one to me. I have got chronic diarrhœa, and I shall die in about three months. I am hopelessly incurable. I have not seen a case get well in Montgomery, and I have seen a great many cases there. It is a chronic disease of the climate. It is endemic all through the valley of the Mississippi. It is what consumption is in New England. When you see in the South a man in vigorous health and middle life gradually wasting away, and at the end of eighteen months drop as a skeleton into the grave, you may take it for a positive fact that he has died of chronic diarrhœa. If in New England you see a vigorous young man, twenty-five or thirty years of age, gradually wasting away, going to his grave as a skeleton, ten to one he has died of consumption. Consumption is comparatively rare here, while chronic diarrhœa is common. A man occasionally gets well of consumption in New England; but from this diarrhœa, unless he can change his climate and whole habits of life completely, he never recovers."

He patiently heard what I had to say, and then he said: "You are thin and emaciated, but I do not at all think that you are going to die. You have got too much vivaciousness expressed in the eye, though your physical frame does not show it. If you will do as I tell you I am sure that you will get well."

I said, "I have consulted medical men in New York and Philadelphia, and everywhere, and nobody has been able to do anything for me."

"Did you never hear of Cooper's Well?" he asked, and I replied that I had not. "Well," he said, "let me tell you about it. It is in Mississippi. This well was dug a few years ago, and you know that, when our army

returned from Mexico year before last, many of our soldiers came back with chronic diarrhœa, the very disease
that you have, and a good many of them died; some, of
course, got well."

I said, "Yes, I have attended several cases and they
all died; none of them ever got well about here. I can
not recall a single case in this part of the State that got
well."

"Well, I will tell you," he said, "what I know of
Cooper's Well. Captain Black, of the regiment in which
my son was a member, was very much worse off than
you are, and he went there, and is as well as ever now.
He went to Cooper's Well, and was cured in a month
or two. My own son Abraham was very ill, he was a
lieutenant, and he was certainly as bad as or worse off than
you seem to be, and he also went there, and to-day he is
as well as ever." And so he went on to enumerate case
after case, giving me a history of six or seven of the
young men that had returned from Mexico, who were in
a desperate state with chronic diarrhœa, all of whom
were cured at Cooper's Well. "Now," he went on to
say, "I believe if you will go to Cooper's Well you will
be cured."

The time soon came for us to part; he continuing on
to Washington City, where he was going as a member of
Congress. He had been detained a fortnight after the
time that he should have been there, on account of the
sickness of his little boy, who had his arm broken, and it
was then in a sling. He had been thrown from a pony,

and the doctor who had charge of the broken arm was not wiliing that the boy should be removed until union had taken place; hence his detention, and hence my good fortune in meeting him as I did. When I arrived at Columbus, of course I was very much elated with what I had heard. I told my uncle what Colonel McLaquelly had advised me to do, and I told my cousin, Bob Kyle, all about it. He said, " Of course you are going to Cooper's Well ? "

I said, " Bob, I haven't a cent of money in the world. I borrowed five hundred dollars to go to New York with, and I thought that would save my life, but I came back no better. I have no money with which to go to Cooper's Well, or anywhere else."

He said, " Never mind that, you are going," and with that he walked into the next room and brought me out two hundred dollars, and said, " You go home and pack up your trunks, take Cousin Theresa, and go straight to Cooper's Well." I did not stay long in Columbus, for I got no better by the visit, and I was very anxious to get home, and to tell my wife the news about this Cooper's Well. So I hurried back, and as soon as she heard of it she immediately commenced getting ready. She said, " We will start the day after to-morrow, and take the baby and the eldest child with us."

When my brother-in-law, Dr. Rush Jones, heard of it, he came in the next day and sent for my wife to have a talk with her. He said: " Marion tells me that you are going to Cooper's Well to-morrow, and that you are going to take Mary and Fanny with you." My wife said that we were. "Well," he said, "I have come here to have a talk with you about it. I have come here to tell you candidly that you must not do it. He is a doomed man, and will die in six weeks. It is impossible for you to take him there; if you do start, you will bring him back in a box."

She said, "If he remains here he will die; if he can go there, there is some hope for him and he may get well."

" But," said he, "he can not get there; he will die on the road. It is impossible. If he does go to Cooper's Well, he is too far gone for it to be of any benefit to him. It isn't worth while; you must not go there."

She said, "I have made up my mind to go, and we are going to-morrow. I feel it to be my duty, and, besides, he has set his heart on it. We shall go, at the risk of his dying on the way."

If we could have gone to Cooper's Well *via* New Orleans, it would not have been a difficult thing for us to do. But, unfortunately, it was at this time the middle of December, when the cholera was in New Orleans, and a man with the diarrhœa, in a cholera atmosphere, stood no chance for his life. The diarrhœa is a premonitory stage of cholera. We were obliged to go to Jackson, Mississippi, directly across the country, where there were very poor facilities for traveling. We went to Selma by boat, and from there we took stage to

Marion, and so on across the country. There had been heavy rains, and the water-courses were high; the swamps were flooded, and the stages would get mired and break down. Once we had to camp all night in a swamp, sitting in the stage until morning, while the driver went for a farmer, two or three miles off, and hired him and an ox-team to drag us out of the mire. In this way we drove into the town of Jackson. We arrived there on the very last day of the month, having taken two weeks to go from Montgomery, a distance now traveled in a few hours by rail. The privations that I went through with on this journey were almost incredible. I was nearly starved to death, living on crackers and milk when I could get them. When I arrived at Jackson, it was on the last day of the month and the last day of the year (1849). It was in the midst of a tremeudous snow-storm, which was a most unusual thing for that latitude. The snow was deep, and it was followed by a heavy, sharp frost, so that the limbs were broken from the pine-trees by the weight of the ice and the accumulation of snow that had been gathered upon them. In many places we had to wait, and at Jackson we remained three days.

At last we arrived at Cooper's Well, having to ride on horseback to Clinton. We found Cooper's Well to be a most God-forsaken looking place. Mr. Cooper, the proprietor, was a Methodist preacher, a circuit-rider. He had a comfortable log house for himself and his family, and a number of log cabins, built on a space of five or six acres

of land, giving the place the appearance of a deserted negro quarter. He had a wife and seven or eight children.
Some of the children, the boys, were nearly grown up.
He gave us a hearty welcome and said that he was very
sure that the water would effect a cure for me. There
was no doctor to consult about the use of the water. He
said that a good many people were injured by the use of
the water, as they were impatient to get well, and consequently took too much of it. But, with a prudent use
of the water, he was was very sure that I would reap substantial benefit from it.

I had been living on stale bread and boiled milk
and could eat nothing else. This diet was continued
for about two days, and then Mr. Cooper told me to
take a glass of the water seven times a day, and then to
increase the doses of it until it began to show some
action on the kidneys. The third day he said, "Now I
think that you can change your diet." I commenced
eating immediately (it was just after the hog-killing season) whatever was set before me; and many things that
I ate I had not dared to touch before. I ate, especially,
fat meat, middle meat, and salt pork—the latter had
been salted perhaps a month before. The diarrhœa was
checked from the time I began to be a partaker of the
water; I had a ravenous appetite, and I drank the water
according to the express directions. I ate as I had never
been able to before. I remained there twenty-seven days,
and gained twenty-seven pounds. I was impatient to get
away, and left too soon. The result of the sudden arrest.

ing of the diarrhœa was to bring on a dropsical effect. My ankles were swollen, my legs were swollen above the knees, and my face and hands were bloated. Still I felt that I was on the road to recovery, and, especially, because the wasting diarrhœa was controlled.

I left there on the 30th of January (1850) for New Orleans, where I remained about a month. I carried with me demijohns of the water from Cooper's Well and continued the use of it, and also contined to eat meat all the time. I spent a month very pleasantly in New Orleans, and got acquainted with my friend Mr. P. T. Barnum, who was then traveling with Jenny Lind and stopping in the same hotel with us. About the first of March I returned home. Everybody was amazed to see me and the wonderful change that had been effected, and all were very happy of course. I immediately plunged into business, and in the course of a week was completely occupied with my professional duties. In two months more I had a return of the diarrhœa, a good deal worse than I had ever had it before, and it grew worse day by day. In July I again returned to Cooper's Well; but the water and the treatment did not have the same beneficial effect that it had upon me during my visit there before. I remained there about two months, and then I concluded that it was best for me to get into a colder clime. So I returned home by the way of New Orleans, and immediately went to New York, where I remained about two months. I was always a little better in New York and Philadelphia than in any other place. Whenever I left

New York and went to New England I was worse. If I went to Brooklyn for any length of time I became worse, and always felt better when I got back home again to New York.

I had supposed that in New York I was better able to control my diet; but subsequent observation proved that that was not the case. The cause of my being better in New York and Philadelphia than elsewhere was the fact of the purity of the water of those two cities. In all New England, where I had been, the water was hard, and hard water was and is very injurious to the irritated mucous membrane of the gastro-intestinal canal.

I returned from New York, in the last of October, a little improved, and dragged through the winter very miserably, and tried to work; but I was not able to do a great deal. True, I was better than I had been; but I was never free from diarrhœa. I was thin and emaciated, and exceedingly irritable. At last I was compelled to go to my bed. I thought that I should die. While lying in bed I wrote out the history of my operations for vesico-vaginal fistula for the press, and sent the article to Dr. Isaac Hays, the editor of "The American Journal of the Medical Sciences." It was published in the January number of that journal (1852), as my last free-will offering to the medical profession before I should quit this world.

It is hardly worth while for me to go into detail, minutely, of the trials, tribulations, and sufferings that

I passed through. In 1852 I had gone to New York, and also during the summer of 1849, 1850, and 1852, with the hope that the change of climate would do something for me, and afford me some relief. In June, 1852, I fell down with a sun-stroke, after a long walk, at the corner of Fifth Avenue and Twenty-seventh Street, and was carried to my boarding-house, at Mrs. Jones's, No. 27 West Twenty-seventh Street. During the month or six weeks before I had improved very much, but this sun-stroke reproduced my disease with the greatest violence, and nothing seemed to control it.

In a state of desperation, I went to Portland, Connecticut, to visit my friend Dr. George O. Jarvis. I remained there a little while, but I got no better. I returned to the city, and went over and engaged board in Brooklyn, which was the worst thing that I could have done, on account of the water, and I grew worse day by day. At last, thinking that I must die, I concluded to go to Philadelphia, as I had some friends there. The idea also was to leave my wife and children among those who could sympathize with them when I was gone. We arrived in Philadelphia, my wife and myself, and stopped at a boarding-house recommended to me in Spruce Street. The next day we got in a buggy and rode up through the Spring Garden District, in various directions, in search of a little house that I might rent, and where my wife could prepare the food that was necessary for me. At the hotels and boarding-houses I could get nothing that was suitable for a man as sick as I was. At last I came to a little house in Vine Street, between Seventh and Eighth, and near the residence of the great artist, Rembrandt Peale. It had on the door "To Let." I applied to Mr. ———, corner of Market and Eleventh Streets. I went to see the proprietor, and asked him the price of the house by the month, and he said twenty-five dollars a month. He asked me for references, and I told him that I preferred to pay in advance. He said, "How long do you want it?"

I said, "I want it as long as I live. I want to rent your house to die in it."

He replied, "Judging by your looks, you will not want it long."

I said, "I shall die within a month or two." We found it unfurnished, so we rented some beds and also some chairs, and two or three tables, and put in it, simply that my wife could get what was necessary for me. I grew worse and worse daily, and at last I was so near dead that I telegraphed for my father, in Montgomery, to come and take charge of my wife and family and take them home. That day there was a severe storm at the North, of hail and wind, and as good luck would have it the storm extended to the South, blowing down all the telegraph-poles, costing Mobile hundreds of thousands of dollars in the destruction of property. So my father did not receive the telegram, and therefore he did not come to Philadelphia.

When I saw that I could not recover, I sent for my friend Dr. Isaac Hays to come and see me. He came very promptly. I explained to him the condition of my affairs, and said to him that I felt that I was going to die, and that I wanted to introduce him to my wife. He said that he thought I had better take cod-liver oil, and not to give up. My wife went out and bought a bottle of cod-liver oil, though we hardly had the money to spare for it. It was placed on the mantel-shelf; I never took it. But this gave me an idea. I said to my wife, "Cod-liver oil is a disagreeable thing to take; pickled pork is a good deal more palatable. Don't you remember with what benefit I used it the first time I was at Cooper's Well, how I ate pickled pork, and how I gained, and how I got well from that very moment?"

She said Yes; and immediately went out and bought some. She boiled it, and then afterward broiled it, or fried it, I do not know which. I had always traveled, wherever I went, with some of the water from Cooper's Well in jugs. So I said, "We will inaugurate the same diet here that we did at Cooper's Well, drink the water, and eat salted pickled pork." So we began it, and, to my great surprise, in four or five days the diarrhœa was under control. This was inaugurated the last of August, and in a month I was able to get up out of bed, and to walk about two hundred yards, with some little help. I happened to pass by a grocery-store one day, when I had been up about a month, and I went in to weigh myself, and I found that I weighed just ninety pounds. Of course, I had been much lighter than this two or three weeks previously.

In the month of October (1852) I was getting well. I then said to myself, "I will not make a mistake this time, as I have done heretofore, in returning to Alabama too soon. I have always gone back to that locality in October, when the weather was still warm. Now I intend to remain at the North till December." We returned to Alabama about the 19th or the 20th of December (1852). I was feeling pretty well. I had no diarrhœa now, and I thought that at last I was cured of this dreadful disease, which I had then had, off and on, for more than three years. On Christmas-Day we went to Mount Meigs, five days after my return from Philadelphia, to dine with our friends the Lucases. There I had a chill. The next day we returned home. The diarrhœa returned, and could not be controlled by any possible means. I grew worse and worse; within a week I was confined to my house, and within one month I was confined to my bed. By that time my throat and tongue were so ulcerated that I could hardly speak, and any nourishment that I took passed through me like water, and almost unchanged. Even milk was not digested.

Early in February (1853) I had given up all hope, and one day the bell tolled. My wife was in hopes I would not hear it. But when it began I called to her from an adjoining room and wanted to know who was dead. She said that it was Mr. Bob Gilmer. I said, "Since I was taken with this diarrhœa, let me see—how many have died? There have been P. D. Sayer, Mr. Ward Allen, Mrs. James Smith, Mrs. Calvin"—and I went on to count up the numbers. I said, " Bob Gilmer is the eleventh or twelfth important person in this community that has died of the disease that I have, since I was taken with it." I said, " They have all died, and I have had a hard struggle for my life, and now I must die too." Of course, my poor wife tried to cheer me as much as she could.

" But," I said, " if I had the physical strength and force, and the moral courage to do what I ought to do, I could get well."

" What, then, ought you to do ? " she asked.

" I will tell you what I ought to do," I said ; " I ought to sell out everything, take my wife and children and go to New York ; because, whenever I have gone to New York I have been better. A few months ago I thought that I was cured. If I could change my climate entirely I believe that even yet I might be cured and restored to health. But that is impossible," I continued.

" But I don't think it is impossible," she said.

I replied, " I have no heart for work, and I can not do anything. I can not undertake the annoyances and troubles we would have to go through to get ready, and it would be a most selfish thing, after all, for me to do. Supposing, after we had broken up here, I should die on the road, or in New York, and leave you and the children, without friends and among strangers, and without money. I hardly think that a right thing for me to do. I had better remain here and die among my friends, where you could get somebody to sympathize with you and to help you in your struggles for life."

" But," she said, " I take a different view of the thing altogether. The whole question can be arranged as you would have it, without giving you a bit of trouble." In two weeks she had arranged everything. She had sold out my interest in the drug-store to her brother, Dr. Rush Jones. I had put five thousand dollars in there four years before. He and Dr. Baldwin, who were partners with me, agreed to give their notes for seven thousand five hundred dollars, payable in twelve months, for my interest. My house and lot were sold for ten thousand dollars, on a credit bearing eight per cent interest. We hadn't many negroes. We had no planting interests, and the dozen negroes we had were house negroes and town negroes — cooks, waiters, and body-servants only. We called them together, and I said, " Now we are going away, never to come back again. You must all select masters with whom you are willing to live, and the man that you select, as a matter of course, will be your master hereafter. We will agree about the valuation."

They all began to weep, and felt very badly over the thought of our leaving them. They said, " Oh, no, master, we don't want to know any other person for a master but you, and we don't want to know any other woman for a missus but Mrs. Theresa. We don't want to be sold. Let us stay here, and we will take Colonel Clauton for an agent, and we will look to him for pro-

12

tection in everything, and pay him the same wages we would pay you. We will take care of ourselves the best way we can, hoping that you will finally be restored, and come back to your old home again among us."

I told the negroes to do exactly as they pleased, and that I would not put any of them in slavery against their will. I consented to their plan, and wished them to be happy, and well taken care of. So all my affairs were arranged and settled so that I could leave. I left some debts behind me; I had made collections and paid off some, and others were still unpaid. I left Montgomery for New York about the first of May (1853), so near dead that no one thought that I would ever get to New York. I had to lie down all the way on the railroad train. The diarrhœa was uncontrolled. We went to Richmond, Virginia, without stopping, the journey being a very fatiguing one for me. I determined to go from there to Rockford Island Springs. We had to go by canal up the James River to Lynchburg, and we arrived there on the second day. I was not comfortably situated there. I stopped at Lexington, and sent to the springs for the water. I remained there a week, but did not derive any great benefit from it, as I had anticipated. I concluded it would be about as well for me to take the water with me as to stay there, and so I left, and went on to New York.

CHAPTER XVI.

I SPENT the summer partly in New York and partly in Middletown and Portland, Connecticut; and then, in September, we returned to New York to seek a home. After looking around, I found one at No. 89 Madison Avenue, between Twenty-eighth and Twenty-ninth Streets, for sale, and bought it for fifteen thousand dollars; the proprietor taking the notes due from Dr. Jones, my brother-in-law, for five thousand dollars, and the other two thousand five hundred dollars I appropriated toward furnishing the house. It was a hazardous thing to do. I had a little money only over and above this, not more than one thousand dollars. I had no friends, no influence, no health, and nothing to recommend me to business. Fortunately, I had published my article on the treatment of vesico-vaginal fistula a year before that, in "The American Journal of the Medical Sciences," and the doctors had read it everywhere, and were very much surprised at the claims set up of rendering this troublesome and loathsome affection easily and successfully cured. They hardly believed it. Whenever I was introduced to any of the doctors, they all knew who I was by that article, and by my previous contributions to the medical literature of the day.

It may be wondered how I lived without friends and without business. Mine is not an isolated example of a man's living in a first-class house, with first-class surroundings, and yet struggling with the most abject want. I had some Southern patients who followed me to New York. They were boarders in the house, and besides these we had some other boarders, so that our house supported me almost by keeping these boarders. Soon after my arrival in New York, I made the acquaintance of Dr. Mott, Dr. Francis, Dr. Buck, Dr. Watson, and indeed all of the leading surgeons of the town of that day and time. Dr. Buck was exceedingly anxious to see me perform some of my operations with the silver suture, and so invited me to go and help operate on a Mrs. Crane, who had lacerated perinæum, and whom he had operated upon unsuccessfully two or three times. I gladly went with him, loaned him my instruments, and showed him how to perform the operation. She was cured in a single week. A week or two after this, Dr. Buck came to me to borrow my instruments to operate on a case of vesico-vaginal fistula in the New York Hospital. I loaned him the instruments, and would gladly have gone with him to assist him in the operation, but he did not invite me. I felt very much hurt by it. I expected that the surgeons in

New York would give me something to do in a branch which I understood so well. But I was disappointed. By and by a patient was sent to Dr. Mott with vesico-vaginal fistula, and he had the kindness to ask me to operate upon it. I did so, in his presence and the presence of his son, Dr. Alexander B. Mott. The case was a very bad one; but the patient was cured. It was the first case ever cured in New York. With my advent to New York, the subject of vesico-vaginal fistula, lacerated perinæum, and the subject of parturition, seemed all at once to interest the profession more than they had ever done before.

Very soon it was heard that Dr. Buck and Dr. Watson and some of the other doctors were performing all these operations very successfully in the other hospitals. I could not advertise; I could get nothing to do; I had no means of bringing myself before the public, or of reaching the profession, because I had no hospital in which to operate or to perform these marvelous operations. As soon as the doctors had learned what they wanted of me, they dropped me. As soon as they had learned how to perform these operations successfully in the New York Hospital and elsewhere, they had no further use for me. My thunder had been stolen, and I was left without any resources whatever. I said to myself, " I am a lost man unless I can get somebody to create a place in which I can show the world what I am capable of doing." This was the inception of the idea of a woman's hospital. If the profession had received me kindly in New York, and acted honorably and gentlemanly and generously toward me, I would not have thought of building a woman's hospital. Some people have given me the credit of coming to New York with the express purpose of establishing a great hospital devoted to the diseases of women and their treatment. When I left Alabama for New York I had no idea of the sort in the world. I came simply for a purpose, the most selfish in the world—that of prolonging my life. I saw that I could not live in any other place than New York, and for that reason, and no other, I came.

Seeing that I must create an institution in which to work, I went at it with all my might. But, even then, my health was feeble; I still had some diarrhœa, and the moral depression under which I labored, and the disappointments that I had in not getting practice or encouragement from my medical brethren, produced a most demoralizing effect upon me. I had become acquainted with Dr. Francis. I told him of the great discovery that I had made; I spoke to him on the necessity of a hospital for the treatment of the diseases of women, in which their improvement could evidently be effected. He took up this subject with great enthusiasm, and advised me to go at once and lay it before Dr. Mott, Dr. Stevens, and some others. I went and saw Dr. Mott and had a long talk with him. He encouraged me in the idea, and said he would be glad to help me in any way that he could. I went and saw Dr. Alexander H. Stevens. He said, "I have read your articles on

' Vesico-Vaginal Fistula ' with the greatest interest in the world, and I think that you ought to have a field in which you can work. Now, the Episcopalians are building a hospital, or about to—St. Luke's ; and I will give you a letter to the Rev. Dr. Muhlenberg. He is its founder, and the leader in the movement. I will recommend him to set aside a ward in his hospital expressly for diseases of women, and that you be made surgeon of it." He continued, " Let me tell you what I will do. I will call a meeting of the profession, at the College of Physicians and Surgeons, and then you can explain all your views to the profession precisely as you have to me, showing the necessity for a new hospital for the treatment of the diseases of women. Thus you will be properly introduced to the doctors of the city, and I have no doubt but that the thing can be accomplished."

" But," I said, " doctor, that is impossible. I can not make a speech. It would frighten me to death to stand up before an audience to speak."

He said, " I do not know why you can not stand up before an audience of one hundred gentlemen and speak as fluently as you can before me. All that you want to do is to tell the tale of the suffering of women in their conflicts with these terrible diseases. You must go there and tell the story of how you made the discovery, and say what it is to lead to in the future, and I think that the profession will take you up with a great deal of warmth."

I said, " You must let me off for a time, my dear doctor, to think about this, but I don't think that I can do it." I had refused, because Dr. Mott had promised to help me, and I knew that he was all-powerful, and that he didn't require me to make a speech. He would indorse and help me all he could. I had performed an operation for Dr. Mott several weeks before this, and I had not seen him since. I went at once to tell him of the interview that I had had with Dr. Stevens, and to ask him to give me the assistance that I wanted to start a hospital. He said that he had thought a good deal about the subject, and that it seemed to be such a herculean task, an undertaking so gigantic, and one so certain to result in failure, that he had concluded to do nothing further in the matter.

I felt exceedingly mortified and disappointed. I went home, and in my heart I blamed Dr. Mott for having deceived me. I ungenerously, perhaps, laid considerable blame upon him, for I really thought that he and his son had seen me operate in consultation, and, having got out of me all that they expected or hoped to, they therefore had no further use for me. Of course, I felt suspicious of everybody, as I was entirely and utterly friendless and helpless. Dr. Francis alone seemed to encourage and stand by me. I became very gloomy and melancholy, and heartily regretted that I had ever come to New York. However, as I had come, there was now no alternative of doing anything, excepting through Dr. Stevens. I then sat down and wrote out deliberately my

thoughts and views on the necessity for the establishment of a hospital for the treatment of the diseases of
women. Then I went in search of Dr. Stevens. By this
time nearly two months had elapsed since Dr. Stevens
had kindly invited me to deliver a lecture before the
medical profession in the city of New York. When I
found him at home I told him that I had come to comply with his suggestion to lecture before the medical
profession of the city. He received me very kindly, and
said, " I have been wanting to see you ever so much
lately, but I did not know where to find you. You remember when you talked to me on the subject, two
months ago, you spoke with such earnestness and enthusiasm that I was completely captivated and carried
away with your idea of establishing a hospital, and I
even gave you a letter to Dr. Muhlenberg, and recommended him to set aside a ward in his hospital, and to
have you appointed surgeon of the same. I wrote it
in good faith, to carry forward the views I expressed to
you. But I am very sorry to say that since then I have
been talking with my friends in the medical profession,
and I find here such a degree of universal opposition to
you and to your enterprise, that I am sorry to say that I
can not now give you the privilege or opportunity of
addressing the profession under my auspices."

Of course, this surprised me greatly, and it was a stab
that I little expected. I do not think that I had smiled
in three months before, not even at home in my own
family. I had become bitter and vindictive, and when

Dr. Stevens addressed me thus I broke out in a sort of sardonic smile or grin, and said:

"Doctor, this is about the first time that I have smiled or laughed in three months. You are the only honest man that I have found since I came to New York in the profession here, and the only one who has dared to tell me to my face that I am persecuted and hunted down. I have felt that I was here under a cloud all the time; that I had no friends, nor one upon whom I could rely, Dr. Francis excepted." I continued, "As to the letter of introduction that you gave me to Dr. Muhlenberg, I will return that to-morrow. I thank you kindly for putting the idea into my head to address the medical profession; I think that I shall do so some day anyhow. You have pointed out to me what is my duty in the matter, and I shall do it."

So I left the doctor with a very heavy heart, deploring the misfortune that had driven me to the city of New York. Some two or three weeks passed over, and I was utterly at a loss what to do. The small amount of money that I had brought to New York I deposited with Henfold, Clay & Co., druggists, with whom the drug firm I was associated with in the city of Montgomery had done business. I found in Mr. Clay a kind-hearted personal friend. I went to see him, to find out how much money I had to my credit with them. I was surprised to find that I had only one hundred and sixteen dollars. I came home and called my wife aside, in order to have a consultation. I told her that I thought we would have to leave New York; that I saw no way in the world for doing what I had started out to do. I told her that I had been to Mr. Clay's, and that we had remaining only one hundred and sixteen dollars, and that it would be better even to go back to Montgomery than to remain in New York under such circumstances as we found ourselves: with bad health, a large family of children, no money, no friends. I did not see how we could possibly go on much longer. She very coolly replied that we must not go back to Montgomery; that we would go into the country, as I had proposed, and rent a cottage until I could live down the opposition of the doctors. She said that she knew that I would eventually succeed in what I had undertaken.

Although it was as dark as it was possible to conceive, she said that she had an abiding confidence that God had not driven us out of our comfortable home in the South, to place us here for an idle and foolish purpose. She further continued that she would never consent to giving up and going back to Alabama. We were reduced to the very lowest extremity. My courage was all gone; but she was as calm and as quiet as possible for one to be. I thought that I would have gone crazy, and I did not know what in the world to do, things looked so dark. And then we had to send our children to the public schools, because we were not able to send them to a private school. Of course, the public schools were good enough; but we would not have chosen the public schools as the place to send girls of ten and twelve years of age; and to see my wife cutting up her dresses, her new fine dresses, to make her children appear respectable at school, and doing her own cooking to save nine dollars a month—all together, I was as near going into an insane asylum as a man ever was, and not go there. Things had come to the very last extremity.

The struggle continued, and at this time I was reduced to such an extremity for the want of means to live on that I felt obliged to rent my house and go to the country, which I wanted to do, and which my wife opposed, and get somebody to take the house and occupy it. The Mrs. Seymour with whom we had boarded previously to my taking the house, was obliged to give up her house—a boarding-house—in Fourth Avenue, and, knowing the dilemma in which I was placed, she offered to take the house and board me and my family for the rent of it; giving the third-floor front room for my wife and myself, and packing the children in the top of the house and elsewhere, as she could conveniently put them, while the rest of the house was given up to the boarders. One whole year of misery was passed in this way. Never in this whole world was a poor family so tyrannized over as we were. We could not get rid of Mrs. Seymour, and had to put up with all her insolence and insults.

At the end of the year I wanted her to leave; but she said "No," that she had possession and was going to hold it. I then had to apply to the courts to have her ejected, and an officer came to put her out. Of course, the heart-burnings and unhappiness attending the association with such a woman were enough to demoralize any family and render them perfectly miserable. This malicious, vindictive woman then sued me for a breach of contract, claiming that she had hired the house for a longer period, and brought in a number of charges against me to the amount of twenty - five hundred dollars. The case was tried before a referee; the evidence was all taken, and this referee was to decide it. He sent for my lawyer, Mr. Benedict, and told him that the case was evidently one of black-mail, but that as I was a perfect stranger, and just starting in an enterprise whereby I would need all the friends it could have, it would be better for me not to accept a verdict against a woman so malicious and bad-tempered, and suggested that the wise thing for him would be to give a verdict of two hundred and twenty-five dollars in her favor. Not that she was entitled to one cent, but her acceptance of that verdict would shut her mouth, and keep her from saying disagreeable things about me in the community; because, as she did not hesitate to swear to a lie, she would not hesitate to tell one.

CHAPTER XVII.

ONE day, just at this time, I happened to meet a man named Beattie, whom I had known very well in Montgomery. I was his physician there, and had attended him at a long spell of sickness. When I met him in the Astor House neighborhood, he inquired how I was flourishing, and I told him my melancholy story —that I could do nothing; that the profession opposed me, all of them; that the influence radiating from the New York Hospital was so powerful that I could make no impression at all. I told him that I could not reach the public; that I could not advertise, could get nothing to do, and I was in a state of absolute starvation.

He said, " Oh, well, you carried everything before you in Alabama, and I have thought that if your health were better, with your energy and working capacity, you would finally do something in New York. But I see it all now. It is the Northern prejudice against a Southern man."

I said, " No, Mr. Beattie, there isn't a particle of political sentiment in it. It is only that I do not belong to any dominant clique in the medical profession in New York. I am alone and solitary; I have no friends, and nobody through whom I can reach the ear of the public."

" Well," said he, " I am sorry that I can not help you ; however, I happen to know the very man here in this city, who, if he takes a fancy to you, can help you. I will bring him to see you to-morrow evening."

Of course, I could not imagine that Mr. Beattie, a comparative stranger, could bring in anybody who could help me, when I had applied to men so strong in the city, and could get no help from them. However, Mr. Beattie appeared about eight o'clock on the appointed evening, and with him came a tall man (Henri L. Stuart by name), with thin, brown reddish hair, a wax nose, and certainly a most remarkable looking man. He was a man of great intelligence, great energy, and as he walked into the room and shook hands with me he said :

" My friend, Mr. Beattie, has told me something about your antecedents and your experience in New York; and I have come here to have a talk with you, and to know what it is all about."

I never felt so much as I did then as if a man had come into my room to take my measure to lay me out. We sat down, however, and I began at the beginning and told him the whole story. I gave him a history of the discoveries that I had made before I came to

New York, and I told him of my affliction and my bad
health; I told him of the treatment that I had received
in the city of New York, at the hands of Dr. Mott and
of Dr. Stevens, and indeed of the whole medical profession; that I had no friends, no money, and no influence; I told him of all the objects and aims I had,
what I anticipated in establishing the hospital, the need
of it, and the benefits accruing to humanity and eventually to science. He himself was an enthusiast, and
seemed to have grasped the whole subject. He said:

"It is very lucky that Dr. Stevens did not stand to
his word, for you to deliver a lecture before the College of Physicians and Surgeons. If he had you would
have been in the hands of a clique. It would not have
represented the whole medical profession, and you would
not have been as strong as you are at this moment,
when you seem to have no friends whatever. Now, I
will tell you what is to be done. We will rent Stuyvesant Hall; we will advertise in the newspapers for the
doctors to attend a meeting, which is to be addressed by
Dr. J. Marion Sims, late of Montgomery, Alabama, on
the necessity of a hospital in the City of New York for
the treatment of the diseases of women. We will invite all the leading doctors in town by special cards, and
they will come to hear you, and will be wise enough to
indorse what you have to say. If you tell your story to
the crowd of doctors that I will get there, as you have
told it to me, we will carry the day. If you don't make
the d—dest failure that a man ever made in this world,

or can make, in one month from now, instead of being a beggar, as you make yourself out, you will be dictator, and command the situation entirely."

I could not understand this man. I could not possibly see how he was to do this wonderful thing. I felt like a child in his hands. He sat down, and wrote out cards of invitation, and ordered seven hundred of them to be printed. He then went down and rented Stuyvesant Hall. I told him frankly that I had no money, and that he must not run me in debt nor ruin me with expenses. He said:

"Damn the expense; never mind the money. We are obliged to have a certain amount of money, let what will happen, and somebody has got to furnish it."

So he went along, but I did not see how he was going to achieve the wonderful thing of which he was sanguine. I did not know who he was, or what his business was, or where he came from. I seemed to be in the hands of a destiny that I could not control.

The cards were issued, and the doctors were invited to meet at Stuyvesant Hall on a certain day of May, 1854. Mr. Stuart had put it off to a certain date, because he said there were public meetings, anniversary occasions, and other gatherings that would interfere with it, and that the people would not come out. And now the mystery surrounding him was soon to be solved.

The day before the lecture was to be delivered he called at my house in the morning, and said: "I want you to go down town with me." I said, "What do you want of me?" "Never mind," he said, "I want you to go with me; so put on your hat, for there is no time to lose." The first place that we went to was to the "Tribune" office. We walked up-stairs, and he introduced me to Mr. Greeley. A poor little backwoodsman like myself was frightened when we came in contact with so great and busy a man as Horace Greeley. He said: "Mr. Greeley, I want to introduce you to my friend Dr. J. Marion Sims, late of Alabama. He has an enterprise here in the interest of humanity, to the public, and to everybody." And in a few brief words he set it forth. Then he said that he would like a few words of a little notice for me in the paper. Mr. Greeley said, "Mr. Stuart, write your notice and send it in." And he did so.

Well, when we walked down stairs, I was frightened at what had happened. We walked along and went into the "Times" office, and there he introduced me to Mr. Raymond. He made the same little stereotyped speech, and received the same invitation to write out his notice. Then, when he came down, he wanted me to go to the "Herald" office; and I said that I was tired of this and I did not like it, and that he might go in and make his speeches just as well without me. He said, "Why, you are my card, and I am playing you off." So I followed him like a dog. We ran up-stairs all the morning, I wondering at the man's audacity and the power which he seemed to exert, and the politeness with which he was received and treated wherever we went. Suffice it to say that he took me into fifteen editorial sanctums, and made the same little speech to every man there in authority. In the "Herald" we saw Mr. Hudson; we did not see the great James Gordon Bennett. In every place that Mr. Stuart went he was treated with the same consideration; in every office the editor promptly consented to what he wished. The next morning the leading papers of the city had little notices under the head of their city news, about four or five lines long, calling the attention of the medical profession and the public at large to the lecture that would be delivered in Stuyvesant Hall that night.

About ten o'clock that morning I was up in the top of the house working away at my lecture, reading it over and becoming familiar with it, and wondering if I would have anything of an audience, and what they would do after they got together, when one of the children came running up and said, "Father, Dr. Mott is in the parlor." I had seen Dr. Mott but once in four months, and that was the time he turned me away in February, and I had felt very unkindly toward him after that. But, as I went down the steps, my heart warmed toward him. I knew what had brought him; that it was the little notice in the newspapers that morning; that he did not want to be left out in the cold if anything was to be done. When I saw him he was as pleasant as possible for him to be, as he always was with everybody, and he said:

"I have come to see you this morning, and to tell you how sorry I am that I can not be with you this evening at Stuyvesant Institute. My daughter, Mrs. Isaac Bell, has just arrived from Mobile, and we have a family gathering, which will· deprive me of the pleasure of being with you. I want to remind you, however, that I indorse your movement, and did the very first time you spoke to me about it, when you came with Dr. Francis's card of introduction. I wish to tell you that I shall be only too happy to do anything I can for you in furthering the objects which you have in view."

I thanked him very much, and told him I had occasion to allude to his name twice in my lecture, and that I could not mention it without honor.

The evening came, and for an hour, from six to seven, there fell the hardest rain that I ever saw fall, and I supposed, as a matter of course, there would be no audience or no doctors there, and that the entire scheme would end in failure. Mr. Stuart and I went down early and had the hall lighted, and I took my seat in the audience part of the house. Presently the doctors began to arrive and to crowd in, so that the hall very soon was full. There could not have been less than two hundred and fifty doctors there. I was very much surprised to see such a gathering of strong men in the profession. There was no formal or other organization of the meeting, and nobody to introduce me. After a while I heard some one in the audience wondering where the speaker of the evening was. Mr. Stuart was sitting near by me, and he said, " This room is about full, the hour for the lecture has arrived, and you had better go on with it. You had better take your place in the lecturer's desk and commence."

I went, and as I walked to the place they took it for granted that I was the speaker of the evening, and that I was the man who was to address them. There was a little welcome in the way of applause, and I began reading my discourse, which took over half an hour, and when it was over I felt that I had done my duty to the profession in laying my views before them, and I then sat down. There had been no preliminary organization; nothing cut and dried beforehand; no consultation with any one. After I took my seat the audience sat still, and everybody waited for everybody else. And then I felt a change come over my feelings. I had gone to that lecture-room full of vindictiveness toward the medical profession. I now saw that the most of the profession were interested in what I had to say, and that a few individuals did not represent its public opinion. A long interval of suspense ensued, and nobody moved. At last Dr. Griscom arose and said:

"I have waited for somebody to take the initiative in this matter; but as there seems to be no previous understanding, or the usual stereotyped resolutions and movers, I would begin the organization of this meeting by calling Dr. Edward Delafield to the chair." Dr. Beedle was requested to act as secretary.

Dr. Griscom went on to approve everything I had said. He said he was glad to indorse everything "which had been so well said by the speaker, and the time had certainly arrived for initiating a movement such as I had proposed." He spoke in this laudatory strain for about ten or fifteen minutes. He showed plainly what was the duty of the profession under the circumstances, and then closed by moving that the chairman be empowered to appoint a committee of ten, five medical men and five laymen, to carry out the plan that had been laid before them for the establishment of a hospital for women. Dr. Gardiner seconded the motion; he made a handsome speech; and there were some other speakers, and the motion was finally adopted. The resolution said that I must be one of the committee of five from the medical profession. The meeting adjourned, with a vote of thanks to the speaker of the evening. I went home happier than I was when I went to the meeting, and with my feelings entirely changed toward the medical profession; for I must frankly say that I was blaming the whole profession for the coldness and position of a few members of it.

The next day Dr. Delafield sent me a little note, requesting my presence at his house. He said he was very happy to assume the responsibility of chairman of the committee to organize the board of councilors, medical and laymen; and he said that, as a matter of course, I would be on that committee, because I was the mover of the whole thing, and then he suggested the names of three others as being suitable for a working committee.

I said immediately, "Doctor, these are good names, and good men; but they do not represent the profession.

I think that you ought to appoint men on the committee who represent the whole profession, because the profession were there *en masse*, and indorsed this movement and went away. The only way that I can see that you can do this properly is, to represent the three medical institutions of the city and the three medical colleges—Dr. Stevens, as president of the College of Physicians and Surgeons; Dr. Green, as president of the New York Medical College; Dr. Mott, of the New York University; and Dr. French would represent the obstetrical branch of the profession. These are all men at the head of the medical profession in the city, and of public institutions, and I think that the medical profession would be satisfied with their appointment."

He said, "Doctor, your views are all correct, theoretically; but for practical working mine is the best. I do not think that you can get Dr. Green and Dr. Stevens to work together in the same organization. There has always been an antagonism in the medical profession to the New York Medical College."

I replied, "Will you allow me to see Dr. Stevens?" And he answered at once, "By all means, see him."

I then said, "It is very likely that under other circumstances Dr. Stevens would not consent; but I, as an outsider, and in an independent movement here, after representing the facts, may be able to amalgamate these elements, which, perhaps, others could not accomplish.

Dr. Delafield did not like this very much, but he was obliged to agree with me, and to my making the attempt to harness these two men together in the same movement. So I was not long in finding Dr. Stevens, when I thanked him for his suggestion and the idea he had given of lecturing before the profession. I also told him of what had occurred, and what we wanted him to do. He said that he would be happy to co-operate with us, and that he had not the least objection in the world to taking a place on the board or committee with Dr. Green or anybody else they would select.

The next day I called on Dr. Delafield and told him that these gentlemen had all agreed to work together harmoniously in organizing the hospital movement. Dr. Delafield was not very well pleased with it; but, as a matter of course, he had to accept. And then it was that the truth of what Mr. Stuart said one evening, when every thing looked dark around us, came to me, that I was no longer a beggar, but a dictator. Hot weather came on by this time, and nothing could be done during the summer. In the autumn I became acquainted with Mr. Peter Cooper, and in him I found a strong friend and adviser. I also became acquainted with Mr. E. C. Benedict. Both these men lent their great energies to the enterprise, and their names were reported to Dr. Delafield as two of the committee of five laymen that were to be selected. Dr. Delafield had lost interest in the institution when he could not control it, and put his own "tools" in the place to run it.

When the autumn came, my friend Mr. Stuart said, " Now you have done with the doctors all that you can hope to do. You have had their public indorsement, and they can not take that back. You must do the work yourself, in your own way, without any regard to anybody else. Now, the way for you to do is for you to start out; tell your same story that you have told to everybody, to some of the leading women of the city, and ask them to do the work. You have nothing to hope from the doctors, or from the profession, or from anybody, but by appeal to the heads and the hearts of intelligent women."

The first woman that I attempted to reach was Mrs. William E. Dodge. I had got acquainted with Mrs. Elisha Peck, living in Fourteenth Street, a very intelligent lady, and she knew Mrs. Dodge. I begged her to see her for me, and interest her in the organization of a board of lady managers for the hospital. She went to see her, and had a long talk with her. Mrs. Dodge said that she had so many irons in the fire already that she did not see her way clear to do anything with any new enterprise, and she had to decline. When Mrs. Peck came back I said to her, " Mrs. Peck, for six weeks I have been trying to get somebody to act as a nucleus around which we could gather the other women to form a board of lady managers for this hospital. I have utterly failed. Why will you not agree to be the first woman to inaugurate the movement, and to stand by it? You fully understand and know all about it."

She said, " I would gladly do it; but I haven't the influence in the community that you want."

13

I said, " It is certainly something to have one honest, true woman of good sense, to whom we can point, willing to indorse and work for the hospital." And Mrs. Elisha Peck, now Mrs. Apperthay, and now the president of the board of lady supervisors, was the first who agreed to stand by me.

Through her I reached others, and eventually I had got about a dozen women who would co-operate in forming a board of lady managers. I wanted very much to see Mrs. Doremus. I had heard of her philanthropy, of her energy, and of her extraordinary efforts in charitable works, but I was told that her health was delicate, that she was feeble, and that she would therefore not be able to give me the time that was necessary. The Home for the Friendless had been organized and managed and run by Mrs. William E. Dodge, Mrs. Stone, with Mrs. Peck as first directress. I went to see Mrs. Dodge, knowing her executive ability, and had a long talk with her. She was a great invalid, confined to her house most of the time, and she had gout worse than any woman that I ever saw in my life—occasionally I had seen a man that had it as badly as she—and altogether, physically, she had more than her hands full to do. But she weighed this matter well. She looked over the list of a dozen or so of names that I had, and she said :

" Your work is a grand and noble one, and it is obliged to succeed; because such an institution as you propose is needed to-day, and it must be built. How I do wish that my own health were such that I could throw all my energies into it, and organize and initiate the movement for you. But that can not be. My advice to you is to go straight to Mrs. Doremus. Those names are good enough in their own way; but, with the exception of three or four, you had better not have had them. They are a dead weight; for they have no social status, no fortune, and they have nothing that will help you in your organization. Pick out three names from this list, and it is all the twelve are worth. Now, my advice to you is, to go with this list to Mrs. Doremus, and see what she can do for you. Lay the whole subject open to her precisely as you have to me, and I am sure that she will grasp it, and organize the work for you immediately."

I saw Dr. Doremus, and asked him when I could go and see his mother. He replied that she was at her home every evening for tea, "and you can go at any time after eight o'clock. If you want to see her this evening I will tell her that you are coming."

I said, "Very well; please prepare the way for me. Tell her that I am coming to talk about my hospital movement." I went promptly at eight o'clock, and went very timidly. She received me very kindly; Dr. Doremus was sitting with her in the back parlor, and she allowed me to tell my story, which was not a very short one. I told it in all its details, and the moment I had finished she said, " These names that you have you must retain, because you have got them. Some of them are valuable; but the majority are not worth anything at all, and are a dead weight; but the way to organize this hospital is to put it on a higher stratum in society. Mrs. David Codwise must be first directress of the institution; Mrs. William B. Astor, second directress; Mrs. Ogden Hoffman, third; Mrs. Webster must be the secretary; Mrs. Jacob LeRoy, treasurer."

"But," I said, "Pray tell me what must Mrs. Doremus be? You seem to be a regular Warwick, appointing kings and leaders, and keeping in the background yourself."

She said, "I will be your chief marshal or chief counselor. I will write a note to Mrs. Codwise, and ask her when you can come to see her. She has for forty years been a leader in the aristocracy of the town, and a woman of great influence and intelligence."

The next day I received a note from Mrs. Doremus saying that Mrs. David Codwise would be glad to see me that evening at eight o'clock. This was on the 5th of February, 1855. I shall never forget with what intense anxiety I mounted the steps to her residence in Twenty-seventh Street. I felt then that everything depended on that evening's visit. Mrs. Codwise was a woman evidently about sixty years of age, and one of the most charming and fascinating women that I ever met in all my life. She was very bright and very intelligent, very kind-hearted, generous, and sympathetic. She saw that I was excited, and nervous, and anxious. I began to tell her my story about the sufferings of women, and what I had done for their relief; about my coming to New

York, and the treatment I had received at the hands of the doctors, or some of them; when, all at once, she stopped me before I had finished my story, and she said:

"Let me say one word to you, and it is this: I am already convinced of the importance of the subject that you are laying before me, and I wish to say to you now, that I will give you all the influence that I can possibly exert in this community to carry forward your views to the fullest extent. Anticipating you in this regard, now I shall be very glad to hear the rest of your story."

Suffice it to say, that Mrs. Codwise entered into the plan with heart and soul, and gave the matter all the thought and time that were necessary to organize the board of lady managers, and to put the work in good running order. This was on the 5th of February (1855), and a meeting of the ladies was called at the house of Mrs. Codwise on Saturday, the 10th of February (1855). I was requested to be present, to answer such questions as might be put to me. It was more for the purpose of introducing me personally, however, than to answer any questions. I was called on to answer a few questions, and to make a statement on the subject, which I did as briefly as possible; leaving it to those whom I had indoctrinated fully in its importance to make such statements and further explanations as they might see fit. The board of lady managers was organized precisely as Mrs. Doremus had said that it should be, and they at once appointed a committee to rent a building, and open a hospital as soon as possible.

Soon after this meeting, when the hospital was organized, at the house of Mrs. Codwise, on this 10th day of February, 1855, notices of it of course appeared in the newspapers. Two or three days after that date, Dr. John Watson called on Mrs. Doremus, and Dr. Gurdon Buck called on Mrs. Codwise. Each of the ladies was to be presented with arguments to show that there was no necessity for the hospital; that they had made a great mistake; that they had been deceived; that the hospital would be an expensive luxury, and a very costly affair, as well as a short-lived one. That the few cases of vesico-vaginal fistula which occurred could be amply provided for in the New York Hospital, and that the surgeons of the New York Hospital were as competent to treat this class of cases as was the man that was then attempting to found the new Woman's Hospital. The visit to Mrs. Doremus was a very violent one on the part of Dr. Watson. He was not at all politic; as a man, he was very dogmatic, very impatient of opposition, and the impression made on Mrs. Doremus was very unfavorable. So he left her, and she was more determined than ever to persevere with the good work that she had undertaken, if it were possible for it to succeed.

Dr. Gurdon Buck was a more moderate man, more politic, and had been not exactly the family physician to Mrs. Codwise, but on one occasion, when Mr. Codwise had had a carbuncle, or some other serious illness, had been called in consultation with Dr. Mott, as an operation was necessary to be performed. Thus the family had had an opportunity of knowing him personally very well, and they felt very grateful to him for the kind professional services he had rendered on a former occasion. His visit to Mrs. Codwise was longer than usual. He went on to praise the cause of the New York Hospital very extensively, and told her of the successful operations they were performing; but forgot to tell her that he owed the whole of it to me. This was a little oversight that I had before supplied on the occasion of one of my visits, and she understood the whole bearing of the question. She was a woman of the world, with large views on every subject, and was too polite to give offense to her visitor; but she had the firmness to tell him that, as first directress of the institution, she should give it the whole force of her influence.

The Woman's Hospital from the day it was opened had no friends among the leaders—among hospital men. I was called a quack and a humbug, and the hospital pronounced a fraud. Still it went on with its work. Its wards were open to any doctor that cared to come, and the operations performed there were seen by most of the leading medical men in the city, and many others from different parts of the country.

CHAPTER XVIII.

During the winter my health was tolerably good; but it was only by extraordinary care that it was kept so. I had to be very particular in my diet. I could eat no salt food, and even butter had to be deprived of its salt. I could eat no condiments, not a particle of pepper nor any vinegar; no fruits, and not a bit of sweetmeats. The least variation from this rigid diet would reproduce the diarrhœa. For six or eight months previous to this I had been in feeble health, and the sudden arresting of the diarrhœa produced dropsy of the lower extremities. In walking on the street, if I ever stumbled once, I would fall flat to the ground, with no power to rise. I well remember one day that I had gone down to Hartwell & Shepard's, in Maiden Lane, to make some purchases. In walking up Maiden Lane to Broadway I had a small parcel in my hand, or rather under my left arm. Under the old Howard House, which stood there at the time, there was a trunk store, opening on Maiden Lane. The merchant had a habit of putting his wares outside the door, and spreading them along on the curb-stone. There was a small valise on the curb-stone, which I did not see. I stumbled over it and fell literally into the gutter, with my face to the curb-stone, with my weight on my left arm, and the bundle under it. I floundered away, trying to get up, but I could not help myself. Presently a policeman stepped up to me and took me by the right hand and raised me up very gently, saying, as he did so, " I am surprised to see a man of your cloth (for I looked quite clerical) in the gutter so early in the day." I said, " I thank you, my dear fellow; but I am as sober as you are. I am a very sick man. I would thank you to help me into that Madison Avenue stage." He did so; but he was quite in earnest in his first supposition that I was drunk.

I have said that I went to see Mrs. Doremus on the fifth of February, 1855. My friend, Dr. Samuel W. Francis, had just lost his eldest son, of typhoid fever, while he was *interne* at Bellevue Hospital, and the dear old gentleman was nearly heart-broken. He resigned his membership in all the societies and all the public institutions to which he belonged, and gave himself up, temporarily, entirely to grief. He wished even to quit the medical practice. On that day, a gentleman living at the corner of Fifth Avenue and Twenty-ninth Street, and one of his old friends, sent for him to see his child who was very ill with the croup. Dr. Francis could not go out, and so told the gentleman to call me to his babe. I was just on the eve of starting down to see

.ͽ. Doremus, and made a hasty visit to the child and prescribed for it. I was twenty minutes behind my engagement. When I had gone from Madison Avenue to Fifth, along Twenty-ninth Street, there was some ice on the pavement. In returning from Fifth Avenue to Madison Avenue, and just opposite No. 12, where the street was covered with snow when I had gone by there ten or fifteen minutes before, the servant at No. 12 had cleaned off the snow, and had left a coating of ice on the stones. On my return I was walking very rapidly, and as I passed from the snow to the pavement my heels slipped and went out from under me, and I fell sprawling on my back, with such violence that it now seems to me that it would have killed me, had it not been for the rim of my stiff old-fashioned stove-pipe hat, which broke the fall.

The shock was very great. I was stunned for a moment, so that I did not know where I was. I climbed up on the steps and sat there a few minutes, and after a while I was seemingly all right again. I went home, at 89 Madison Avenue, which was just around the corner, and waited there till I thought I was completely recovered, and then made my visit to Mrs. Doremus, which I have already related. But a few days after this blow the diarrhœa returned. It increased in spite of all my remedies and dietetic precautions.

The Woman's Hospital was inaugurated at 83 Madison Avenue, on the first of May, 1855. For a month before I had been in bed almost all the time. I was very weak and exhausted, and the committee appointed to locate the rooms for the hospital chose the place they did because it was in close proximity to my house, with a view to saving me as much exertion as possible. At the inauguration of the hospital I was very feeble, but still I was determined to do the work. Very soon I commenced performing one operation a day. The hospital was full from the day that it was opened. We had about thirty beds. It was a charity; there were no " pay-patients " admitted. One clause of the by-laws provided that the assistant-surgeon should be a woman. I appointed Mrs. Browne, a widowed sister of my friend Henri L. Stuart, who had been so efficient in organizing the hospital. She was matron and general superintendent.

The hospital was kept open all summer, and I did what work I could; but I did not entirely recover from the diarrhœa until the autumn. The work was well and efficiently done, notwithstanding my bad health. Patients were applying, and coming from a distance, in larger numbers than could be accommodated. The hospital had been opened about six months, when I told the board of lady managers that I must have an assistant. They were glad to accommodate me, and told me to select the man that I wanted to assist me. When I first went to New York, Dr. Frank U. Johnson was the leading practitioner of the city, and, next to Dr. Francis, perhaps one of my best friends. He had a son, Dr. F. U. Johnson, Jr., who had just graduated. I offered him the appointment of assistant-surgeon to the hospital. He said that he would be very glad to accept it, but that he was soon to be married, and was going to locate in the country near Cooperstown. I then offered the place to Dr. George F. Shrady. He, too, was about to be married, and for some cause or other he did not see fit to accept it.

Soon after this, a young friend of mine at the South, whom I had known from her early girlhood, Miss Kate Duncan, was married to Dr. Thomas Addis Emmet, of New York. As I was looking for an assistant, I did not know that I could more handsomely recognize the friendship of former days than to appoint the husband of Mrs. Emmet as my assistant. So, to the accident of good fortune in marrying a beautiful Southern young woman, Dr. Emmet owes his appointment to a position which he has long and honorably filled in the Woman's Hospital.

The first anniversary of the Woman's Hospital was held at Clinton Hall, in Astor Place, on the —— day of January, 1856. From this time on the hospital flourished. As soon as the hospital was opened, the notices of the work done there brought me business to a great amount, and very soon my private consultation rooms were filled. Soon after the hospital was organized, on the 10th of February, notices of it were published in the newspapers, and the public began to know considerable of its object.

Twelve months had rolled around when the board of lady managers and working friends of the institution saw that it had been inaugurated at a most opportune moment, that it was an instrument for effecting an immense amount of good, and that the necessity for a larger institution was of prime importance. Then it was that steps were taken to get a charter from the State for the "Woman's Hospital of the State of New York." This new hospital was to be on a grand scale; it was to be under a board of governors, composed of twenty-seven of the leading men of the city, while the board of lady managers of the present working hospital were to be transferred to the new organization, when complete, as a board of lady supervisors, having the general control of its domestic affairs.

The charter of the Woman's Hospital was obtained in 1857. Hon. James Beekman was my chief adviser and coadjutor. I spent a great deal of time at Albany that winter, neglecting my private business very much, and leaving Dr. Emmet in charge of the hospital, and also in the care of some of my private business. I had to make frequent visits to Albany, to lobby and to hire help among the members of the Legislature, and, as a matter of course, my affairs at home were very much neglected. I recollect returning from Albany, and Dr. Emmet saying, "It seems to me that you are spending too much time in Albany. A larger hospital than the one we have is hardly necessary. It is rather a heroic undertaking, and it seems to me that you ought to be a little more selfish; for the present hospital is good enough for your purpose."

Of course I had larger views than this, and I said that I did not establish the hospital solely for money and aggrandizement. As soon as I saw the necessity for a greater one, with a larger board of surgeons, I was anxious to establish it. The hospital was unpopular, because it was a one-man power, and because all the advantages that accrued were to the surgeon and his assistant.

The most difficult thing I achieved, in connection with the founding of the Woman's Hospital, was the procuring of the land on which the building to-day stands. This land belonged to the city, being the old Potter's Field in time of the cholera in 1832. At that time the city could not alienate any of its domain without the consent of the Legislature. The Legislature had to pass an act authorizing the city to give away any of its property when it chose to do so. First, then, it was necessary to go before the Board of Aldermen, and get them to pass a resolution asking the Legislature to pass an act authorizing the city to make the asked-for transfer. This I accomplished, after a great deal of hard work and political wire-pulling; Dr. Mott, Dr. Francis, and even the dear old lady, Mrs. Doremus, besides Mr. Beekman, appearing before the Board of Aldermen, to testify as to the workings of the hospital, and as to the needs of a larger institution.

Mr. Beekman and myself, as soon as the ordinance was passed, went to the Legislature, and had that body pass the necessary act authorizing the city to give away the land to us. Then, with this authority, we came back to the city fathers, and they passed the ordinance deeding the land to us, which only awaited the signature of the mayor. It was passed on the very last day of the season, and the last day of the year (1856). It was the year in which Mayor Wood went out of office as mayor. He was busy that night, signing documents that were necessary to have his official signature before his term expired; and in the hurry of the moment the act giving the land to the Woman's Hospital failed to receive his official signature—not because he was opposed to it, for he was in favor of it, warmly in favor of it, but because, in the hurry of the hour, his secretary forgot to bring it to his notice. The work had thus to be done all over again.

A new Common Council came into power, and we had to get this new board to pass another ordinance, asking the Legislature to give the grant again. We had to go before the Legislature for a new act, which was passed after the same lobbying, and this was brought back to the city authorities, who then agreed to give us the title to the land. But Tiemann was now the mayor. Personally he was in favor of the Woman's Hospital; but on economic grounds was opposed to it, and hence vetoed the bill. I knew very well that I had influence enough in the Common Council to have the bill passed over his veto. He saw that I was about to do so, and he sent for me for a consultation in reference to it. He said:

"I want to have this land given to you; I believe in the Woman's Hospital, and I would like to see it firmly established on a grand scale. But there are so many people asking land from the city for various purposes, there is such a disposition to 'grab' and steal, that, on principle, I am obliged to oppose you in order to keep the others away. Now, if you will agree to give us fifty beds, forever, for the use of the city poor, I will agree that you shall have the property."

Of course, I acceded to it, telling him that if I were not able to give him fifty beds for the use of the city after the hospital was well established, it would be hardly worth the time I had bestowed upon it. Thus we got the title to the land on which the hospital was erected.

Full titles were obtained for the land in April, 1858. It was situated between Forty-ninth and Fiftieth Streets, and Lexington and Fourth Avenues, comprising a whole block. As before stated, it was the old Potter's Field during the time of the cholera in 1832. The west half was full of dead bodies, which had been buried in tiers of coffins eighteen deep. The president of the Board of Governors, Hon. James W. Beekman, got possession of the property, and obtained permission to remove the bodies. It took nearly all summer to accomplish it. Twenty-seven thousand bodies were removed from this piece of ground, less than two hundred feet square. They were neatly replaced in new wooden boxes, and then reburied on Ward's Island. It had been twenty-five years since they were buried. There was nothing offensive in the exhumation, and no sickness occurred among the men that were employed to do the work of removal and dis-interment. There was no necessity for disturbing the eastern half of the lot, where there were a few isolated graves only, the reason for this being that the solid rock came very near the surface at this portion of the block.

When the charter was obtained for the Woman's Hospital the Board of Governors had a meeting, selected an architect, and adopted a plan of the building. Mr. John W. Rich was selected as the architect, at the earnest solicitation of Mr. Robert B. Minturn. A goodly number of the Board of Governors were not satisfied with Mr. Rich; but still his nomination and election were pressed so strongly by Mr. Minturn that he was finally appointed. He drew the plans of the hospital, modeling it somewhat after St. Luke's. I was opposed to the plan and wanted them to adopt the pavilion system; but no decided change in the plans was made. In 1861, I went abroad for the first time. I should remark that after the autumn of 1855 I had no attack of diarrhœa, which had followed me from 1849 to 1855—just six years. I had recovered speedily from the attack that was brought on by the fall in the previous February, to which I have referred. After that time my health was reasonably good, and I had no return of the serious illness that for six years had stuck to me, off and on.

It was in June (1861) that I went abroad, because I needed a little holiday. I had worked very hard and was tired out; but I went more particularly to investi-

gate the hospital treatment in the Old World. The results of my investigation went to show the superiority
of the pavilion system over the block system. When I
returned home Mr. Rich was dead, and Mr. Harrison
had been selected to take his place as architect of the
hospital. He and I were in perfect accord as to the
plans which he drew, which I submitted to the Board of
Governors, and they were adopted.

CHAPTER XIX.

THE first point I touched when I went abroad was
Queenstown. I landed there on the 31st of August
(1861), and went at once to Dublin. There a hearty
welcome awaited me from my Irish brethren. I remained about ten days in Dublin, and was dined and
fêted to satiety. Dr. McClintock was then Master of
the Edinburgh Rotunda Hospital. He received me kindly, and introduced me to the leading members of the
profession. I was glad of an opportunity to see many
cases in the Rotunda Hospital. None welcomed me more
warmly in behalf of my work than the chief of obstetrics in all Ireland, Dr. Fleetwood Churchill. All were
anxious to see me perform my operations for vesico-
vaginal fistula; and after a while a case was found, on
which I operated with satisfaction to all present. I was
in Dublin about ten days; and every night I had to dine
with some of the leading men of the day. Once, I

was invited to a great dinner given by Dr. Stokes to
about twenty guests. Among the company was the
great Irish lawyer and member of Parliament, Mr. Butt.
He was one of the wittiest men I ever heard talk in all
my life. He kept the table in a roar of laughter all the
time, and I wondered how a man could have such an in-
exhaustible fund of anecdote as he had, which he told as
I know that no other man could have done. They were
a party of great eaters and great drinkers, and they were
very much surprised that I ate so little and drank nothing at all. They wanted to know if I were a typical
American, and representative of my country. I told
them that I was an anomaly—a *sui generis;* it was my
idiosyncrasy, and that I could as well have been an Irishman as an American, and that I deserved no credit for
my peculiarities and temperate methods of living.

In coming to Europe, the man that I most wanted to
see was Professor Simpson, of Edinburgh. His labors
and contributions to the literature of the day were the
most valuable that had been made to the growing science
of gynæcology. So, in leaving Dublin, I went by way
of Belfast to Edinburgh, where I was warmly welcomed
by Simpson, Syme, Christison, and Matthews Duncan.
Matthews Duncan was a pupil of Simpson, a young man
just married and laying for himself the foundation upon
which he has subsequently built such a magnificent professional career. I had performed many of Simpson's
operations; I was the first to operate according to his
method for dysmenorrhœa. He had represented the

operation as being attended with no danger. I had had serious hæmorrhages follow it—two of an alarming character—and I thought that possibly I did not perform the operation precisely as he did. So I was anxious to see as much of his practice as I could, and particularly one of his operations on the cervix uteri. Fortunately, he had a fitting subject for the operation in a young married woman, about thirty years old, who had come from India expressly to consult him. I saw that he performed the operation in theory only, but making a more profound sensation than I had ever done. Yet he insisted that he had never had a case of accident after this operation.

Christison, was then no longer a young man, but of wonderful endurance physically. I shall never forget his walking me to the top of Arthur's Seat and down again. I was awfully fatigued, but he did not seem to mind it in the least. I saw a great deal of Dr. Syme, and saw him operate repeatedly. I have seen, all over the world, great surgeons operate, in my own country, in London, and in Paris; but I have never seen such an operator as Dr. Syme. He was a man of remarkable diagnostic powers, infallible judgment, and was wonderfully rapid and precise in execution. All this was necessary before the introduction of anæsthetics. With the introduction of anæsthetics the rapid, brilliant operator has disappeared. Syme was rather reticent; but, somehow, he took a wonderful fancy to me. I was with him at his country-place frequently, dining with his family without ceremony. When I was about to take my leave for Aberdeen, I timidly, one day, while sitting in his office, asked Dr. Syme if he would have the kindness to give me a card of introduction to Professor Keith, of that city. He surprised me very much by saying, " I shall do no such thing." He looked up, to see how I would take it, for I was really surprised, and immediately finished his sentence by saying, " For a man that would not receive Marion Sims on the presentation of his own card would not receive him on the presentation of mine." However, he gave me the card of introduction smilingly.

When I got to Aberdeen, I was surprised to find that Simpson was not the god in his own country that he was abroad. When I told them of my accidents following his operation on the cervix uteri, and that he had none of the sort, they laughed at my credulity. They gave me the name of a doctor living not ten miles distant from that city, whose wife had been operated on by Dr. Simpson, and she died within forty-eight hours afterward. Of course, this surprised me exceedingly, and when I returned to Edinburgh I spoke to one of the eminent surgeons of the town, who was a friend of Dr. Simpson's, and not an enemy—for the doctors of that city seemed to be divided into two classes, those who were the friends of Dr. Simpson and those who were not—and this gentleman told me that he knew of one death following the operation, and that in Dr. Simpson's own hands.

I subsequently returned to Dublin, where I related what I had heard in regard to the dangers of the operations in Dr. Simpson's hands, and some of the doctors there said: "We did not tell you before you went to Edinburgh, for we saw that you had an exalted opinion of Dr. Simpson and his work, and that to such an extent that we were not disposed to spoil your ideal of the man." Then I was told of the case by Dr. McClintock himself: that he had sent, about four years before, a patient from the Isle of Man to Simpson for treatment; that the patient was operated on by him in his usual manner, and that she died in three or four days—whether from hæmorrhage, or from peritonitis, he never knew; but certainly death followed the operation. And yet Dr. Simpson claimed absolute immunity from any bad results in this operation.

Simpson was exceedingly anxious to see me operate for vesico-vaginal fistula. He had performed the operation two or three times himself, and was anxious to see my method of operating, but he had no patient for me. In London I was received as cordially as I was in Dublin or in Edinburgh. Spencer Wells, Henry Savage, Routh, and others of the Samaritan Hospital, all gave me a hearty and cordial welcome. I was called upon to operate on a case of vesico-vaginal fistula in the Samaritan Hospital. The case was a difficult one. The operation was satisfactorily done; but the patient died five or six days afterward. This was the first patient that I had ever lost by this operation, and I had performed it hundreds of times. The post-mortem examination revealed the fact that the ureters had been closed by the suture, and death resulted from kidney complication.

I arrived in Paris about the first of September (1861). I soon made the acquaintance of my friend Dr. Johnstone, who had long been a resident in Paris, though not then a practitioner of medicine. He was devoting himself to literary pursuits, as the well-known correspondent of the "New York Times," under the *nom de plume* of "Malakoff." He was an Ohio man, educated in New York, and went to Paris when he was quite a young man. Dr. Johnstone informed me that the operations associated with my name had never yet been successfully performed in Paris. Jobard de Lamballe had performed, or rather operated, over and over again, and had had public learned discussions on the subject; but nobody had ever seen any successful operations for vesico-vaginal fistula by him.

I was in Paris only a few days when Dr. Huguier of the Beaujon Hospital called and invited me to visit the hospital. I did not then speak a word of French. It was at Dr. Johnstone's suggestion that I was invited, I believe. Dr. Huguier was exceedingly anxious to see the operation, as Dr. Johnstone had informed him that the operation in my hands was uniformly successful, which he greatly doubted. He had a case of a fistula, just in the neck of the bladder, which I supposed was favorable for an operation; but it was not, for it had been operated upon previously by some one unsuccessfully.

On the day appointed for the operation, it was noised abroad among the doctors of all the hospitals that I was there, and about to perform an operation for Huguier. Drs. Nélatou, Denonvilliers, and other distinguished surgeons left their hospital services and came to the Beaujon to witness it. It was raining, and the light was very bad. I was then forty-eight years old, and I had never used spectacles for operation. But, with Dr. Nélaton's head between me and my patient, it was impossible for me to see without glasses, and so, for the first time, I put them on. Suffice it to say, the operation was performed to the satisfaction of Nélatou, Huguier, and all who witnessed it. At the end of a week the patient was cured, which was a great surprise to all of them, for they did not believe that the case was possibly curable.

A few days after this, Dr. Vernier kindly invited me to visit his ward at the St. Louis Hospital, where he had a case of vesico-vaginal fistula of enormous dimensions, and in which the base of the bladder was almost entirely destroyed. The fundus of the bladder was prolapsed through the fistula, and protruded externally from the body, thus inverting the bladder. This was supposed to be absolutely incurable; but, really, it was much easier to operate on, and a cure was much more certain, than in the case that I had operated on for Huguier. When that case was cured at the end of a week, it created a regular *furore* in the Paris hospital circles.

Very soon after this Professor Loquier, of the Hôtel Dieu, hearing of what had been done at the Beaujon, and

14

also at the St. Louis hospital, kindly invited me to come and perform an operation on a patient of his. Here I performed in the amphitheatre, in which Joubard de Lamballe had performed all his operations. I operated on a case which was supposed to be very difficult to cure—by any of the older methods it would have been impossible to cure. Suffice it to say that this operation was performed in the presence of distinguished surgeons and a large concourse of students, and in a week's time the patient was entirely cured. I had had three cases in succession, which greatly added to the interest in this new departure in surgery, and as a matter of course it was the theme of professional gossip of the day in that city.

Soon after this I was invited by Velpeau to go to La Charité and operate on a young woman, who had been the subject, so it was said, of seventeen previous operations by Joubard de Lamballe, all of which had resulted in failure. He had been able to reduce the size of the fistula about one half, but it was now large enough to pass the finger through easily into the cavity of the bladder. This was a great occasion. Velpeau was incredulous about the success of the operation, though he had been told that three cases had been operated on successfully. He stood at my back and carefully watched every step of the operation. There were many distinguished surgeons present, including Nélaton (one of the great surgeons of the day). Young Mr. Souchon, who was then a medical student in Paris, and a pupil of Vel-

peau. He was *interne* at La Charité. He translated to
Velpeau every step of the operation, although he could
see for himself. But when it was finished Velpeau took
me by the hand and thanked me very much. He said
he would watch the day of the taking out of the sutures
with a great deal of interest. I assured him that the
case would certainly be cured. He found the sutures at
the end of a week just as I had placed them. I was
called on for a history of vesico-vaginal fistula, and the
method of operating. I spoke in English, and my young
friend translated very rapidly in French. This was considered the highest triumph possible for me, being the
fourth successful operation in three or four weeks.

Soon after this operation, Dr. Deroubaix, surgeon to
King Leopold of Belgium, and the first surgeon in Brussels, came to Paris. He said he had heard a great deal
of what I had done in the hospitals of Paris in regard to
indoctrinating the profession for vesico-vaginal fistula,
and that he wished me to come to Brussels and demonstrate the operation in the hospitals there. I accepted
his invitation and went to Brussels a few days afterward.
I went into the hospital at nine o'clock in the morning,
and was operating until twelve at noon, or even later in
the day. I performed three operations that morning, to
illustrate the different varieties of this terrible infirmity.
The operations were satisfactorily done; but one of the
patients died about a week afterward. The post-mortem
showed that the operation was done satisfactorily and
was perfectly successful; but the nurse, in using the

catheter, had driven it through the posterior wall of the bladder around into the peritoneal cavity of the bladder, resulting in death—an accident which would not have happened in the hands of an ordinary nurse accustomed to such cases.

However, the doctors were so well pleased with the operations that they gave me a big dinner, and made speeches at me, not a word of which did I understand. They elected me a corresponding fellow of the Royal Academy of Medicine, and recommended my name to the Government for the Legion of Honor.

I then returned to Paris, intending to go to Vienna to show the operations there. I have forgotten to mention the fact that, about three or four years before I went to Paris, an American surgeon had gone there claiming to be the author of the operations for vesico-vaginal fistula. He gave me some credit in having initiated the work, but claimed for himself the honor of perfecting it. He even claimed my speculum and all the instruments as his own. He had set the blade of the speculum at a little more of an acute angle with the handle, and he had put an ivory handle to the tenaculum, instead of ebony. He used what was called a " button " for the fastening of the silver wire. He had operated only once in Paris. The operation was only a partial success; for very soon after the sutures were removed there was an absorption of the line of union, the fistula opening and the urine escaping. So his operations were pronounced a failure. Of course, there was

no enthusiasm over it, because he had not succeeded.
Nobody had been able to follow his method, or to cure
a single patient during the whole four years preceding
my advent in Paris.

I had now performed four operations, in four of the
most prominent hospitals in Paris, and before all the
leading surgeons of the city, and my work was the
theme of conversation among medical men everywhere.
Men attending the hospitals wrote to different parts of
the world, even to Russia and back to my own country,
about the work that I was doing in Paris.

Very soon after the operation for Velpeau, in La
Charité Hospital, Dr. Mungenier, who had taken a great
interest in me and my work, and who, with Dr. Johnstone had been prominent in introducing me to the
surgeons of hospitals, brought me a woman about forty
years old who had had a vesico-vaginal fistula for more
than twenty years. She had been seen and examined by
many of the leading surgeons of Paris, and pronounced
incurable. She had also been seen by the American
surgeon who preceded me in Paris three years previously, and who had refused to operate upon her. The
case was certainly a very bad one. The whole base of the
bladder was destroyed, the mouths of the ureters were
plainly visible, and the urine could be seen passing in
little spurts from these narrow openings. The bladder
was inverted and hung outside of the body, in a little
hernial mass as large as a child's fist. Her condition was
very deplorable, and my friend Dr. Mungenier was very

much surprised when I told him she could easily be cured by a single operation. He said, " But I can't get a bed for her in any hospital." I replied, " That makes no difference; I will take her to the Hôtel Voltaire and engage a room and will pay the expenses myself, just to show you that I can cure her."

He was very much surprised that I should be willing to do this, and then he said, "I can bring many of the leading surgeons from the different hospitals to see you operate if you will let me. I agreed to it, and the operation was performed at the Hôtel Voltaire on the 18th of October, 1861. I was greatly surprised to see what a number of leading physcians were not only willing, but anxious, to witness the operation in private practice. Among them were Nélaton, Velpeau, Civiale, Baron Larrey, Sir Joseph Oilliffe, Campbell, Huguier, and others of the most distinguished men of Paris, numbering to about seventeen or eighteen. Dr. Johnstone gave the anæsthetic. The operation required about an hour; the fistula was closed to the satisfaction of everybody present. In one week's time the sutures, twelve in number, were removed and the patient was found perfectly cured.

As a matter of course, these five successful operations in three or four weeks in the great city of Paris, created a *furore* among the profession in regard to the curability of an affection which they had until now supposed to be totally incurable.

Having thus demonstrated clearly the principles and

success of the operation in the hospitals of Paris, I was on the eve of going to Vienna to do something in that city, when Dr. Campbell, the great *accoucheur* of Paris, told Dr. Nélaton that I was about to leave. Dr. Néla-ton asked Dr. Campbell to see me and beg me to remain for a few days, till he could go for a patient to come to me from the south of France. The patient had been seen six or eight months previous, and pronounced perfectly incurable. "But," said he to Dr. Campbell, " since I have witnessed what I have in the hands of Dr. Sims, and since I have heard of the success attending his operations in other hospitals, I think that he can cure almost any case of the sort. I am anxious to get his opinion in the case of this lady, who belongs to the higher walks of life." Of course I was too good a tac-tician to let such an opportunity as this pass without im-proving it, and I immediately sent word that I would await the arrival of his patient from the country. I did not get to Vienna at all, as a consequence.

His patient arrived in due time. She was about twenty-one. She had been delivered two years before. The child had *hydrocephalus*, the pressure of its enor-mous head produced a sloughing of the soft parts of the mother, which resulted in, seemingly, a total destruction of the base of the bladder. She was young, beautiful, rich, accomplished; and, as Dr. Nélaton had told her six months before that she was absolutely incurable, she was praying for death, but in vain, for patients seldom die of afflictions of this kind. In all my experience I have never seen a case of this kind which was attended with such extreme suffering. The constant discharge of the urine had created an inflammation and excoriation of the external parts with which it came in contact, in some places producing sloughings as large as a pea. It looked like localized small-pox. She was obliged to take anodynes in large quantities to relieve the burning pain attendant upon her sufferings. She passed sleepless nights and restless days, and was altogether one of the most unhappy women I have ever seen.

On examination of the case I saw that it was exceedingly difficult. At first I was almost disposed to say it was incurable, but after a more thorough investigation I said to Dr. Nélaton that I was sure she could be cured; that it would require a little preparatory operation which would take a week or ten days, and the radical operation would be performed afterward, and I was convinced she could be restored perfectly. I went on to explain to him how the operation was to be done, thinking as a matter of course that he simply wanted my opinion on the question. He heard me patiently and said, " I understand everything that you say, but I don't feel competent to do the work. I have not the experience nor the skill of manipulation that you possess, and, if you will kindly take charge of my patient and perform this operation in my stead, I shall be greatly obliged to you." As a matter of course I accepted the case, which prevented me from making my proposed visit to Vienna.

The first operation, as I had indicated to Dr. Nélaton,

was performed in the country, and in two weeks afterward the radical operation was performed at St. Germain, an hour's distance from Paris. Dr. Nélaton, Dr. Johnstone, Dr. Campbell, Dr. Beylard and Dr. Alan Herbert were my assistants.

Dr. Campbell was the great *accoucheur* of Paris at that time. He was in the habit of giving chloroform to his patients in labor, and was selected by the family to give the chloroform because of his known reputation in using it. The operation was begun at ten o'clock in the morning of the 19th of December, 1861, Dr. Nélatou sitting by and watching every stage of it with the greatest attention. At the end of about forty minutes all the sutures were introduced and ready to be secured. Just at this time I discovered a certain amount of lividity in the mucous surfaces, and I called Dr. Nélaton's and Dr. Johnstone's attention to it, and said, "It seems to me the blood is stagnating." I asked Dr. Campbell if the pulse and respiration were all right; he said "Yes, all right; go on." Scarcely were these words uttered when he suddenly cried out, "Stop! Stop! No pulse, no breathing." And sure enough the patient looked as if she was dead. Dr. Nélaton was not in the least disconcerted. He quietly ordered the head to be lowered and the body to be inverted, that is, the head to hang down while the heels were raised in the air by Dr. Johnstone, the legs resting one on each of his shoulders. Dr. Campbell supported the thorax, Dr. Herbert went to an adjoining room for a spoon with the handle of which

the jaws were forced open, and I handed Dr. Nélaton
the tenaculum, which he hooked in the tongue, pulling
it out between the teeth, and gave it in charge of Dr.
Herbert, while Dr. Beylard was assigned to the duty of
making efforts at artificial respiration. Dr. Nélaton ordered and overlooked every movement. They held the
patient in this inverted position for a long time, making
artificial respiration, before there was any manifestation
of returning life. Dr. Campbell, who published an account of the case subsequently, said in his report that it
was fifteen minutes, and that it seemed an age. My
notes of the case, written a few hours afterward, make
it twenty minutes that the patient was held in this position. Be this as it may, the time was so long that I
thought it useless to make any further efforts, and I said,
"Dr. Nélaton, our patient is dead, and you might as
well stop all efforts." But Dr. Nélaton never lost hope,
and by his quiet, cool, brave manner he seemed to infuse
his spirit into his assistants. At last there was a feeble
inspiration, and after a long time another, and by and
by another; and then the breathing became regular.
When the pulse and respiration were well re-established,
Dr. Nélaton ordered the patient to be laid on the table.
This was done very gently, but the moment the body
was placed horizontally the pulse and breathing instantly
ceased. Quick as thought the body was again inverted,
the head downward and the feet over Dr. Johnston's
shoulders, and the same manœuvres as before were put
into execution. Dr. Campbell thinks it did not take

such a long time to re-establish the action of the lungs and heart as in the first instance, but it seemed to me to be quite as long, for the same painful, protracted and anxious efforts were made as before. Feeble signs of returning life eventually made their appearance. Respiration was at first irregular and at long intervals; soon it became more regular, and the pulse could then be counted, but it was very feeble and intermittent. When they thought she had quite recovered they laid her horizontally on the table again, saying "She's all right this time."

But the moment the body was placed in a horizontal position the respiration ceased a third time, the pulse was gone, and she looked the picture of death. But Dr. Nélaton and his assistants, by a simultaneous effort, quickly inverted the body a third time, with a view of throwing all the blood possible to the brain, and again they began their efforts at artificial respiration. It seemed to me that she would never breathe again, but at last there was a spasmodic gasp, and after a long time another, and after another long interval there was a third, and then a fourth more profoundly; there was then a long yawn, and the respiration after this became tolerably regular. She was held in a vertical position until she in a manner became semi-conscious, opened her eyes, looked wildly around, and asked what was the matter. She was then, and not until then, laid on the table, and we all thanked Dr. Nélaton for having saved the life of this lovely woman. In a few minutes more the operation was finished, but of course without any more chloroform. The sutures were quickly assorted and separately secured, and the patient put to bed. On the eighth day thereafter I had the happiness to remove the sutures, in the presence of Dr. Nélaton, and to show him the success of the operation.

I have detailed the circumstances of this interesting case at great length, because I believe it goes as far to establish the proper method of resuscitation from chloroform narcosis as anything possibly can. If the recovery had been complete and perfect with the first effort at reversing the body, there might have been a doubt whether the vertical position was really the cause of resuscitation ; but when the horizontal position was again and again followed by the cessation of all signs of life, and when life was again and again re-established by a process that favored the gravitation of the blood, poisoned as it was with chloroform, to the brain, the inference is very clear that death in such cases is due to syncope or cerebral anæmia.

Some years ago there was a story current in Paris that Dr. Nélaton had derived the hint of reversing the body in chloroform poisoning from a discovery accidentally made by his little boy, then some seven or eight years old—that his little son had killed some mice with chloroform, and without thought or reason he had taken up a dead mouse by the tail and was twirling it around, when to his surprise, it begun to manifest signs of life, and soon recovered entirely, while the mice left lying were dead; and that the great surgeon was thus taught an important lesson by his little boy. This is a very pretty story, and it seems a pity to spoil it, but lately when in Paris I called to see young Nélatou, who is now a doctor of medicine, and I asked him for the facts of the mouse story. He said that when they lived on the Quai Voltaire the house was infested with mice; that great numbers were caught in traps almost daily; that he was in the habit of killing them with chloroform, by covering the trap with a napkin and pouring the chloroform on it, and that his only idea was that of its being an easy death for the mice. One day, when he had given a happy dispatch to some mice, his father happened to come into the room, and seeing the dead mice he told his son that, if he would take up one by the tail and hold it with the head downward, it would revive, while the others that were permitted to keep the recumbent position would not. He did this and found it was true; and he told me that he had when a boy performed this experiment on mice some forty or fifty times or more, and always with the same unvarying result. He says that he has often heard his father speak not only of the case that occurred at St. Germain, but of other cases that he had saved before the time of the mouse story, which dates back to 1857.

In America *accoucheurs* use chloroform and surgeons mostly ether. I believe there has not as yet been a single death from chloroform administered during labor, while deaths from it in general surgery occur constantly, and for unimportant operations. There must be a reason for this. I believe it can be explained only on the theory that death from chloroform is due to syncope or cerebral anæmia. Now, we know that in active labor there can be no cerebral anæmia, for every pain throws the blood violently to the brain, producing fullness and congestion of the blood-vessels, thereby counteracting the tendency of the chloroform to produce a contrary condition. It may be said that the recumbent position has some influence in determining the safety of chloroform in labor; and so it has.

Chloroform given intermittingly is thought to be less dangerous, but patients in labor are often kept for hours under its influence with impunity, and occasionally it is necessary to produce complete and profound narcosis in some obstetrical operations; and yet I believe I can safely repeat what I have already said, that no woman has yet died in labor from the effects of this anæsthetic. In puerperal convulsions, where the brain is believed to be overcharged with blood, and that, too, when the blood is known to be poisoned by urea, we formerly bled the patient, and we do so now, but one of our chief remedies is chloroform, which acts by resisting spasmodic movements and by producing that very state of cerebral anæmia so necessary to a successful result. Whether puerperal convulsions are less frequent in labors under chloroform than in those without it, I do not know. I believe that obstetricians may take lessons from Nélaton's method of resuscitation.

We should not be satisfied with simply placing the head low, but, in addition to the means usually adopted, we should invert the body and throw what little blood there is left in it wholly to the brain. Whether death from chloroform is due to cerebral anæmia or not, it is safe to adopt Nélaton's method in all cases of supposed or threatened danger; and I think the safest plan is to relinquish the use of chloroform altogether except in obstetrics. The frequent cases of death from the use of chloroform in surgical operations that have occurred among us, even of late, should warn us to give up this dangerous agency, if we can find another that is as efficient and at the same time free from danger. Ether fulfills this requisite to a remarkable degree; but, while it is safe, it is offensive to the physician and bystanders, as well as to the patient. Chloroform is delicious and dangerous; ether is disagreeable and safe in purely surgical cases. Since the publication of Dr. Nélaton's method of resuscitation from chloroform narcosis, many valuable lives have been saved by it in different parts of my own country and elsewhere in the world.

CHAPTER XX.

Soon after Dr. Nélaton's case was cured I returned to America, sailing from Queenstown on the Inman steamer Kangaroo, on the 25th of December, 1861, and arriving in New York on the 11th of January, 1862, after a stormy passage of seventeen days. When I left home in July previously, we were marshaling forces North and South for battle. On my arrival in Europe we heard of the battle of Bull Run. On my return, in the following January, I was obliged to provide myself with a passport to come into my own country. When I got home I found that we were in the very midst of a great civil war, and I was so unhappy by the state of affairs then existing that I made up my mind to take my family abroad, and we sailed from New York on the Great Eastern on July 18th, 1862.

My programme was to establish my family in Paris, and I thought I would remain there six months in the year, in the summer time, and then return home for six months to practice my profession to make money to support them. I was so sure of coming back again to America in the autumn that I had paid for a return ticket in advance on the Great Eastern; but, as soon as I got to Paris, I found that the work I had done there the summer before in the hospitals and for Dr. Nélaton, had given me so much reputation, that I had no trouble at all in getting business enough to support my family, without the necessity of returning to New York for that purpose. Sir Joseph Olliffe was my great friend, and through him I was called in consultation to some of the highest personages in the land. Thus I was detained abroad quite unexpectedly; but viewing the political condition of the country and the disturbed state of affairs, I easily resigned myself to the force of circumstances and remained abroad, thinking every year that I would return.

Through Sir Joseph Olliffe, I became physician to the Duchess of Hamilton, who was then very ill, and in 1863 I went with her to Baden-Baden to spend the summer. She gave me a beautiful château to live in, ready furnished, one which had never before been occupied by any but royalty; and here I took up my abode for the summer.

When I went abroad I thought I would occupy my leisure moments in writing my work on the Accidents of Parturition, and, as I knew I was to spend the summer at Baden-Baden, I took all my material, manuscript and drawings, for the purpose of writing the proposed book. About the middle of June, 1863, I began it. I had piles of manuscript and piles of illustrations, and commenced classifying and arranging the material, working very hard for two days. The weather was excessively hot and exhausting, and at last I said to myself, " This work is too heavy ; I am not equal to the task during such extremely hot weather. I will lay it aside until the autumn, and then I will set to work in earnest to write my great work," which I hoped and expected would send my name down to posterity. And then, said I, " Between now and October I will occupy my time in writing a pamphlet on the subject of sterility. I don't know a great deal about it, but I know more than anybody else, and I am sure that a pamphlet on this subject will be welcomed by the profession everywhere." With this intention I dismissed the heavy work and commenced the lighter one of writing a pamphlet. I went on with the subject, and instead of its ending in a pamphlet form it became a book on all the diseases of women, leaving out the subjects of ovariotomy and the accidents of parturition, but embracing everything else in the department of gynæcology. This book was entitled " Clinical Notes on Uterine Surgery." It was so radical and revolutionary in all the methods adopted, and so startling in the results claimed in the treatment of many affections, that the profession did not at first readily accept its teachings, but in a few years it completely revolutionized the subject of gynæcology, and even now it is received everywhere as authority. Before that time there was not a professorship of gynæcology, worthy of the name, connected with any of our medical schools, and now we have professorships of this department in every medical school in the country, and, indeed, throughout the civilized world.

I have always said this book was a mere accident; that I never intended to write it. The book that I went to Baden-Baden to write has not yet been written.

While at Baden-Baden, the Duke of Hamilton went with his friend Lord Howard one night to the opera. After the opera they went to the Maison Dorée, as is the custom in Paris, for a supper. Between one and two o'clock they left the Maison Dorée to return to their hotel, and the duke, as he started down the stairs, tripped and fell a distance of twenty feet, head foremost, turning in his fall so as to strike the back of his head on the floor at the bottom of the stairs. He was taken up insensible, and carried to the Hôtel Bristol, and immediately a telegram was sent to the duchess at Baden-Baden. Although she was very ill, she at once undertook the trip back to Paris, and I accompanied her with the family. On arriving in Paris, the duke was still unconscious and remained in that condition for several days, when he died, without having recognized any member of his family. The Duke of Hamilton was a handsome man of the Byronic order. He was a handsome likeness of Lord Byron, and his whole life was Byronic, but unpoetical.

It was at the Hôtel Bristol that I was presented to the Empress Eugénie. She came every day to see the duke, and I was surprised and delighted to see her efficiency as a nurse, to see her gentleness and kindness, and skill, and management, in giving directions for the comfort of the poor insensible duke. When the duke died, the emperor sent his remains to Scotland in a ship of war. The empress invited the duchess and the Lady Mary Hamilton to go to St. Cloud, where she was spending the summer. This was about the 6th of July, 1863. On the 5th of April, 1863, the emperor, having heard of my work in Paris, sent for me to consult me about the empress's health. I arrived at the appointed time and found his majesty waiting. I sat and talked with him about half an hour, about the political affairs of my own country as well as about the empress's health. He spoke in the tenderest and most affectionate terms of the memory of his mother; told me how she had suffered in the last days of her life; of the manner of her death, and how anxious he was about the empress's health; and he said that her majesty would send for me in a day or two for a consultation. I supposed when I went to see him that I would feel a little embarrassed, but his manner was so gentle and kind that I really forgot that I was talking to the emperor, and after I left I was mortified at remembering that I had never once said " Sire," in addressing him. He spoke remarkably good English, with a slight German accent.

The day after my visit to the emperor, the empress was taken with diphtheria, and I was disappointed in not seeing her at the time that I expected. She was confined to the house for about a month, and was not able to go out a great deal until she went to St. Cloud, about the

1st of June. The day after the duchess went to St. Cloud I was sent for, and installed in the palace, to be near her, and render her any professional services she might need, and she needed a deal of care. While there I saw a great deal of the empress. I was the guest of the Duke de Bassano, who was the lord chamberlain of the empress. The Duke de Bassano spoke very good English, and so did all the members of his family. There was no formality at St. Cloud. The emperor was at Vichy. The first day of my arrival, when I was sent for to come to dinner, I was told it was not necessary to appear in a dress-coat. At the Duke de Bassano's table there were about fifteen persons present, ladies-in-waiting at the court, and gentlemen-in-waiting. I did not speak a word of French at that time.

I remained at St. Cloud a fortnight. During that time I had the professional supervision of the empress's health; saw her every day and every evening. Just before breakfast, and dinner, the guests of the Duke de Bassano, the ladies- and gentlemen-in-waiting, would arrange themselves in a drawing-room adjoining the dining-room of the duke, and the empress would come in and have a pleasant word to say to every one, a bow and a smile for each, and pass along to her own dining-room, which was in a different part of the pavilion, where she dined with the Duchess of Hamilton, her daughter Lady Mary, and the prince imperial. The prince imperial was then about seven years old. After the empress had passed on to her own dining-room, then the party of the Duke de Bassano followed, and filed off to one side into his dining-room. Almost every afternoon we would get in carriages and drive in one direction or another. Occasionally we would sit under the shadows of the trees, or in the porticoes of the palace, and engage in lively conversation.

I remember one evening, when the sun was about an hour high, the carriages were driven up, the empress, and the Duchess of Hamilton and her daughter, and a lady-in-waiting, were in one carriage, and the other ladies and gentlemen were in three or four others. I had been invited to take a seat with two ladies and a gentleman in an open phaeton, and, just as I got into the phaeton, the empress, whose carriage was twenty steps distant, cried out, "O doctor, we are going to take a long drive this evening; we are going to Versailles, and we shall not get back before nine o'clock. It may be cool in the evening, although it is hot now, and you had better run up-stairs and get your overcoat." I mention this to show how thoughtful and considerate she was of the comfort of everybody around her. She was beloved—idolized, as it were—by all her household, and all the court circle, and by everybody that came in contact with her. I knew the nurse very well that was with her when the prince imperial was born. The empress was very ill, and she was bed-ridden for a long time, and I have heard the nurse say that she had never heard her say a cross or disagreeable word, or complain of anything, during the whole of this long illness. I have sat at the table night after night, for two and three hours at a time, and heard the empress and the Duchess of Hamilton talk upon every imaginable subject. I was amazed at the profundity and the universality of her knowledge. We talked of science, of politics, of religion, of philosophy, of art: no subject escaped her, and I was very much surprised to see how much she knew of individuals, of persons that she never had seen, and even of the scandals of the day. The Duchess of Hamilton remained here about three weeks, and then returned to Baden, and I went with her, and remained there until the month of October, when I returned to Paris, and took up my abode in the Rue de Surène, where I resided in 1864, and part of 1865.

I had been now in Paris two years and was making a very comfortable living. So far as that was concerned I was perfectly satisfied. I was one of those benighted southerners who thought that the war between the States would necessarily result in a dissolution of the Union. After Mr. Lincoln was re-elected president, I said to myself, that prolongs the war for another four years. I made up my mind not to return to New York until the war should be ended; but if it should last through another administration I could not afford to remain in Paris and educate my children under such circumstances as to unfit them for the duties of life at home; and as I felt confident that the war would be prolonged for another four years I determined to remove to London. I went to London and took the advice of some of my friends there, and among them Mr. Ernest Hart, who said that he thought there was a field for me; that my name was well known to the profession throughout the country, and that, if I would contribute to the medical journals some original articles on my peculiar methods of operating, etc., he thought it would attract sufficient attention.

France has produced many great surgeons, but I presume that Trousseau was the most distinguished physician she has ever had. Some years ago, at one of the anniversaries of the Woman's Hospital, the Rev. Dr. Adams made an address to the board of lady managers, and, mentioning the handsome things said of the hospital and its management, he alluded to my labor, saying, "When I go through these halls, and see the numbers of sick women who have been restored to health by the marvelous skill of your surgeon, after long years of suffering and sorrow, I feel sure that he ought to be the happiest man in the world." I saw Dr. Adams a few days after this and thanked him for his kind words, and said: "Your conclusion that I was one of the happiest men in the world was correct, but your premises were not. I am one of the happiest men in the world, but it is not because I cure these poor people who would never have been cured but for my labors and my

discoveries and inventions. It is because I am happy at
home." And I illustrated this by telling him of the
great Trousseau, one of the greatest physicians of the
age, a man endowed with physical beauty as well as fine
intellect, the philosophic physician, the classical *littéra-
teur*, the elegant teacher, the successful practitioner. He
was without a rival. I had never known such a grand
man who was purely a physician; and yet he was a very
miserable man, and why? Had he not reached the
highest distinction in his profession? Had he not the
largest following of students at the Hôtel Dieu? Was
he not exhibited as the highest authority in medicine
all over the world? His lectures were translated into
all languages; he was read and esteemed as much in
England and America as in France and elsewhere on
the Continent; and then he was the leading practitioner, the great consultant, the fashionable doctor in
Paris, and had accumulated a large fortune. Everybody
spoke well of him; everybody admired him as a man;
his private character was above all reproach; he had
no children whom he could not recognize as his own,
as unfortunately too often is seen in Paris among the
highest classes. As the world saw the man, they had
the right to think and to say that he ought to be one
of the happiest of men. True, he was not court physician. Smaller men, men far inferior to him in every
point of view, occupied this high position, but every
other ambition of his life had been fully gratified; and
yet he was unhappy, and why? His wife was an ele-

15

gant and accomplished woman, of great beauty and fine intellect, but they were separated. He had a daughter, one of the most beautiful women in Paris, who married a man too much her senior. They were incompatible and separated. He had an only son, who was a scape-grace. He was a gambler and everything else that was bad. His father was worried to death with his dissoluteness and foolish extravagance, and had to pay enormous sums of money to extricate him from his disgraceful orgies and gambling complications. He was married to a fine woman, who ought to have made any man happy, but he neglected and made her miserable. How, then, could the great, the good Trousseau have been happy with such unhappy family surroundings? No! rest assured if there is any real happiness in this world it must be in the home, in the family circle, and not alone in public applause.

In October, 1863, I was in attendance on Mrs. ——, daughter of Mr. W. W. Corcoran, the banker-philanthropist of Washington. She had a long, serious illness, and I called Trousseau and my friend Sir Joseph Olliffe in consultation. Trousseau, unlike most French doctors, was always punctual to the minute. Sir Joseph and myself, who were united in our admiration of the man, always asked him to appoint an hour of the next day to suit his convenience. On one occasion he said, "Well, gentlemen, I shall have the pleasure of meeting you to-morrow at thirteen minutes after four." We accepted the hour, but I thought to myself a Yankee or New

York man would have said ten or fifteen minutes after four and not thirteen. The next day I observed closely, and sure enough Trousseau was exactly on time. I afterward took the liberty of asking him why he appointed the consultation at thirteen instead of fifteen minutes after four. He took it in good part and said, "Well, I knew I would leave my office at such an hour for such a place; that I would surely get through my consultation there at four, and that it would take my coachman less than fifteen minutes and more than ten minutes to drive here. Indeed, I knew it would take just thirteen minutes, as I had several times timed him, and so I made the appointment accordingly and not from any affected eccentricity. Time is too precious to be wasted, and two minutes here and there, when added together, are often of much value in our work." With all Trousseau's grand qualities of head and heart he had also his little weaknesses.

In September, 1861, I met the Stewart family, of Mobile, in Paris. There were many Southern refugees there during our great civil war. Mrs. Stewart had a severe attack of bronchitis and asked me to prescribe for her. She was at the Hôtel Vendôme. I said, "It is better to send for some physician who is familiar with the endemic condition of the climate. Send for the best; send for Trousseau." "But," said Mrs. Stewart, "I would like to do so but he is such a great man, and so busy, I fear he would not respond to a stranger at a hotel." I said, "I will go for him myself, and I am sure he will come and see you." So I went. He then lived in the Rue Basse-du-Rempart. His consulting rooms were crowded by fashionable, well-dressed people. I sent in my card and he saw me at once. I told him my message, and he went to see Mrs. Stewart at the hour appointed. He examined her closely, auscultated her lungs, and said she was not seriously ill, that she was undergoing a climatizing process, which would run its course in a few days, that it could not be cut short, but would terminate at such and such a period. In the mean time he would look in on her in two or three days, to see what progress she was making, and guard her against any accidental complications, which possibly might arise, but which he did not anticipate; and he ended by writing an order for asses' milk, "which is to be sent to 12 Rue de Surène; and he said that the asses would be driven to the door of the hotel to-morrow morning at seven o'clock, and that she must drink a pint of the milk warm at breakfast. With this he rose to leave, and Mrs. Stewart bade him good-by, with thanks for his kindly courtesy, and laid the fee in his hand. At this moment Mrs. Stewart's youngest daughter, about eight or nine years old, a charming little spoiled child, who was very anxious about her sick mother, ran up to the doctor and caught him by the hand, and said, "Doctor, ain't you going to give my mamma any medicine; nothing but asses' milk?" "No, no, my child; nothing else; your mother needs no medicine." "Why, I never saw such a doctor, a doctor like you. I thought you were such a great doctor you would give my mother some medicine and cure her quick. I never heard of a doctor just giving asses' milk and nothing but asses' milk. That ain't going to cure her." The great man's pride was doubly wounded by this persistent little child, who dared to assault his dignity and to question his skill; and he pushed her away gently and walked off, evidently much hurt by this little American *enfant terrible*. Trousseau did not return to see Mrs. Stewart. She sent for him two or three days afterward, but he didn't respond to the call. He doubtless justified his conscience from the knowledge that she was suffering from a malady that would run its course without endangering her life.

In the autumn of 1866 it was known that Trousseau's health was failing. On New-Year's day, 1867, his friend, Sir Joseph Olliffe, went to see him, and found him very much changed. He said, "Sir Joseph, I have carcinoma of the pylorus, and of course my days are numbered. I can now take nothing but milk. It is now a war between waste and supply, and I have been making a calculation of the probable time of the end, and I think I shall last until about the 20th of June." He died within a week or ten days of this date. He was a philosopher and died like one, but how embittered must have been his last days. He had not seen his son for a long time before he died. About a fortnight or three weeks before this event his son went to one of the gambling hells of Paris and lost all his money, and more than he could pay besides. He became desperate, rushed madly from the scene of disaster determined to end his miserable exist. ence; but, on second thought, he concluded, when he got into the cool way of the Place de la Concorde, to write parting lines to his wife and mother. On reaching his apartment he accordingly wrote to each that he had been unworthy of them, and that he would be no more by the time they received his notes. They naturally supposed that he had committed suicide. His poor father died soon after this, and his unworthy son saw a notice of his death in a London paper the next day; and I saw the tall, handsome, wretched man bending heart-broken over his great father's coffin in the Madeleine, whence he followed it to its final resting-place in the Père Lachaise. We are happy or unhappy in this life, as our children choose to make us. The joys, amenities, and pleasures of home, with health, make life worth living. But these must abound and be enjoyed by all who come in contact with us. We must not only be happy in our own homes, but must do all the good we can outside of these and try to make others happy too.

CHAPTER XXI.

DUBLIN, *August 18, 1861.*

Here I am again in my beloved Dublin. The Social Science Congress is in session, under the presidency of Mr. Brigham, and yesterday afternoon all its members were invited out to Phœnix Park and entertained at the Zoölogical Gardens. About five o'clock P. M. Pratt and I were sauntering along one of the graded walks of the beautiful garden, when who should meet us but my old friend Sir William Wilde, the great oculist of that day and time. He was not expecting to see me. He stopped suddenly, letting drop the lady's arm that was leaning on his, and raising both hands aloft he exclaimed, "Why, my dear fellow, is that you, you great unshaved humbug!" (I had not shaved, true enough, that day.) "Where did you come from ? Well, well, come and dine with us this evening." "At what hour ?" said I. "At six o'clock, sharp six." Looking at my watch and seeing it was only forty-five minutes from that moment, I said, "My dear sir, that would be impossible. I would be most happy to do so, but I have not time to go to the hotel and fix up and put on a dress-coat." "But," said he, "who the devil cares about the coat? It is you that I want, and as for your coat you may pull it off and hang it on the back of the chair; and you may turn your breeches wrong side out if you will, but I must insist on your wearing them." So he invited Dr. Pratt to go with us, and we arrived there a few minutes after the appointed time. After dinner we all went to the reception given by the president of the Royal Irish Academy to the Social Science Congress in the halls of the Irish Academy. There was a perfect jam. Everybody was there. Lady Wilde turned over a young widow to me and a young lady to Dr. Pratt. The widow and myself got along famously, but Tom and his partner were not very sympathetic. She was a strong-minded woman, who was devising ways and means of elevating her sex, opening up new channels of occupation for young unmarried women; a radical in politics, pitching into slavery particularly, and wishing to reform the world generally. And poor Dr. Pratt had to stick to her the whole evening. She paraded him up and down, and when he, too, had on a pair of boots that pinched his toes unmercifully. He tried to seat her, but she would not be seated. They were generally close to the widow and myself, and the young lady and myself occasionally had a cut and thrust. On one occasion she was wondering at my youthful appearance. I insisted that I was but thirty. She said, "You must have been married very young." "Oh no, not very; I

was twenty-four," said I. "How old was your wife?"
"She was nearly twenty-one years, quite old enough to
get married. "But," she said, "young ladies very often
marry much younger in America." I said, "Yes, often
as young as seventeen or eighteen." "Still," she replied,
"they grow after marriage." I said in the most innocent
way imaginable, "You would be surprised to see how
some of them grow in the course of one short year."
Just at this moment Sir William came rushing up and
hurried me off to the lord-lieutenant, as everybody calls
him. He is a courtly-looking gentleman, about fifty-five
or six. On being introduced, I found myself trying to
bow as much in the stiff Northern style as I possibly
could, but the princely old fellow took the starch out of
me at once, for he held out his hand and shook mine in
the most cordial Southern way. . . .

On Monday we went to the Social Science Congress
meeting, and saw and heard Lord Brougham and others,
and at night we went to a reception given by the lord-
lieutenant in Dublin Castle. It was a grand affair.
The enormous suites of apartments, corridors, etc, were
filled with well-dressed gentry, with now and then a
sprinkling of nobility, but the latter could not be distinguished from the former unless pointed out by some one
who knew. The lord-mayor was there, wearing his in-
signia of office, a massive gold chain as large as the little
finger, around the neck. It is external to the coat and is
passed around three times and looks at a little distance
nearly as wide as the hand. The Earl of Carlisle, the

lord-lieutenant, who gave the entertainment, had hanging from his neck some sort of ornament two or three
inches in diameter which was a mass of diamonds.   I
didn't notice it until the lady who accompanied me called
my attention to it after he passed.   On being introduced
to him, he said, " O, I remember you very well, Dr.
Sims, having seen you on Saturday evening at the
Academy."   He is the man for the place.   He has a kind
word for everybody and makes everybody feel easy.   As
he moved off, being pushed on by the crowd that was
pressing behind, he called out, "You are going in the
right direction if you wish to see the Yankees."   I did
not understand his meaning, but it was explained when I
met some familiar looking, close fitting caps and straight
jackets.   After we had passed a little distance the widow
said, " You must be, I am sure, a very distinguished man,
if I may judge from the lord-lieutenant's kind reception of you."   I told her, " He remembers me by the
brief conversation last Saturday night on the subject of
the distracted state of my country."   I tell you all these
little things because I know you are more interested in
my personal adventures and experiences than in any en-
cyclopedian account of cities, rivers, mountains, statues,
etc.   Lords and ladies look at home much the same as
any of us.   The Earl of Carlisle is very prepossessing in
appearance and manner.   The lower part of his face is
not handsome ; the upper is.   He is graceful and affable,
and is said to be very large-hearted.   Lord Brougham is
one of the most remarkable men now living in the king-

dom. He is eighty-two years old, and is the perfect counterpart of old Father Bears and the Rev. Mr. Bangs, of the Methodist Church. Lord Talbot de Mahilide looks like a good Southern planter.

To go back to the widow and the party. We had a very pleasant evening. She pointed out to me the dignitaries and magnates, and occasionally showed me some good-looking fellow that she had jilted because she could not help it. She married an old man for his money, who died in good time and left her eight hundred a year. Eight hundred a year is no mean sum here. One of my doctor friends tapped me on the shoulder, as we were walking along, and whispered, "You have got a widow with eight hundred a year." She had married for money, and now she was about to be paid off by so many willing to marry her for money. Lady Wilde told me she had refused forty-six young men last year, some of them ten years her junior. I know you are tired of the widow, but I must tell you one more incident: As we went home in a cab at midnight she took regular hysterics on account of the cabman driving so fast. She cried out, "Stop the cabman; he is driving too fast!" She was sitting on a back seat, and the young lady and myself were in front. I tried to quiet her. She didn't swoon, for I was not sitting by her and of course there was no chance for her to fall into my arms. The more I tried to pacify her the less pacified she got. There was no reason, no sense in her carrying on. I got tired of it and laughed at her fears most heartily. She said these drunken cabmen often turn over their cabs and break the people's necks. And she said Mr. So-and-so had his leg broken and suffered terribly. "Oh," said I, "what a lucky fellow. Just to think what a happy man to get his leg broken, so that he could lie up at home away from the troubles of business, and have his wife to pet him." "But," said she "I have got nobody to pet me if my leg is broken." "But," said I, "I will pet you if you get your leg broken. I will rub it and stroke it, and splint it and bandage it, and cure it•up so nicely for you that you will almost be willing to have the other leg broken." This killed all her hysterics, and brought her to her senses. She laughed outright, and said I was the oddest fellow she ever met. I made this discovery: That the way to cure hysterics in a widow with eight hundred a year is to talk about rubbing her leg. Whether rubbing it will cure it or not, I really do not know.

You can't imagine how many people are talking to me about settling in London. I have not the remotest idea of ever leaving New York, but would you believe it, that more than two prominent doctors have insisted on my going to London. The great Syme, of Edinburgh, told me that if I would go to London to live he would insure me more than I could make in New York, with less labor. And a few nights ago I was introduced to a physician here, who told me that London was the place for me ; that they need such a man there as I am. Compliments certainly! And yesterday Sir William Wilde said that if I would go to London and settle down that I would make a fortune. But don't fear. I have not the remotest idea of it. New York has done well by me and I will stick to her just as long as she will let me. The queen arrived here this morning. I have missed seeing her, and will go to the Curragh, an hour's ride by mail, to see her review the troops to-morrow. Failing to lay eyes on the blessed woman to-day, I thought it would be very unloyal not to sacrifice one day to testify my admiration for this purest of women and best of queens.

I have already said that I was treated very kindly by Derolebaix, surgeon to the King of Belgium, and the other members of the profession whom I met in Brussels when I went over to wait for the vesico-vaginal fistula in their hospitals. And I have mentioned the fact that they have elected me corresponding Fellow of the Royal Academy of Medicine, and they recommended my name to the government for Knight of the Order of Leopold the First. I then never had any public recognitions abroad, and not many at home, and of course I was exceedingly anxious to obtain this from the Belgian government. Of course this must go through a certain form before the end can be reached. After I had been at home about a month, say about the 1st of February, 1862, I received notice from Brussels that the government had created me a Knight of the Order of Leopold the First. Whenever any European government confers such an honor on a foreigner it must, as a matter of course, be through the minister representing his government. At that time Mr. Sanford was the American minister at the Court of Brussels, and he objected to my receiving this honor, and gave as a reason that I was a rebel and an enemy of my country, and therefore was not entitled to any honor of the sort, even when conferred for scientific claims. I was exceedingly mortified when I heard this news, and immediately determined if possible to circumvent Mr. Sanford. Mr. Henry J. Raymond, of the "Times," had always been my friend, from my first experience in New York. He had been a friend of the Woman's Hospital movement; he was one of its advocates and advisers; Mrs. Raymond was one of the first lady-managers and had always taken a deep interest in it and in me. Mr. Raymond was then all-powerful with the authorities at Washington. I thought that I would have nothing to do but to speak to him, and that he would write to Mr. Seward, and that through his agency I would receive the honor that I so much coveted. My political sentiments were never hidden from anybody, but I was not a politician, and could not help my sentiments. I had a conversation with Dr. Horace Green, who was a warm personal friend of Mr. Raymond's. Dr. Green, at a family dinner party, invited Mr. Raymond and myself there, with the view of giving me an opportunity of speaking to Mr. Raymond, after dinner, on the subject which was so near my heart. After I had laid the whole story before Mr. Raymond, telling all that he knew, that I was a southern sympathizer, but yet, as a man of science and as a citizen of New York, as loyal to the Government as he himself was, I wished him to bring his influence to bear on the Secretary of State, Mr. Seward, so that I could obtain the honor I wanted. I don't think I was ever so surprised in all my life as when, after hearing my story and request, he turned sharply on me and said: "I don't think any man holding the sentiments that you do has any right to expect any favors of any sort from the Government under existing circumstances." I detail this to show what bitterness and unreasonableness existed in the minds of the great leaders of that day and time. I never obtained the honorable order from the Belgian government until the summer of 1880, when my daughter, Mrs. W. Graham Sandford, the wife of Mr. Sandford, who was then Secretary of Legation of the British Embassy at Brussels, laid the facts before the minister of state that I have already detailed, and the Government then granted me the honor, which was accepted by Mr. James O. Putnam, then representing the American Government at the Court of Belgium.

DUBLIN, *August 25, 1861.*

The queen arrived here yesterday, on her way to visit the troops at the Curragh. I thought it would be too bad to leave without laying eyes on the little woman. I did not happen to see her driving around town, and my disappointment determined me at once to remain here and go to the review at the Curragh. Yesterday, the 24th, was the grand review of the troops there, some twenty-five or thirty miles from Dublin, on the road toward Cork. The Curragh is a great camp for training soldiers. The barracks make quite a town of one-story houses on either side of the central street, a mile and a half long. The occasion was a grand one; everybody was there. It is said that there are from eighteen to twenty thousand troops, and there was an immense throng of spectators. The day, for Ireland, was a fine one—for us it would have been called bad. It rained very hard twice during the parade, which lasted from ten to three. People here don't mind getting wet. I learned to stand and take it like an Irishman. I never wanted a horse as badly in my life. If I had been mounted, I could have charged over and around the Curragh in any direction with the others. I can imagine very well that in battle men may forget themselves in leading a charge, for we had all the excitement of battle without the carnage. We saw the commanding general on an eminence in the distance, glass in hand, surveying the field. He was surrounded by his staff. Presently an aid was flying on his charger, as swift as the wind, gave an order, and instantly thousands of soldiers were in motion, changing the whole scene, and in a very short space of time another and another aid would be sent in another direction, which soon wheeled the serried columns of infantry, changing the position of flying artillery, or moving light dragoons, so rapidly that the whole column, more than a mile long, was soon placed at right angles to its former position. We had the booming of cannon, the rattling volleys of infantry, the terrific charge of thousands of dragoons. The noise of these was like thunder, and seemed to me would be dreadful in an open plain in attacking ranks of infantry. There were many ladies and gentlemen on horseback. They didn't care at all for the rain, though it poured in torrents for a little while. They seemed all excitement, and were charging in all directions, not fearing cannon, musketry, or anything else. . . . But to return to the Curragh. You ask, did I see the queen? When we stopped first to survey the line of soldiers, we were on an eminence about the center of a great plain, which is continually undulated, and so uneven in some places as to hide the movements of the troops—all hill and dale. After nearly three hours of standing, talking, and gazing at the waves of soldiers, I said to a gentleman accompanying me, " I came here expressly to see the queen. I have stopped three days for that purpose. I fear I shall be disappointed." " No, you won't," said he, "here they are coming." At that moment the guard came dashing along, followed by the queen's carriage, drawn by four fine bays with riders. The carriage was open. It stopped within twenty or thirty steps of us, with the right side toward us. They had to look over our heads to see the charge of cavalry. The queen seemed to enjoy the scene like a true woman. Three of her children were with her, one on her left, and the other two, whom I could not see, were on the front seat. They were all dressed in deep mourning, and behaved themselves quite as well as any well-bred ladies

would with us. The queen is a fine looking woman, and
were I an Englishman I could be vociferously eloquent
with her as my theme. Taking her in all the relations
of life, as wife, mother, Christian, and queen, no such
woman ever graced the throne or so honored her sex;
but, poor thing, she is queen and therefore not free to do
as she chooses about anything. She who has, nominally,
great power, is really powerless. Over her own actions
she is cramped with royal formulas. The other day her
servants petitioned her to go on a picnic, or rather she
planned a picnic excursion for them, to Wicklow, a
beautiful region of country not far from Dublin, and
they petitioned her to allow them to ride in open Irish
jaunting-cars, instead of closed carriages. She said, "Certainly, ride in the open jaunting-cars. I should like the
privilege of doing so myself, if the British people would
not feel outraged by it." The queen was accompanied
by the prince consort, on horseback. I have never seen
a finer looking man. This was only four months before
his death.

PARIS, *September 16, 1861.*

This morning we went to the Hôpital Lariboisière,
which is altogether the finest hospital I have ever seen.
We had been following Chassaignac around the wards for
some time, and just as he got through he turned suddenly around and came toward me. He discovered that I
was a stranger, and, bowing and stopping a moment, his
instrument maker, Mr. Mathieu, who happened to be
present, introduced me. He grasped me warmly by the

hand and commenced, "Ah! Monsieur Marion Sims,"
and he talked away at a terrible rate, in a very compli-
mentary manner, not a word of which did I understand;
but the students and doctors all gazed at my confusion,
as if I had been nicely dissected or was undergoing a
brilliant *écrasement*. He was exceedingly polite to me,
and kept me by his side for the two hours that he was
lecturing and operating in the amphitheatre. I learned
something from him about the use of the *écraseur*, and
I confess that I was greatly profited by what I saw.

PARIS, *Friday, September 20, 1861.*

I am utterly amazed at the ignorance of French
surgeons on some subjects. For instance, in hospital
practice almost all cases of amputation die. I am
very sure I see the true cause, and if I had time I
would pitch in for a complete revolution in the art of
dressing wounds here. Don't repeat this to anybody,
for it looks too presumptuous; but I am sure that the
same surgery in New York would be, other things
being equal, attended with the same results as here.
Everybody is kind and polite to me. I went to the
Société de Chirurgie the other evening with the great
Chassaignac, the inventor of the *écraseur*. He lionized
me quite as much as I could comfortably bear. Fortunately for me it was all in French, and I did not wince.
Huguier, the man I mentioned in my amputation paper,
has been very polite to me, and I am to operate for
vesico-vaginal fistula for him, at the Hôpital Beaujon,

to-morrow morning, at nine o'clock. To-day I am at the Hôpital St. Louis, by invitation of Dr. Verneuil, who invited me to operate there on a case next Monday at nine o'clock—both cases just bad enough and just good enough; would not have them otherwise. How rejoiced I am every day that I obeyed your injunctions in coming abroad. I only wish I had more time here. The fields are rich, the harvest is ripe. I have prepared my amputation paper, and it is now in the hands of the translator. Chassaignac will read it on Wednesday next before the surgical society, and on Wednesday following he will read my paper on vaginismus. I am now at work on it; but as I have only a few minutes more to get this off in time, I will drop professional subjects, though I know I can not interest you in any way half so much as to tell you the pleasant and profitable things that daily occur to me, whose very existence is wrapped up in your own.

PARIS, *September 24, 1861.*

On Saturday we operated at the Hôpital Beaujou. It was difficult for anybody else, but easy for me, lasting thirty-five minutes. I was honored by the presence of Nélaton, Gosselin, Huguier, and Denonvilliers. The operation was satisfactory and successful; and when Dr. Nélaton bade me good-by, and thanked me, he said he had been very much surprised to hear that I had cured more than two hundred cases, but after seeing this operation he was not at all surprised. Dr. Ordronoux, of New

York, and Dr. Johnstone, of Paris, interpreted for me. Yesterday I operated at the Hôpital St. Louis, for Verneuil, before a very large class. Dr. Johnstone interpreted ; and to-day I was waited upon by Dr. Péan, who came at the request of some of his students to solicit me to operate for them on the cadaver, for which they offered me one hundred francs apiece. Of course I declined the money, but accepted the honor, and I am to go to Mont Clair on Thursday to perform the operation.

To-morrow my paper will be read before the Société de Chirurgie, and next Wednesday the second paper will be read.

PARIS, *October 2, 1861.*

My two surgical cases at the Beaujou and the St. Louis have been cured. All the young men are in ecstacies about them, while the older appear to be satisfied. I went to see the great Civiale, the great lithotriptist, and he gave me letters to Munich, Vienna, and Berlin, and invited me to operate for him in his wards. He said he had no case just now, but would soon have one for me. This morning I saw Velpeau at the Charité for the first time. He said he had heard a great many surgeons speak of me and of my operations, and that he would be glad to see me operate, and he would save the first case for me that presented itself at the Charité. Frenchmen don't ask strangers to visit them, or to dine or breakfast with them, as do the English and Americans; but Dr. Campbell, who is Scotch by birth, invited me to meet Baker Brown, of

London, and others at dinner two days ago. We had a glorious social English dinner, at which everybody spoke French but myself. Baker Brown said that he had felt quite hurt when he learned I had passed through London without calling to see him. He is a splendid fellow, but the greatest blower I ever met; belches out everything he knows, and thereby shows there are many things he does not know. He is a cute, cunning fellow, but everybody can see through him. In London he is not liked; he is looked upon as unreliable, but I don't think they do him justice. So it is! A man may have a few eccentricities, or foibles, or weaknesses, and he is like a poor woman with leucorrhœa—it weakens him all over. I also met another great surgeon of London yesterday, Sir Henry Thompson, who invited me to operate at the University Hospital, where he and Erichsen are the surgeons. Of course I will not throw away such an opportunity. Besides this, I have received messages from other surgeons in London to make them a visit. I called on Mr. Dayton, our minister, the other day. He is a very elegant gentlemen. I asked him if he had any discretionary powers in issuing passports, or if he was obliged to exact the oath under any and all circumstances. He said he had no discretionary power whatever, and at my request showed me a copy of the oath. I had a very pleasant visit, explained to him that everything I had in the world in the shape of property was at the South, that the Confederate Congress had passed a sequestration act, and that I could not in justice to my wife and children take an oath that would result in the confiscation of all I had. He said it was surely a hard case, and regretted that his government did not allow its ministers some discretion under the circumstances, and said he most certainly would help me if he could. I replied that I was an honest man, could not do anything that was not honorable, that I would not, as some had suggested, go by way of Canada and sneak stealthily home by some unfrequented route, nor would I take another man's passport and go into Boston under a fictitious name, as some had suggested, but feeling sure of my honest purpose, being wholly incapable of the slightest treasonable act, I had determined to go home like an honest man, fearing no harm; for it is true that "the wicked flee when no man pursueth."

PARIS, *October 18, 1861* (*Friday*).

This 18th of October, 1861, has not by any means been the happiest day of my life, but, with perhaps three exceptions, the proudest. The first exception was the day, the 23d day of July, 1833, on which you gave me the rose-bud through the garden fence. We were then young and alone; there were none to approve or condemn. A few seemingly long years rolled tardily over and at last brought the second era, the happy day, the 21st of December, 1836, on which you became my wife. Family and friends were there to yield assent. Many perfectly happy years passed rapidly, and, together we climbed up the hill of life until, almost at the top, came the first anniversary of the Woman's Hospital, the 9th of February, 1856. You were not there, but New York was, and from that day your husband's American reputation was fixed, and your hopes were fulfilled, and your ambition gratified.

To-day Velpeau, Nélaton, Civiale, Ricord, Chassaignac, Follin, Huguier, Debout, Baron Larrey, Sir Joseph Olliffe, Campbell, Johnstone, and many others honored me with their presence at the Hôtel Voltaire, Quai Voltaire, No. 19. I had one of the most difficult operations I ever performed. The patient was a very bad one, short, fat, and nervous. Chloroform was administered by Dr. Johnstone. It acted very badly; the patient became slightly hysterical, and uncontrollable, and chloroform was for a while suspended. Some thought it dangerous to continue it; to stop it was to stop the operation. Velpeau strongly advised against continuing to give it, but Johnstone proceeded, and gave enough to produce quiet, and the operation was performed. It took about forty minutes. It was one of the most difficult that could be. Everybody was delighted except me. I never had so many obstacles present at one time in any one case. I have had as bad patients, but then the operation was not so difficult; and I have had a few as difficult, but they were in docile patients; but here everything was wrong except my presence of mind and confidence. But all obstacles were so quietly and so thoroughly overcome that everybody congratulated me on encountering them.

The triumph is complete, and you may feel secure as to the full and perfect recognition of my claims throughout all Europe. Not only now, but often while I sit in the midst of the decorated *savants* of this great city, my thoughts turn instinctively to the wife of my bosom, who, as the mother of my children, is a thousand times dearer to me than she was in the spring-time of life, as the play-mate of my childhood and the idol of my youth. To your gentle care and loving kindness and wise counsels I owe all that I am, and I feel that, with all my successes, all my triumphs, with the prospect of lasting fame, I am far, very far from being worthy of you ; for when I have told you thousands of times that you were too good for me I have been in earnest. But while I feel a secret, unexpressed gratification at the extraordinary result of my visit here, which would not have been made but for your persistent entreaties, let us not forget the great Author of it all. I have done nothing, but have been led along, I know not how, and have followed blindly, confidingly, and patiently. Nothing has been done just as I would have had it, but all has turned out, or is turning out, better than I could have devised.

Tuesday, October 22, 1861.

Time enough has elapsed for me to find out something of what the doctors say and think. It seems that my operations are all the talk among them. The great Velpeau is anxious for me to operate before his young men at the Charité, and the young men are absolutely

16

running down women to find out if they are fistu-lous.

Civiale invited me to go to the country with him and dine on Sunday. There were twelve or fifteen of us, and I was the only one who did not speak French. Tom Pratt and Dr. Oldfield, an Englishman, were there. I had a very pleasant but rather stupid time, as I did not speak French. Civiale begs me to become his pupil and learn the art of lithotripsy. I have a great mind to write you what he said. It looks well enough on paper when you alone see it, but not to others when repeated. On Saturday last I went to the Hôpital Necker, where the great Civiale is on service. I was standing in a row with some medical students, and the old gentleman passed by, bowing to the students as he walked along. As his eye caught me, he stopped suddenly and came up to me, and, taking me by the hand, he launched forth a terrific tirade which I took to be something compli-mentary, but could not understand a word he said. Of course I bowed very humbly, but could make no reply. Pratt was not with me, but a young Englishman standing by said, " Well, doctor, I must translate that for you; it is too good to be lost; it is this : ' I beg to render you my homage. You are a true surgeon. Such gentleness and firmness, such dexterity and skill, such judgment and courage, I have never seen before combined in such exact proportions in any one man. What a great litho-triptist you would have made. Come and be my pupil.' " When we were riding in the cars on Sunday, with Civiale, out to his country-place, he said to Tom, "Is it so, that the doctor has received six thousand francs for an operation in private practice?" Tom said, "No, sir; he has not received six sous." "Well," said Civiale, "the doctors are talking about his great fees, and about his wonderful operations." So you see I am discussed in private circles, as well as in hospitals, and clinics, and societies. Yesterday I had a delightful visit from Sir Joseph Olliffe, who came to congratulate me on the operation on Friday, and to ask to see the next operation I am to perform. You can hardly imagine the *furore* and enthusiasm the doctors are passing through now on the subject of my operations. To-night I dine at Dr. Preterre's. It seems that the occasion was to bring me in contact with some influential *littérateurs* in the profession, who have set their heads together to do me justice in French, or rather Continental, medical literature. How providential it all seems.

I am now unexpectedly finishing this letter in London. Dr. Campbell received a letter the other day from Baker Brown, saying that he wished me to come to London to perform an operation for him, and, just as I was making up my mind to come, Professor Gosselin wrote me that Mr. Curling had written to him to come to London to operate on a case for him. So, under this double inducement, I left Paris last night and arrived here at six this morning. I must tell you that the case I operated on last Friday is perfectly cured. You know that I dreaded London, for I feared that they would not receive me so kindly there as elsewhere, but I have been mistaken. I have not been treated better anywhere than in London, and here they are ready to do me ample justice at once. I saw Baker Brown operate for ovariotomy to-day. It was splendid. He performed several minor operations, and asked my opinion about a difficult case or two. He called for a speculum, and when it was brought he held it up and said, " Dr. Sims, I believe this is your speculum." I replied, " Yes sir, and I am glad you have found it out, for you have not done me justice in applying the name of another man to that speculum." There were twenty doctors present, and I spoke pretty sharply but not rudely. He felt it, and said very promptly, " I understand that you have been breathing vengeance against me because I called this speculum by another man's name; and here, before these medical gentlemen, I wish to make the *amende honorable*. I have been imposed upon and deceived, and so has the profession at large, not only here, but all over Europe, by your countryman who pretended to have been the inventor of the speculum; and I acknowledge that I have done you injustice, but I did it ignorantly. I shall rectify the error, and will hereafter do you the justice that is due you." Of course he acted very nobly in speaking out like a man before the whole crowd.

PARIS, *November 1, 1861.*

The unfortunate state of political affairs at home places us in a very precarious position. I feel that we are not worth one dollar to-day. Let us do as we always have done, accept our position as we find it, and look continually to Him who overrules all things for the best. Financially the war ruins us. I have nothing but wife, children, health, reputation, and plenty of labor. So far a man is blessed. I am content, nay happy, and truly thankful that I am so well off. Our property in New York is valueless to us, and will soon be worth nothing. Our property at the South yields nothing, and may all be lost under the sequestration act. If we remain in New York, the probabilities are that it will all go into the Confederate treasury. If we take the oath of allegiance to the Northern States, it is absolutely certain to be confiscated, and I will be worse off pecuniarily but better off professionally. I am just as well satisfied, just as cheerful and happy, as I can be under the circumstances. You know I always have a happy faculty of accommodating myself to any position in which I may be placed. I wish you to go and see Mr. Simeon Draper, and tell him that I came over here to remain six weeks; that the Government, since then, requires every American citizen to get a passport and to take the oath. Tell him that my father and all my family are rebels, that they are fighting for the Confederate government, and that I sympathize with them ; that if I did not I would be, as a man, totally unworthy of the confidence that he and all the good people of New York have placed in me for the last eight years. That however much of the rebel I may be at heart, he knows very well that I am as incapable of doing a trai-

torous act, against the flag under which we live at the
North, as a five-year-old child would be. My sentiments
I can not help, for I lived forty years of my life at the
South. The companions of my youth are the leaders of
the great Southern rebellion. My father, now seventy-
three years of age, is one of its soldiers; our whole family are in arms; your father and mother, my mother, and
one of our beloved children have graves on Southern
soil, and how under heaven could we be otherwise than
as we are, unless lost to all sense of humanity. Give this
letter to Mr. Draper to read, and after that, if he gives
you his assurance that I shall not be subjected to any
indignity or annoyance on my return home, let me know.
If he hesitates one second, let me know it, and my resolution is taken. Somehow or other you have on one or
more occasions been placed in the position of assuming
great responsibilities in piloting our little life-boat, and
your presence of mind, your judgment, and your courage
have always been equal to the emergency, and I have the
most unbounded confidence in your wisdom. You are
again placed in that trying position; and now, under all
the circumstances, I ask you this question and leave it to
your decision: Do you think it would be wise for us to
remain in Europe until the war is over? Think of this
and write me your decision, and what you say that will I
do. If our two furnished houses could be rented for
enough to pay off their mortgage, interest, taxes, etc., and
leave something over, it would be better than living in
them, for here we can live in a cottage in the suburbs of

Paris for very little, while I could give my time to the preparation and publication of my works, which the world outside of the Woman's Hospital is sadly in need of. I would have some time to devote to you and the children, and really I don't think the change would be a very unhappy one. Is it not strange to hear one speak so calmly about such a sad reverse of fortune? I suppose if I were put in Fort Lafayette I would make a virtue of necessity, and turn it all to the best account. But, if we go into voluntary exile here, it would not be an exile of want or destitution by any means. Turn me loose to-day anywhere in Europe, and I shall be able to support you all in a modest and unpretentious style. I feel that I have now equally as much influence in Europe as in my own country. You can not imagine what an interest I have created here by my professional labors; and in six weeks from this I could sit down anywhere and draw patients in abundance. This grows out of the fact that Paris is like New York. It is to Europe what New York is to our whole country. One of my friends and counselors said to me yesterday that my Parisian baptism is my salvation in Europe. I have already operated four times, and in all cases successfully. I operated to-day for Velpeau, at La Charité. It was a great occasion. Many distinguished men were present, and a large class of students. The case had been previously operated on about seventeen times by Joubard de Lamballe. Velpeau, Malgaigne and Denonvilliers were perfectly delighted. After the operation, I said if the young men wished it I would make any explanations or answer any questions they might ask. I was too modest to say I would deliver a lecture. The young men took their seats, and Velpeau, Malgaigne, Denonvilliers, Trélot, and a host of other old fellows sat by me. As I talked, Mr. Soucon, a medical student from New Orleans, a student of Professor Stone's, sat by and translated as I spoke, and everybody seemed perfectly satisfied with his rendering of the subject. I never saw such complete satisfaction in all my life. Malgaigne, who is nicknamed the "Barking Dog" because he snarls and growls at everybody, sat there patiently all the time, occasionally asking a question on some point that he did not comprehend, and when he left he shook my hand, and thanked me cordially over and over again, and everybody said that he was never known to speak well of any one, or to any one in a familiar way before. They consider my triumph over him as an era in surgical polemics. Colonel Robert E. Cox was there, and he says the lecture was one of the best that he ever heard. That grows out of the fact that a man can not afford to say a silly thing, or to waste words, when they are to be rendered in another language.

APPENDIX I.

It has been deemed proper to include the following letters of Dr. Sims in this volume, as they mark two great transition periods in his career; one the period of his struggling advance, the other that of assured triumph.

The Fourth of July address is included, as it serves to illustrate the breadth of his views upon current political topics, and to prove that the great surgeon, who had been decorated by crowned heads in many lands, was also by conviction and sentiment a true American.

But a few out of the many memorial resolutions and addresses, published upon the occasion of his universally lamented death, are here included. It would be impossible to include all within the compass of a book of reasonable size, and hence those only are given which are not only tributes to his professional character and achievements, but to his virtues as a man, to whom the duties of life were more than life.

Requesting the Mother of his Betrothed to consent to their Marriage.

LANCASTERVILLE, *June 12, 1835.*

MRS. JONES,

DEAR MADAM: The relationship existing between your daughter Theresa and myself I feel in duty bound to disclose to you. That I have not done so before was not, I assure you, owing to any want of respect for you personally, or for your authority and natural right to be consulted in such a matter, but rather to the peculiar circumstances under which I have been placed. In these may be found some apology for what I know to be a transgression of right, and of your rights.

Theresa and myself have mutually plighted our faith to each

other, and, I need scarcely add, it is our earnest and anxious desire to obtain the approbation of yourself, and the approbation of those who with you have a reasonable and just right to control the affair in any way. I do not propose marriage immediately—circumstances render it inexpedient—for I wish first to give you an earnest of what I may hereafter be; but of that enough, till I am satisfied on the first point.

I know that, as a mother, holding the dearest interest and welfare of an affectionate child at heart, you will give the subject that mature consideration which it deserves, and I hope that it will not be long till I hear the result of your deliberations, and am relieved from the suspense which necessarily oppresses the mind in a matter of such importance, and one, too, of doubtful issue.

I am, with the highest esteem, your obt.,

J. Marion Sims.

In Search of a Home in the West before getting Married.

Mount Meigs, Alabama, *November 3, 1835.*

My dear Theresa: I arrived here last night after a three weeks' siege of it. Myself and father are both very well. We had a delightful time for traveling, with the exception of the dust, which was exceedingly unpleasant, as we had not a drop of rain from the time we left Columbia. I stood the slow mode of moving along remarkably well, and walked nearly the whole way from Columbia here, not riding more than two or three miles a day on an average. I visited Mr. Adams to-day. He was very polite to us, but neglected to invite me to call at his house, consequently I have not seen his wife.

To-morrow I expect to visit Messrs. Carter, Ward, Crockett, and Lanier, and from there I shall go to see Mr. String. Next week I set out on a tour through some of the districts west of this. I design going across to Perry and Greene Counties, then down through Marengo and Wilcox, thence through Lowndes and Montgomery, back to Mount Meigs. In this range of country, somewhere, I hope to find a resting-place. Mount Meigs is a fine stand for a physician, and I have been strongly advised to remain here; but I shall not be in a hurry about locating. It's best to take time and look well. I have one very serious objection to this place: it is unquestionably one of the most dissipated little places I ever saw.

At this very moment there are about a dozen or twenty men, of the most profane cast, drunk and fighting, in the street below my window, with a negro playing a banjo (I believe it is so called) in their midst. I am informed that this scene is not at all uncommon here. This is, unfortunately, the character of almost all the little towns and villages in these new counties.

If I should not find a place in Alabama that I like, I shall direct my course to Mississippi. In selecting a home, I shall always remember that there is only one whose happiness is the darling wish of my soul. I shall not only look around for a place of making money, but, if possible, I will locate where there is good society, and consequently there can be social enjoyment.

I am happy to say I have been in the finest sort of spirits ever since I left home. You, Theresa, should not indulge in melancholy reflections. Whenever you are about to take the "blues," go over and plague Cousin Nancy till you laugh yourself out of them. Although I am so far removed from you, you'll suffer me to prescribe in this instance, if you please.

I wish, if you please, you would get the last letter Aunt Sally wrote me, from Cousin Ann, hand it to my father on his return home, and after that keep it till I visit sweet old Carolina again.

Remember me most affectionately to your dear mother and family. Tell Cousin Mary Ann, etc., for me. I expect to write again before I get to my home. Till then good-bye, Theresa.

J. Marion Sims.

Mount Meigs, Alabama, November 13, 1835.

My dear Theresa: I know you will be surprised when I tell you I have at length concluded to make this place my home. When I wrote last I had not visited or consulted with any of my friends about the affair. I have been prevailed upon by strong solicitations to locate myself here without looking any further. What I then told you of Mount Meigs is literally true, though I judged altogether from superficial appearances. There are a great many vagabonds (if I should judge from appearances) that frequent this place for the special purpose of frolicking, which has given it a desperate character abroad. It, however, has its redeeming qualities. Mount Meigs will, in the course of twelve or fifteen months, be a very desirable place, because the society will in that time be excellent. There

is a very large spring in the immediate vicinity (say five or six
hundred yards distant) at which several gentlemen are now making
preparations to build. Colonel Campbell, Colonel Keen, Mayor
Ashurst, his brother, and brother-in-law Ward Crockett, will all
build at the spring. Crockett's house will be finished in the course
of the winter. I expect to board with him. In addition to the
above-named gentlemen, there are other families at Mount Meigs.
Mr. Lucas and his step son-in-law Mr. Charles, who married Miss
Fanny Taylor, of Columbia. Upon the whole, I think I have made a
judicious selection as far as society is concerned. It was on your
account, Theresa, that I at first rejected Mount Meigs, and it was on
your account that I afterward concluded to remain here. As to
the prospects of making a living here—I set up in opposition to one
of the most popular men in the county or perhaps State—he is exceedingly popular as a man, and equally so as a physician, and no
doubt deservedly so. I shall ever feel grateful to my friends Lanier,
Adams and Crockett, for the interest they seem to manifest for my
welfare. Mount Meigs has generally been considered very healthy,
but the vicinity is a rich, densely-populated country, and withal
sickly. If, with such opposition as Dr. Lucas, I can support myself
and pay my debts next year, I shall think that I have done a fine
business, though some of my sanguine friends say that they will insure two or three times that much. To-day I bought all of Dr.
Childers's books and medicines, he is going to Mobile; about sixty
years old and very eminent in his profession—has been practicing
here for the last year—he has a great many friends and is using
his influence for me. I have already found several valuable friends,
but my dear Theresa I must take leave of you again. Do write to
me soon, don't put it off, it's my last request, Theresa.

J. MARION SIMS.

MOUNT MEIGS, ALABAMA, December 31, 1835.

MY DEAR, DEAR THERESA : Why in the world don't you write to
me? I can't conceive what possible shadow of excuse you can have.
Heretofore you had valid reasons for not writing, but now the
whole affair is known at home, and you can leisurely sit down and
write to me at any time you please. Theresa, you must excuse me
for writing so ardently. You have been from home, from friends
and relations, you know what it is to look anxiously for some in-

telligence from them, and look in vain. You must therefore be in some measure conscious of the painful anxiety of mind I now labor under. Theresa, I say no more than the truth when I declare that you are nearer to me than any brother or sister I have (and heaven knows I love them dearly). Is it, then, a matter of surprise that I should beg, entreat, and even chide, because you appear to forget me? I know you have not forgotten me, but I speak of appearances. Of course I would feel easier and more happy if you would from time to time give me some evidence of continued attachment. I am certain that you are constant; don't construe what I have said into any apprehension on my part of a want of the most untiring constancy in you—far from it. I could not possibly believe that any one could bear with such Roman fortitude, that you, Theresa, have endured, with such unflinching firmness—the strenuous opposition you have encountered—and at this late hour retreat. I could not believe it. Think not, then, that I have any doubts. I only wish you to make certain, more sure. It has been nearly three months since I left home and I have received but two letters, one from sister a few days ago, and a few scratches of the pen from brother Wash. Not one word from you to cheer me on in the path of duty and to comfort what few leisure hours I have. But you have already become tired of this scold. I repeat, Theresa, you must excuse me. All the time I can spare from my studies and practice I spend in writing to my friends. What I tell you about my prospects and practice is confidential—it would look like vaunting to speak candidly about it to any other individual than yourself. My friends accumulate hourly. My practice increases daily—in fact I have as much as I want, and so far I have more than divided the practice with Dr. Lucas, my opponent, who is one of the most popular men in Alabama. It is not sickly, but I am constantly employed, there's not a day but I have something to do. I have the glorious consolation of knowing (to a certainty) that, by a very simple operation, I have saved one man's life who was left by older physicians to die. In his neighborhood the people believe in me, but I begin to feel almost ashamed of writing in this tone. I fear you'll set me down as an egotist. Theresa, I believe that generally I express my opinion too freely to you, but you must look over these little things. It's human nature. We must always have some one to confer with, some friend into whose attentive ear we can pour our secret thoughts and speculations; but I must stop this apology for my egotism, merely because I fear I shall make bad worse.

Theresa, be not angry with my importuning you. Will you write to me? "I pause for a reply." I shall wait for an answer. Give my love to your dear mother, and sister Mary. Let me, through you, congratulate my friends Mr. and Mrs. Thornwell.

For the present I take leave of you, Theresa.

J. MARION SIMS.

MOUNT MEIGS, *January 10, 1836.*

OH, my dear Theresa, can you forgive me for the scold I gave you last week? I have repented it fifty times to-night since the reception of your dear, long-looked-for letter. I have read it with the greatest avidity, and read again and again, and am not yet tired. Theresa, if you could but imagine what immense pleasure and gratification it is to me to hear from you, I feel confident that you would not let me remain another three months without writing to me. It seems to make my spirits more buoyant, and is an additional stimulus to industry.

In this little Mount Meigs—which is nothing but a pile of gin-houses, stables, blacksmith-shops, grog-shops, taverns and stores, thrown together in one promiscuous huddle—I say in this trifling place, our engagement is talked of by everybody as currently as in old Lancaster. How in the world it got out I can't divine; some great wide-mouthed fool from Carolina stopped a few days ago at the post-office and inquired for me. He gave the young men at the office (who are very particular friends of mine) our whole history, courtship, and the time that was appointed for solemnizing the marriage ceremony; in fact, he appeared to know as much or more about it than I do. He told the young men his name, but they forgot it. Whoever he may be, he is most assuredly an uncommonly smart fellow. However, I am perfectly satisfied about it. This evening, as I was telling Mrs. Adams that I had written to Rush and gave her compliments, etc., to him, a lady sitting by (Mrs. Shellman) exclaimed, "Well, when you wrote to Miss Jones did you give her my love." I need not say what my predicament was, or whose face could have lighted a candle. I got out of her clutches the best way I could, which was by acknowledging everything she said, for it was all the truth. You may now consider yourself presented with the love, etc., of Mrs. Shellman; she is a fine little woman and always says what she thinks.

I have spent an intolerably dull Christmas, for I was the whole time in the sick chamber. Ward Crockett came near giving up the ghost about that time, but is now well. There was a ball in the town of Montgomery about a week ago, but I did not attend it. There were one hundred ladies and as many gentlemen at it; I had but little temptation to go, though some of my warmest young friends persuaded me very strenuously. On such occasions I always think of Cousin Nancy and the advice she gave, and I have frequently thought of her, and as frequently endeavored to follow the wholesome advice. It was this: "Never sacrifice duty to pleasure." I always considered it my duty as well as interest to be ever found at my post, and could therefore leave home on no other pretext than that of professional business. As it is very late, and my fire burnt down, I must for the present say *farewell.* That's a doleful word, and I never like to pronounce it, much less to write it.

Theresa, be sure you write to me soon, let it not be more than *two weeks* at the utmost. Remember now, my dear Theresa, *two* weeks is the limit.

I remain, with the same ever fond, endearing attachment,
Good-bye, Theresa,
J. MARION SIMS.

P. S. I am now boarding with Mr. Adams. Mrs. Adams is the same pleasant little woman that she ever was. Remember me affectionately to your *dear mother* and *all* the Conguss folks. I should be glad to receive a letter from our sweet little cousin Mary Ann. Do let me know how Wash is getting; he was very sick, you know, when I left home. I hope he is convalescent, at least I think he is not dangerous; inquire of his *physician,* if you please.
Again, good-night, Theresa.
J. MARION SIMS.

It's strange that you have not received a letter from me in five weeks—I have written four, I think. J. M. S.

MOUNT MEIGS, ALABAMA, *January 30, 1836.*

MY DEAR THERESA: I am certain you can't divine the object of this letter. You may expect me in old Lancaster about the 16th or

18th of February, and, as soon after that as is perfectly convenient, I wish to have a final adjustment and consummation of all our love matters. Be ready, prepared for our wedding and for Alabama, and you will make me the happiest man.

O, Theresa, I do long to see you, my dearest girl!—Be ready, Theresa!

Till I see you, good-by, my dearest, dearest Theresa.

J. Marion Sims.

Mount Meigs, Alabama, January 30, 1836.

My dear Mrs. Jones: I must acknowledge that I feel somewhat embarrassed in addressing you this letter. Nothing but a false delicacy, combined with some uncertainty in my movements and success, caused me to postpone an explicit understanding relative to the proposed connection that I hope to form in your family. You know that I have been long and devotedly attached to Theresa, that this attachment has existed, as it were, from childhood, and that it has been strengthened by long cherished and intimate friendship. Two years and a half have elapsed since our mutual faith was plighted, and I have naturally looked forward with interest and anxiety to the final consummation of this, the first darling wish of my soul. My circumstances and prospects you as a mother have a right to inquire into. I have succeeded in making arrangements that I knew nothing of when I wrote to Col. Witherspoon a few days ago. I have obtained a lot, and have lumber ready cut to put up a comfortable little house, which I presume can not be finished before the first of May or June. Till then I have procured board in a private family. I will be in Lancaster on or before the 18th of next month, February. It will be out of my power to remain longer than 10 or 12 days, because I can't do so without making considerable sacrifices here.

My dear Mrs. Jones,

I remain your ever affectionate friend and faithful

J. Marion Sims.

Mrs. E. I. Jones, Lancaster, S. C.

Mount Meigs, Alabama, April 1, 1836.

My dear Theresa: I am once again safe at home after a long and tedious, but withal delightful siege of traveling. In Philadelphia I spent ten days very pleasantly indeed. I've taken Aunt

Sally and all her little family by surprise. I found Virginia well and in good spirits. She has improved very much in every respect. I never thought that she had a strong constitution, but the severe northern winter did not appear to impair her health in the least— on the contrary she has grown considerably, looks better, and her general health is excellent. Aunt Sally says that she is talented and very studious. She performs well on the piano and sings delightfully. I shall not praise her any more at present, but merely say that, by her amiable deportment and sweet disposition, she has won the affections of every young lady and child in the school.

I called on Miss Rogers and all my acquaintances in the city. They invariably inquired whether I was married or not. I would have liked to answer in the affirmative, but doubtless it will be better, after a short lapse of time, that circumstances prevented it for the present, for "whatever is, is right." I gave Aunt Sally the present you sent her, with which she appeared to be delighted. She spoke frequently and affectionately of you, regretting very much that you did not visit Philadelphia last fall. She says that she never expects to see you as long as she lives.

I send you by Rush a small memento which I requested him to give to you, *provided* Mrs. Jones interposes no objection; but, if *possibly* there should be any, *of course* you'll not want it. Theresa, the wind blows favorably now, all opposition is happily done away with, and everything is peace and harmony. You can scarcely imagine what the state of my mind is now, compared to what it was last year this time. Then it was racked with doubts and misgivings, and perplexed with anticipated evils; now it is comparatively calm and easy. I know that the time will come, and speedily (for it's limited to nine months), when all will be settled. I know, too, that your precious mother is better reconciled: and this makes me more contented, for there is no sacrifice so great that I would not make to conciliate her. When I think of her situation, that of a tender, doating mother, I say to myself, "Do as you would be done by," and whenever I have had the philosophy to call this golden rule into action I feel certain that I never experienced any regrets in consequence. I believe I heard you say that you liked a *matter of fact* letter, and not one filled with moralizing, etc. As I have no news to communicate that would at all interest you, I must instead of facts give you ideas, though they may be expressed so incoherently as not to be comprehensible always. However, the chain of connection is plain in my own mind, though it may appear a confused affair to another. Then excuse.

This is the first day of April. April fooling is in great fashion here. Mrs. Judkins sent me up to see Miss Shellman, saying that she had the most excruciating toothache, and wished me to go and extract it. I assure you I felt rather awkward when I went with my instruments and found that I had been "*fooled.*"

Next Monday, the 4th of April, is, I believe, your birthday. I shall not forget it, neither can I forget, among many other fond recollections, that on that day—1836—I was completely and totally "*used up.*" However, all's well now, and I am amply repaid for all such cruel acts, though they were not altogether voluntary. Have you heard anything from Wash or any of the volunteers since their arrival in Florida? How is Cousin *Marian?* I expect her to write to me as well as yourself.

Theresa, remember what I told you. Write to me. Give my love to Mrs. Jones and family.

Good-by, my ever dear Theresa.

J. MARION SIMS.

MOUNT MEIGS, ALABAMA, *April 13, 1836.*

MY DEAR, DEAR THERESA: I had the *blues* most horribly last night. I could not help thinking of *home*—of *you.* During my absence from Alabama a friend of mine was married, and his brother gave him a party last evening. I shared his hospitality, but, indeed, a small portion of pleasure fell to my lot. I feel now, when in the company of young ladies, that I can't possibly do or say anything calculated to interest or please, and, therefore, only take pains not to excite the displeasure of any. This feeling of indifference it is impossible for me to master; but this is as it should be, for I exult in saying that my heart is inthralled, that it belongs to *one only.* This being the case, it is not unnatural that I should manifest so little solicitude about the company of others, indeed, their *presence* only serves to remind me more forcibly of the *absent,* and, therefore, did I say that I was afflicted with a slight paroxysm of the *blue devils. . . .* The party was small and select. The young ladies generally looked "*pretty fiercely,*" I may say handsome; their manners open, frank, and pleasant, not being trammeled with too great a show of formality and etiquette. The minds of the mass of them were not, however, *extremely well cultivated*, though they could make a noise on the *piano*, dance gracefully, dress splendidly, and talk nonsense enough for anybody's use—unfortunately, nowadays, these accomplishments, as they are termed, instead of being thought superfluous, or rather supplemental, are made the very basis of female education—but I commenced to give you an idea of these *Alabama lassies*, and not to write a dissertation on education. A few of these misses, as is usual in such a *crowd*, were thought to be beautiful—what a pity that girls generally will tell, by their actions, that they are aware of the fact!—this was the case with some of these, and, *of course*, they were rather too "airy" to please such an old gentleman as myself. But, to be serious, I could not help contrasting with these the *one* I love. Theresa, I never was in the habit of praising you to your face. I know you have too much sense to suffer flattery, and I too high a regard, too much love for you to attempt such a thing. I am wholly incapable of it. Truth in commendation is not flattery, even though it should be misdirected. I say that the contrast involuntarily arose in my mind. How I hate affectation and coquetry. "Love is blind" I know; but I must say that such things could never elude my observations. Theresa, I have told you more than once that I *love* you; yet words vainly essay to convey an idea of the degree and intensity of that *love*. Should I say that time, space, and a thousand new faces could not effect a change in my present sentiments, you, I am certain, would believe me sincere, though you might answer that I was human, and frailty was natural. What on this earth ought to make one happier than the idea of being sincerely loved? I *ought* to be satisfied, for I feel certain that I am loved for *myself alone*. I am poor, very poor, and you have always known it; yet I rejoice in this poverty when it buys such love as yours. I have nothing to boast of, nothing, Theresa, but you. These are not unmeaning words. I speak as I feel, but, heaven knows, not half as much. Think me not romantic, I never was, but delight in reality, be it ever so sad.

I have called on Mrs. Howard again. "All's well." She appears to be contented; but I assure you there is a great difference between her situation here, for comfort, and the one she enjoyed in old Lancaster. We have to make a great many sacrifices, and en-

dure many privations, by moving to this or any other new country.
I am no ways backward in telling you the truth, for I am anxious
to prepare your mind for the worst. If there is to be any disappointment I want it, if possible, to be agreeable. About a week
ago I received a letter from Brother Wash. It was written with
his characteristic brevity, and dated at Volusia, March 24th, and
says: " If I am not *killed*, it is uncertain which way I shall return
home. Write to me at St. Augustine and inform you whether you
are married or not. If you are, it is possible that I may pay you a
visit before I return home. Give my love to *Marian* and *Theresa*,
and tell them *farewell* for me—farewell." (Signed.)

I shall ever regret that I did not go with Wash and my friends
to Florida. *My brother is there.* It is not always prudent to say
what we think; but, when I think of old H——'s treatment of
—— and Wash on the eve of his leaving home, it makes me too
hot. I never can forget or forgive that act in the old colonel. I had
more charity for him than to suppose for a moment that he could
possibly be guilty of such an act of cruelty. A Turk would not
have done more! I am anxious to hear from you. I have not
heard from —— since I left there. Farewell, my dear Theresa.

J. MARION SIMS.

MOUNT MEIGS, ALABAMA, May 11, 1836.

THERESA, my dearest girl, your precious letter was duly received,
for which you have my acknowledgment—a thousand thanks. I
would certainly have answered it before this time but (as I suppose) you are aware that the mail has been stopped, in consequence
of the disturbances in the Creek Nation. The whole country is in a
perfect uproar. Women and children are flying in every direction,
for the last two days. The road here has been strewed with these
helpless creatures, leaving their houses and homes to be plundered
by the ruthless savage. Most of the chiefs are friendly, but they
say that they can't possibly control their young warriors, and that
a fight is inevitable. About four hundred men from this section of
country will march into the Nation to-morrow or next day, which
I think will act as a most powerful sedative on these infurated, hot-
blooded animals. Our village is crowded to-night with women and
children who have fled from the Nation. *Forty* or *fifty families*
have crossed Line Creek to-day. Really it is a melancholy specta-

cle to look at them, to hear them describe the situation of the country and the consternation of the inhabitants. If such scenes as this are not sufficient to stimulate to action, and to fan into a flame the last latent sparks of chivalry, I don't know what would be. *Any* man who would openly refuse, under such circumstances as these, to march to the rescue of his fellow-citizens, would not justly be entitled to the protection of the community in which he lived, much less to the affection that any *fair friend* might bear him. But you have heard of " *Ulans and rumors of Ulans*" till you are tired of it. You have already suffered painful anxiety enough about your friends and acquaintances who went to Florida, without having your feelings too much excited or your sympathies too deeply enlisted by a description of our suffering here. Tell Rush that, if he wishes to visit this country this spring, he can't now come as a *traveling* gentleman, but he can come in the capacity of a "knight-errant." It is thought that there will be ample room now for a display of gallantry; that those restless young spirits, panting for glory and military renown, may now have an opportunity of evincing their courage and immortalizing themselves. Think not, though, that I am one of these adventurers. I am satisfied with doing my duty in giving protection and assistance to the defenseless inhabitants—but I promised to say no more about wars. However, it may turn out, as everybody says, that there will be a first-rate chance of getting a fight out of the Indians. Some of those young fellows will have fun over these if there's fun in fighting. If Major G. put this letter in the post-office after he got there, please let my father know these facts. I have not time to write to him at this moment. Two of his last letters have been received.

Remember me kindly and affectionately to your dear mother and Rush and all of my friends. Promise to write to you whenever I have a chance of sending the letter to any place in Georgia.

Farewell, Theresa. Ever yours. Love to "Marion," and tell her " blessed is he (she) who holdeth out to the last." Again, farewell, my dearest Theresa. J. MARION SIMS.

TUSKEGEE, ALABAMA, *June 4, 1836.*

MY DEAR THERESA: I have just time to drop you a few lines. I write by a company of engineers returning to Columbus. This morning our company was (as they call it) honorably discharged.

I have been long enough in the service to become tired of it. We lived well indeed, not suffering any of the privations to which our Florida volunteers were accustomed. The only thing we lacked was a chance of fighting. I never saw men so hungry for a fight in my life, but I suppose that it will be the least troublesome of all the labors that those who remain will have to undergo.

I presume you have heard by this time that Mr. Thifer arrived safely at home. He had a hard time of it. He was out three days and nights without a mouthful to eat, etc. A minute history of what he had to suffer would make one's heart ache. I had an account of the affair from one that was with him. His trunk has been seen lying by the road-side (being labeled), but it was torn open and everything taken out.

I shall in a few minutes leave here for Mount Meigs. Excuse this scratching if you please, we have to do as we can in camps. Give my respects to my cousins, friends, and remember me most affectionately to your dear mother.

For a time farewell, my dear Theresa.

J. MARION SIMS.

MOUNT MEIGS, ALABAMA, *June 24, 1836.*

MY DEAR, DEAR THERESA: I have just this moment received brother Wash's letter dated the 1st of June. Sorry indeed am I if I have inadvertently given you uneasiness by not writing more frequently. I wrote to *you* by Major Gibson, a day or two before he marched to the Nation. A few days afterward I wrote to father and Rush, and, when we were discharged, I wrote again to my father and *yourself*. These letters were intrusted to gentlemen soldiers going on to Columbus, who promised to place them in the post-office there. I presume that ere this time they have all come to hand, if they had not when brother's letter was received. Wash gave me a tremendous scolding. It's all just enough. After enumerating what I must write to you about, brother says: "Tell her all that a lover can tell, or all that a lover can ask." With regard to the Creek Ulan, we are here altogether ignorant of what is going on in the Nation. Various and innumerable contradictory rumors are flying through the country. We don't know what to believe. Report says that this portion of the army was within a few miles of the camp of the hostile Indians last week, and intended attacking them immediately; that when they went there the Indians had *decamped,* that they took some negroes that the Indians had stolen, with five hundred bushels of corn and three hundred head of cattle, together with some fifty or sixty prisoners, one of the head chiefs among them.

I fear that it will be a long time yet before peace and tranquillity are restored to this section of country, though let not this frighten you, for it must not prevent our connubial arrangements in the fall. I am just as safe here, and as much out of danger, as *you* are in Lancaster. Think me not premature, Theresa, if I here speak of appointing the wedding-day, etc., for it takes a letter so long to travel from here to Carolina, it's well enough to begin in time. I find that I can't leave this place before December, which I expect to early in the month, so that I may spend the Christmas holidays in old Lancaster. I would suggest the appointment of any day (Sunday excepted) between the 10th and 20th of December, provided it meets your approbation. I beg you when you write to me to define some particular day for the occasion, as it will be too late after I get there to do so and make the necessary arrangements. I hope now that you will not *forget this.* You might possibly *neglect* to say anything about it for a time, but I don't think you can easily forget.

Wash seems to be in a desperate way; I wish you would prescribe for him. Tell him there's nothing like *patience* and *perseverance.* I have tried in my own case and found it beneficial. I would, therefore, strenuously recommend it to all those afflicted in like manner; such medicines frequently answer an admirable purpose, when harsher remedies have proved totally inefficient, if not detrimental. It's a hard case. I know it troubles your mind in some degree, for you can not but sympathize with individuals so unfortunately circumstanced, particularly when you feel so much interest in their personal welfare and future happiness.

Remember me, Theresa, most affectionately to your precious mother and her dear family. Tell Rush to write to me, if he has not already done so. Let me hear from you, if you please. Give me all the news, for I have had nothing particular from *home* lately.

Farewell, my dear, dear Theresa.

J. Marion Sims.

Mount Meigs, Alabama, *July 20, 1836.*

My dear Theresa: It is now midnight. I have just returned from the country, and found Dan Clarke at the hotel. The opportunity is so fine that I would be committing a criminal act if I did not take time to write you a few lines.

I am in perfectly good health, and, as usual, in very fine spirits. You have seen that the Indian war is probably at an end; three or four days ago about three thousand Indians were taken from Montgomery, on board of two steamboats chartered for the purpose, to Arkansas. The war was completed much sooner than I anticipated, but I can't conceive that any or much praise is to be awarded to the whites in consequence. The credit of bringing it to a close is principally due to two friendly chiefs, Opothlo - Yohola and Jim-Boy.

I have been very tardy about building my house, etc.; the fact is, the Creek war distracted the whole country so much that it was impossible for me to do anything about it. I could not procure a lot with which I was pleased, and thought I had better postpone buying for a while. I had rather go to housekeeping than to "board out," and shall consequently rent a house and lot, provided it is perfectly agreeable to you, which I shall presume to be the case unless you say otherwise.

When you write, pray don't forget the few little "preliminaries" I mentioned in my last letter. I should like to have all these little affairs adjusted and understood.

"What in the world" is the reason that Rush has not answered my letter? Not the scratch of a pen have I received from him since we parted in New York. Has he forgotten me? Is it accidental or is it intentional? It can't be. He must either not have received my note, or else his answer is written and never come to hand. Do tell him to write to me, his friend.

Remember me dearly to Cousin Nancy and my never-to-be-forgotten friend Mr. Thormule. Tell Cousin Mary Ann to walk Spanish and Charlie not to walk crooked. Give my love to your dear mother, and sister Mary. Do write to me, my dear Theresa, for I am almost crazy to hear from you.

Good-night. Farewell, Theresa.

J. Marion Sims.

MOUNT MEIGS, ALABAMA, *August 21, 1836.*

MY DEAR THERESA : I received your very affectionate letter this morning, together with one from Sister Marion, and Aunt Sally, which have kept me on the "grin" all day. I don't know what would have become of me if they had not come to hand at the time, for Rush had left me for "Sweet, sweet home" about two hours before. I scarcely can tell how the last week has slipped away. Rush (my dearest friend), I must say, has been as liberal with me in his visit as I could have asked, considering he had been absent so long and was so anxious to get back. He ran around with me eight days, and when he left I had on (I am told) a face about a yard long, but my gloominess was wholly dissipated on the reception of your kind letter. Indeed, Theresa, if you only knew how much you could and have contributed to my happiness and contentment by writing, I feel confident that you would most assuredly exercise your pen more frequently. Don't understand me as complaining now, for I have already done that sufficiently. I would give anything, at least something handsome, if I could only recall the scolding letter I wrote you by your brother Rush. You will receive this though before he can get home. Consider, then, that I recall everything in the shape of a quarrel which I have unfortunately written by him. I am sorry that I did not put it off a while longer, but really I had despaired of ever receiving the scratch of a pen from you again. I say that I recall, for "I know that you, too, are of a forgiving disposition." It gives me the greatest pleasure imaginable to know that you have spent your time so agreeably during the summer, for naturally enough I am only happy in proportion as I know that you are so ; there is nothing surprising in the sympathy existing between two kindred souls, particularly when they are on the eve of being amalgamated, united into one. It was certainly from a knowledge of this that we are told in divine revelation to "laugh with those that laugh, and weep with those that weep." But I perceive that I am becoming grave.

Your Uncle Wash and Miss Raigan! Well, I was truly a little surprised, but very agreeably so. I say to him, Davy Crockett like, "go ahead." We will certainly have "big doings" in old Lancaster this fall if Rush and Miss Mourning, your Uncle Wash and Miss Raigan, etc., etc., should make it out. "The more the merrier," as the saying is, and I don't care how many there are. Why don't

17

somebody spur George up. I suppose, though, that he is too much devoted to his profession to be guilty of any thing like this kind of gallantry. I am sorry for those Lancaster boys, they are as bad off for some object to bestow their affections on as the young men of Alabama; they would do well to import a few lassies, or at least, to transport them. I should like very much to see the young man in Sumter you say looks so much like me, for I have never yet seen a piece of flesh I thought myself to resemble except one, and he was as ugly as sin and wicked as Satan; physically, perhaps, there was a resemblance, but, morally, I must say there was none, for (I think) I am not half as bad as I used to be. I don't allow that Sumter youngster to look like me, and—but no matter—I feel mischievous this evening anyhow, am a privileged character in the way of talking and writing. Sisters, Virginia, Aunt Sally and all were very well on the 8th inst., and had nothing to do but visit, as this is the month of vacation. Father had paid them a visit of five days, and they were delighted. Sally tells me to "have patience," that "December" will be here before long, etc., she says she has bought you a "bridal present" which she intended sending by father. The appointment of the special day you have so kindly and liberally given to me, that I designate "Wednesday, the fourteenth of December," provided, etc. Remember the fourteenth. I presume you will have four attendants, as it is the order of the day (it will suit me perfectly whether we have half a dozen or none at all). I expect Rush, Frank Massey, Bill Davis and Le Massey, all doctors. That will be a real physical wedding. I have said nothing to Rush about it as yet; I can talk to anybody else with greater freedom on this topic, and yet with him I am always under the greatest restraint. "'Tis strange." I am not tired of writing, but I suppose you had as leave stop reading. I therefore accommodate you. Give my love to your dear mother. I expect to trouble her with a brief letter some day, provided I can bring my courage up to the point.

Farewell, my dear Theresa.

J. Marion Sims.

Mount Meigs, Alabama, *October 10, 1836.*

Oh, my dear Theresa, I received your very affectionate letter day before yesterday, and you can't possibly imagine the effect it had on my spirits. Since I wrote to Brother Wash, I am sorry to say I have had a second relapse; however, it lasted but four days, and I am now improving rapidly. I am able to walk across my room (which is about 12 feet), and can sit straight in bed (without a prop) whenever I eat. You may perhaps think this is getting along slowly, but I assure you I feel proud that I am able to say this much. I was taken sick on the 3d of September, and have been prostrated ever since, a span of five weeks. I am reduced to nothing but skin and bones; it could not have been otherwise, for I have been literally physicked to death. Once, while so sick, I thought that I was going to die. When in health I have always been of the opinion that I could face death without any dread, but there is a grand difference between one's feelings while blessed with a strong and healthy constitution and when the body is emaciated, worn down by disease, and covered with a cold, clammy perspiration, with a mind correspondingly prostrated; then is the time that death appears in all its terrors to the mind of him who feels conscious that his course of life has not been in consistence with all the just principles of moral and religious rectitude, and then the idea of dying among strangers. Oh, it's terrible beyond description! I have written till I feel very feeble and must conclude. As soon as I am able to travel from here to Carolina I intend to leave here, but it will be some considerable time first, perhaps not before the 20th November. If I should improve faster than I expect, I shall come sooner.

Rease Prin and the doctor passed through this place last night. Mr. and Mrs. Howard and most of their family have been sick, but are now well or improving. McKinzie's family have all been healthy. I am extremely sorry indeed to hear that Dr. Brown is dead, and that Lancaster has been so wretchedly sickly. Dr. Tom's match surprised me no little I assure you. How do Dr. Wash and Sumter make it? Have the colonel and the Sumter widow made a bargain or not? Rush will understand why I have not written to him. Please give Rush, your dear mother, and sister Mary, and all the family my love. I received a letter from Sister Miriam this morning dated 29th September. All were then well, though at a loss to know why I had not written to them. When I get straight I'll make the mails groan with letters, for time lost must be made up.

I must bid you adieu, my head grows dizzy.

Farewell, my dear, dear Theresa.

J. MARION SIMS.

Letter to his Father after his Removal to New York.

79 MADISON AVENUE, NEW YORK, *August 8, 1855.*

MY DEAR FATHER : At last I have some good news to write you, such as I never expected till within the last month. I confess I am surprised at it, and perhaps you may be so too. I am still not only living, but feel like a tolerably sound man *again.* I have never been so nigh well since I lost my health, last March was five years ago. I know I can not write you better news than this, and nothing that should unite us more perfectly in lifting our hearts in thankfulness to Him who orders all things wisely and well.

It is strange how often I have been raised up, when it seemed impossible for me to live ; and yet not strange when I see the finger of God directing so plainly a destiny which I pray may be profitable to others on earth, and profitable to me in eternity. These afflictions are necessary to my spiritual welfare, they are necessary to my usefulness here, and are not the result of mere accident. I know full well that I have a mission to fulfill—one to which my life is most willingly devoted—but which should not interfere with my looking forward to a purer existence hereafter.

You and I, my dear father, have both been very bad men, considering we were almost faultless in all the duties and relations of life. We have been mere *moralists.* We thought ourselves as good as anybody, and far better than most people. We never dreamed of our own sinfulness and utter unworthiness. Instead of looking to a Saviour for help, we have felt in our own hearts a plea of self-righteousness, which makes us occupy a more dangerous ground than the out-breaking sinner. Because it is hard for us who are good moralists to see our depravity, while the blasphemer and law-breaker may all at once be perfectly overwhelmed at the contemplation of the enormity of his transgressions.

When we occupy such a dangerous position, one so securely fortified, how are we to be brought to terms? How are we to acknowledge that we are rebels, that we have taken up arms against our Father? He has said that nothing but an *unconditional surrender* will suit Him, and He has pointed out the only way that He will receive our approach. The Saviour is the way. But have we chosen the way? or have we come up presenting our own merits and pleading our own justification? Fathers are generally forgiving

—you know that—for you have had to forgive much. But Our Father in Heaven is more forgiving than all others. He has to use different means with his several rebellious children, according to circumstances. With those who are strongly fortified on the almost unapproachable hill of morality, nothing but the strongest artillery will do any good—small arms are of no use. They are only scorned, laughed at. It requires long guns of the largest size.

Our lives, my dear father, have been very similar. Our successes and contented lot in early life and our *moral* sort of religion were alike. Our reverses of fortune and our afflictions have been similar, occurring about the same period of our career.

Father, these reverses and afflictions are the long guns, whose work of demolition should long ago have brought us to terms. See what afflictions I have passed through in the last four years. Till the death of our little Merry I knew no great trouble (save the one that gave you and me so much unhappiness). Since then what have I not suffered. My physical diseases were not so great as Job's, but then they seemed almost more than I could bear. With these came the maltreatment and persecutions of my own brothers-in-law; then money tribulations; then disappointments in men; then an exile from home and friends; a separation from the father whose declining days I had fondly hoped to have rendered pleasant and happy; then difficulties, disappointments, obstacles and tribulations here, which, superadded to my real physical sufferings, almost drove me to the mad-house; all troubles of such countless variety that I care not to recall them except in general terms. But I see the finger of God in all, and I feel that it was absolutely necessary for me to have passed through precisely what I have to make me what I am. One blow less would hardly have produced the desired effect.

I have said, father, that our lives and fortunes have not been dissimilar. My own happy lot and subsequent reverses I have briefly recounted. Bear with me while I as briefly bring to mind yours. I tread upon sacred ground, but it is one that a dutiful son may well survey with an affectionate father. You were a good moral man, fulfilling admirably all the duties of life. As a son, husband, father, master, private citizen or public officer, you were faultless. You know it. You felt it, and in your heart you told your Heavenly Father so. You rested your claims to a better world hereafter upon your own good deeds here. You felt not the need of a Saviour (I judge, of course, from your past life, and by looking into my own heart), for they who feel the need of a physician call out for help.

God prospered you. He gave you health. He blessed you with a wife who was a model for her son. He gave you a most interesting family of children, in whom your heart was wrapped up, and for whose education you labored and sacrificed yourself as only a good father could do. He gave you warm and true friends. *No man ever had better*. He gave you success in all the mere earthly objects of life. But did all this bring you nigher to the good Giver of all these good gifts. Did you feel that they came from Him. Did you feel that in yourself you were unworthy, that you could not come directly to Him pleading your own good works, and that you must approach Him through a Mediator and feel your need of a Saviour. I can not recall any evidences of this during this time of prosperity. God wanted to bring the heart of so good a man as you nearer to Him. Intrenched as you were on the great hill of morality, he could not do it by any very gentle means. Having tried all other means, the heaviest artillery was opened upon you. The death of a beautiful boy, ten years old, was the first Absalom! How it wrung your heart! Scarcely less than did the death of Absalom, the brat of poor old David! Was this all? oh, no! would to God it had been enough. The batteries were opened, and nothing but an unconditional surrender would be sufficient. What next? A few unimportant reverses, a few disappointments in men, much anxiety about worldly affairs, defeat, annoyances, all in quick succession, and then came the great and fatal blow—the death of my mother.

79 Madison Avenue, New York, *December 23, 1854.*

My dear Theresa: We are all getting on as well as it is possible for us to do in your absence. We try to do the best we can. Knickerbocker is less fretful to-night than he has been at any time since you left. Of course you know he has been fretting only because he misses you, and not in consequence of the vaccination, for that is drying up. Mrs. McC. washes and dresses the little fellow every morning. I don't see him as often as I expected. Mary brought him down yesterday afternoon after her return from school. She says they had a big time at the school yesterday. The presentation to Miss Miller of a silver pitcher by her pupils was made, when

she resigned her charge, amid a general bellowing of the young
animals. I hope her successor may be as competent and as good
as she is. It's a great loss to us to part with her, and I can not but
feel very anxious about the new superintendent.

Granville went to Flatbush to-day, and begged me to let him stay
with Johnny during the whole vacation, till Tuesday week, the 2d
of January, but I told him it would not be proper for him to tire
the good people out entirely, and he must come home on Wednesday. You and Harry, Sharpey and Fanny all being absent, makes
quite a vacuum in our family circle. Mary and Eliza are nice girls.
They behave with great propriety. They are quiet and dignified.
They remain mostly in their rooms, occasionally sit awhile in the
office. I can't help praising them up a little even to their mother.
You very well know that I am not in the habit of praising either
of them, so you may feel sure that it is from no disposition to flat-
ter. I am making up my mind to change their music teacher, although I have not mentioned it to either of them. Having the opinion that I do of madame, and knowing what you think of her, I
don't think we should retain her as a teacher after this quarter.

Cold! cold! gloriously cold! The weather is magnificent. It
has been intensely cold ever since you left. First-rate hog-killing
time. I know they would be glad of a touch of this sort of weather
round about Montgomery. It is now midnight, and it is sleeting
hard—too cold to snow—but, while I am luxuriating in the cold, it
carries distress into the haunts of the poor. The distress here can
hardly be imagined. Several meetings of mechanics out of employ
have been held in the park, and some most inflammatory speeches
made, where the speakers were loudly cheered when they spoke of
oppression of capital over labor, and the necessity, if it came to the
worst, of bursting the doors of storehouses and taking what they
want.

What a contrast between this country and the South. Here we
have vagrancy and pauperism, and all its attendant ills of vice, crime,
and degradation, which we never see in a slave population. Here
I feel that the time may come when a man may not be secure in the
accumulation or enjoyment of wealth. The great and good Peter
Cooper says that the millionaires of this country have much to dread
from the popular voice; that the time may come when the masses
may vote away, confiscate, as it were, their hoarded wealth—but

this is not the theme for a letter to you. We are here and can't help ourselves. Providence has placed us here and will, I have no doubt, take care of us.

I have been to see Mrs. Peck to-night. She is as courageous as ever. I find that she is not only interested in the hospital movement, but she is feeling great interest in my own business. She wanted to know whether I would go to see a lady friend of hers, who had been complaining for some time and was not wholly satisfied about her condition. So you see how the great movement will operate when we get it properly started; but money! money! money! How are we to live till I can get properly at work—I have but two dollars; don't like to call on Mr. Clay for any more. My clothes are not good enough for me to make the appearance that I ought, considering my claims and pretensions, so I am obliged to have a decent suit, but how it is to come I don't know. Although I write thus, don't think for a moment I am despondent; I never felt more confident of success or more cheerful. I am not gloomy. I feel a power within me that is irresistible. I feel that I am in the hands of God, that I have a high and holy mission to perform, that his blessing has already crowned my efforts, and that He will in due time raise up friends to assist me in my labors. This is coming about daily. How differently am I situated from what I was three months ago, and I am gaining power almost hourly.

24th.—Have been to hear Dr. Adams to-day. The new church at the foot of Madison Avenue was dedicated. Went there again to-night to hear Dr. Bethune, but the house was so crowded that I could not stand the heated, contaminated air of the place. I rather liked Dr. Adams. The church is a good one to hear in, and I would be willing to have a pew there if they are not rented at too great a price.

Mrs. Greer has volunteered to call in her carriage some morning soon, and take me down to Amity Street, and introduce me to some rich, working women who will help me with the hospital. One of the Councilmen called on me with Mr. Stuart yesterday, but I was not at home. I am to see him soon. Mr. Stuart is to introduce me to the Mayor this week, and to several of the Councilmen, so you see the work goes bravely on. It would have ruined everything if I had left here for a month.

I pray God you may be able to arrange our affairs so as to secure the daily bread for a year to come. About the negroes—well, I think it best to sell them. We are bound to do it some time, and I don't see why it should be procrastinated. They might not sell as well as they would some time ago, but I reckon they would bring good prices if they were sold on time with good security; but do as you and Mr. Lucas and father may on consultation think best. We must live, and my present position must be maintained here, let it cost what it may. I can't back out, nor would I if I could. The prize is too great, too glittering, not to be grasped when it seems so easy to do it.

It is Christmas eve and midnight. I have just been up to the children's room. They are fast asleep, and have hung up stockings near my bed for old Santa Claus. How they will be disappointed in the morning. Well, I must get them something to-morrow. Negroes and children always expect liberal presents on Christmas. I was too busy yesterday to think of such things, and to-day being Sunday puts it out of my power, even if I had money. What do I care for money—I have what is better than money, and what money can not buy, I have health. I feel that I have an honest heart, and a mind intent upon great and good purposes. I have a loving, confiding wife. I have dutiful and healthy children. I have friends a plenty, the comforts of a good home, and an almost illimitable prospect of future usefulness. Good God! was ever man more blessed on this earth. Why, then, should I feel uneasy a moment about a few hundred contemptible coppers, when I know that this scarcity is but temporary, and that the time must soon come when I shall have an abundance.

Kiss Harry for me. Remember me to father, Mr. and Mrs. Lucas, and the lots of friends you may see, and believe me, my dear wife, ever your devoted husband, J. MARION SIMS.

Mrs. ELIZA THERESA SIMS, Montgomery, Alabama.

79 MADISON AVENUE, NEW YORK, *December 25, 1854.*

MY DEAR THERESA: I have been at home all day. Mr. Stuart dined with us. We have had rather a stupid time of it. Mr. R. and myself played a game of chess just before dinner. It was too hard work, and I told him he could not rob me of another hour and a half so profitlessly. He made the chess a Christmas present to

Mary. To Eliza he gave a neat breast-pin, to Carrie some candies. The other girls went down to see Mrs. Swezey this afternoon. They took tea with her, and Mr. S. came home with them. Carrie and the Kissam children went next door, and with the Green children have had quite a frolic since tea, while Mary and Eliza have been up-stairs with Knickerbocker. I am fully repaid for your absence, by having an opportunity of finding out more of our two oldest children. It is odd that a father should know so little of his children, and unfortunate that he should be so incapable of understanding and appreciating their true worth. Mary and Eliza both exhibit so much good sense, such decorous deportment, such gentleness and such affection for each other, that I am quite in love with them. Willie is the best boy in the city. He improves daily. It is really ridiculous to see Mrs. McCerren curling his hair—hair that is so rudimentary that it requires a microscope to see it. His arm is getting well. I think he is two or three pounds heavier than when you left. Tell my Alabama boy that there is danger of the old Harry being supplanted by old Knick.

Our household is getting on very well. The children were all allowed to dine at the first table to-day, and they behaved very well. Mrs. S. gave them a big dinner. The Catholics had a great time last night. They had high mass at midnight and did not get home till about two o'clock, and poor old Mrs. D. has had the mulligrubs all day. Truly, I have never seen any one whose religious duties so mortify the flesh as do her fastings and prayers. She was never intended for a Catholic. She is so only by accident and a forced habit.

I was complaining to you yesterday about my clothes. To-day I hunted up a coat that was laid aside last spring, and Mary Doyle gave it a good scrubbing, so that I have determined to make it carry me through the holidays rather than ask credit or borrow any more money, although I am satisfied that I ought to dress better than I do. But I feel that a clear head and a good heart are far better than fine linen and fine clothes. It's good to be poor, provided that poverty does not oppress and wholly crush us out. I am just about poor enough to be stimulated to extraordinary efforts; yet I feel that if I was a little more distressed I could hardly bear it. God in His mercy has, in my case, most assuredly tempered the wind to the shorn lamb. Am I not peculiarly blessed? Does not the light shine in upon our darkened path as we never dreamed of seeing it? Is not the finger of God visible in all our afflictions? Is He not blessing us more than we deserve? Oh, what a glorious thing it is to feel, to know, to realize that you are a blessed instrument in the hands of God for the accomplishment of good! When I pause to consider what I have done here, and how it has been effected, I can not but acknowledge that an overruling Providence has wisely directed all things for the best. When I look back and remember how my heart quailed before the dangers that surrounded us, how I was just on the eve of surrendering all as lost, how despair almost drove me to madness, and when I call to mind your gentle tones of encouragement, your blind and implicit reliance upon Divine Providence, your high moral fortitude and self-sacrificing efforts, dare I say I would have had it otherwise? No, no. It is all for the best, and the time is not far distant when we shall rejoice that we have passed through this period of tribulation; when we shall really laugh at the remembrance of the tears of bitterness that were then shed. Was ever a man's wife more literally his ministering angel? Every period of my life, from youth to the present hour, attests the fact. All that I am and hope to be I owe to you. How different would have been my destiny but for the influence exercised by you!

Indeed, my dear wife, I fear I am hardly a worthy husband; but it is not in my nature to be a better one.

May God bless you in your mission, and return you safely to your family, is the prayer of your devoted husband,

J. MARION SIMS.

Mrs. ELIZA THERESA SIMS, Montgomery, Alabama.

79 MADISON AVENUE, NEW YORK, *December 29, 1854.*

MY DEAR THERESA: The more I think of the negroes, the more am I satisfied that it is wholly to their advantage to have good homes. Let them understand that is impossible for us to keep them, that our necessities will compel us to a sale at no distant day, perhaps in less than a year, and that it is better for them to have homes of their own selection than to be sold under a mortgage to the highest bidder, for then they may fall into the hands of traders and be carried clear off. If we could afford to keep them, we would be glad to do so, but already are there mortgages on some of them, and there is no telling when they may be foreclosed. It is true that the evil day may be postponed for a little while longer, but it is certain to come, and we only consult the interests of the negroes by asking them to select homes now.

Cupe must be sold, it matters not how things go, and all the rest had better make up their minds to it. As to Abby's coming here, I am satisfied it would not suit her. She would never be happy here, and then we would have to let her go back again, and really, in our embarrassed circumstances, the luxury of gratifying her would be entirely too expensive. If we had our own house, so we could give her a comfortable room and make her happy, we might think of bringing her. It seems to me the best plan is for them all to select their homes, and, if the persons they severally wish to live with are not able to pay down the purchase money, they can be sold on any reasonable time, by having payment secured by undoubted paper. If they determine not to do this, they must take the consequence, and absolve us from blame, if by-and-by they should find cause to regret it. Let them understand our straitened circumstances, that we are obliged to live, that we have now no means but by sacrificing property, if our friends do not step forward and help us, and they will certainly see the dilemma in which we are placed, that the proposition to sell them is not one of choice, but of dire necessity. Let them know that it would be to our advantage to retain them, as it would afford us an income from their hire which would be of great assistance to us. Let them know, too, that it lacerates our hearts as much it does theirs to be compelled to the course we suggest. As you are there among them, I see that you have a difficult task before you. My heart aches at its contemplation.

The Sayne children are here. All's well. Knick is doing finely. He will captivate you completely when you get back again. His hair grows finely. I should suppose it was at least a quarter of an inch long. You can see it without holding him sidewise in the sun. Tell the Alabama boy that the Knickerbocker brother sends a heap of love to him and wishes to see him. I hope Harry is a good boy, and that he will return home greatly improved by his extensive travels.

I don't know what to make of Dr. J. He has not written me a word about Mrs. S. in a week. I suppose, however, that she is doing well or he would be clamorous for my presence up there.

Mr. R. calls for the letter, so I must close. I can't pretend to particularize, where we have so many friends, but just remember me with gratitude to all. To them I owe everything. But for their just appreciation and tender care of me, when I needed it, I could have done nothing. No man ever had better or truer friends, and no man's heart was ever more bitterly wrung at separating from such. But it is all right. This expatriation, as it were, almost made me mad, but now I would not have it otherwise.

May God bless you, my dear wife, and return you safely to your affectionate husband,　　　　　　　　　　J. MARION SIMS.

Mrs. ELIZA THERESA SIMS, Montgomery, Alabama.

79 MADISON AVENUE, NEW YORK, *December 31, 1854.*

MY DEAR THERESA : It is near midnight, and the old year is flickering out. Ah! what saddening thoughts are always associated with the death, even of time. The birth of the New-Year brings with it bright hopes, the realization of which depends more upon ourselves than we are apt to imagine. While we regret the misspent time of the old year, let us resolve to profit by past experience, and improve every moment of the new. We will soon be old. What we do in this life must be done quickly. Look back. Eighteen years have we been *one.* Our lives have glided smoothly, happily. We have lived for each other. Mutual confidence and mutual love have made us as happy as it is possible for mortals to be. We have been blessed with dutiful, fine children. We have had all the comforts, nay, even the luxuries of life. We have had more than the average degree of health. We have been blessed with friends, and the great objects of life with us have been eminently successful. Have we not much to be thankful for? Have we been really sufficiently so? Have we done our duty to our children, to ourselves, to our God? We have not. We have well and faithfully fulfilled all the other relations of life, but the moral culture of our children we have neglected, our own religious promptings we have smothered, and the whisperings, nay, the loud calls of the Holy Spirit we have slighted. Do we not then stand self-condemned? What, then, is to be done? Repent and give our hearts to God. Let us try to do this and we shall feel that we are in the line of our duty. Why hesitate? Why wait a moment? A public profession of the religion that I know glows in your heart is all that is needed. The power of your example will do more for the moral elevation and religious culture of the rest of us than whole volumes of sermons. Your whole life is a sermon. Why not, then, preach it? Your heart is full of religion. Why not, then, openly declare it? If you do not take the first step forward, then we shall remain in the darkness and doubt. But do you say there is no church here for you to unite with? This poor excuse can not exist after this. At last I have found the house of God I was willing to visit a second time—the man I was glad to hear more than once. It is Dr. Adams. You can not but be pleased with him. Religion is a matter of culture. The preached word is as necessary to the growth of grace as is rain to the growth of grain. Ah! my dear wife, we have been too happy in ourselves to give much attention to spiritual affairs. But, while we are still happy, let us not longer forget what is so palpably our duty.

January 1, 1855.—Five hours of quiet rest have infused new life into me for the day. What a beautiful, bright, glorious day! The sun is just rising, and all nature favors the gay season. Everything is frozen up; the streets are therefore dry and favorable to pedestrians. The air light, bracing and life-giving. What a day is this in New York! Who will rejoice more than the ladies when its rollicking jollities are over? Would you suppose I had the names of forty-eight on my list of calls? I expect to get to about half a dozen places. You know how I hate mere idle compliments, bowing in and bobbing out. I would not go at all, but I may have a chance to drop a good word somewhere for the advancement of the *cause*, the cause of poor suffering woman. This is at the bottom of my breast, it is at the top of my throat, it fills my brain. It is the grand moral object of my professional life. For this I work, for you I live.

Your affectionate husband,

J. MARION SIMS.

Mrs. ELIZA THERESA SIMS, Montgomery, Alabama.

79 MADISON AVENUE, NEW YORK, *January 7, 1854.*

MY DEAR THERESA: Your welcome New-Year's letter was received yesterday, and afforded me great gratification to see how much better you are attending to the great objects of your mission than I could have done—while it would certainly have been almost ruinous for me to have left here. The work goes on bravely. Last night Mrs. Hutchings took me to see Mrs. Dr. Marvin, a lady who was instrumental in founding and managing the "Home of the Friendless." She lives in Brooklyn, but is on a visit at Mrs. Stone's, who is one of the Fifth Avenue aristocracy. I never felt better, and they gave me scope to explain all my plans. Mrs. M. will become a co-worker, and will join Mrs. Peck and others, and I think, from the great interest manifested by Mrs. Stone, that she too will join in the movement. To-morrow morning, at half past nine o'clock, I am to call at Mrs. Stone's to accompany Mrs. M. to see Mrs. Hawkins, who was the prime mover, the real mother of the "Home." I pray God to give me wisdom, the power of language, and tact to enlist her and others on the side of this great humanitary movement.

Next to you and our children stands in my affections the success of this glorious mission. When I look into my heart I do not see that my motives are at all selfish. The only selfishness that I feel is the desire to do good, to be a benefactor of my race, and I sincerely pray that my labors may be blessed, so far as they tend to relieve suffering humanity, to advance the cause of science, and to elevate the condition of the medical profession. You can understand me. The world may not. It is a glorious thing to feel that you are above the dross and glitter of mere pageantry. Money is trash, and may be blown away by the wind. Honors are evanescent, and may be snatched by another. Even reputation may be tarnished by the slanderous tongue of an envious villain, but the proud consciousness of rectitude, coupled with true benevolence, lives in the heart of its possessor, and is as immortal as the soul itself.

I have heard to-day three good sermons. The morning and evening services at Dr. Adams's. I like him very much, and I am sure you will be pleased with him. The pews there are to be sold on Wednesday night. I fear they will exclude us poor folks from the church. I hope, however, we shall always be able to find a place there whenever we wish to worship with them. The afternoon service I attended at Dr. Van Ness's in Twenty-first Street near Sixth Avenue, where the Rev. Mr. Cuyler preached to young women on their Christian duties and destiny. It was a very eloquent address. Mr. B. generally goes to church with me. I have become quite attached to him, and also to Mr. D., who I find to be a very clever fellow indeed.

I received a letter from Mrs. Watkins two days ago. She had arrived safely; found all well. She was a show in Huntsville, and seems to have been lionized. Mrs. Coles, her cousin, will come on as soon as she hears that there is room in the house for her.

The children are all well, and Willie is the best child I ever saw. Mary stuffs him all the time. She keeps him chock full. He has no time to be bad. He eats and sleeps, laughs and grows fat. You will hardly know him when you get home, and I am sure he will hardly know you either. He is the admiration of the household, and tell Harry he is becoming quite a pet with his papa.

Remember me, my dear wife, kindly to all our friends, and, believe me, your devoted husband, J. MARION SIMS.

Mrs. ELIZA THERESA SIMS, Montgomery, Alabama.

P. S.—We are all as anxious to have you at home as you can be to get here, but don't you think you had better take a week longer and make a pop call on Aunt Betsey and Sister Mary. Think of it. J. M. S.

79 MADISON AVENUE, NEW YORK, *January 2, 1855.*

MY DEAR THERESA: Your letter of the 26th makes me easy on a very important matter—the money for which Mr. Lucas is my security, and what I owe him. Certainly this removes a great weight from us, and I can not feel thankful enough in being blessed with so good a friend. I know you will do what is exactly right in reference to the negroes. Sell what are necessary for immediate purposes. They will be sacrificed, but no matter, we must live, let it cost what it may.

Times are tight, but, thank God, we have good friends, some means, and a stout heart. I have never felt firmer. Indeed, I am getting stronger in my position every day. I have had several consultations since you left. To-day saw a case of ovarian disease.

I have just returned from a visit to Mrs. Gilbert, the wife of the elegant and efficient clerk of the Board of Education. She volunteered to help me in the hospital movement, and is willing to take a place on the Executive Committee. She is a working woman. Has brains as well as a heart. To acquire so efficient a woman is a good evening's work for the great cause. I did not get through with my calls yesterday, and that was the reason of my calling on

Mrs. Gilbert to-night. I told you in my letter yesterday that some good would come out of these New-Year's calls. Two days in the year mark us as a peculiar people—the 1st of May and the 1st of January. On May-day everything and everybody is *en déshabille*, but on New-Year's day all is prim and tidy.

But for Dr. Stillman I should have made a booby of myself staying at home all day, after calling on three or four of our neighbors. He came in and said I was going to do a very stupid thing if I remained at home, and so with him I had to go. We called together at Mrs. Dodge's, Peter Cooper's, Curtis's, and some others of the upper-ten, when I got fairly in for it and continued calling till after nine o'clock. And I found out that the ladies, after getting everything ready, are really disappointed if their friends do not come. So you see Dr. Stillman saved me from making the silly mistake of staying at home. I went to thirty-three places, and got home more sober than some of my friends. Mary and Eliza received your calls, and entertained your friends with sweetmeats and hot coffee. I had long cozy times at Mrs. Pryor's, Mrs. Kate Emmet's, Mrs. Clay's, Mrs. Hutching's (tell Miss Martha they all looked well there), and at Mrs. Crane's.

Well, I must brag a little about Knick. He is the best boy of his age in New York, and he grows so rapidly you will not know him when you get home. Mrs. McCerren takes great pains with him, and makes him look very nice indeed. I think him much better-looking than Harry was at the same age.

There's luck in leisure. I hope Miss Mary will have a good time of it, and that her home will be as good as she deserves, and her life as happy as it is possible for a married woman's to be.

Sorry to hear that *Puss* has been *Taylored*, but of course this gives Mrs. W. a fair chance to come out, as she could not now be a rival of her daughter.

I go to Portland to-morrow. Hope I shall get a letter from you before I leave.

The children started to school to-day. They like Miss Miller's substitute pretty well. I hope she will prove worthy of her high trust.

Two things I want you to do. Get Mr. Powell to put up some new pine (heart pine) boards at our little Merry's grave, to mark the place yet a while longer. I hope we will soon be able to get

Mr. Swezey to put up something handsome for us in the way of a monument. The other is, to bring with you your picture, painted when you were seventeen years old. Don't forget it. You can roll it round something. Well, take a sheet of pasteboard and roll it up so as to make it about six inches in diameter, and then roll the picture round this. Don't forget it. I have set my heart on it. I just want to see how much better-looking you are now than you were at seventeen, that's all. Take your time to come home. Make your visit as agreeable as it is possible under the circumstances. Don't let anything either there or at home mar the pleasure of the trip. Your affectionate husband,

J. MARION SIMS.

P. S.—Shall go to Connecticut to-morrow. Can not write again for two days.

79 MADISON AVENUE, NEW YORK, *January 15, 1855.*

MY DEAR THERESA: Yesterday was Sunday. I had received a message from Mr. Thorpe (Tom Owen, the bee-hunter) the night before to call over to Brooklyn and see Mrs. T., who had been sick for the last six or eight weeks. I went early, and after I fulfilled my mission I stepped across the street to hear . . . thunder. His church is a plain brick one, with a gallery extending forward covering nearly half the area of the ground floor, and giving it very much the appearance of a theatre with its parquette below and amphitheatre above. It was crowded, and he was playing to an appreciative audience. His preaching is simply acting. I am sure it is not prejudice in me when I say I can not believe that he possesses the first ray of spiritual religion. He seems to me to be a purely pulpit demagogue, and I judge not from any preconceived opinion of the man, but from yesterday's observation of him.

But, enough of this, the sworn but harmless enemy of his country. I intended to go to church in the afternoon (as I had gone to the theatre in the morning), but I missed it. I had to call and see Jos. Greer, and Mr. G. and myself got into an old-fashioned southern talk about everybody and everything that we knew in common, and so the time whirled on so rapidly that as I returned home the people were returning from church. But Mr. B., Mr. D., and myself all went last night down to Twelfth Street, near Sixth Avenue, to hear the Rev. Dr. Murray, of Elizabethtown.

Well, the hospital movement. Every spare moment of my time is put in. On Saturday morning Mr. Stuart took me over to see Alderman Tucker, who immediately comprehended the whole scheme, and is to come here at nine o'clock to-night to have a long war-talk on the subject He says he will introduce me to all the aldermen and councilmen that it is important for me to know, so that everything shall be prearranged and well understood before it comes up before the Council. Alderman Tucker lives right opposite Mrs. S. in Thirtieth Street, so as I was in the neighborhood I called to see her. She seems to feel like she had known us always, went into regular ecstatics at seeing me, asked a thousand anxious questions, promised to introduce me to the wife of Alderman Mott, and insisted that I should go and see Mrs. Doremus, which I have determined to do. So I called at Professor Barker's to see Dr. Doremus and inquire when I might find his good mother at home; and by this accidental call I have made a friend of Mrs. B., and the doctor has promised to introduce me to some two or three other ladies who will co-operate. My whole plans have received an impetus and assumed an importance by my labors since you left that they did not possess before.

The children are all well, and Knick is the best boy in the city. Although we are as anxious for you to get home as you are yourself, still let not our condition hurry or divert your plans. A week longer is as nothing *after it is gone.* So make yourself as happy as you can and come when you get ready. The children all send love to mother and Harry.

Believe me, my dear wife, ever your devoted husband,

J. Marion Sims.

Mrs. Eliza Theresa Sims, Montgomery, Alabama.

79 Madison Avenue, New York, *January 24, 1855.*

My dear Theresa: Your letters of the 16th to Mary, and of the 17th to me, arrived yesterday. I have felt distressed, first, because Harry has been sick, and, second, because it necessarily detains you from us longer than we expected; but I have been more distressed because I was so sure that you would get off by the 22d that I had ceased to direct letters to Montgomery, and the last two written had been dispatched to Lancaster, supposing that they would meet you there. Thus you have been so long without letters that I fear you will make yourself unnecessarily anxious about home. We are all in a magnificent state of preservation, especially old Knick, who fattens daily, and is said to be not only good-looking, but the best child in the city. Fannie and Carrie Sharpe, Eliza and Mary are all well; but Mary has had a cold, for which I have kept her at home a whole week. She is now over it, and would have gone to school to-day but for the grandest snowstorm I ever witnessed. It began to snow early this morning, and continued the whole day without the slightest intermission. We had no snow last winter as deep as this. Notwithstanding it is more than a foot deep, I have to-night walked nearly three miles and have talked about two hours. I encountered a real old hardshell, a regular old fogy, to-night, in Mrs. Mason of Second Street, who has been for upward of thirty years one of the managers of the Marion Street Lying-in-Asylum. She couldn't co-operate or sympathize with any movement that was not based upon the fact of the " patients being able to produce a certificate of good character." You ought to have seen the good old woman with her narrow-minded views pitch into the "Woman's Hospital" movement as soon as she welcomed me. I think you would have felt a little provoked; but if you could have seen the change in her tone when I left you would have been amply repaid, for we parted first-rate friends. She invited me to come and see her again, and recommended me to see Mrs. Codwise and some other ladies, and said, as she now fully understood the principle of action, she would take great pleasure in recommending to all her friends to aid in getting up the Woman's Hospital.

To-morrow night I am to spend at Mrs. Benedict's, with Mr. Gilbert and Mr. Stuart, when we are to draw up just such a charter as we want granted by the Legislature. The next night I am to go with Mr. Peck to see General Mather, who is one of the Peter Cooper reformers, and is an influential man in the Board of Councilmen. To-morrow, at ten o'clock in the morning, the owner of one of the brown stone houses, adjoining the one in which Mrs. Seymour lived year before last in Fourth Avenue, is to call and see me about renting said house for the temporary Woman's Hospital. Mrs. Peck went all through the house yesterday, and said it would answer first rate, and I shall take it at a thousand dollars. So you see everything goes on bravely. I am getting on with the doctors most magnificently. Professor Gilman called to see me the other day, and invited me to deliver a lecture on my operations before his class. I accepted the polite invitation, and will do it on next Saturday week, by which time, perhaps, you may be at home. You can't imagine how our friend Stuart crows over the "fighting of the chickens," as he terms it. His whole energies are now bent on our hospital plans, and he brings me daily in contact with such men as I could never reach but for and through him.

Thursday Morning, 25th.

This is a glorious morning. It is bright and beautiful. I am now at the midday of my life. The sun will soon turn toward the horizon, and I must work hard to make my life useful. I have no time to waste. If I should be blessed with health I can not calculate on accomplishing anything after sixty; indeed, in fifteen years I shall be a real old fogy. "Now is the day and now is the hour." What I do must be done soon. I don't doubt for a moment the success of the great object of my life. I only fear the failure of my health; but I am now well, and I pray God to continue his blessing on my efforts. Give me health, and even without money I shall accomplish wonders with the aids now at my command. I shall write again to-morrow, although you may not get the letter. I am only sorry that I did not continue to write to you at Montgomery.   Truly your devoted husband,

J. MARION SIMS.

Mrs. ELIZA THERESA SIMS, Montgomery, Alabama.

79 MADISON AVENUE, NEW YORK, *February 18, 1855.*

MY DEAR WIFE: Only a line can I write, because your letter of the 10th received to-day is so absolutely imprecative and imperative on late hours that I dare not disobey your gentle mandates, which you very well know I have always heeded as a good husband should.

Whatever you do about the negroes is all right. I don't allow myself a moment's thought, further than the anxiety I might naturally feel about the trouble it gives you, my model wife.

I was glad to hear that my poor, puny chick had at last ventured to eat one dinner. I hope she has continued steadfast in the good work.

I was rejoiced to hear you say you would run over to Columbus to see Aunt Betsey. Can't you write for Tan to come and see you before you leave? As anxious as I shall be for your return, let me implore you not to come home without calling to see sister Mary, if you should lose a fortnight's time by it; also go to Columbia.

We are getting on first-rate. The musical little "Nightingale" is the only one here that don't miss you. Willie is a little sick. It's his teeth; nothing more. The rest of us well, but, my dear Theresa, I am in the greatest state of alarm about our dear good friend, Mrs. Doremus. I have been wretchedly unhappy about her all day. She is very ill, but, as sick as she was, she allowed me to go to her room at 10 o'clock last evening to report to her the good success of my mission before the grave and reverend seigniors of the State Senate. She was too ill to see me to-day. I have been down twice to ask after her. Mrs. Codwise saw her yesterday. Ah! two such children of God can afford to talk calmly of death and a glorious eternity, as they did. Their lamps are all trimmed, and so should ours be.

How happy should we feel in the friendship of two such good mothers.

If I don't have time to write to-morrow (and I hardly think I shall), Mary will write to let you know about Mrs. Doremus.

It's late, and I must close. Remember me very kindly to all friends. With love to ma and the children, believe me, my dear wife, ever your devoted husband, J. MARION SIMS.

Mrs. ELIZA THERESA SIMS, Montgomery, Alabama.

79 MADISON AVENUE, NEW YORK, *February 22, 1855.*

MY DEAR THERESA: Mary wrote you yesterday, but I find she did not send her letter, which annoys me considerably, for, between us, you ought to have had a letter at least on alternate days.

We are all well, literally so, not half-way so. Nightingale and Willie are real pictures, while Harry is a rushing reality. We are getting on well, and, as anxious as we may be to have you at home, let me entreat you not to return till you have made a visit to Aunt Betsey and sister Mary. This I insist on, and I would like it very much if you could make up your mind to run over to Columbia for a day, but this I will not insist upon.

I have just got home from a tour of observation and civil engineering. Have made visits to-night to Governor Raymond, Mr. Benedict, Dr. Wilkes, Dr. Francis, Dr. Mott and Dr. Hosack, and with the four first named have been maturing our plans of operation. It seems that Providence has given power over the very men that are absolutely indispensible to the success of our great scheme.

I have a part for each to act, and no one of the mighty combination could well be substituted for the other. Benedict is wiser than all.

I can hardly, my dear wife, realize the truth of the great drama that is now being enacted. Why we should have been translated from our happy Southern home and warm-hearted friends and placed here under the circumstances now surrounding us is truly enigmatical.

Let us bow with humility to the will of Him who in His wisdom has ordered all this, and as you used to say "for the best," even when it seemed to my dull vision to be for the worst. Do you still think it was for the best? Ah, it is best for us individually, only if it humbles us.

It is late and I must stop. Do you ever see aunty? If so, remember me most affectionately to her. Also to other friends.

Love to ma and the children, and believe me ever your devoted husband,

J. MARION SIMS.

Mrs. ELIZA THERESA SIMS, Montgomery, Alabama.

Letters written on his First Trip to Europe.

QUEEN'S HOTEL, ABERDEEN, SCOTLAND, *Saturday, August 10, 1861.*

LOOK at the map, my dear wife and children, and you will see that I am above the 57th degree of latitude, in a most delightful country and fine climate, except that it rains too much. This has been one of the most profitable days I have spent since I left home, and I would be amply repaid for my trip, were I now to return without going further or seeing more. You know how I have fretted and worried about not getting the hospital up long ago. If I had succeeded as I desired, the whole structure would have been wrong in principle, and ruinous in its practical workings. Now I shall return with enlarged views of hospital hygiene and hospital structure, and I can not but congratulate myself on what I supposed to be very hard luck. Truly a good Providence overrules all our actions, whether we will or not.

When I left Edinboro yesterday, I asked Professor Syme for a letter to Professor Pirrie here, and he said: "No." For a moment I was startled, but he finished the sentence by saying: "It's entirely unnecessary, for the man in this kingdom who don't know you on presenting your card, and who won't be glad to see you, is not worth your seeing;" and sure enough, when I got here, the splendid Dr. Pirrie gave me the heartiest sort of a welcome, and said immediately: "You'll dine with me at five to-day," and of course I said yes. At ten o'clock went to the Royal Infirmary (which means a hospital with three hundred beds), where I saw Professor Keith perform a half dozen surgical operations, as I have seldom ever seen equaled anywhere. After this he showed me the hospital, and expatiated largely on its unfitness for its purposes, pointing out defects, suggesting remedies for them, etc., etc., all of which will be exceedingly valuable in constructing our hospital. I leave here to-morrow (Sunday) for Dundee, where there is a very fine new hospital, which I am told has defects that I must avoid.

Dr. Simpson asked me to operate on a case or two when I return to Edinboro. I shall then go to Glasgow, and return to my precious Dublin for a few days, where I have to perform several operations. I forgot to tell you in any of my former letters that Dr. Denham, a distinguished Dublin man, took me to see a lady requiring my opinion, and when I shook hands and said good-by she slyly let drop a guinea into my palm. I said, "Oh no, madam, I can't take your money. I do this for my friend, the doctor." The doctor immediately said, "You must take it." I still declined. The lady looked confused and surprised. The doctor whispered in my ear, "You must take it, she will be greatly mortified to receive your valuable opinion gratuitously." So I took it. I thought it very funny, and wished it was the habit at home to get a guinea slipped into a fellow's hand every time he deserved it.

The doctors here keep no books, patients pay at every visit, and always pay a guinea ($5). I saw the great oculist and aurist, Mr. Wilde, haul out of his pocket, the day before I left Dublin, a great handful of one-pound notes which he had received during the day. All the doctors I have met as yet are well to do, live in the very best style, and many of them are very rich; but, if I write more in this vein, you may fear that there is danger of my setting my face toward the service of Mammon. Not wishing to distress you in the least, I shall change the subject.

Sunday, August 11.

I fully intended to leave here to-day on the 12.23 train, the only one on Sunday. I wrote some letters to Dublin during the morning and went out at eleven to mail them. When I got into the street (Union Street), which is the Broadway of Aberdeen, it was crowded for nearly a mile (its whole length) with well-dressed church-going people. After depositing my letters in the post-office, having an hour to spare, I concluded to follow the crowd to a church I had visited yesterday. A very young man (just twenty-five) was occupying the pulpit. I surveyed the church and the people, and concluded to stay twenty minutes. They were singing when I entered; the sexton offered me a seat, which I refused, preferring to stand in the aisle just at the entrance. A placard hung by the door which I would like to see in all churches, because it assures a stranger a polite welcome, viz.: "Strangers will please apply to the pew-openers, who will furnish seats as soon as the service begins." On the walls and pillars, in various conspicuous parts of the church, were hung black-boards, about twelve by fourteen or fifteen inches, marked as in this diagram, so that the congregation could see the psalms to be sung. Of course there was no organ, nor instrumental music of any kind, and the choir, instead of being placed away off in a gallery, was at the foot of the pulpit, a very appropriate location.

Psalm.	Ver.	T
XXXIV.	I.	80
XXXIX.	I.	77
XlVI.	I.	29

They were singing (as I said) the xxxiv Psalm when I entered, then came the long prayer and reading from the Scriptures, in which I found myself interested. The preacher was a good and emphatic reader. I liked him. He was just the size of and the very picture of Uncle Jo Kyle; then was sung the xxxix Psalm, very and excessively dolorous. I looked at my watch, thought I must go. Then came the reading of the 3d chapter of St. James, which was the text dwelling upon the evils produced by the tongue:

18

"The tongue, no man can tame." The eloquence of the man chained me to the spot where I stood. I looked at my watch again, said to myself, "I'll stay ten minutes longer, then I will have twenty minutes to run to the hotel, pay bill, and be off." The time rolled on. I looked at my watch, indeed held it in my hand, the hands moved on, then it lacked eighteen minutes of the time of starting, then fifteen minutes, and then I said why should I hurry away from this enchantment when there is no need of it, so I deliberately resigned myself to my pleasant fate, and heard the most eloquent sermon I have listened to for years. I do not regret it. Looking at my watch I saw that the sermon was about thirty-three minutes long. I could have listened to the little fellow three or four times as long with comfort and profit. I shall go at two o'clock to hear the same man again.

Sunday, 10 P. M.

This has been the most Sabbathical Sunday I have spent for many months. True to the hour I was at church again, and heard a very fine sermon, twenty-six minutes long, from Psalm xvii, 14th verse. After church returned to the hotel, where we had a *table-d'hôte* dinner, and, as the servant just this moment brings in my bill, preparatory to my leaving at five o'clock in the morning, he tells me a very funny thing. Six of us sat down to dinner. It appears that the gentleman at the head is the president and master of ceremonies, the one at the other end is vice-president. As soon as we sat down (I on the president's right) he says, "Stranger, will you join us in a glass of wine?" "Certainly, with pleasure," said I. Well, we ate away, and drank wine, and I, feeling quite unwilling to be behind my liberal neighbors, ordered a large bottle of champagne. They looked a little surprised, but drank my wine. Well, I was very well satisfied. We had a splendid dinner, a good time, they pitched into Yankeedom generally, and I let them. Dinner over, the president said, "Waiter, the bill." It was brought, looked over, and passed round the table for each man's inspection. It amounted to the round sum of 7s. 6d. apiece, or $1.87½. When I got the bill I insisted on paying for my own bottle of wine, but they said "No." So the whole bill was equally divided. I didn't like much the idea of treating them at their own expense, and didn't know till just this moment that there was a joke anywhere. The waiter says: "Well, sir, they are having a hearty laugh down in the coffee-room at the way they were sold to-day." "Ah!" said I, "how is that?" "Why, sir, they took you to be green, and their game was to have a good wine bill, and make you bear your proportion of the expense, but when they saw that you didn't care, and ordered more expensive wine than any of them would, and then wanted to pay for it yourself, they thought it the best joke of the season and acknowledged themselves beat at their own game." I was very innocent in all of it. They told the waiter I was a regular take-in, for they thought I didn't know anything till they got me to talking—but enough. After dinner I called on Dr. Pirrie. He was out, but I had an hour's talk with Mrs. Pirrie. She is greatly interested in our Fulton Street prayer-meeting. It seems to me there is a book giving an account of this prayer-meeting from its beginning. If there is I was going to say send it, but let it alone till I get home again.

Your devoted husband,   J. M. S.

EDINBORO, *Tuesday, August 11.*

I LEFT Aberdeen early yesterday morning, arriving at Dundee at 11. Visited the infirmary (all hospitals here in Scotland are called "Royal Infirmaries"), saw several medical gentlemen, who were glad to meet me. Left at 5.40 P. M. and got here at 10. Soon after which young Dr. Simpson called, and we went to see an old lady with vesico-vaginal fistula upon whom the doctor had operated unsuccessfully two or three times. She weighs about three hundred and fifty pounds, and is not at all a good case to operate upon and leave in the hands of others for subsequent management.

I telegraphed Tom to come up here to-day, and expect him this evening. The railroad ride from Aberdeen tired me a good deal, but I am getting on well. Received your first letter, which cured me of my little feeling of home-sickness. If I can only be assured that you won't starve while I am away I'll take my time, and will not let a week or ten days stand in the way of investigations. If the doctors treat me half as well in London as elsewhere, I shall remain there at least a fortnight, which will be a week longer than I expected. As yet I have learned nothing from any man—I am sorry to say it—but I hope to get some ideas from Simpson. If I don't I shall be disappointed in my visit here.

Give my love to all the children. Kindest remembrance to the servants, and to all friends. I don't particularize, but mean all. Don't worry about me. I am doing well, not fretting about any. thing at all.

　　　　　　Your devoted husband,　　　　　J. MARION SIMS.

　　　　　　　　　　　　PARIS, THURSDAY, *November 21, 1861.*

MY DEAR WIFE: I wrote you not long ago that the 18th of October was one of the proudest days of my life. I have now to tell you a different story, for Tuesday, the 19th of November, was certainly one of the most fearfully anxious. I operated on the Countess de F. Tom was not present. He had gone to Liverpool. Nélaton, the great Paris surgeon, Campbell, the great obstetrician, Béclard, the accomplished Franco-American physician, and Johnston, the splendid fellow and good friend I have so often mentioned before, and Tom's friend, Mr. Herbert, a young Englishman, were present and assisting. Upon Dr. Campbell was imposed the responsibility of the chloroforming. The operation was begun at 10 o'clock, with the expectation of its lasting about an hour. Everything went on well, and in fifty minutes it was nearly finished. There was nothing to do but to secure the silver sutures. Just then I noticed a very livid appearance of the tissues, and called Dr. Johnston's attention to it. I asked if all was right, was answered "Yes, go on." But almost immediately Dr. Campbell said "Stop a moment. Let her head hang down." He ordered Nélaton to support the head, and Johnston to raise her feet perpendicularly in the air, while he supported the body and shoulders, and Béclard attended to forcing the respiration by pressing the thorax and abdominal walls. Young Herbert was sent for a spoon, with the handle of which her locked jaws were forced asunder, and Nélaton called for forceps to pull the tongue from the top of the wind-pipe. A tenaculum was handed, the tongue hooked up and held firmly. And I, imagine poor me, standing like a very statue of sadness and sorrow, calling out mechanically every now and then, "My dear Dr. Campbell, is there any hope of saving her?" She was to all intents and purposes dead. They held her in this inverted position for twenty minutes, trying to force the respiratory function. It appeared to me to be useless. At last she breathed, and breathed again. It was very poor breathing, but better than none at all. The doctor said: "Don't be alarmed, she will recover." After a while they laid her

on the table in the recumbent posture. But soon, almost immediately, the breathing ceased again, and the pulse stopped too, as it
had done before. Again they quickly inverted the body, and again
long, painful, protracted and anxious efforts for resuscitation were
repeated as before—but now she seemed more dead than before,
and I thought spontaneous respiration would never again return;
but, thanks to the brave men who had her in charge, for they never
ceased their efforts, and after a seeming very long time, they were
repaid by feeble signs of returning life. Respiration had some
regularity, the pulse became countable, though very weak and sometimes suspended. My heart began to pour forth involuntary thanks
to God for her recovery. They laid her upon the table again, saying, "It will all be right now." But in a few seconds the respiration ceased a third time, her pulse was gone, and she looked the
perfect picture of death. Then I gave up all as lost. But Campbell and Nélaton, Béclard and Johnston, by a consentaneous effort,
quickly inverted the body again, thus throwing all the blood it contained to the brain, and again began their heroic efforts at artificial
respiration. It seemed to me she would never breathe again, but at
last there was a spontaneous spasmodic inspiration, and after a while
another, and by-and-by there was a third. They were very "far
between." I thought there would never be a fourth one, but there
was, and then there was a long yawn or gaping. Dr. Béclard said:
"Her pulse comes again, but it is very feeble." Nélaton ejaculated:
"The color of the tongue and lips is getting more natural in appearance." Campbell said: "The vomiting is favorable, and see, she
moves her hands, she is pushing against me." But I was by no
means sure that these symptoms were not merely signs of the last
death struggle. She was still in the inverted position, with the jaws
pried open and the tongue held out with the tenaculum. Presently
Johnston said: "See here, doctor, she is safe now, see how she
kicks." Feeling somewhat assured, I said: "Let her kick. I want
her 'to be alive and kicking.'" Soon they all said: "Oh, she is safe
now." I replied: "For God's sake keep her safe then. Don't put
her upon the table again till she is conscious." They held her then till
she kicked in good earnest. I have heard of ladies "kicking," and
once as you know, my dear wife, I had a little experience of it, but
the most interesting feat in that way that I have ever known was this
by my dear dying-dead, but now living, little Countess de F. The

operation was finished. It was one of the most difficult I ever exe-
cuted, and certainly the most difficult, take it all in all, that I ever
performed on any one in the upper walks of life. Of course, it is
needless to say, it was completed without further recourse to the
use of chloroform. Dr. Emmet always gives me great credit for
foresight, skill, etc., but he says, added to this I am the luckiest man
in the world. He will see that my luck did not desert me in this
case, but it was luck based on the intelligence, kindness, coolness,
courage, judgment and perseverance of four of the bravest men I
ever saw. It seems to me now that she could hardly have been saved
in any other way, and it would be difficult to get together four other
men as competent to the task. Campbell and Nélaton were the
responsible men, but if she had died the whole blame would have
fallen upon your poor husband. To them is due the credit of saving
her, and to them let the credit be given. But let us not forget to
thank God for her restoration, and to bless Him for this great de-
liverance.

I have given you the facts. I can not and will not try to tell you
the heart-rending agony through which I passed during the nearly
two hours of anxious, persevering effort for her resuscitation. But
the best part of the story is to be told. Although it has been but
forty-eight hours since the operation, I am able to pronounce the
verdict of a perfect cure.

To-day I told her that hereafter, whenever I am asked how
many children I have, I will not make my usual stereotyped answer
"Nine," but will say "Ten," for she seems almost like one of ours,
and I tell her she shall be next to my own dear little Florrie. If
you could only see her, you could not help loving her. She is now
bright and cheerful, and hopeful and happy, thankful and joyous.
As she lies in bed her happiness is manifest to all. She warbles as
innocently as a little bird. She sings out and reminds me so much
of our own Mary. Tom thinks her very much like Mary. And
now, my dear wife, having unburdened my heart to you, let us not
cease to thank our Heavenly Father that He blessed the means for
her recovery, and saved your husband from murdering her or being
accessory to her death. Tell Emmet I am done with chloroform,
will never again operate on any patient under its influence, and believe it ought to be banished from ordinary or general use. It is
too dangerous. No one was to blame yesterday. It was given with

caution and care, but the blood evidently became chemically changed by it and unfit for the circulation. It was one of those unfortunate occurrences that may happen at any time, and have happened hundreds of times, with chloroform, but never to my knowledge with ether. With these facts, were I again to use this dangerous agent, and it to produce a fatal result, I could not hold myself guiltless morally, nor should I be in the eye of the law. My hands are then, henceforth, washed of chloroform and devoted to ether.

I shall be here eight or ten days longer, and then go to London, where I expect a good time for ten or twelve days at least. I am dreadfully disappointed at not hearing from home by the last steamer. I ought to have received a letter to-day. Certainly looked for my passport; I have a bet of a dozen cigars that I shall get a passport. A good many say I won't get it, but I am sure of it; for if they refuse such a thing to two such men as Raymond and Benedict they must all be insane, and the sooner we prove it the better for the country. But I shall not abuse anybody yet. I will wait for another steamer.

Friday, A. M.

I have been running all day after hospital doctors and instrument makers, and so finish this in a hurry. I am well, first-rate, but I have fallen off some in spite of Jenny Emmet's views to the contrary. I shall try and send my photograph next week. I need the lager-beer, don't like wine any better, but am obliged to take it with the water.

Kiss my little ones and the larger ones, and remember me very kindly to my friends, who are still friends notwithstanding my political faith, which I could not change under any circumstances, for I can not help being honest.

God bless you, my dear wife. You'll hear from me again before I go to London. Always your devoted husband,

J. MARION SIMS.

PARIS, *Friday, November 29, 1861.*

MY DEAR WIFE: I received no letter last week, but got yours of the 9th November yesterday, the contents of which were truly welcome. I was delighted to hear that you were all well and enjoying yourselves fairly. Am glad to know that Professor Bedford was kind to Granville, and proud to hear that my boy is at work in earnest, pleased to hear that Father Connelly was on a bust, and that my friend Dr. Miliano called. It was he, because I went with him on the 3d of October to the École de Médicine, and there pointed out a statue that looked like Willie. I hope he went again to see you. But with all these pleasant little things I will not pretend to hide my disappointment at not receiving by the mail my passport, for I fully expected it, and can't understand why it was not forwarded on the application of Mr. Raymond and Mr. Benedict, but I shall not fret the least bit about it, for good will come of all this. How, I do not exactly see, but we will know by-and-by.

I am happy to say my little patient the countess is beautifully and perfectly cured, never had a single unpleasant symptom after her recovery from the chloroform. I leave here on Sunday or Monday for London, where I hope to have a good time for ten or twelve days. I am pressed on all sides to stay here, but I go to London, and next week I hope to hear from you. I am anxious to go home, but a great many sensible people say I am foolish. Even Mrs. Murray S., who is a great New York woman, says I ought not to go home till the war is over, but everything will depend on your letter. I have such unbounded confidence in your judgment, that whatever you say I must do will be done. Were it possible I should spend a hundred dollars in telegraphing to you, and consider it a good investment, but that is out of the question. I shall not speculate further, but wait the arrival of your letter. The Countess de G. wants me to stop in Paris. Yesterday she received nine letters before breakfast from her relations, congratulating her, and rejoicing with her over the restoration of her daughter. She says if I will only stay, all her friends will be my friends, and she knows that I will get a plenty to do, and she says that she is sure I will not desire to go home again if you were all over here, but I can't imagine myself becoming a permanent "*voulez-vous.*" I am quite willing to go it for a year, just for the sake of the children. It will be capital invested for them, and the publication of my works here and in England would be worth the time, which would not be lost—but here I am again speculating before the arrival of your doubtful letter.

I have been at St. Germain now since the 10th. Altogether, here and at the Château de Granery, I have been the guest of the countess four weeks, and it is the pleasantest time I have had since I left my happy home. I am quite domesticated and hate to leave. Whenever a countess or other dignitary calls, Madame la Comtesse says, " Come, doctor, you must put on the dignity now." Of course, I get immediately as stiff as possible, and look as grave as a Presbyterian preacher just about to say, " Let us pray." All of which tickles my little patient very much, but she soons calls out, " Now, doctor, that's too tiresome, please be yourself again." Last evening the abbé, I mean the priest, came in, and madame sent word in to Leontine that she would bring him into her room, and she expected her and the doctor to be very dignified. So I put myself in attitude, the old fellow was ushered in, introduced, and we bent our bodies at each other, but he staid too long for me, as we had to dine together, and then sit for an hour afterward. He came to inquire for the success of the operation, and appointed a day next week for a great mass in the little chapel for her happy recovery. They are all very good Catholics and go to church daily. Yesterday morning I removed the last of the sutures from my patient. Was on the eve of going to the city, had been in my room some fifteen or twenty minutes looking over some instruments, etc., and just as I was about going out I saw a box setting on a little table by the door of exit (I had entered by a different one). On the box was a bit of paper with the words : " From the most grateful of mothers to the kindest of doctors." I had some curiosity to look into it. It is the most beautiful dressing-case I ever saw. I haven't time to describe it, but you'll see it. It is too fine for use, and I expect it to descend down in the family. Therefore it is a thing to will. Besides the many beautiful and useful things in it, there was a large roll of yellow paper which I took to the city. Mr. Monroe told me that there were several thousand francs' worth, and as an earnest I send you a portion of it in plain English. The others were of course in French.

The foregoing was written at St. Germain, and I expected to finish it in Paris. But the day is so dark that I can scarcely see how to get on without gas-light. It is a London day.

There is great excitement among Americans here on the subject of the Slidell and Mason arrest. If there is to be war between Great Britain and the United States I must make a straight shoot for home, Fort Lafayette or no Fort Lafayette.

By the time this reaches you I hope all will be right with Mary.

Kiss her and all the dear children for me. How I would like to be with you. Kind remembrance to Emmet and all other friends.

In haste. Your devoted husband,

J. MARION SIMS.

The day we celebrate. Americans love it as their natal day, and the free world admires it as the birthday of a nation of freemen.

Response to Toast on board Steamer Atlantic.

ON BOARD STEAMER ATLANTIC, *July 4, 1871.*
Bound for Europe.

MR. CHAIRMAN, LADIES AND GENTLEMEN: I fear your committee have made a mistake in delegating to me the honor of speaking to this patriotic sentiment. Not that I yield to any of you in my love of country, but that, like my brothers of the army and navy, I and my brethren of the medical profession are little given to speech-making.

This day reminds me that nations are but masses of individuals, that individuals, as a rule, know their birth-day, anticipate its anniversary with pleasure, and celebrate it with joy and gratitude. This privilege, so precious to us individually, is not often vouchsafed to nations. Even our beloved motherland, Great Britain, the stronghold of civil liberty, can not tell the time at which she reached its full fruition. With her it was gradual, the growth of generations, yea, of centuries. But with us it is otherwise, for we know not only the year, the month, the day, but the very hour in which we sprang from a tottering state of dependence and thraldom into one of independence and liberty.

John Adams said at the time, that this day would ever be hallowed by Americans, and that they would celebrate its annual return with speeches, and bonfires, and all manner of rejoicings. And so it has been, and so it shall be, as long as our country claims to be the land of liberty. It was said this morning, by my friend Mr. Train, the eloquent orator of the day, that the fourth of July was annulled by the bombardment of Fort Sumter. Sir, the thunders of Fort Sumter were but the premonitory throes of a labor that ended in the new birth of one of the mightiest nations of the earth, for we can now truly say that we have been born again. If you applaud so vociferously this sentiment from a citizen of New York, let me tell you that it is from the heart of a red southerner, for I was born in South Carolina, was wholly educated there, and lived there till I was a full-grown man; that I was contemporary with Davis, and Stevens, and Toombs; that my political teachers were Thomas Cooper and Turnbull, Mr. Duffie and the immortal Calhoun; that I was for many years an intimate personal as well as political friend of Yancey; that in later years I was in the kindest and most sympathetic relations with Mason and Slidell; and that I sympathized heart and soul with the South in what you miscall a rebellion.

With this record, if I can hail and celebrate this day, as every American should, who here shall dare repudiate it? Rebellion, did I just now say? Why, sir, this term as applied to our late struggle is false. Our civil war was a real war between what had been sovereign and independent States; a war of principles and a war between political equals. From the very foundation of our Government, from the days of Jefferson, and Madison, and Hamilton, and Jay, we had incorporated into our Constitution two great antagonistic principles that have been continually threatening our existence as a nation. These principles have been variously interpreted by parties—on the one side representing the rights of the States, and jealous of the powers delegated by these to the Federal Government, and on the other by a party advocating a strong central Government, and ever ready to encroach upon the rights reserved to the States. These principles, thus underlying all parties, by whatever name called, have been at unceasing war ever since the adoption of our Constitution. We fought them out on the tariff; we fought them out on the bank question; we fought them out on internal improvements; we fought them out on the territorial questions; and on a variety of side issues.

And in our great civil war these questions of the rights of States, and of the power and authority of the central Government, were the real questions of the day, all others being incidental and sidiary. While they were general and theoretical all But as soon as they became sectional and practical Southern States, standing upon their reser formed a new federation, and thus the old federations fought out in contended for in the le beaten here as we b

seem, in this great struggle for national existence, the country did
not produce a single man, North or South, who rose to the dignity
of true statesmanship. Not one man who grasped the whole subject in all its bearings and issues. Why, sir, every movement at
the North was one of temporary expediency, every step at the South
one of utter desperation. North and South were alike blind and
mad. Each equally sowed the wind, and each alike reaped the
whirlwind. But God Almighty rode in the tempest and directed
the storm, and its result was according to His will. The questions
at issue were too mighty for the puny intellect, but He in His wisdom decided and overruled all, and they were settled in a way not
foreseen by any. And now, sir, under these circumstances, what is
our duty to ourselves and to our country? We now have a Government that is no longer a rope of sand, one that is felt to be a
real power, not only at home, but a leading power among the nations of the earth. I am proud of my country abroad, but ashamed
of it at home. The humiliation of the South is inexcusable. Its
ruin is unjustifiable. But, notwithstanding all this, when I calmly
survey the past, when I closely inspect the present, and when I
look into the depths of the future, I must in all sincerity say that I
now think the worst thing that could have happened for the country at large would have been the success of the cause to which my
heart and soul were honestly and earnestly given, and conversely,
that the best thing that could have happened under the circumstances for the cause of civil liberty, not only in our own country,
but throughout the civilized world, was the success of the principles
based upon a strong central Government.

Sir, we of the South are a congenial people. Have you of the
North been magnanimous or generous to a fallen foe? to a prostrate
brother? No, sir, you have ruled us with a tyrant power. You
have been merciless and vindictive. You have forced upon us conditions humiliating to our pride and subversive of our rights. You
have confiscated our property and disfranchised our best citizens.
You have robbed us of civil liberty, and degraded us politically below the level of the meanest slave that ever wore a shackle. But, if
I reproach you with injustice, and injury, and wrong-doing, don't
for a moment suppose that I justify the South in the course she has
pursued since the war. In her it is folly to talk of the lost cause.
It is puerile to sulk and to play the part of abstention. Let her citi-

zens now show to the world that they are men, that they can understand the great problems now before them, that they can rise and
prove themselves equal to the emergencies of the times. Let them,
like sensible, practical, honest men, accept the issues of the war, the
fifteenth amendment and all. Then we shall have universal amnesty,
and equal rights under the Constitution, not as it was but as it is.

Colonel George Francis Train and others got up a Fourth of July
celebration on the steamer Atlantic, White Star Line, 1871, when a
few days out from New York for Liverpool. I responded to the
toast, "The day we celebrate," etc., and was requested to write
out my remarks, which I did the following day.   J. M. S.

APPENDIX II.

HALL OF THE MEDICAL SOCIETY OF SOUTH CAROLINA,
 CHARLESTON, S. C., *December 19, 1883.*

AT an extra meeting of the Medical Society of South Carolina, the following preamble and resolutions were unanimously adopted:

At the announcement, some weeks since, of the sudden demise of Dr. James Marion Sims, the hearts of the people of this, his native State, and of his professional brethren at large, went out in tender sympathy and in gushing grief.

This national bereavement assembles us this morning, while women everywhere weep in grateful remembrance over his bier, to pay the customary tribute, with more than ordinary impressiveness, to the memory of our illustrious great! Our great, we call him, since he stands pre-eminent above all her sons in the sacred domain of his professional usefulness and humanity, and because, through his fame, he has bequeathed a bountiful legacy to which we, more particularly, exultingly lay claim.

Before a strictly professional audience, like the present, there is no necessity to rehearse those triumphs of genius and of skill which have for many years pointed to J. Marion Sims in the world's estimation as to the father of Gynæcology, and could have secured for him such munificent rewards as to have constituted a princely fortune, had he claimed for himself alone any one of his many ingeniously invented appliances, instead of delegating them, with generous liberality, to suffering humanity; for in this special department his stream of mind and invention seemed perpetual.

But, alas! is it not always so where genius finds itself affiliated with a great mission?

Does not everything become subservient to the full fruition of our plans? Do not all things subscribe to life's grand consummation? In the great unrest of active discovery and invention there is no affluence of time to be devoted to the search after or accumulation of wealth.

How often do we find this the case among original geniuses in the varied departments within the commonwealth of knowledge?

We are told that Farraday's income, from commercial analyses and other sources, at one time amounted to more than £1,000, when Science, that harsh mistress, seduced him, as her child, from the acquisition of fortune, by revealing new secrets from Nature's manuscripts day by day, until his professional receipts fell to less than £150, and left him at last relatively poor.

When the French Commissioner from Europe urged Agassiz somewhat importunately, while the latter was engaged with his heaviest work in Cambridge, to accept the proposals of Napoleon, with their imperial inducements, as the means then offered him of amassing wealth, his memorable reply was: "I find in America a wide field of discovery before me; you must say to the Emperor that I have no time left me to make money." Indeed, Marion Sims's absorbing thought was to devise hitherto unrevealed methods peculiarly his own, and new instruments for securing the most permanent recoveries.

In the accomplishment of these great ends he continued to dazzle the professional mind throughout his remarkable career. It is not too much to affirm, as we well know, that the benefit our departed colleague conferred upon the suppliant female patient everywhere has for all future time thrown open the doors of organized "Hospitals for the Incurable," wherever these may have been established, and has said to suffering woman, in all humility and in the language of the Great Physician: "Take up thy bed and walk." But, when the wonderful results of this life mission are consorted with the unaffected simplicity and affectionate impulses of his genial nature, we realize the influence he possessed for good, and the eminence to which he so rapidly attained.

But, alas! this much beloved and eminent colleague and friend, whose death convenes the present assembly, has terminated his useful, distinguished, and brilliant career.

Ripe in years, and decorated with honors which an appreciative and admiring profession extended him, he has passed away from those who loved him, and has left scattered over his entire country friends, admirers and competitors, who for nearly half a century have been guided by his counsels, influenced by his example, and instructed by his doctrinal teachings.

It is when Death, Life's triumphant hero, has robbed us of the good and the great, that we realize the magnitude of our loss, and the void which can not be readily filled.

When we recall the excellences of his character and the evidences of his genius, how irretrievably sad will be his absence from among us.

In accordance, therefore, with the object of this meeting, we present the following resolutions:

Resolved, That, in the death of Dr. J. Marion Sims, we, his professional brethren, lament the loss of an affectionate colleague and a most able and ever-willing counselor.

Resolved, That in recognition of his important disclosures in certain departments of our science, and in the impulse he has given to its electrical advancement, the people at large mourn the death of a most distinguished citizen.

Resolved, That, in view of the world-wide reputation of the deceased, which virtually constitutes him an honorary member of every American medical organization, a blank page, with its customary badge of mourning, be inscribed to his memory in the records of our society.

Resolved, That a copy of these resolutions be transmitted to the members of his family.

Resolved, That the proceedings of this meeting be published in the " News" and " Courier. "

From the minutes.

(Attested,) P. Gourdin De Saussure, Secretary.

APPENDIX III.

Tribute to the late James Marion Sims, M. D., LL. D., by W. O. Baldwin, M. D., of Montgomery, Alabama, November, 1883.

The following tribute to the memory of the eminent surgeon and physician, the late Dr. J. Marion Sims, who recently died in the city of New York, was spoken at a *Memorial Meeting of the Medical and Surgical Society of Montgomery*, and by that body ordered to be published in the "Montgomery Advertiser." It was afterward reprinted in "Gaillard's Medical Journal," January, 1884. At the request of some of the friends and admirers of Dr. Sims it is now published in pamphlet form, with a few additional facts and reflections by the author; who desires to say that, while some of the prominent facts and incidents in the life of this great man have been briefly glanced at, others of almost equal importance have not been noticed at all. All of these, when collected and fully detailed, will form a large volume of the deepest interest.   W. O. B.

Sketches and Reminiscences of the Life of Dr. J. Marion Sims, as given at the late Memorial Meeting of the Medical and Surgical Society of Montgomery, by W. O. Baldwin, M. D., of Montgomery, Alabama.

After the introduction of appropriate preamble and resolutions, with addresses from other gentlemen, Dr. W. O. Baldwin said:

Mr. President and Gentlemen: In my somewhat lengthened life it has often been my lot to mourn the death of loved friends and associates, and to feel those bitter heartaches which spring from lost companionship and cherished affections. One by one, I have seen many such whose lives had become a prominent part of my pleasures here pass to the spirit land; but seldom in all my life has my heart been so filled with gloom as since the morning when the wires brought us the news of the death of my old and loved friend, the companion of my youth, Dr. J. Marion Sims.

I am sorry, Mr. President, that I am unable to pronounce a fitting eulogy, as you have requested of me, upon the life and achievements of this truly great physician and good man. This duty belongs to an abler tongue than mine, and to opportunities more ample than I possess. Rest assured, however, that the task will be performed in due time. The world accorded to him while living the praise of genius, and the still higher praise of consecrating that noble and beneficent genius to suffering woman. The world will not forget such a benefactor. Death has enhanced his claims'on our justice, our sympathy, our veneration; and thus life and death will combine to secure him a proud niche in that temple of fame whose gates already wait to receive him.

I probably know more of Dr. Sims's personal and professional history while he lived in Alabama than did any one else now living, except his brother-in-law, Dr. B. R. Jones.

So far as I can learn his history, there was nothing particularly striking in his character up to the time when he settled in this city in the fall of 1840. I hear from persons who knew him almost from his childhood, that when a boy he was not particularly remarkable for traits of character which distinguished him above other boys of his age. In his classes at school he stood fairly well, but was not precocious, and attracted no particular attention beyond his handsomely-chiseled face, his delicate physique, and his genial and playful turn of mind.

After graduating at the renowned College of South Carolina, he studied medicine in the office of Dr. B. C. Jones, at Lancaster, a small village in the district in which he was born, and about ten miles from his native spot. He afterwards attended lectures at the Medical College at Charleston, South Carolina, but received his diploma at the Jefferson Medical College of Philadelphia. After graduating he returned to Lancaster, and for a short time offered his services to practice medicine in that village. As is often the case with young men attempting to pursue their profession in the towns where they had passed their boyhood, he did not meet with great encouragement, and, remaining there but a short time, he removed to this State (Alabama) and located, in the fall of 1835, at Mount Meigs, a small town twelve miles from Montgomery. At this place he remained about two years, during which time he returned to Lancaster (in 1836) and married Miss Eliza Theresa Jones, who still survives him. Returning to Mount Meigs with his wife, and remaining a year longer, he removed to Macon county in 1837, and settled in a neighborhood near Cubahatchee Creek, and not far from a little place called Cross Keys. From this place he came to Montgomery in 1840, bringing with him his little family—consisting of, I think, his wife and two little girls. It was at this juncture of his life that I first knew Dr. Sims. He was about six years my senior, yet we soon became intimate friends, I suppose partly from the fact that I was nearer his age than any of the other physicians of the place, and the additional fact that neither of us was overwhelmed with business, and had plenty of leisure to cultivate each other's society. I thought he was the most winning and captivating man I had ever met, and I soon learned to love him as I did my own brother. Meeting a reciprocal feeling of attachment on his part, our intercourse soon ripened into confidential relations, which were not disturbed during his residence in this place.

When Dr. Sims located in Montgomery, he had scarcely any income except from his profession, and, that being quite limited for the first year, he was sorely troubled, for a time, to meet his current expenses.

But his was not a nature to be long discouraged. He was all zeal, energy, and pluck. Within a few months after he located here, the operations for club foot and cross-eyes, the latter of which had but recently been devised by Deiffenbach, in 1839, and practiced successfully by him, were creating quite a sensation in Columbia, South Carolina. Dr. Toland, then of that city, and now of San Francisco, had but recently returned from Paris, and was making quite a reputation as a surgeon by performing these operations in Columbia. I heard Dr. Sims read from a newspaper, published in that city in 1841, the first accounts he had ever seen of the operation for cross-eyes, commenting most favorably upon Dr. Toland's success. This, I believe, was the starting-point of the great success of Dr. Toland as a surgeon.

Dr. Sims immediately procured for himself a neat case of eye instruments, and was not long in finding cases of each of these unseemly deformities upon which to try his skill.

I was present at his first operation for each. They were attended with beautiful success, and being novel were much talked about. He was, even at that day, a remarkably neat operator, and I think handled the knife with more grace and skill than any man I have ever known of his age. His first successes brought him other cases, until within one or two years he had about finished up and straightened all the cross-eyes and club-feet within forty or fifty miles of Montgomery. This proved to be his stepping-stone to general surgery, and within a few years more he had the largest surgical practice in the State, excepting, perhaps, that of Dr. J. C. Knott, of Mobile. He was a bold, fearless, and dashing operator, and would undertake almost any case that another surgeon dare encounter.

At this day we had no such thing as specialties in this part of the country, and a man who could operate for cross-eyes would be trusted to operate in the most formidable surgical diseases, and was also considered a good physician in all the various departments of medicine. So that his surgical reputation in turn brought him into general practice, and very soon he had the largest family practice that had ever been done in this place by any physician up to that time. His services were sought by all classes of people, and in all kinds of cases. He was frequently, though still a very young man, called into consultation with the oldest and most experienced physicians of the place, men who had long been established in practice. He was immensely popular, and greatly beloved, so that he was a formidable rival to the best established physicians, and with all these facts it would not be greatly surprising if he did not always escape criticism. But, when such things were carried to his ears, they never made the slightest difference in his feelings or his deportment toward the authors of them, but he would meet and pass them with the same kind word and pleasant smile which were always his custom.

When Dr. Sims came to Montgomery we had no medical society for the report of cases and the discussion of medical subjects. Very soon after he located here he took an active part in the formation of the old medical society, and was from that time one of the leading members in its affairs, and much of the *esprit du corps* which has since distinguished the physicians of the place was due to his example and influence.

While he lived here he performed almost all the important surgical operations known to the science at that day. He was from the first a hard student, and thoroughly methodical in keeping notes, records, and histories of his cases, in reading medical journals, and in keeping up with the medical literature of his day.

After the first year of his residence here, he kept a private hospital, in which to care for his surgical cases. This, after he first became interested in his speculum, and in uterine surgery, he devoted exclusively to females, and especially to such cases in uterine surgery as were calculated to test the value of his speculum, in which he was already deeply interested.

I do not remember the precise year, but it was after he had acquired his great local reputation as a surgeon, that he became earnestly engaged in working out what was at first known as his duck-bill speculum, the vaginal speculum, which now bears his name, and which was the foundation of the brilliant reputation which he subsequently achieved. He interested his medical friends in the country in hunting up for him difficult cases of uterine diseases which had resisted treatment in the hands of other physicians, and he was delighted when among these he could find a case of vesico-vaginal fistula, that loathsome disease of woman, which had previously been regarded as the opprobrium of surgery, and which physicians rather shunned than courted. He became enthusiastic in this, as he was in all his pursuits, and was not slow in finding cases of this disgusting disease, particularly among the slave population, whose management in accouchement was generally confined to the ignorant midwives of their own color. His efforts promised success from the start, sufficient to encourage him to continue his labors. Failures did not dishearten or repulse him, but he worked on and on, sometimes performing dozens of operations on the same case, until final success was achieved. During all this time he was devising methods and plans for procedure in his operations, and was inventing instruments and appliances as collateral aids to his speculum. Of all his labors, trials, and achievements in this direction, I think he has somewhere published a statement—probably in the "American Journal of Medical Sciences," or it may be found, perhaps, in his book entitled "Notes on Uterine Surgery," which I have not looked at lately.

If my memory serves me correctly this brings us to about the year 1850, when, in the midst of his investigations, his health failed him, and he gave up much of his time to visiting different health resorts in order to regain it. This was a serious drawback to him, and came near ending his life. Having no regular or fixed income, and receiving now but little from his professional services, his financial affairs suffered greatly, and he again became hard pressed for ready means to support his family, which had grown to be larger and much more expensive than when he came to Montgomery.

About the year 1851 or 1852, I think it was, he began to entertain the thought of leaving Montgomery. The plea which he gave for wishing to remove to New York was that he believed this climate was unsuited to his health, but it is also probable that his desire to find a larger field in which to display his discoveries in that department of surgery to which he had lately been devoting his time had much to do with his desire to change.

From the time he reached New York to make it his home (I think in 1853), most of you are probably as familiar with his movements as I am, and I shall not attempt any further connected account of him.

I will say, however, after further and fully demonstrating the value of his speculum and various other instruments and devices used in his operations, and displaying his own superior skill in the use of them, he devoted himself to the thought and purpose of founding, through his exertions, a great charity, in that large metropolis, for the treatment of the diseases peculiar to women. You all know of his labors in that direction, for they are now a matter of history. You all know how faithfully he labored with some of the great and benevolent of his own profession, and how he besought and obtained their aid ; how he appealed to the hearts and enlisted the help of the influential, the opulent, and the philanthropic; how he visited and obtained from the Legislature of the State a donation of fifty thousand dollars; how he besought the city fathers for municipal aid, and procured through them a grant of land from the city which constitutes the site on which the hospital now stands; how he, with ceaseless and tireless energy, worked and planned, with a devotion and singleness of purpose rarely met with, until the Woman's Hospital was an accomplished fact. This act of his alone shows what a magnetic power he must have possessed. How he, a stranger, he who had scarcely emerged from the obscurity of a country life and himself in poverty, could so move the hearts of the people of a great city such as New York, and make himself the first and final cause of a great enterprise which, like the Woman's Hospital, should be a blessing to his race, proves how earnestly and untiringly he must have exerted his powers of persuasion over the minds of men. His efforts in the scheme of establishing this hospital, strange to say, were not always without opposition from quarters where it should have been least expected. And yet this opposition probably aided him in his work, and was one of his credentials to genius and goodness. True men often owe no little of their power and success to the hostility, jealousy, and littleness of others. He was not only a man of genius, but he was a lovable man, full of personal magnetism, full of kind and tender instincts, alive to the romance that redeems life from commonplace and routine, and abounding in those high impulses which make their subjects benefactors because they are enthusiasts in the pursuit of truth. No man could be an hour with him and not feel the simplicity and fervor of his nature, the straightforwardness of purpose and intent which went into all his intercourse with others, and the absorption of his whole being in the work he had set himself to accomplish.

Dr. Sims's health was never robust, and yet he could endure an amount of prolonged physical exertion which was remarkable for one of his apparently delicate physique. He had lived beyond the age of three score and ten, and yet his death was a great surprise to those of us who knew something of the elasticity of his constitution and the great care he always took of his health. I have seen much of him within the last fifteen years; I have been with him often in New York, and have met him at various other places, and twice during that time he has paid long visits to Montgomery. I was led to believe that he would probably reach fourscore and ten, so perfect seemed his physical and mental preservation. When I saw him last he looked as if he had not more than reached the meridian of life, and he told me he thought he would live to be ninety —though at that time he had no idea of any organic trouble about his heart. Only a few days before his death I received two letters from him, written on two consecutive days, in which he says: "You can't imagine how disappointed I am that I could not make you all a visit this fall. But if I live another year you may count on seeing me in Montgomery. But for that dreadful pneumonia, I would certainly have lived to be ninety. But my heart gives me so much trouble that I have given up the idea of longevity; still I hope to hold on a while longer." While he was in Rome last, in one of my letters to him, I begged him to stop his wandering, cosmopolitan life, and settle down in New York, and die there when it should please Heaven to end his days. In his reply, under date of Rome, January 14, 1883, he says: "I spend most of my time in Europe, because my life is more pleasant here; my fees are much larger, I make more money, my work is lighter, and I have more leisure." And in the last of the two letters referred to above he again refers to the same subject, and says: "I can not follow your advice and settle in New York. I could not possibly do the work here. I must go, and will sail on Thursday, the 8th, on the Celtic. I shall remain about three weeks in Paris, on my way to Rome." During the latter part of the summer my letters from him were written at the residence of Mr. Yulee, formerly United States Senator from Florida, but now living in Massachusetts. While there he was occupied chiefly in dictating to a stenographer his autobiography. He sent me advance sheets as they had been printed by a type-writer. It consists of a brief history of his life, modestly told, interspersed with little anecdotes and life-stories which no one could tell so well as himself, if at all. It is deeply interesting, and reads like a romance. He did not expect to complete it before he reached Europe, but I sincerely hope he brought it far enough up to make its completion an easy task for one of his children.

Dr. Sims's domestic relations were most fortunate and happy. The wife who survives him, and who now sits in the tearful and hopeless agony of her grief within the precincts of Madison Avenue, was the sweetheart of his boyhood. She was a loving and cheerful companion, a wise counselor, a true helpmeet; and throughout his brilliant but checkered and eventful life she shared his prosperity with joy and gladness, and bore his adversities with becoming patience and resignation; but at all times, and under all circumstances, she was to him "like the ivy to the oak, which clings closest in the storm." It was beautiful to see him in the sanctuary of his own home, when surrounded by his wife and children, and to witness their common devotion, where, even in his advanced age, he seemed as the "big brother" of the family. And when in their youth, with but two little children hanging upon their hearts, I used to visit them at their modest little home in this place, they made a picture of sweet and confiding domestic bliss which has not, in all these changing years, left my memory. At that time I had no matrimonial ties nor expectations, but their intercourse, I am sure, left a charm and a lesson on my heart which has not been without its pleasures, as well as profits. In later years he expressed to me the same chivalric and tender devotion to his old sweetheart, and assured me that all he was in this world was due to his fortunate selection of a wife.

As an author Dr. Sims stood well. He was never a voluminous writer on any of the subjects of which he treated. His work entitled "Notes on Uterine Surgery" was his largest, and was quite a respectable volume. It was printed in London in 1866, and was reprinted in several languages. It created quite a sensation, from the number of original, novel, and valuable lessons which it taught. It also met with some sharp criticisms. and, perhaps, it was not entirely free from blemishes. But, had he lived according to his expectations, he would have corrected all these in good time, as it is known he was engaged in rewriting it, and had already completed several new chapters, and had revised others. Take it, however, as it stands, and with all its defects, there has been no work published on uterine surgery within the last century that has been as full of original thought and invention, or that has contributed so largely to the advancement of gynæcology as this book has done. I will not attempt to go into detail about his writings. Although I am somewhat familiar with them all, I have no list of them with me. Though his contributions were not long they were not infrequent, and many valuable essays on different subjects were furnished by him to the medical press of his day. It is not the length or the number of the books, however, which a man may write, but it is the originality and the value of the material with which he fills them which make them desirable. His were all terse, original and eminently practical. His style was peculiar; it was altogether didactic, and it was his own.

I can not, either, undertake, in the short space of time allotted to occasions like this, to go into detail in enumerating the number of instruments which he invented, or the operations or operative procedures which he devised or planned, but their number was immense, and shows how fertile of ingenuity was his brain and how busily and skillfully it must have worked. He does not seem to be entitled to priority in the discovery of metallic sutures, but he was certainly

19

entitled to great credit in their revival and the vast prominence which he gave them.

Dr. Sims was never connected with a medical school, but only because he did not desire it. There was probably no institution of the kind within the limits of all this country that would not most gladly have given him a professorship could he have been induced to accept it.

Dr. Sims's clients, especially in Europe, seem to have been people of great wealth, and, from his acknowledged superiority in his special department, he was able to command the largest fees, and yet he never became rich. He also had a proper appreciation of the value of his services, and usually demanded an adequate honorarium where his patient's purse could afford it, but when it came into his possession it seems that it was either lavishly spent or unwisely invested. (We are glad to learn, however, he left a competency for his family.) He was also a man of large charities. But it is unnecessary to dwell upon these minor points in his life. The day which made him great was the day when the idea of his speculum first dawned upon him —that day when he first conceived the thought of throwing an abundance of light into the vagina and around the womb, and at the same time obtaining ample space to work and ply his instruments. This alone is enough to carry his fame down to the remotest ages, and his historian will need no more brilliant facts than these on which to rest the immortality of his name. This instrument caused his name to flash over the medical world like a meteor in the night.

Gynæcology to-day would not deserve the name of a separate and cultivated science, but for the light which Sims's speculum and the principles involved in it have thrown upon it. It has been to diseases of the womb what the printing press is to civilization, what the compass is to the mariner, what steam is to navigation, what the telescope is to astronomy, and grander than the telescope because it was the work of one man. Those great philosophers, Galileo, Gregory, Herschel, and Sir Isaac Newton, all claim and deserve successive parts of the telescope. Sims alone discovered his speculum, and, like Minerva from the brain of Jupiter, it sprang from his hands alone, full fledged and perfect when he gave it to the world. His work was so complete that it is said that no alteration or modifications which have since been made upon it, up to this time, have been regarded as improvements. The distinguished Dr. Emmet, of New

York, who is peer to any living gynæcologist, and whose reputation is world wide, has been heard to say, within the last few years, that so perfect was Sims's speculum and other instruments, that he had never been able to improve upon one of them. No man can divide the honor of his speculum with him, and he deserves to be called the father of modern gynæcology.

Thus, starting amid the sloughs and swamps of Alabama, having for his patients the most humble in the land, often spending his nights by the bedside of the sick found in the slave huts of these localities, without family influence, himself poor and with nothing to aid him save a strong will and a careful preparation, combined with a devotion to purpose, he rose by the splendor of his own genius above all obstacles, and before he has reached the meridian of life we find him one of the acknowledged discoverers and benefactors of the world, and ranking as one of the foremost men in his own country. A few years later we hear of him in all the great capitals of Europe; sometimes the guest and pet of emperors, often receiving honors and distinctions from learned and enlightened scientific bodies, courted by the *élite* of his own profession, sought by the nobility, and receiving titles and decorations from courts representing and boasting the foremost civilization the world has ever known.

I believe that before the next decade shall have passed away, when time with its silent throb shall have buried those antagonisms, rivalries, and jealousies which often spring up around the paths of great discoverers, it will be the settled verdict of the medical men of the world that Sims has lived to a greater purpose than any man in any age who had preceded him in his special department.

Gentlemen, there is one page in the life of this great man, one scene in the living panorama of which he constituted a part, that I would fain not disturb, and one on which I would prefer to drop the mantle of oblivion, were it not that it is already a matter of history, and perhaps it is due to the memory of Dr. Sims that I should refer to it. I alluded to the night when, as one of the surgeons, he last met the governors of the Woman's Hospital, and which closed forever his connection with that institution.

It is said that republics are ungrateful, and it therefore should not be surprising if even the governors of charitable institutions should sometimes forget their greatest benefactors, and smite the cheek of him whose hand was chiefly instrumental in calling them into existence. The Woman's Hospital was Dr. Sims's bantling. The creation of its germ and the conception of its possibilities were the outgrowth of those discoveries which emanated from his brain alone, and its final success was due to his untiring exertions. He was proud of his work ; he was proud of the child of his own life, and when the Woman's Hospital was completed he regarded it as the largest pearl in all his greatness—the central jewel in his crown of glory. But while it was the glory of his life it was its humiliation too!

Those governors, who were in fact but little more than figureheads so far as the privileges and duties of the surgeons were concerned, had taken upon themselves the privilege of regulating the affairs of the operating-room, and of saying to the surgeons that only fifteen guests or spectators should be permitted to be present at any one operation. Dr. Sims took this occasion for telling them that he had not obeyed this order of theirs, and would not, and that if they insisted on enforcing this rule his resignation was at their disposal. He claimed the right to invite such numbers as his own judgment and inclination might dictate.

Their action in assuming to restrict his privileges, in this respect, he regarded as without authority. To a man of honor their action must have been offensive.

In effect it accused him of being ignorant of the surgeon's duties in the sick-room, and of wanting in a proper regard for the feelings and sensibilities of his patients. All this made it insulting and galling to him, and especially as he knew it to be an unauthorized invasion of his own prerogatives, inherent to the office which he held, and altogether outside of their accredited duties.

All the world over, the creed of common courtsey which exists between the laity and profession makes the physician the autocrat of the sick-chamber, and the privilege of the surgeon, as to whom he will invite to his operating table or room, has never before been restricted. If it was wrong to invite all who desired to attend, or all whom the surgeon might wish to witness his operation, why invite fifteen? It was not necessary to invite any! The hospital service afforded all necessary assistance. If it would not offend the sensibilities of a woman to have fifteen guests present, would it shock her modesty very greatly to have eighteen, or twenty, or fifty, or a hundred, or any number that the room could accommodate conveniently? Besides, it is well known that the patients in this hospital are rarely ever seen by the spectators until after they have been placed upon the operating-table and under the influence of an anæsthetic, when the table is rolled into position. Another and even stronger reason exists against this restriction. To serve all the purposes in the interest of woman of which this hospital was capable, it was doubtless intended, or in contemplation by Dr. Sims from the first, that it should be used as a school, so far as possible, for teaching physicians from the country, or city, or other cities, or from other States or nations, who might temporarily be in New York for the purpose of studying that class of diseases, and would like to see these operations.

But suppose these governors could find nothing in all these facts to make them retrace their steps, could they find nothing in the fact that Dr. Sims thought they were in error, and wished them to reconsider their unjust and unwise action? Could they not have conceded something to the opinions of the man who had created the hospital, who had devoted fifteen or twenty of the best years of his life to its service, who had passed many weary days and sleepless nights in the promotion of its interest, and had carried it upon his heart as none of them had ever done? They knew he had placed himself in a position, in relation to the order which they had issued, from which he could not recede without loss of dignity or even honor; they knew he did not wish to sever his connection with the hospital, and they knew he did not wish his resignation accepted, and yet, with a heartless and cruel inflexibility, they refused to abolish their miserable order and accepted his resignation; thus stabbing him in the most vital spot of his life, and mortifying him as nothing else had ever done.

In this difficulty Dr. Sims had the sympathy of a large portion of the medical men of America. And, as an expression of their sentiments in this direction, the American Medical Association, at its very next meeting, unanimously elected him its president. He was elected in Louisville in 1875, and presided at the meeting held in Philadelphia the succeeding year, known as the "centennial session." This was the very highest honor which could have been paid him by the medical men of his own country. While Dr. Sims in every way deserved this high compliment, and was himself an honor to the position, I yet have reason to know that he was selected at this particular time over other distinguished aspirants, not only that they might thus express their admiration of his exalted worth, but also in approval of the manly, dignified and honorable position which he had assumed and maintained in his controversy with the managers or governors of the Woman's Hospital.

When the names of these sickly sentimental governors shall long since have passed into oblivion, and their foolish rules and regulations, in connection with this hospital, shall have been wisely forgotten by the world, the name of Sims shall be known and read of all men as its great founder and patron, and emblazoned all over its walls "from turret to foundation stone" as its ensign-armorial and shield to guard it against evil and unwise spirits.

Nor can posterity accept the imputation as true or just, that the man who had planned, and schemed, and worked, even in the midnight solitude of his office, that his life might finally achieve this good to woman, could be false to any of the proper delicacies or courtesies due to her sex. I will not pursue this subject further—it is not a pleasant one to dwell upon. He is now far beyond the cruel malice or petty jealousies of those who bore a part in inflicting this mortification upon him; and the manhood which recognizes the great value of his life will see to it that his name does not suffer neglect in the grave.

The friendship and affection which valued his exalted worth and appreciated the beauty of his life would not shadow his claims to the admiration and gratitude of the world by exaggerating them, or by saying that he possessed none of the weaknesses common to human nature. He no doubt had his share of these. It is known to his friends that he was sometimes fretful, impatient, and intolerant about minor matters or little crosses, and, when vexed or angered, did not usually attempt to conceal his displeasure. He was at times excitable, jealous of his rights, and keenly alive to any encroachment upon his claims to those discoveries which he thought belonged exclusively to himself, and when he considered them unjustly invaded he was offended, and outspoken to a degree beyond the reserve usually found in men of less mercurial dispositions. I do not refer to these things as faults, for they, like his other traits, but go to prove that he was a man without guile or deceit—too honest to dissemble, too noble to disguise. Vices he had none, or if he had I never knew them. If he had faults they were harmless to others, and deserve the name of frailties or foibles rather than faults, and were to his brilliant life only as the spots on the sun are to the splendor of that luminary.

For nearly half a century our friend pursued his profession with an energy and devotion which were as inspiring to himself as they were beneficial to medical science and the welfare of humanity.

The selfishness of renown had not a charm for him. Distinction he valued, as every high-minded professional man values it, for its influence and intended usefulness. It came to him without the least resort to doubtful means, and it remained to him as an inalienable possession. No wreath upon his brow was other than a garland of just and honorable fame; and, when death came, it had no frost to wither a leaf in the chaplet that two continents had woven for his crown. His splendid reputation is perfectly secure. It rests on such virtues, such talents, and such works as give to the name of SIMS a mutual pledge of IMMORTALITY.

Pardon me, gentlemen, for a little personal allusion to myself connected with Dr. Sims.

From the time when Dr. Sims located in Montgomery up to the period when he left to cast his lot in the great city of New York, he was my warm and devoted friend and my loved companion. He was open and confiding to his friends. I was proud of his confidence and affection, and gave him in return the full measure of my own. The fact which I am about to refer to is known to but a few only of the older members of this body, and is this: A few weeks or months after he had removed from Alabama to New York, a little misunderstanding grew up between us, which resulted in our estrangement, and for many years afterward all intercourse between us ceased. This has always been to me one of the bitterest episodes of my life, and memory never recalls the event without a feeling of sadness and regret. In this rupture I was probably more to blame than he, and I have no doubt that, had not our paths in life widely diverged at this time, the heart-burning which our separation had caused to last for long years would have been forgiven and forgotten in a few days.

In 1868 I made a visit to New York, and while I was there he returned from a prolonged visit to Europe. The first time we met was at the opening of the Bellevue Hospital Medical College, when Dr. L. A. Sayre was to deliver the introductory address. We were each, without the knowledge of the other, invited to go on the rostrum, and were to meet in the faculty room to join the professors for that purpose. I did not know that Dr. Sims was in the room, and at the time I entered he did not observe me, but soon I felt some one clasp me around the neck with both arms, and looking I observed my long-lost friend Sims, who only said, "Baldwin, my old friend." We had no words of explanation, but from that moment all feeling of resentment left my heart, and again I loved him as a brother. Since then our intercourse, by letter and otherwise, has been constant, confidential, and free.

I look back now upon my association with him as one of the providences of my life, and his death as one of the bitterest afflictions.

Dr. Sims's Return to Montgomery in 1877.

It is known that the first advancement of Dr. Sims toward the great distinction which he afterward attained commenced in Montgomery, where he resided for a period of twelve years. In the year 1877, after an absence of nearly twenty-five years, he returned to his old home to make a visit to his friends. The physicians of the place, members of the Medical and Surgical Society, in anticipation of his arrival, made arrangements to receive him in a manner becoming his rank in the scientific world. The proceedings on this occasion were published in the "Montgomery Advertiser," but as this paper had but a limited circulation outside of Alabama, and as the proceedings contained some interesting historical facts, and incidents of a pleasing character, as related partly by Dr. Sims himself, it has been suggested that it would not be out of place to add them to this memoir, for distribution among those friends who never met with them before, as forming a portion of this brief sketch of his life W. O. B.

[From the "Montgomery Advertiser."]

Arrival of Dr. J. Marion Sims.—The Courtesies extended to him while in Montgomery.

Dr. J. Marion Sims, the distinguished Gynæcologist and founder of the Woman's Hospital of New York, arrived in our city on Wednesday evening, and was met at the depot and escorted to the residence of his brother-in-law, Dr. B. R. Jones, by the committee of four from the Medical and Surgical Society of Montgomery: Drs. R. F. Michel, W. C. Jackson, J. B. Gaston, and James Berney.

On entering the drawing-room, Dr. Michel addressed the distinguished visitor as follows:

"As chairman of the reception committee of the Medical and Surgical Society of Montgomery, I come with these gentlemen, Dr. Sims, to welcome you to the city, and to tender most earnestly our heart-felt congratulations on seeing you once more upon the soil of your former scenes of labor in the profession you have so much adorned by your intelligence, learning, and skill.

"To tell you how gratefully we have watched your advancement to the very first rank of your profession, not only in this country, but in the Old World, is but to reiterate what you so well must understand.

"The members of our society (of which you are an honorary member) have requested us to solicit your presence at a banquet, to be given in honor of your arrival among us. Please, therefore, select for this purpose an evening most suitable to your convenience."

Dr. Sims, with much feeling, replied that, on visiting his old homestead, in South Carolina, he was taken sick, and had not, up to this time, entirely recuperated his strength. However, after thanking Dr. Michel for the kind and complimentary manner in which the invitation from the Medical and Surgical Society of Montgomery had been conveyed, he accepted the courtesy, and selected Tuesday evening, March 20th, as the time most convenient for him to meet the members of the society.

At the hour appointed last evening, the beautiful hall was well illuminated, and the walls, decorated with drawings illustrating different important problems in physiology, gave to the entire room a most scientific appearance.

Dr. Sims was presented to the society by Dr. Michel, when Dr. B. R. Jones, president of the society, said:

"Dr. Sims: Sir, it is with no ordinary feelings of pleasure that I welcome you to the hall of the Medical and Surgical Society of Montgomery. With a large portion of its members you are personally acquainted; the others have known you by reputation. They and we have felt proud as we have watched your advancement to the highest honors of our profession.

"Sir, we have ever claimed you as one of us from the foundation of the Sydenham Medical Society of this city, of which, during its existence in former years, you were always one of its most active members, and in the organization of this society you were elected one of its first honorary members. But, sir, I will leave it to one, and the only one left, of your *confrères* when you commenced your medical career in this city—Dr. William O. Baldwin— to address you in expression of our high gratification in having you again with us."

Dr. Baldwin, who had been selected by the society to receive the distinguished *savan*, as he had been many years ago his intimate associate and companion, addressed him in the following beautiful and dignified language:

"Dr. Sims: As the representative of the Medical and Surgical Society of Montgomery, I am commissioned to tender you a hearty welcome to our hall, and to the courtesies and hospitalities of our association, in honor of the distinguished services which you have rendered to the science of medicine and surgery.

"I feel myself incompetent, sir, to express to you in fitting terms the just pride which the members of the medical profession of our State, and especially those of the Medical and Surgical Society of Montgomery, feel in the renown which you have won since you left our borders. Yet, it is perhaps proper that one of the few remaining of the brotherhood with whom you were associated in youth, and who witnessed the promises of your morning life, should be selected to tender this testimonial of our appreciation of your labors.

"After an absence of twenty-five years, you are again in the halls of the first medical society to which you ever belonged. Sir, your eyes will wander in vain over this assembly in search of the faces of most of those with whom you were accustomed to meet and exchange friendly greetings in former years, and you will recognize but few whose hands you grasped as you departed from our midst upon the great mission of your life. I am pained to remind you that most of those who then answered to roll-call in this society have passed from the stage of this world's action, and now sleep the sleep that knows no waking.

"Sir, we claim you as an Alabamian. South Carolina may assert the honor of having rocked the cradle of your infacy, and of having nurtured your boyhood, but it was here in Montgomery that your greatness had its first dawning. It was here that your genius found its earliest expression, and it was here it first took its flight and asserted its claims to the applause of strangers. It was here that your sleepless industry, your anxious toil, and your sublime fidelity to purpose, carved out those surgical devices and appliances which have made your name so justly famous, and it was here that you first reduced those inventions to that practical utility in the treatment of the surgical diseases peculiar to woman which has not only challenged the admiration of the great and learned in your own profession, but has also won the homage of the crowned heads of Europe, and made your name a familiar word in all the great capitals of the civilized world.

"It is surely no small honor or trifling subject for pride and congratulation to the State which claims to be the mother of your early manhood, to see that the enlightened courts of the Old World, with their splendid civilization, have recognized the vast resources of your genius and the importance of those great discoveries which have justified them in ranking your name among those of the foremost men of the age, and in conferring upon you honors, titles, and decorations due only to those who, by their achievements in science, literature, art, or statesmanship, have accomplished some grand purpose in life, or conferred some lasting benefit on mankind. It is, therefore, eminently proper, upon your visit to the home of your youth, after an absence of so many years, that your early companions, associates, and friends of the medical profession should desire to greet you, and pay you that homage which is so justly your due. We wish, sir, to congratulate you upon the success of your labors and the usefulness of your life, as well as upon the splendor of the fame which these have given you.

"Indeed, sir, to those who, like myself, are familiar with the difficulties and struggles of your early professional career, the grand success of your life would seem almost as a romance were it not for the solid and lasting benefits it has conferred upon humanity.

"Let me also congratulate you upon the fine preservation of your physical and mental health. I am glad to see that Heaven has dealt so lightly and kindly with your person; yet you are no longer the youth with whom, though somewhat your junior, I commenced my professional career. Often, in the solitude of my own quiet life, I have called to mind those good old days when we were young together, and as I looked through the vista of the years that have since passed, and remembered your hopeful and cheerful enthusiasm, and your ardent devotion to your profession, which often excited me to greater zeal and effort, I could not wonder at the heroism you have displayed on other fields, or the brilliant reputation you have achieved."

Then, turning to the members of the society, Dr. Baldwin said:

" The association of things always affects us. A page or a leaf torn from the book of memory, which we have carefully stored away in youth, becomes most precious when circumstances arise which bring to mind the most trifling fact there recorded.

" A review or contemplation of the life of one with whom we ourselves entered the world derives a larger interest from the fact that we were personally observant of the adventures, enterprises, and resources which contributed to its success, and finds additional entertainment if we can call to mind the livery or outward appearance and habit with which it rushed into the world to work out the destinies awaiting it. In this connection, I well remember a friend with whom I associated much about a third of a century ago, when we were young doctors together—moved by the same sympathies, hopes, and ambitions, and striving in friendly rivalry for a prize in the same noble calling. He had a handsome face, with a benevolent, lively, and winning expression of countenance, dark eyes, chestnut hair, figure erect, slender and boyish-looking, mercurial in his disposition, enthusiastic in his pursuits, unaffected in his address, kind in his deportment, and always willing to do or say something to make others feel pleasant and happy. With these traits he possessed more personal magnetism than any man I ever met. It seems to me I can see him at this very moment with his captivating, boyish tricks, and his other engaging levities, which, being practiced only on proper occasions, never failed to make him a most charming companion. One of the pictures of his daily life here, now most vivid upon my memory, is that one wherein I have seen him seated in his curiously fashioned buggy, which he playfully called his ' Grecian Galley,' with his mettlesome little sorrel mare between the shafts, with her shining red coat, her gay white face, and her sinewy, white legs, looking as proud as Juno. I think he called her ' Kitty Jumper.' His buggy was, indeed, a queer and notable-looking little land craft, and, by the way, was the first four-wheeled vehicle ever used in Montgomery for the purpose of practicing medicine. At first this was quite a displeasing innovation upon the customs of our staid old physicians, as previous to that time we had all been going on horseback, with doctors' saddle-bags, or in the old-fashioned two-wheeled sulky, and considered these the proper paraphernalia of a physician as he was seen going his daily rounds. We soon, however, found this innovation of the young doctor to be only a marked improvement upon our primitive mode of locomotion, as the world has since done with his innovations upon science, except that we could never come quite up to the style and fashion of this particular vehicle, which probably never had a duplicate.

" Thus seated in his buggy, with his little negro boy by his side, and panoplied with a medicine-box and case of surgical instruments at his feet, I well remember the picture as it used to pass rapidly to and fro in our streets, with the doctor's whip nervously waving over his little favorite, as if he did not intend to lose any practice through the lazy habit of slow driving.

" But all things upon this earth must change. Time, with its ceaseless and silent throb, at length dissolves every living panorama, and that which constituted my picture has not escaped this all-pervading law.

" The buggy, the horse, the medicine-box, and perhaps the case of surgical instruments, it is reasonable to suppose, have long since turned to dust and ashes—the little negro, it is to be hoped, has reached the dignified position provided by the ' Fifteenth Amendment '—while he who formed the central figure in the picture, the young doctor, still lives, as the renowned originator and founder of one of the noblest charities ever erected to woman—the Woman's Hospital of New York. Through his own unaided efforts he has achieved results which have throbbed a new life into the science of gynæcology, and awakened for it an interest and influence which have extended far beyond the confines of his own country, and indeed to the outer borders of civilization. For original invention and operative skill, he stands in his special department with but few rivals and no superior, and has had more honors and distinctions conferred upon him by his own and foreign countries than any living American surgeon ; and now, at the age of sixty-four years, I will venture to say, has as much metal and pluck as had the little spirited mare which so proudly carried him in the days of his youth.

"I have referred to these little incidents in the early life of my old friend, chiefly because they bring pleasant reminiscences to my own mind, and partly because they demonstrate the fact that the germs of great thought and inventive genius, which are destined to receive the admiration of the world, can as well be hid under a light, happy, careless, and sometimes seemingly thoughtless exterior, as in the recesses of that grave and severe mind whose outward look is that of stern and dignified reserve."

Then, turning again to Dr. Sims, he said:

"Sir, you may not be able to fill up the blanks in the picture I have drawn, but I believe there are some within the hearing of my voice, and many old citizens outside of the hall, who will have no difficulty in that respect.

"In conclusion, sir, permit me to say that, if your achievements within the the domain of science, or if your exalted worth as a benefactor of your race, should hereafter rear the monumental marble to perpetuate your name as a great physician, still those simple, unaffected, kind and genial qualities of the heart, so peculiarly your own, and so well remembered by the companions of your youth, will ever with them constitute the charm and glory of your life as a man.

"Let me again welcome you to our city and to the arms and hearts of your old friends, and express the hope that the Providence which has watched over and prospered all your efforts, will still spare you many years of active, useful life, and shed upon your pathway its richest bounties."

In response to Dr. Baldwin's remarks, Dr. Sims said:

"MR. PRESIDENT AND GENTLEMEN OF THE MEDICAL AND SURGICAL SOCIETY OF MONTGOMERY: I thank you with all my heart for this kind reception, and you, sir, for the kindly manner in which you have been pleased to speak of my labors. A warm personal friendship of nearly forty years naturally gives a roseate hue to your recollection of by-gone days. It is seldom given to any man to live to see himself fully understood, and his labors fully appreciated. On this score I certainly have no cause of complaint, for wherever I go, whether in our own country or in the Old World, the same generous recognition awaits me; but not so demonstratively as here on my return to my old home, the scene of my early struggles. Sir, if I were a conquering hero, or a great statesman, you could not vie stronger with each other in trying to do me honor. But when such an ovation is given to a mere doctor, even if he is in deeds a philanthropist, and in heart a patriot, it seems almost paradoxical.

" Forty-two years ago I left my native State—South Carolina—to seek a home in Alabama. I intended going to Marengo County, but circumstances conspired to arrest my progress.

" The head and front of this conspiracy was my old friend Dr. Charles S. Lucas, who is with us this evening. He was the first friend I ever made in Alabama, and has remained my friend ever since. Many little incidents have occurred in the last few days to touch my heart—first, the visits and congratulations of my medical friends; second, of my lay friends; third, of former patients; fourth, of my former slaves; and, fifth, when my octogenarian friend, Dr. Lucas, heard I was here, he mounted his horse and rode fifteen miles to see me. We met, and our tears were mingled for auld lang syne.

" Well, I remained two years at Mount Meigs. The late Dr. Bolling A. Blakey, of Macon County, then offered me a partnership, and, accepting it, I went to Macon County, and lived there three years, and, in 1840, I came to Montgomery. You claim me as an Alabamian, and rightly, too, for all that I am I owe to Montgomery and to the people of Montgomery. I am frank to acknowledge my allegiance, and can do it without treason to my native State. When I came among you I was young, inexperienced, in bad health, and very poor. I had nothing whatever to recommend me—nothing but honesty, industry, and determination to succeed. You received me kindly, and with the greatest hospitality. You were to me good Samaritans. You literally fulfilled toward me the command of our Saviour—for 'I was naked and ye clothed me; an hungered and ye gave me to eat; thirsty and ye gave me drink; I was sick and ye visited me,' and if I had been in prison I am sure you would have liberated me as soon as possible. Your Crommelins and your Pollards gave me houses to live in till I was able to procure one for myself. Your merchants gave me credit for food, and raiment for my family, when I had not a dollar in the world to pay for them. And no young man was ever treated more kindly by his seniors in the profession. How, then, could I ever be otherwise than grateful and loyal to those who were my friends when I most needed friends?

"I have long felt that I belonged to a generation that is past and gone. But never till this moment have I realized this solemn fact more intensely. In looking round this room I see that you, sir, and I are the only survivors of the noble band of brothers who were our companions in 1840.

"Sir, as I said before, you and I are the only survivors of the men of 1840. You are many years my junior, and I hope and pray that you may long live to advance the science you have done so much to adorn, and to exert among your brethren the benign influence that has characterized your whole life.

"Again, gentlemen, let me thank you for the distinguished honor you have conferred upon me."

After these interesting proceedings, Dr. Sims was escorted by the members of the society, in procession, to the mansion of Dr. Baldwin, on Perry Street, this gentleman having kindly tendered his house to the Medical Society as the best place for the banquet they had prepared for their distinguished guest.

The company sat down to the table about ten o'clock, and from then on until a late hour there was literally "a feast of reason and a flow of soul." In the center of the table was a beautiful stand of flowers, and above it a wreath, in the center of which the word "Sims" was most artistically arranged in flowers. Many toasts were offered and appropriately responded to. Altogether the evening was one long to be remembered by all who were present.

APPENDIX IV.

Dr. A. F. A. King, chairman, presided.

Dr. T. E. McArdle, secretary.

Dr. King stated that the regular order of business would be suspended, in order to devote the evening to hearing the report of the committee appointed last week to prepare resolutions relative to the late Dr. J. Marion Sims. He said that while the profession throughout the world would mourn the loss and honor the memory of so great a man, he was glad to know that this society would not remain silent. While unprepared to attempt any adequate eulogy of Dr. Sims, he regarded him as an extraordinary genius, whose name would remain immortal in the annals of medicine. Among the greatest luminaries that adorn the professional firmament, Sims appeared as a comet, leaving a path of light that would forever reflect luster upon the medical art. Reading only lately the old treatment of vaginal fistula, he referred to the great boon conferred upon the victims of this malady by the inventive genius of Dr. Sims. In conclusion, Dr. King called attention to portraits of the deceased, kindly loaned by Dr. Busey, and then called upon Dr. Garnett for report of committee.

Resolutions presented by Dr. A. Y. P. Garnett, Chairman of the Committee.

Whereas, The Medical Society of the District of Columbia having heard of the death of our illustrious countryman, Dr. J. Marion Sims, with profound sorrow, and being impelled by feelings of the sincerest sympathy and warmest admiration for the lamented dead, desire to record the expression of their sentiments by the following resolutions:

Resolved, 1. That the sad intelligence of the sudden and unexpected death of Dr. J. Marion Sims, flashed throughout the civilized world with electric speed, has communicated to us a shock well calculated to overcome us with emotions of unaffected sorrow and abiding regret.

Resolved, 2. That as Americans we feel justly proud of the brilliant and distinguished career of this eminent physician, whose original and valuable achievements in the domain of surgery, as well as his wisdom, superior skill and rare tact in other departments of his profession, illustrated a genius and intelligence seldom vouchsafed to mortal man, and which challenged the admiration of the scientific world, and deserved the gratitude of suffering humanity.

Resolved, 3. That we shall ever recall the man as one who combined an unusual and attractive beauty of manly form, with a refinement and gentleness of manner, and a genial cordiality of deportment, betokening the "kind, true soul within," which seldom failed to win and fascinate all with whom he came in contact, calling forth the grateful love of woman, and the admiring friendship of man.

Resolved, 4. That among the galaxy of eminent men of our country in scientific achievements, Dr. J. Marion Sims stands forth a grand, central light, illuminating the world of science, and fully receiving not only due recognition and reverential observation from the *savans* of Europe, but royal homage from crowned heads, and grateful tributes from titled peers.

Resolved, 5. That although he had attained the period allotted to man, of three score years and ten, we deplore his loss, because we believe that the light of his genius had not grown dim with years, but that to him we might still look for future discoveries of hidden truth in the yet unexplored regions of medical science, which can only be penetrated and made manifest by a genius like that of Sims.

Resolved, 6. That a copy of the foregoing resolutions be sent to the family of the deceased as a respectful offering of our sincere sympathy and condolence.

ALEXANDER Y. P. GARNETT, M. D.
J. M. TONER, M. D.
SAMUEL C. BUSEY, M. D.
WILLIAM G. PALMER, M. D.
W. W. JOHNSTON, M. D.

Remarks of Dr. A. Y. P. Garnett.

In presenting these resolutions, Mr. President, which are intended to express the sentiments of this body, I can not refrain, sir, from adding a few words on behalf of myself individually. I enjoyed the honor of the acquaintance and friendship of Dr. Sims during the last five or six years of his life, and therefore claim the privilege of paying a tribute to this noble man as I knew and apprehended him.

I shall not attempt to present even a brief biography of the illustrious dead, nor is it my purpose to review the numerous and brilliant achievements which illustrated his rare powers and adorned his professional career.

The portrayal of these I leave to others who are more familiar with the history of his whole life, and who have doubtless rendered themselves better competent than I am to descant upon these themes.

Viewed from a social standpoint alone, we find him as much appreciated in the *salons* of European society, where his merits made him the petted favorite and envied recipient of royal honors, as he was the distinguished cynosure in the arena of professional effort. Almost unequaled in polished refinement and gentle fascination of manner, no one could be brought within the sphere of his magnetic influence without feeling the attraction and acknowledging the presence of an extraordinary being.

From the first moment of my acquaintance with this singularly gifted man, I felt attracted to him by a mysterious and irresistible charm, never before experienced in the presence of a stranger, and, almost unconsciously to myself, I conceived from that moment an interest which was destined in a short time to develop into lasting sentiments of friendship.

It was evidently through his superlative qualities of character and heart, and rare grace of manner, combined with his irresistible personal presence, that he won the exceptional popularity he everywhere enjoyed amongst men and women, not only in the higher circles of society, but in the humble walks of life.

A prominent and beautiful feature of his character was the kind and sympathetic interest he always manifested in the younger members of his profession. Were I familiar with the private history of his life I could doubtless there find many incidents illustrating this admirable trait. In view of the circumstances which call forth my remarks, it can not be deemed egotism for me to give an instance of his kind thoughtfulness which considered others, even amidst pressing cares and outside duties, because it came home to myself during his recent visit to this city.

Though in Washington for only a few days, he did me the honor to call several times at my office, and conversed fully and freely of his plans and purposes in regard to his contemplated residence in this city; yet he did not forget to make especial inquiries after the health of my son, with whom he was personally acquainted, and to evince great interest in his professional plans. I can see now the earnest and interested expression of face with which he turned to me and said, when about leaving: "Be sure to make your boy come to see me; write and tell him to keep out of Charity Hospital, and send him to me." This interest was manifested toward the young doctor, not merely to the son of his friend.

Apart from the many personal associations which bound me to Dr. Sims, I may be pardoned, I trust, for referring to one incident of his life, while in Europe during the late civil war in this country, which not only enhances the feeling of respect that I entertain for him now that he is dead, but served also as a bond of union between us during his life:

I allude, Mr. President, to the efforts made by the United States Representative at the Court of Belgium to induce King Leopold to refrain from bestowing the honor of his order upon Dr. Sims, because he sympathized with the people of his own section in their struggle for self-government. All that official influence, inspired by political and sectional malevolence, could accomplish was exerted against him, on the sole plea that he was loyal in heart to the South; and this sinister influence so far prevailed that the order of decoration (intended for merit and distinguished ability, that should have received just recognition from even a national foe) was actually deferred for a time.

I can not repress, sir, the pride I feel that this great and good man was a native of the South, and that I can stand here to-night and claim for that section of this Union, although remote from the great centers of medical learning and the best opportunities of clinical observation and experimentation, the proud honor of having given to the profession the bold and intrepid pioneer in the art of gynæcology, in the person of McDowell, of Kentucky, as well as that genius, skill and perseverance which developed it into a science, in the person of J. Marion Sims, of South Carolina.

Biography read by Dr. J. M. Toner.

James Marion Sims, M. D., was born in Lancaster District, South Carolina, January 25, 1813, and died suddenly of heart disease at his residence, 267 Madison Avenue, New York, November 13, 1883. He was a descendant of the great Scottish chieftain, Rob Roy MacGregor. His birth-place was in the vicinity of the dividing line between North and South Carolina, near where President Andrew Jackson first breathed life. Having received a good preparatory education at the common school and from private tutors, he also became well grounded in the classics and acquired a knowledge of French, which he spoke and wrote with readiness. At a suitable age he entered South Carolina College, and graduated in letters in 1832. His medical studies were pursued first in Charleston, South Carolina, then in Philadelphia, Pennsylvania, where he received the degree of M. D. from the Jefferson Medical College in 1835. The following year he began practice near Montgomery, Alabama, and a year later he removed to that city, where he acquired a large and lucrative business. In 1845 he communicated to the profession some new views on "Trismus Nascentium," which he published in the "American Journal of Medical Science," in 1846, and a second paper on the same subject in 1848. In following the professional labors and life of Dr. Sims it should be borne in mind that he was scholarly and well-read in his profession, a good general practitioner, a careful diagnostician, and a fearless and dextrous surgical operator, before he developed the specialty of gynæcology. Although this is well known to the older members of the profession, it is fully manifested by the subjects which early engaged his attention as an author. His first five contributions to medical literature were upon diseases and operations of interest to the general practitioner and surgeon. It was not until 1852 that he published any account of his discoveries and operations, which he followed with such eminent success, and which justly brought him such distinguished honors.

In 1845 his attention was especially called to the subject of vesicovaginal fistula, which previous to that time had been much neglected

by surgeons, or deemed incurable. Dr. Sims conceived the idea of
relieving its victims by a surgical operation. To this end Dr. Sims
established at Montgomery a private hospital, into which he received
patients suffering from this accident, and after many efforts and
modified operations he, in 1849, fully established the fact to the profession that his operation was a success. The devotion and earnestness with which he pursued this branch of surgery led to the invention of a number of new and important instruments and devices
to accomplish the results desired, some of which bear his name.
Among them is "Sims's speculum," and the use of "the silver wire
suture," which, instead of the silk thread, was of great value. Subsequently he used the silver wire suture in all operations where
sutures were required. Owing to unceasing toil his health failed in
1850, and in 1851, while confined to his room from a severe and protracted indisposition, which he and his friends feared would terminate in death, he wrote his famous paper on "Sims's Operation for
Vesico-Vaginal Fistula," which was published in the "American
Journal of Medical Science" for January, 1852.

The good results which had been obtained in his hospital for the
especial treatment of diseases and accidents to which women are
liable, reports of which were, from time to time, published in the
medical journals, awakened in the profession much interest, and
patients were sent to consult Dr. Sims from all parts of the country.

A change of climate, on account of his health, as well as to find
a larger field for professional work, led him to remove to the City
of New York in 1853.

Although his health was not fully restored, he, with the encouragement of some of the leading physicians, within a year commenced
the founding of a woman's hospital in that city, which through his
energy, efficiency, and surgical skill, and under the patronage of
some forty of the first ladies of New York, became, in 1855, an
established fact. To bring the subject directly before the profession
of the City of New York, Dr. Sims determined to deliver an address
to the profession and the public on the necessity of a hospital for
women. The following is a copy of the call which was published in
the leading city papers:

"Lecture on the Necessity of Organizing a Great Hospital in this
City for the Diseases Peculiar to Females.—The undersigned will deliver a lecture on this subject at the Stuyvesant Institute, No. 659

Broadway, on Thursday evening, the 18th inst., at 8 o'clock. The medical profession and the public are respectfully invited to attend. J. MARION SIMS, M. D., 77 Madison Avenue."—From the New York "Tribune," May 17, 1854.

As this was a most important juncture in the professional career of Dr. Sims, we will be pardoned for referring to the effect of the lecture, as he chose to call it, upon the profession and the public. The New York "Post," and also the New York "Times," on the morning of the 19th, each had brief notices of the meeting, cautiously commending its objects:

The following is from the New York "Times" of May 19, 1854: "Dr. Sims on a Hospital for Females.—In spite of a heavy shower that fell just at the hour when the meeting was announced to open, the lecture-room of the Stuyvesant Institute was nearly filled last evening with persons who were present to hear Dr. Sims on the reasons why a hospital should be established in this city for the treatment of the diseases peculiar to females. A large proportion of those present were physicians. Some of the 'solid men' and a number of ladies were in attendance, too. The doctor spoke with great earnestness, and directly to the point, at times becoming eloquent with his subject.

"He aimed, by the history of a Southern institution with which he had been connected, and its results, to show how much might be done in this city, and how great was our need. The attention was undiminished to the close, and it was evident that the right impression had been made.

"On sitting down, Dr. Griscom, of the New York Hospital, after a few complimentary remarks, moved that those present organize themselves into a business meeting, and nominated Dr. Edward Delafield to the chair, and Dr. Edward Beadle as secretary, which was seconded by Dr. Gardner, and which motion was unanimously confirmed.

"Dr. Griscom, in the course of his remarks, said that the interests of humanity united in demanding such a hospital. He remarked that a large percentage of the cases of insanity in our insane asylums is due to the neglected diseases of females.

"A resolution of thanks to Dr. Sims was unanimously passed, and another resolution approving of the project, and that a committee of ten persons—five physicians and five laymen—to devise ways and means to accomplish it be appointed, was also passed.

"The committee is to be named by the president, and hereafter announced through the press. Meanwhile the project will be discussed by the profession, and we trust not ineffectually. The labor of establishing a new hospital in this city is not a trifling one. But there is a demand for more hospital room for these special diseases —a most urgent demand. We trust that the benevolent will turn their attention this way."

The project and the address is commented upon in "The American Medical Monthly" for June, 1854, page 479, in the following language: "On the evening of the 18th ult., 1854, a number of professional men and others, about two hundred, among whom were conspicuous five ladies, attended the Stuyvesant Institute by invitation, to hear Dr. Sims's argument in favor of a hospital for the reception and treatment of diseases peculiar to women.

"The lecturer traced the history of his operation for vesico-vaginal fistula, and related in a pleasing and effective manner the various steps by which he had attained progressively to the present excellence in the performance of this great achievement in curative surgery.

"It was a striking narrative. The obstacles and difficulties he encountered and from every quarter, the failures and disappointments which mortified but did not subdue him, the discouragements of friends and the sacrifice of time, money, bodily and mental labor, would have been sufficient to defeat a less resolute will, to try a faith not sustained by the soundness of the principles which directed him, and the sufficiency of the science on whose altar he was laboring to place the trophy of perserverance, ingenuity, and devotion.

"At the conclusion of the lecture, Dr. Delafield was appointed chairman of the meeting, and Dr. Beadle secretary, when two resolutions were unanimously passed, one expressive of accordance with the views propounded by the lecturer, the other appointing a committee of ten, comprised of five medical men and five lay members, to devise a plan for accomplishing so desirable an object as the establishment of the institution then so eloquently advocated."

The committee of ways and means was composed of Drs. J. W. Francis, Valentine Mott, Alexander H. Stevens, Horace Green, J. Marion Sims, Peter Cooper, Hon. Erastus C. Benedict. An appropriation of $2,500 was obtained from the City Council, to which was added funds raised by the ladies, a house was rented for temporary use, and the hospital opened in May, 1855.

The New York "Medical Times" for June, 1855, page 368, has the following: "Woman's Hospital.—A building on Madison Avenue, No. 83, having been rented for the purpose of this institution, it was formally opened on the 2d of June, 1855, being the first hospital of the kind in New York. Dr. J. W. Francis, one of the consulting physicians, presided, and delivered an appropriate address commendatory of the object. The other prominent speakers on this occasion were Drs. E. H. Dixon (of the 'Scalpel'), D. M. Reese, and Horace Green. There were at the time nineteen patients under treatment."

Dr. Sims had been elected attending surgeon, and Drs. Mott, Stevens, Francis, Delafield, and Green, a consulting board. The institution was patronized by patients from all parts of the country. The success attained by the treatment given, and the important operations performed in it, speedily demonstrated its usefulness and the need for an enlarged establishment.

During the sessions of the New York Legislature of 1857–1858, Dr. Sims, aided by influential gentlemen of New York City, obtained a charter for "The Woman's Hospital for the State of New York," and received from the city a grant of a block or square of some 80,000 feet of ground, and an appropriation of $10,000 to assist in erecting suitable buildings for hospital purposes near the Central Park, opposite Columbia College.

Dr. Sims made a careful study of hospital designs and plans, and finally recommended the pavilion system as the best suited to the purpose.

The first pavilion, with a capacity of seventy beds, was completed and occupied in 1866. Largely through Dr. Sims's personal efforts, and the merits of the work done in the hospital, aid was at different times obtained from the State to the amount of $60,000 for the institution. A second pavilion was opened in 1876, and the combined capacity of the two pavilions is 260 beds. This hospital is at once a grand monument to the genius of Dr. J. Marion Sims, and to the humanity and medical progress of the age. In 1861 Dr. Sims first visited Europe, chiefly to study hospital construction and its sanitary requirements. His arrival was everywhere heralded by

20

encomiums of praise for his valuable discoveries and surgical skill, and he received from the profession in all the large cities and hospitals of Europe such a welcome as has rarely or never been given to a medical man. He was pressed to operate in many of the leading hospitals, and by surgeons who themselves enjoyed world-wide reputations.

Dublin, London, Paris, and Brussels were each in turn the theatre of his surgical triumphs. He operated in nine different hospitals in London, and perhaps a greater number in Paris. His successes were so noted and brilliant that he speedily received decorations from the Governments of France, Italy, Germany, Spain, Portugal, and Belgium as a public benefactor. Indeed, he received two medals from the Government of Italy.

From France he received the Order of the Knights of the Legion of Honor, from Belgium the Order of Leopold I, and from Germany the Iron Cross.

Having returned to America in 1862, after a brief stay at his home, he revisited Europe, to place his children at school, but with the intention of returning to his practice in New York, which had grown to be large, responsible, and remunerative. But as soon as it was known that Dr. Sims was again in Paris, patients flocked to him in such numbers from all parts of the world as to fully occupy his time, and rendered it next to impossible for him to refuse treatment, and it was not till 1868 that he again returned to New York and resumed his practice, his family remaining in London.

At the opening of the Franco-Prussian war in 1870, Dr. Sims happened to be in Paris, and was the prime mover in organizing what is known in history as the Anglo-American Ambulance Corps, and was made its surgeon-in-chief. The organization did good service at and after the battle of Sedan, which led to the downfall of Napoleon III. He was placed in charge of Mayory Hospital, with over four hundred beds, and served faithfully and efficiently for a month, when he resigned the position and returned to Paris. He was one of the escorts who attended Marshal McMahon from the field when wounded by a shell.

The incident was gracefully remembered and acknowledged by the Marshal, who gave him one thousand francs to purchase delicacies for those confined to the hospital. A report of the services and operations of the Anglo-American Ambulance Corps was made by

Dr. Sims's first assistant, William McCormack, now Sir William McCormack, and was published in London in 1871.

I am unable at this time to give a full list of Dr. Sims's contributions to journalistic medical literature. Whenever he wrote he had something to say which the profession was ready and anxious to hear from so original and able an exponent of the art and principles of medicine. The following is presented as an approximate list of Dr. Sims's publications. Most of his writings have been translated and published in the French, German and Italian languages:

"An Essay on the Pathology and Treatment of Trismus Nascentium, or Lockjaw of Infants." 8vo, pp. 21. Philadelphia: Lea & Blanchard. 1864. From *Amer. Jour. Med. Sc.*, April, 1846, Vol. II, p. 363.

" Removal of the Superior Maxilla for a Tumor of the Antrum. Apparent Cure. Return of the Disease. Second Operation. Sequel." Illustrated by woodcuts. *Amer. Jour. Med. Sc.*, April, 1847.

" Osteo-Sarcoma of the Lower Jaw. Removal of the Body of the Bone without External Mutilation."—*Amer. Jour. Med. Sc.*, October, 1847.

" Further Observations on Trismus Nascentium, with Cases illustrating its Etiology and Treatment."—*Amer. Jour. Med. Sc.*, July, 1848, pp. 59 to 78.

"Further Observations on Trismus Nascentium, with Cases illustrating its Etiology and Treatment."—*Amer. Jour. Med. Sc.*, October, 1848, pp. 354 to 366.

" On the Treatment of Vesico-Vaginal Fistula." With Illustrations.— *Amer. Jour. Med. Sc.*, January, 1852.

" On the Treatment of Vesico-Vaginal Fistula." A reprint. 8vo, pp. 28. New York. 1853.

" On the Treatment of Vesico-Vaginal Fistula." By J. Marion Sims, of New York, late of Montgomery, Ala. Philadelphia: Blanchard & Lea. 1853. Pp. 28.—A review in the New York *Med. Times*, December, 1853, p. 104.

" Two Cases of Vesico-Vaginal Fistula, cured by J. Marion Sims, of New York, late of Montgomery, Ala."—New York *Med. Gaz.*, January, 1854, p. 1, with an illustration.

"A case of Vesico-Vaginal Fistula, with the Os Uteri closed up in the Bladder; cured by J. Marion Sims of New York, late of Montgomery, Ala., with an Illustration Exhibiting the Parts."—*Amer. Med. Monthly*, February, 1854.

" A Case of Vesico-Vaginal Fistula resisting the Actual Cautery for more than Seven Years; Cured in Thirteen Days by the Author's Process."—New York *Med. Times*, May, 1854.

" Vesico-Vaginal Fistula of Seven Years' Duration; Cured in Thirteen Days by Sims's Method."—From New York *Med. Times*, 1854; *Amer. Jour. Med. Sc.*, July, 1854.

"A New Uterine Elevator, with Illustration."—*Amer. Jour. Med. Sc.*, p. 432, January, 1858.

"A Review of Silver Sutures in Surgery. An Anniversary Discourse before the New York Academy of Medicine." Pp. 20. Philadelphia. 1858. Reprinted from *North Amer. Med. & Chir. Rev.*, July, 1858.

"Silver Sutures in Surgery. An Anniversary Address before the New York Academy of Medicine." November 18, 1857. 8vo, pp. 79. New York: S. S. & W. Wood. 1858.

"On the Poisonous Properties of Quinia, with Remarks by William O. Baldwin." 8vo. New York, 1861.—From *Med. Gaz.*, New York, 1861.

"Amputation of the Cervix Uteri." 8vo, pp. 16. New York: Horn Book and Job Printing Office, 1861.—Extract from "Transactions of New York State Medical Society, 1861."

"Vaginismus." A paper referred to in the "Transactions of the Obstetrical Society of London, 1862."—New York *Med. Jour.*, July, 1862.

"Influence of Uterine Displacements upon the Sterile Condition." Read before the British Medical Association, 1865.—*Med. Times and Gaz.*, August 19, 1865 ; *Amer. Jour. of Med. Sc.*, October, 1865.

"Chronic Inversion of the Uterus." Read before the Obstetrical Society of London, October 4, 1865.—*Brit. Med. Jour.*, November 18, 1865.

"Lister's Antiseptic Methods in Ovariotomy." New York *Med. Rec.*, October 9, 1865.

"Procedentia Uteri." Read before the Obstetrical Society of London, December 16, 1865.—*Lancet*, December 16, 1865 ; *Amer. Jour. Med. Sc.*, April, 1866, p. 554.

"Clinical Notes on Uterine Surgery, with Special References to the Mangement of the Sterile Condition." 8vo, pp. 401. New York: Wood & Co. 1866.

"Ovariotomy. Pedicle Secured by Silver Wire, after the Failure of the Actual Cautery to Arrest Hæmorrhage. Safe Cure."—*Brit. Med. Jour.*, July 19, 1867 ; *Amer. Med. Jour. Sc.*, April, 1867.

"On the Nitrous Oxide Gas as an Anæsthetic ; with a Note by J. Thierry-Mieg."—*Brit. Med. Jour.*, April 11, 1868.

"Illustrations of the Value of the Microscope in the Treatment of the Sterile Condition." Read before the Midwifery Section of the British Medical Association, August, 1868.—*Brit. Med. Jour.*, October 31, 1868, p. 469, concluded on p. 492.

"The Woman's Hospital Anniversary." Address delivered at the Woman's Hospital, New York, November 17, 1868. 8vo, pp. 11. New York: Baker & Godwin, printers. 1868.

"On the Microscope as an Aid in the Diagnosis and Treatment of Sterility." 8vo, pp. 25. New York: D. Appleton & Co. 1869. Read before the New York County Medical Society, February 7, 1868.—From New York *Med. Jour.*, January, 1869.

"Ovariotomy. Pedicle secured by Silver Wire. Ligature. Cure."—*Brit. Med. Jour.*, April 16, 1869.

" On Ovariotomy." 8vo, pp. 85. New York: D. Appleton & Co. 1873. —From New York *Med. Jour.*, December, 1872, and April, 1873.

" On Intra-Uterine Fibroids, with Illustrations of Methods, etc." 8vo, pp. 27. New York: D. Appleton & Co. 1874. Reprinted from the New York *Med. Jour.*, April, 1874.

" On Nélaton's Method of Resuscitation from Chloroform. Narcosis." Read before the Surgical Section at the Annual Meeting of the British Medical Association, in Norwich, 1874.—*Brit. Med. Jour.*, August 22, 1874.

" Anæsthesia in Obstetrics. Nélaton's Method of Resuscitation from Chloroform. Narcosis." Read before the British Medical Association, August 22, 1874.—*Amer. Jour. Med. Sc.*, October, 1874.

" Utero-Gastrotomy." A communication to the New York State Medical Society, 1875.—New York *Med. Rec.*, February 15, 1875 ; *Amer. Jour. Med. Sc.*, April, 1875.

" Lecture on Vesico-Vaginal Fistula."—*Pac. Med. and Surg. Jour.*, San Francisco, Cal., 1875.

Same reprinted in *Med. Herald*, Leavenworth, 1875.

" Address as President of the American Medical Association, January 6, 1876."—" Transactions of the American Medical Association, 1876."

Reprinted by Collins, Philadelphia, 1876.

" Legislation and Contagious Diseases; an Extract from the Inaugural Address delivered before the American Medical Association, at its Twenty-seventh Annual Meeting, in Philadelphia, June 6, 1876." 8vo, pp. 14. Philadelphia: Collins, printer. 1876.—Extracted from " Transactions of the American Medical Association."

" Legislation and Contagious Diseases ; an Extract from the Inaugural Address delivered before the American Medical Association, at its Twenty-seventh Annual Meeting, in Philadelphia, June 6, 1876." 8vo, pp. 16. London: Spottiswoode. 1876.

" Epithelioma of the Cervix Uteri." Read before the British Medical Association, August 2, 1876.—*Brit. Med. Jour.*, August 20, 1876. Pp. 277.

" The Woman's Hospital in 1874. A reply to the Printed Circulars of Dr. E. R. Peaslee, T. A. Emmett, and T. Gaillard Thomas's Address to the Medical Profession, May 5, 1877." 8vo, pp. 24. New York: Kent & Co., printers. 1877.

" Discovery of Anæsthesia." With engraved portrait of the discoverers, Dr. Crawford W. Long and Horace Wells. Pp. 14.—*Richmond Med. Monthly*, 1877.

" The Discovery of Anæsthesia." Pp. 20. Reprinted from the *Richmond Med. Monthly*. J. W. Ferguson & Son. 1877.

" Professor Lister's Introduction on Antiseptic Surgery. Letter from Paris." Paris, October 10, 1877. Pp. 608.—*Brit. Med. Jour.*, October 27, 1877.

" Battey's Operation." 8vo, pp. 31. London, 1878. Edited by Frichos. Reprinted from the *Brit. Med. Jour.*, December, 1877.

" Extracts from an Essay upon Battey's Operation, in the *British Medical Journal*, December, 1877." 8vo, pp. 2. (N. P. N. D.)

" Remarks on Battey's Operation."—*Brit. Med. Jour.*, December 8, 1877, p. 793; continued in December 15, p. 840; December 22, p. 881; concluded December 29, 1877, p. 916.

" Cholecystotomy in Dropsy of the Gall Bladder. Case operated in April, 1878."—*Brit. Med. Jour.*, June, 1878.—*Gaillard's Medical Journal.*

"Remarks on Cholecystotomy in Dropsy of the Gall Bladder."—*Brit. Med. Jour.*, June 8, 1878, p. 811–815.—*Gaillard's Medical Journal.*

" The Operations of Simpson and Sims for Stenosis of the Cervix Uteri compared." Read before the British Medical Association, at Bath, August 8, 1878. Reported in *Brit. Med. Jour.*, September 7, 1878, p. 365.—*Gaillard's Medical Journal.*

"Surgical Instruments exhibited at International Exhibition in Paris: Uterine Curette, Bistoury Holder, Uterine Dilator." Illustrated.—P. 704 *Brit. Med. Jour.* for November 9, 1878.

"On the Surgical Treatment of Stenosis of the Cervix Uteri."—Extracts " American Gynæcological Society." Vol. III., p. 54. 1878.

"On the Extraction of Foreign Bodies from the Ear."—*Brit. Med. Jour.*, London, December 14, 1878, p. 868.

" On the Surgical Treatment of Stenosis of the Cervix Uteri." With discussion.—" Transactions of the American Gynæcological Society, 1878." Boston. 1879. Vol. III.

" Cholecystotomie pour l'Extraction des Calculs dans l'Hydropsie de la Vesicule Biliare." Trad. de l'Anglais par Fontain et Bargemont.—*Rev. de Lit. Med.* pour 1878. Vol. III. 1879.

" History of the Discovery of Anæsthesia." New York. 1879. Pp. 14. Portrait. Reprinted from *Virginia Med. Monthly*, 1879.—*Gaillard's Medical Journal.*

" On Syringing the Ear." Letter.—*Brit. Med. Jour.*, February 1, 1879.

" A Forceps Case." Letter—*Brit. Med. Jour.*, February 22, 1879.

" Remarks on Abscesses of the Liver, made before the Medical Society of Virginia, at its Tenth Annual Session, held at Alexandria, October 26, 1879." 8vo, pp. 6. (N. P.) 1879.

" The Treatment of Epithelioma of the Cervix Uteri." 8vo, pp. 41. New York: Wm. Wood & Co. 1879. Reported from *Amer. Med. Jour of Obs.*, N. Y. Vol. XII. 1879.

" Cholecystotomy." Translated by Dr. Spaak.—*Jour. de Med. Chir. et Phar.* Brux., 1879. Reprinted in other French and foreign journals.

" Diagnosis of Abscesses of the Liver by Symptoms of Cerebral Hyperæmia, with some remarks on the Treatment of Hepatic Abscess by Aspiration." " Transactions of the Virginia Medical Society, 1879." The same in the *Southern Practitioner*, Nashville, 1880.

" The Bromide of Ethyl as an Anæsthetic." Read before the New York Academy of Medicine, March 18, 1880, with discussion. 8vo, pp. 22. New York. 1880. Also *Medical Record*, N. Y., 1880. — *Gaillard's Medical Journal.*

" The Treatment of Epithelioma of the Cervix Uteri."—*Amer. Jour. Obs.*,

N. Y., 1879. Reprinted in *Gaillard's Journal, N. Y.*, 1880. Also printed in French in the *Annales Gynæcologicales pour* 1880. Also in pamphlet, February, 1880.

"Bromide of Ethyl as an Anæsthetic." Reprinted in the New York *Record*, April 3, 1880.—*Brit. Med. Jour.*, May 14, 1880.

"Thomas Keith and Ovariotomy." 8vo, pp. 16, Part I. New York: W. Wood & Co. 1880. Reprint from *American Journal of Obstetrics*, New York, April, 1880. Vol. XIII.

"Pregnancy Vomiting." 8vo. pp. 8. New York: G. P. Putnam & Son. 1880. Reprinted from the *Archives of Medicine*, June, 1880.

"Thomas Keith on Ovariotomy." New York. 1880. W. Wood & Co. 8vo, pp. 16. Portrait. .

"Bromide of Ethyl as an Anæsthetic." — *Gaillard's Medical Journal*, New York, 1880.

"Thomas Keith and Ovariotomy."—*Amer. Jour. of Obs.*, New York, 1880.

"Surgeons in Public Journals (Thomas Keith, the great Scotch Ovariotomist)."—*Med. Rev.*, New York, 1880.

"Annual Address as President of the American Gynæcological Society, 1880." Boston. 1881. Vol. V. *Gaillard's Medical Journal.* "Transactions of the American Gynæcological Society."

"Pregnancy Vomiting."—*Archives Med.*, New York, 1880. The same, 8vo, pp. 8. Putnam & Son. 1880.—*Gaillard's Medical Journal.*

"Remarks on the Treatment of Gunshot Wounds of the Abdomen in Relation to Modern Peritoneal Surgery."—*Brit. Med. Jour.*, London, 1881.— *Gaillard's Medical Journal.*

"Supplementary Remarks."—*Brit. Med. Jour.*, London, 1882, p. 180. Further remarks, pp. 222 and 260.

"The Recent Progress of Peritoneal Surgery."—*Med. Rec.*, New York, 1881.

"The Surgical Treatment of President Garfield."—*N. A. Rev.*, N. Y., 1881. Article on "Sterility in Women."—*Johnson's Cyclopædia*, 1877.

"Remarks on the Treatment of Gunshot Wounds of the Abdomen in Relation to Peritoneal Surgery." Read before the New York Academy of Medicine, October 6, 1881.—*Brit. Med. Jour.*, December 10, 1881, p. 925; continued December 17, 1881, p. 971; February 11, 1882, p. 184; February 18, 1882, p. 222; February 25, 1882, p. 260; concluded March 4, 1882, p. 302.

"Treatment of Syphilis."—*Brit. Med. Jour.*, March 10, 1883, pp. 448 and 450.

As Dr. Sims was a frequent contributor to the current medical journals, a more careful study will greatly increase the list. And he was an active or corresponding member of many medical societies in America and Europe, besides being an honorary member of the Edinburgh, Brussels, Berlin, Christiania, Paris, and Dublin societies, a Fellow of the Obstetrical Society of London, and numerous other medical and scientific bodies at home and abroad.

He was a member of the Alabama State Medical Association, New York County and State Medical Society, New York Academy of Medicine, New York Neurological, Pathological, and Surgical societies, and an honorary member of the Connecticut State Medical Society, Virginia, South Carolina, and California State Medical Societies.

Dr. Sims became a member of the American Medical Association in 1852, as a delegate from the Alabama State Medical Association; and, in 1858, attended for the Woman's Hospital of New York. He also attended meetings of this organization in 1860, 1872, 1874, 1875, 1876, 1877, 1880, and was president of it in 1876. He was also a member and president of the American Gynæcological Society, and has contributed ably to its transactions. His skill and experience in the obstetrical art led to his engagement to attend the accouchement of the Empress Eugénie, of France, and also to attend the Empress of Austria. His practice in Europe was largely among the nobility, from whom he received large fees and valuable presents. The doctor visited Washington city but a few months ago, and selected and purchased a most eligible site for a residence, and looked forward to the enjoyments of home in that city a few years hence, when he should retire from active practice.

He was, when here, in apparently good health, and certainly looked remarkably well, but spoke of the necessity he was under of being careful as to diet and exposure.

Wishing to avoid the rigor of our winters, he proposed to visit Italy, and anticipated a delightful visit to Rome, where he spent last winter. Some three years since, Dr. Sims suffered from a severe attack of pneumonia, since which time, in cold weather, some unwelcome heart symptoms were from time to time observed. Hence, for the past two years, he has passed the winter months in the south of France and in Rome, and the remainder of the year in other parts of Europe and the United States.

Dr. Sims was united in marriage, December 21, 1836, to Eliza Theresa, daughter of Dr. Bartlett Jones, of Lancaster, South Carolina, who, with seven children, survives him. His son, Henry Marion Sims, is in active practice, and most abundantly inherits the ability and skill of his father, whose memory the whole medical profession loves to honor, for by his genius the science and the art of medicine has been advanced as much, if not more, than by any medical man of the present century. Dr. J. Marion Sims's name will stand in the history of the progress and discoveries in medicine, associated with Harvey, Morgagni, Laennec, and other grand characters, who have heroically and successfully devoted themselves to the science and the art of medicine for the benefit of mankind.

Biographies of Dr. Sims were published some years since in Johnson's "Universal Cyclopædia," in "Physicians and Surgeons of the United States," and in the "Virginia Medical Monthly," from all of which the material for this sketch has been freely drawn.

An excellent portrait, engraved by R. O. Brine, from a photograph by Kurtz, was made some years since. It exhibits the doctor at about the age of sixty, and wearing his decorations. It also contains a *fac-simile* autograph. A fine marble bust of the doctor was, in March 12, 1880, presented by the surgical staff of the Jefferson College Hospital to the Alumni Society of Jefferson College. This society has presented it to the trustees of the Jefferson College Hospital, and it now occupies a conspicuous place in the hall of that institution. In commemoration of the founder of the Woman's Hospital of New York, a fine marble bust of Dr. Sims was presented to the institution by Mrs. Russell Sage, a few days since, on the twenty-ninth anniversary. The bust was cut by Dubois, of Paris, and is a good likeness of the great apostle of gynæcology, and a splendid work of art.

Dr. Sims's funeral took place, in an unostentatious manner, from the Madison Square Presbyterian Church, where he was one of the oldest pew-holders, on Friday, November 16th, and was largely attended by the medical profession and leading citizens of New York. The Rev. Charles H. Parkhurst, minister of the church, conducted the services, and eulogized the character and achievements of Dr. Sims in merited and glowing terms. The interment took place in Greenwood Cemetery. Peace to his ashes!

Remarks of Dr. Joseph Taber Johnson.

Mr. President and Gentlemen: When John Hancock, President of the Continental Congress, signed his name to the Declaration of Independence in 1776, it is said that he wrote his signature in characters so large and so loud that the cry for liberty, which they represented, was heard around the world.

It may be said with equal truth and propriety that when Marion Sims fell so suddenly into the arms of death, the shock was felt wherever women suffer or surgery is practiced.

Hancock, by his eloquence, wisdom, and example, stimulated not only his associates but posterity to patriotism, learning, and noble deeds. Sims, by his brilliant genius, patient industry, wonderful skill, and dexterity saved the lives of many, and made the burden of life less irksome to countless numbers of this and future generations. Who shall say that the former is more deserving of fame than the latter?

Poets sing that he who dries a tear or saves a pang to suffering woman has rendered a service more praiseworthy than to have fought a battle or captured a ship.

Those who have advocated great principles or instilled pure and noble thoughts into the minds of a people; those who have conquered the enemy of the state; he who by his conquests has added to the territorial possessions of his sovereign; statesmen who have originated, and by their zeal and ability carried through the Congress or the Parliament measures for the relief of the oppressed— all these have received just praises and adulation during their life, and monuments have been erected to perpetuate their memories after they were dead. Equally, if not more, are they benefactors of their race who devise means for saving life instead of destroying it, who by their genius rid the world of a scourge or a plague, as well as they who destroy an army or take a city.

Prominent among the benefactors of mankind would I see the honored name inscribed whose useful deeds we have met together to recount, and whose virtues it gives us a melancholy pleasure to commemorate.

If the sad procession could speak to us to-night—which would have gladly and mournfully followed his mortal remains to their last resting-place—made up of those directly benefited by the skill of this great master in surgery himself, and by the much greater host of those indirectly owing their relief from pain and misery to him, there would have been no uncertain voice to proclaim that this beloved name should occupy a position among the highest and noblest upon the pillar of fame.

Honored, as few have been in our land, by the presidency of the American Medical Association—that great representative body of physicians—and with the same distinction by the American Gynæcological Society, elected also to membership in scores of medical and scientific societies—these distinctions exhibit the esteem in which he was held by his countrymen, and also the fact that they delighted to do him honor.

As his reputation increased, so great became his fame that no city, State, or country could retain him within its narrow boundary, and, before his too sudden death had taken him from us forever, he had been the reluctant recipient of the most flattering evidences of the regard of the great and the noble in many countries in Europe. Kings and queens actually besought him to accept their orders and decorations. The order of Knight of the Legion of Honor was conferred upon him by the French Government, and he was subsequently decorated by the King of the Belgians, also by the Italian, Spanish, and Portuguese Governments.

One of the most remarkable elements in his character, Dr. Emmett said to me only a year ago, was the cool and ready ability which he always exhibited in an emergency. His unequaled and wonderful quickness to appreciate how best to turn to good account some unlooked-for occurrence during the progress of a grave operation had been a constant surprise to him.

This was exemplified in his operation upon a French countess whose life had been despaired of by the best medical talent in Paris. Sims, believing she could be cured, operated—in her weakness and prostration—in the presence of many celebrated physicians, and, when about to close the wound, after the skillful removal of the cause of the malady, she apparently expired under the combined effects of shock and anæsthesia, whereupon a bystander sarcastically remarked: "Yes; your operation is successful, but your patient is dead. *We* could have done as well as that."

Sims had staked everything upon this, his first prominent operation in France, and, stung to the quick by the sarcasm of this skeptical Parisian, he dropped his knife and sprang upon the operating-table, remarking, "No, she shall not die," seized her by the feet and swung her head downward until the anæmic brain, with the aid of gravity, became supplied with blood. Nervous power was generated to cause the heart to send a vascular supply to the lungs. The patient drew a long breath, and the mysterious machinery of life moved again slowly into action—and the countess lived. The operation proved to be a success, and Sims's reputation was won.

Hanging the head downward, in cases of suspended animation from chloroform poisoning, was not entirely new or original with Sims, but his cool, quick, and successful grasp of the situation was the culminating climax which won to him the hearts of the French people, ever fond of courage and dashing display when crowned by success.

It was not, however, by stage effects, parade of wonderful cures, or the industrious importunities of partial friends or grateful patients, that Sims's glorious and phenomenal reputation was made.

This was founded upon the everlasting rock of solid scientific attainments, and upon those rare elements combined in one man which go to make up, round out, and complete the character of the Christian gentleman. It is said of him that no woman ever distrusted him, while his exceptional purity of speech and life, together with the personal magnetism of his smile, his words, his manners, attracted many to him and held them chained with the silken cords of love, gratitude, and esteem.

Gaillard Thomas says: "If all that Sims has done for gynæcology were suppressed we should find that we had retrograded at least a quarter of a century."

This, coming from the now most prominent, original, and justly celebrated gynæcologist in America, and scarcely second to any throughout the world, is praise indeed, and, were it not a sad pleasure to his friends and professional admirers to enumerate his many achievements for science and humanity, and his many estimable qualities of head and heart, it would be a sufficient eulogy, as it epitomizes whole discourses, and might constitute an appropriate epitaph to inscribe upon his monument.

I have left it to others to describe his operations and to speak of the era in gynæcology inaugurated by the invention of his speculum, and the use of silver-wire sutures in vagino-plastic surgery.

It gives me a peculiar pleasure, however, to speak of this great man, who has brought such relief to suffering womankind, whose reputation is world-wide, who was courted by kings and princes, decorated by foreign governments, elected to honorary membership in many European societies, and whose name is embalmed in the hearts and memories of thousands as a gynæcologist.

As a gynæcologist he began his career in Alabama, in 1836. In 1849 his fame in that State culminated in the perfection of his method of operating for the cure of vesico and recto-vaginal fistulæ. In 1853 he moved to New York, and in addition to the building up of an extensive and lucrative practice as a gynæcologist, he succeeded in establishing one of the largest and best-regulated hospitals in the world, devoted to the exclusive practice of gynæcology.

As a gynæcologist he visited Europe, and it was in this capacity that unparalleled honors were literally showered upon him, and it has ever been in the acquisition of his fame that he wrote, spoke, and practiced gynæcology.

The grand universal school of Medicine claims him with pride as one of her brightest and most particular stars, and is now everywhere engaged in her journals and societies in doing honor to his memory. The more particular division of Surgery claims him as one of her most skillful and renowned operators, and every professor of surgery has ere this spoken to his class of the glory of his career. But, Mr. President, though Medicine universal may claim him, though surgery more especially may claim him, it is the specialty of Gynæcology which *owns* him, which cultivated and produced him, which he honored in his life and which *loves* to honor him in his death.

It is sad to think that his last years were too full of cares, occupation, and ill health to permit him to finish the great literary work of his life, which would recount for the benefit of posterity the various steps by which he reached the elevated plane upon which he stood. He said to me in his parlor at the Arlington Hotel, during his recent visit to Washington, in answer to my regrets that its publication had been so long delayed, with a sadness and pathos in his voice which I shall never forget: "My dear doctor, I shall never live to complete it. There are plenty of others to take up the work where I leave it, and I have more important things to do in the little of life remaining to me than to write of what I have done in the past."

There is a sadness also in viewing the elevation of any man to a plane so high above his fellows that he has no equals of whom to take council, or for daily, friendly intercourse; but this sadness has its alleviation in the contemplation of our honored, loved, and trusted friend, standing so high in the clouds, upon the topmost round of the ladder of fame, that it was but a step for him *over* into the confines of that celestial country where the weary are at rest for ever.

Remarks by Dr. W. W. Johnston.

The great apostle of hero worship has said that "Universal history . . . is at bottom the history of the great men who have worked here. . . . All things that we see standing accomplished in the world are properly the outer material result, the practical realization and embodiment of thoughts that dwelt in the great men sent into the world, the soul of the whole world's history, it may justly be considered, were the history of these." Is this doctrine true, or is it not nearer the truth to hold that great men do but utter the thoughts of thousands *not great*, and "that all things that we see standing accomplished in the world are the practical realization and embodiment" of the strife and travail of the unfamed, often of the unknown? Events make men, and are not made by them. It took many years of discontent and liberty-craving in England to make a Cromwell. He came to the top as the ablest representative of the long-suffering spirit of rebellion against tyranny and intolerance. He did not make the revolution. The revolution made him. But none the less honor is due to those great names which mark the epochs of the world's history. That these great men did embody in themselves the power and intellect of thousands, gifted with intelligence and aiming at the same ends, is the highest tribute to their genius and fame. Their deeds, however, rank not as miraculous outbursts of genius, but take their place in the orderly procession of events which mark the evolution of man's growing dominion over ignorance and nature.

The knowledge of the diseases of women lay sleeping during centuries. The structure of society in Catholic Europe and among the Arabs, by the peculiar relations fixed between men and women, put a stop to all scientific and practical investigation. Even after all barriers were removed, the time was very long before a real gain was made. The time was ripe when Sims patiently began to work out problems which were essential to operative gynæcology. Even slavery had its uses in the pursuit of his ends. Who can tell how many more years the progress of the art might have been delayed, if the humble negro servitors had not brought their willing sufferings and patient endurance to aid in the furthering of Sims's purpose.

In looking at the after-life of the successful surgeon, we are apt to overlook the struggles with many obstacles during the earlier years of his life. The soul of Sims must have been a supersensitive one. We know that beneath a quiet exterior there slumbered emotions which were the necessary accompaniment of his delicate cerebral organization. Such men do not go through life without many crosses. That tenderness which drew all men and women to him was the expression of an impressionable nerve-tissue which reacted to the slightest touch of harshness as to a wound.

The life of Sims marked an epoch in medical history. He lived to see a new science born, to watch it grow into the perfection of exact beauty and proportion, and he died with dreams of great things yet to be done filling the chambers of his capacious mind.

After which Dr. J. M. Toner read a carefully prepared biography of Dr. Sims, which appears in the first department of this number. The resolutions reported were unanimously adopted, and then this historical meeting in connection with Dr. Sims silently adjourned.

NOTE.—An eloquent and handsome eulogy was pronounced by Dr. S. C. Busey, but no report of his remarks was made.

THE END.

THE STORY OF MY LIFE.

By the late J. MARION SIMS, M. D.   Edited by his Son, H. MARION-SIMS, M. D.   12mo, cloth, 472 pages. $1.50.

"Marion Sims, by himself and through others, has restored to society and to happiness an ever-increasing multitude of sufferers, condemned, before he opened the way of escape, to life-long wretchedness. For himself he achieved such renown that his name is a household word in medical circles the world over. But the story is more than an autobiography: it not merely illustrates the evolution of a South Carolina country lad into one of the most useful and conspicuous of modern benefactors; it is local history interpreting rural life in that section fifty years ago."—*New York Evening Post.*

"The book opens with a very interesting introduction, in which Judge T. J. Mackey pays a deserved tribute to the distinguished surgeon, and recapitulates the achievements upon which his professional fame rests, and which have won him recognition in Europe and America as the foremost clinical surgeon of the age. Dr. Sims was born in Lancaster County, S. C., and though the greater part of his life was spent away from his native State, South Carolinians have a right to feel a personal pride in the reputation he won."—*Charleston News and Courier.*

"The claim of Dr. Sims to the regard of posterity rests on a number of professional achievements conferring honor on both himself and his country. First, he invented the silver suture and applied it successfully to cases of fistula, until then deemed incurable. Second, he invented what is known as the 'Sims Speculum'—the most effective now known. Third, he made an exposition of the pathology and true method of *trismus nascentium*, or the lock-jaw of infants. Fourth, he was the founder and organizer of the Woman's Hospital of the State of New York, the first institution ever dedicated exclusively to the cure of the diseases of women. Fifth, he made valuable contributions to medical literature. The story of a life so full of usefulness to his fellows will have a permanent value, and will be widely read by all who admire the benefactors of the human race."—*Troy Daily Evening Times.*

"The medical profession will find a peculiar interest in this volume, in which the great physician tells the story of his career, and of those brilliant discoveries and inventions which have given renown not only to him, but to the entire body of American medical science. In his special departments he enlarged the scope of surgery for the whole world, and it is not too much to say that his name will stand in the completed history of the science as one of its illustrious creators. He was not less distinguished for the simple virtues and noble heroism of his character in private life, than for his successes in his profession, and this testament from his hand will commend him to the love and reverence of thousands who have only known him hitherto through the reports of fame."—*N. Y. Home Journal.*

"The late Dr. Sims probably obtained a wider reputation than any other American physician. His brilliant discovery in a highly important but obscure department of surgery won the admiration of his profession in the New and Old Worlds. His fame culminated in this country as far back as 1855, when the Woman's Hospital was established in New York for the sole purpose of curing by his method a trouble that had previously been deemed incurable. The leaders in the New York fashionable society of that day took charge of this truly philanthropic work. They were assisted in it by our most distinguished local physicians and surgeons, who freely testified to the extraordinary merit of Dr. Sims's discovery. For nearly thirty years this institution has been one of the crowning mercies of New York. Dr. Sims in this work tells the story of his life with the utmost fullness and frankness. Aside from his claims on the gratitude of womankind, the doctor had a history well worth telling. In Paris, London, and other capitals of Europe, he was thrown into much brilliant society, and of this he jots down his recollections in a fresh and amusing manner."—*New York Journal of Commerce.*

For sale by all booksellers ; or will be sent by mail, post-paid, on receipt of price.

New York: D. APPLETON & CO., Publishers, 1, 3, & 5 Bond Street.

LOUIS PASTEUR:

HIS LIFE AND LABORS.

BY HIS SON-IN-LAW.

TRANSLATED FROM THE FRENCH BY LADY CLAUD HAMILTON. WITH AN
INTRODUCTION BY PROFESSOR TYNDALL.

12mo, cloth, $1.25.

"Never was man of science more fortunate in his biographer. The book has the interest of a novel joined to that of heroic biography. The translation is excellent."—*N. Y. Commercial Advertiser.*

"The book as a whole is much more a sketch of the man's work than of the man himself; and the work is great work."—*N. Y. Evening Post.*

"Pasteur's discoveries have so often been almost sensational in their brilliancy and unexpectedness, and have so frequently ministered to the comfort, health, and material prosperity of mankind, that the story of them has all the interest of a well-wrought fiction."—*New York Examiner.*

"The results achieved by Pasteur are so far in advance of those obtained by any of his contemporaries that he may be safely placed where the last century placed Newton."—*Springfield Republican.*

"To give a complete description of the contents of the book would be futile but the 'Studies on Wine and Beer,' 'Attenuated Virus,' the 'Etiology of Splenic Fever,' and descriptions of the laboratory of the celebrated Normal School and experiments in hydrophobia, will probably draw most of the reader's attention."—*New Haven News.*

"The picture of Pasteur leaning over the foaming head of a mad dog held motionless by attendants and suffocating with fury, and at a distance of a finger's length sucking up into a narrow tube some drops of the saliva, is truthfully illustrative of his earnest and fearless love of science throughout his life. Hydrophobia has been his latest study. As regards the attenuation of the rabid virus, and the rendering of an animal by inoculation proof against attack, the success of M. Pasteur is assured. The volume describes in detail and with clearness the labors of a bold pioneer in scientific experiment, whose contributions to scientific knowledge and to the happiness of humanity are among the most valuable of his period. The narrative of what he has done and is doing is a most important one."—*Boston Globe.*

"The discovery of corpuscles which produced a disease from which all the silk-worms in France were dying, and of the means of preventing their spread, made Louis Pasteur famous in France twenty years ago. His more recent discoveries of disease microbes and of the power to render contagious diseases harmless by inoculation have made his name known from one end of the earth to the other."—*Philadelphia Inquirer.*

For sale by all booksellers; or sent by mail, post-paid, on receipt of price.

New York: D. APPLETON & CO., Publishers, 1, 3, & 5 Bond Street.

MAXIMS OF PUBLIC HEALTH.

By O. W. Wight, M. D., of the Detroit Board of Health.   16mo, cloth,
75 cents.

"The appearance of this hand-book is most timely. There is a vague apprehension that the cholera may visit the United States next year. Everybody
wants to know what to do for the exclusion or limitation of the dread disease.
Dr. O. W. Wight, to whom we owe these 'Maxims of Public Health,' speaks
with the voice of authority. He has been for six years Health Officer of Detroit,
and has made epidemics the subject of patient and earnest study. Here we have
the fruits of all his experience and observation. His book ought to be placed in
the hands of every person connected in any way with health boards in all parts
of the country. It is invaluable for instant reference in an emergency. Dr.
Wight proves his competency to speak on this subject by the emphasis he puts
on cleanliness of houses and streets as the best safeguard against pestilence."—
New York Journal of Commerce.

"Dr. Wight is to be commended, not only for reiterating the dangers to which
we are subject, both in city and country, from unsanitary surroundings, but
because he has clothed his thoughts in virile, understandable English. He has
the ordinary scientific view of filth as the breeder of certain contagious diseases
—scarlet fever, typhoid fever, diphtheria and the like—but has a new idea concerning the removal of sewage before it putrefies. As he puts it in the preface,
'the only way to get rid of sewer-gas is not to make any.' It is a pleasure to
read his thoughts ; they can not be other than a great boon to the unprofessional
man, for whom they are specially written."—*Hartford Evening Post.*

"The intelligent householder who has no time, perhaps no inclination, for
systematic studies, may read these maxims with a quick comprehension of their
import, and find hints that will save himself and his loved ones unspeakable
pain and sorrow. To say nothing of his success as a medical practitioner, Dr.
Wight gives in this valuable book the result of six years of personal experience
in sanitary administration. We heartily commend it to the careful reading of
all who would be prepared to ward off any epidemic that should make its appearance in their midst, or who would have everything about their premises of the
most healthful character."—*Boston Home Journal.*

"Dr. Wight's heart is at his pen's point in every page of his book, and he is
as exhaustive upon every phase of human life and suffering and exposure and
economy, as he is on the school."—*St. Paul Dispatch.*

"A little volume which condenses within less than two hundred pages a vast
amount of sanitary science. . . . The book is evidently the result of long and
close attention to the subject, and, being designed for the general reader, it gives
the results of investigation and experiment without burdening them with details of the processes by which they have been reached. It is a book which should
be studied by all."—*Chicago Daily Times.*

"This is a timely and most instructive as well as interesting series of para-
graphs on sanitary subjects, which ought to be read in every household and
board of health."—*Newark Daily Advertiser.*

"He plunges into the subject of city drainage, handling the topic with such
skill and precision as prove him a past master of hygienic science. Every
possible phase of house, stable, and city drainage, and sanitation, is explained
and discussed."—*Detroit Evening News.*

*For sale by all booksellers ; or will be sent by mail, post-paid, on receipt
of price.*

New York: D. APPLETON & CO., Publishers, 1, 3, & 5 Bond Street.

WOMEN, PLUMBERS, AND DOCTORS;

OR, HOUSEHOLD SANITATION.

BY MRS. H. M. PLUNKETT.

Showing that, if women and plumbers do their whole sanitary duty, there will be comparatively little occasion for the services of the doctors.

With 50 Illustrations - - - 12mo, cloth, $1.25.

CHAPTER-HEADS.

HYGIENIC HOUSES.	SEWAGE AND PLUMBING.
UNDER THE HOUSE.	SEWER-GAS AND GERMS.
ARRANGEMENT OF THE HOUSE.	OVERLOOKED CHANNELS OF INFECTION.
LIGHTING THE HOUSE.	OUR NEIGHBOR'S PREMISES.
WHOLESOME WATER.	PUBLIC SANITATION.

"Here is a really profound and thorough investigation into the causes of half the diseases that afflict humanity. If dwellings were built in the right places, properly constructed and furnished, and then carefully looked after, sickness would rarely occur in such houses. Mrs Plunkett cites numerous facts from the experience of herself and others to prove all she says. She tells many touching stories to illustrate the fatal results of ignorance and neglect of the laws of health in American homes The book is very interesting, aside from its instructive and useful character. It is full of pictures showing the contrasts of good and bad plumbing, complete and defective drainage, etc. The reading of practical books like this one will do much to educate our people in the art of making homes healthy and happy."—*New York Journal of Commerce.*

"After a few pages on sanitation in general. Mrs. Plunkett describes the dangers which lurk in wet house-sites and inadequate foundations, and then proceeds with the arrangement of the house for securing sufficient warmth, ventilation, and sunshine. The next chapter deals with lighting, and contains many facts in relation to dangerous burning-oils that every housewife should thoroughly know Various ways in which water may become unwholesome are told, with directions for tests and measures of protection. The requirements of a good system of plumbing are stated, examples of defective work are given, and some explanation of the nature of sewer-gas and disease-germs is added. As many eminent physicians have declared that cholera will certainly come to America in 1885, a memorandum of the New York State Board of Health relating to the prevention of the disease has been introduced, together with directions for home treatment, including recipes for medicines The book, though aiming especially to interest women, is addressed to all readers who desire a popular and practical presentation of this important subject; quotations from the writings of able physicians and sanitarians have been freely used, and evidently care has been taken to make a useful and reliable book"—*The Popular Science Monthly.*

"Mrs. H. M. Plunkett has written a book that will prove a blessing in thousands of households, if only its important lessons are heeded. She clearly shows why women should understand the details as well as the theory of sanitation, and furnishes all information to enable them to possess such an understanding."—*Boston Home Journal.*

"The work is well written, and the diagrams showing the perfect and imperfect work are simple and easily understood; it is well worth perusal by every father, and more particularly by every mother of a family, showing, as it does, where most of the seeds of disease germinate."—*Rochester Post and Express.*

For sale by all booksellers; or sent by mail, post-paid, on receipt of price.

New York: D. APPLETON & CO., Publishers, 1, 3, & 5 Bond Street.

JELLY-FISH, STAR-FISH, AND SEA-URCHINS.

Being a Research on Primitive Nervous Systems.

By G. J. ROMANES, F. R. S.,

Author of "Mental Evolution in Animals," etc.

12mo. Cloth, $1.75.

"A profound research into the laws of primitive nervous systems conducted by one of the ablest English Investigators. Mr. Romanes set up a tent on the beach and examined his beautiful pets for six summers in succession. Such patient and loving work has borne its fruits in a monograph which leaves nothing to be said about jelly-fish, star-fish, and sea-urchins. Every one who has studied the lowest forms of life on the sea-shore admires these objects. But few have any idea of the exquisite delicacy of their structure and their nice adaptation to their place in nature. Mr. Romanes brings out the subtile beauties of the rudimentary organisms, and shows the resemblances they bear to the higher types of creation. His explanations are made more clear by a large number of illustrations. While the book is well adapted for popular reading it is of special value to working physiologists."—*New York Journal of Commerce.*

"Six years have been consumed in these investigations and experiments, and the result is a condensed statement of probably all that is known at present concerning these curious and beautiful fishes "—*New York Evening Telegram.*

"A most admirable treatise on primitive nervous systems. The subject-matter is full of original investigations and experiments upon the animals mentioned as types of the lowest nervous developments."—*Boston Commercial Bulletin.*

"Dr. Romanes is above all clear in his statements ; the general reader for whom he writes in this volume, as well as the zoölogist, can find pleasure and instruction in what he has to say. The highly nervous organisms of which he treats are so familiar outwardly to the people, that what an eminent scientist writes after careful and intelligent investigation will be received with much more practical interest than the same scrutiny with extinct monsters."—*Hartford Evening Post.*

"A curious and instructive study of a low order of animal life. to which even the young naturalists who go for the summer to the sea-shore will be attracted. The book is meant, however, for something more than entertainment. The complicated and beautiful structure of the little marine animals is explained and illustrated very cleverly, and in a way to increase the wonder and admiration of the reader."—*Philadelphia Evening Bulletin.*

"Mr. Romanes's latest book discourses of ingenious experiments and original discoveries, and opens a field that has hitherto remained an unknown land to the general reader."—*Boston Saturday Evening Gazette.*

"May be read with delight and profit by all studious persons."—*Boston Beacon.*

"Mr. George J. Romanes has already established a reputation as an exact and comprehensive naturalist, which his later work, 'Jelly-Fish, Star-Fish, and Sea-Urchins,' fully confirms. These marine animals are well known upon our coasts, and always interest the on-lookers. In this volume (one of the International Scientific Series) we have the whole story of their formation, existence, nervous system, etc., made most interesting by the simple and non-professional manner of treating the subject. Illustrations aid the text, and the professional student. the naturalist, all lovers of the rocks, woods, and shore, as well as the general reader, will find instruction as well as delight in the narrative."—*Boston Commonwealth.*

New York: D. APPLETON & CO., 1, 3, & 5 Bond Street.

Origin of Cultivated Plants.

By ALPHONSE DE CANDOLLE.

12mo. Cloth, $2.00.

"The copious and learned work of Alphonse de Candolle on the 'Origin of Cultivated Plants' appears in a translation as volume forty-eight of the 'International Scientific Series.' Any extended review of this book would be out of place here, for it is crammed with interesting and curious facts. At the beginning of the century the origin of most of our cultivated species was unknown. It now requires more than four hundred closely printed pages to sum up what is known or conjectured of this matter. Among his conclusions M. Candolle makes this interesting statement: 'In the history of cultivated plants I have noticed no trace of communication between the peoples of the Old and New Worlds before the discovery of America by Columbus.' Not only is this book readable, but it is of great value for reference."—*New York Herald.*

"If general and lasting usefulness is to be accepted as the test of meritorious achievement, it might do us no harm to remember that within the last two thousand years man has not won from nature by discovery and cultivation a single species of food staple comparable with wheat, rice maize. the potato, and the banana, some of which invaluable conquests can indeed be proved to have been made more than forty centuries ago. This is one of the suggestive facts contributed by botany to the history of the birthplace and evolution of civilization, and which are discussed in the light of the ripest and most accurate investigation by the well-known Genevan scientist, Alphonse de Candolle. in the 'Origin of Cultivated Plants.' Of the one hundred and twenty to one hundred and forty thousand species in the vegetable kingdom, man has detected properties sufficiently precious to make it worth while to cultivate the plants on a large scale, and for use in less than three hundred instances."—*New York Sun.*

"Not another man in the world could have written the book. and. considering both its intrinsic merits and the eminence of its author, it must long remain the foremost authority in this curious branch of science. Of the 247 plants here enumerated. 199 are from the Old World, 45 are American, and 3 unknown. Of these only 67 are of modern cultivation. Curiously, however. the United States, notwithstanding its extent and fertility, makes only the pitiful showing of gourds and the Jerusalem artichoke."—*Boston Literary World.*

"The volume, though not large, is evidently the result of great study and research. Botanists in all parts of the world, travelers, herbaria, works on botany, history, archæology, and philology, have been all called upon to contribute to the results. The author justly remarks in his preface that 'the knowledge of the origin of cultivated plants is interesting to agriculturists, to botanists, and even to historians and philosophers concerned with the dawnings of civilization.' "—*Albany Cultivator and Country Gentleman.*

"In a word. all that can be recorded of the plant kingdom is given in the four hundred and fifty and more pages of the volume, and a good index aids materially the readers. All flower-lovers can find substantial information about their favorites in the work."—*Boston Commonwealth.*

"It is an exhaustive treatise on the habitat and origin of all the useful plants known to medicine, cookery, and science. One is here informed that the turnips come from Siberia, that the strawberry grows wild in Europe from Lapland to the isles of Madeira and Greece gooseberries come from the Caucasus, and wheat from the region of the Euphrates. Rice was known 2.800 years B. C. in a ceremony in which the Emperor of China plays a conspicuous part."—*Cincinnati Enquirer.*

New York: D. APPLETON & CO., 1, 3, & 5 Bond Street.

FALLACIES:

A View of Logic from the Practical Side.

By ALFRED SIDGWICK, B. A., Oxon.

12mo. Cloth, $1.75.

This book is intended mainly for the general reader. That is to say, it requires no previous technical training, and is written as much as possible from the unprofessional point of view.

"A book intended for popular use, and one now very much needed in these days of half education, when so many persons are the prey of illusions. It treats mainly of the methods of proof, shows what evidence is, and the different sorts needed to produce belief, and what are the fallacies most suited to deceive."—*Hartford Courant*.

"Like all the others in this series, this volume is intended for the general reader, but the trained logician will find it useful and suggestive."—*New York Herald*.

"An important treatise on a topic that deserves the attention of all thinking people. The author writes mainly for the general reader; no previous technical training, but only a fair degree of intelligence and application, is needful to follow the train of his thought."—*Cultivator and Country Gentleman*.

"Even among educated men logic is apt to be regarded as a dry study, and to be neglected in favor of rhetoric; it is easier to deal with tropes, metaphors, and words, than with ideas and arguments—to talk than to reason. Logic is a study; it requires time and attention, but it can be made interesting, even to general readers, as this work by Mr. Sidgwick upon that part of it included in the name of 'Fallacies' shows. Logic is a science, and in this volume we are taught the practical side of it. The author discusses the meaning and aims, the subject-matter and process of proof, unreal assertions, the burden of proof, non-sequiturs, guess-work, argument by example and sign, the *reductio ad absurdum*, and other branches of his subject ably and fully, and has given us a work of real value. It is furnished with a valuable appendix, and a good index, and we should be glad to see it in the hands of thinking men who wish to understand how to reason out the truth, or to detect the fallacy of an argument."—*The Churchman*.

"Its perusal would save many a man from being misled "—*Louisville (Ky.) Christian Observer*.

"The author has bestowed much labor upon the production, and the originality of his ideas is refreshing. He holds that to combat fallacy is the *raison d'être* of logic, hence, instead of touching logic directly, he treats, in a systematic manner, of those fallacies which logic combats."—*Harrisburg (Pa.) Telegraph*.

New York: D. APPLETON & CO., 1, 3, & 5 Bond Street.

THE ORGANS OF SPEECH,

And their Application in the Formation of Articulate Sounds.

By GEORG HERMANN VON MEYER,

Professor of Anatomy at the University of Zürich.

With numerous Illustrations. - - - 12mo, cloth, $1.75.

" At once philosophical and practical, suitable as a text-book in a medical college or for reading at home. Persons engaged in philological studies, and all professional musicians, will find it full of extremely useful facts and suggestions."
—*New York Journal of Commerce.*

" This volume comprises the author's researches into the anatomy of the vocal organs, with special reference to the point of view and needs of the philologist and the trainer of the voice. It seeks to explain the origin of articulate sounds, and to outline a system in which all elements of all languages may be co-ordinated in their proper place. The work has obviously a special value for students in the science of the transmutations of language, for etymologists, elocutionists, and musicians."—*New York Home Journal.*

" The author perceives in the sounds made by animals meanings analogous to words, and in support of this is the fact that in the legends of all nations an important part is played by wise men who understand the language of the brute creation. With patient thoroughness Professor von Meyer describes minutely the vocal apparatus, and the sounds produced by the complex combinations of its simple parts."—*Cincinnati Commercial Gazette.*

" It is surprising to note what different sounds, and shades of tone and meaning, can be produced by volition in the use of the human organs of speech."—*Hartford Daily Times.*

" The book presents a happy combination of the Teutonic thoroughness of treatment with the method and lucidity of statement which especially distinguish French scientists. The author's expositions are remarkable for their clearness and avoidance of technicalities ; while their meaning is rendered more apparent by the use of numerous diagrams."—*Edinburgh Scotsman.*

" The work is a thorough and exhaustive one."—*Boston Commonwealth.*

" The author's plan has been to give a sketch of all possible articulate sounds, and to trace upon that basis their relations and capacity for combination."—*Philadelphia North American.*

" A treatise of remarkable interest."—*Boston Transcript.*

" Ought to be welcomed for the varied, new, and original interpretations contained in the book."—*Harrisburg Telegraph.*

New York: D. APPLETON & CO., 1, 3, & 5 Bond Street.

Printed in Great Britain
by Amazon

18064728R00276